ANTHONY KALDELLIS

The Byzantine Republic

People and Power in New Rome

Harvard University Press

Cambridge, Massachusetts, and London, England   2015

Fifth printing

Library of Congress Cataloging-in-Publication Data

Kaldellis, Anthony.
  The Byzantine Republic : people and power in New Rome / Anthony Kaldellis.
    pages cm
  Includes bibliographical references and index.
  ISBN 978-0-674-36540-7 (alkaline paper)
  1. Byzantine Empire—History—527-1081. 2. Byzantine Empire—Politics and
government—527-1081. 3. Legitimacy of governments—Byzantine Empire. 4. Power
(Social sciences)—Byzantine Empire. 5. Republicanism—Byzantine Empire.
6. Monarchy—Byzantine Empire. 7. Authority—History—To 1500. I. Title.
  DF571.K35 2015
  949.5'02—dc23   2014011695

To Carolina López Ruiz
with love and admiration

Contents

Preface

The goal of this book is to present an original argument regarding the nature of what we call "the Byzantine empire" as a political society. In discussing the Byzantine political sphere, scholarship has focused almost exclusively on the emperor and has tended to accept at face value the theological grounds for the legitimacy of his power often claimed by the court. This picture, I will argue, is partial and even misleading. Byzantium must first be understood as a republic in the Roman tradition. As I will explain in Chapter 1, by "republic" I mean a regime in which only popular consent could authorize the allocation of power, which could be used only to benefit the totality of the Roman people (whom we call the "Byzantines"). According to this definition, and following most political theorists down to the Enlightenment, republics and monarchies were not incompatible. By contrast, what we (and not the Romans) call the "Republic" was only one specific type of regime by which the *res publica* or *res Romana* was governed in one phase of its history, namely, by the senate, consuls, and popular assemblies. Byzantium was a republic in the broader sense. The Roman people remained the true sovereign of the political sphere, and they both authorized and de-authorized the holding of power by their rulers. The latter, "the emperors of the Romans," must be understood in relation to the political sphere constituted by the totality of the Roman people. The *politeia* was the Byzantine Greek translation and continuation of the ancient *res publica*.

This project is part of a two-pronged effort to rehabilitate the Roman dimension of Byzantium and the Roman identity of the Byzantines themselves. The sequel and companion book will argue, according to both the evidence and theoretical models that have prevailed in the social and historical sciences since the mid-twentieth century, that the Byzantines not only "called themselves Romans" (as our field evasively and grudgingly puts it) but actually were that: Greek-speaking, Orthodox Christian Romans to be sure, but Romans still. The present volume, by contrast, will not focus on identity claims but will use political theory and the peculiar framework of Byzantine politics to argue that the Roman people in their Byzantine phase constituted a political sphere whose contours were recognizably republican. In my usage, which follows that of the Romans, "republican" refers to underlying ideologies of power and notions of popular sovereignty; it does not have to do with the structure of offices ("the Republic" was not called that by the Romans, but is a modern term for a period and a specific mode of governance).

George Ostrogorsky, who wrote a standard history of the Byzantine state (first published in 1952), unobjectionably claimed that "Roman political concepts, Greek culture, and the Christian faith were the main elements that determined Byzantine development."[1] But while the field generally concedes that "Rome" had something to do with Byzantium, it has never been specified exactly what that was. What were those "concepts" that Ostrogorsky referred to? Part of the problem stems from the origins of Byzantine Studies as a field of research. In western Europe, this research took place within the ideological parameters set by many political and religious institutions that had a stake in the Roman legacy. Since early medieval times the Byzantine claim to Rome had been rejected and polemically denied. The field of Byzantine Studies inherited the claims of that polemic as obvious facts and so had to devise ways of referring to the eastern Roman empire that were different from what it called itself. Thus we have been saddled with "the empire of the Greeks," "the empire of Constantinople," and "Byzantium," for Rome proper belonged to the (Latin) West. But Rome and Roman claims are written all over the Byzantine evidence. Given the extreme reluctance in the field to admit that the Byzantines *were* Romans, this evidence has been interpreted in one of two ways. The first is to equate those Roman concepts with the theology of empire applied by the bishop Eusebios of Kaisareia to Constantine the Great. This effectively folds the Roman dimension into the Christian one; many leading historians today still maintain that Byzantium was Christian *rather than* Roman,[2] not that it was both but in different ways. Thus Ostrogorsky's three pillars have been reduced to two. According to a recent book, "it has also been common to regard

Byzantine culture as based on two elements: the Greek . . . and the Judaic and Christian tradition."[3] The other option is to regard the Roman aspect as a function of imperial propaganda, limited to titles and diplomacy.[4] It survives in the view that the Byzantines were Roman insofar as they were the subjects of the emperor, as if they derived their Roman identity, such as it was, from his title (the exact opposite was in fact true).

This is a revisionist book: it aims to question established opinion and proposes alternative models that better explain the facts, or explain facts that established models avoid. To this end, it does not repeat things that are repeated often enough elsewhere. Readers who want to read about Byzantium as an Orthodox society should look elsewhere: there is no lack of books on that topic. But in my view the dominant Orthodox model is not only one-sided, it is not viable. This book, then, stems from a growing realization that the Byzantium described in most modern scholarship diverges from the society one encounters in the sources, sometimes widely. A formulaic definition of "Byzantine political theory" has been constructed out of mostly modern concepts, projected onto the culture, and recycled since the 1930s. Scholars are content to recite this model as a general definition of the culture before they move on to study the particular aspects that interest them. The latter focused research is of high quality, but the general framework into which it is pressed has never been subjected to critical scrutiny. The field ought to be more worried than it is that the basic studies that are still cited as authoritative for Byzantine political ideology were written by European scholars coping with, or trained in, the crisis of the 1930s, and that they valorized theocratic over populist political ideologies.

Our "insidious governing image"[5] of Byzantine political ideology would have it that the emperor and the so-called imperial idea—a type of political theology—held absolute dominion within, and also completely filled up, the political sphere, and that the position of the emperor was understood and also legitimized in relation to God. To quote a leading scholar: "The empire was held together by a strong ideology based on its court and capital at Constantinople. This ideology revolved around two axes: the imperial power and the Orthodox religion."[6] "Ideology," according to most versions of this position, played out in a metaphysical realm between emperor and God to which imperial subjects had no access and upon which they gazed in awe and submission. Historians also used to stress "the exalted position of the emperor, who dominated and controlled the entire life of the empire . . . The power he wielded was vast, unlimited, and subject to no higher authority."[7] Recent scholarship has played down this absolutism by recognizing that the emperor was not quite so powerful in practice and his rule was not recognized as absolute by his subjects, even though the foundations for imperial power are still understood in religious terms.

An alternative view will be defended here, one that has been proposed in the past, albeit in a preliminary and underdeveloped way, by Hans-Georg Beck in the 1960s and 1970s. This book will propose that Byzantium had a complex political culture in which different ideological systems were superimposed, one Roman, republican, and secular and the other late Roman, metaphysical, and eventually Christian, and they occupied different sites of the political sphere. In itself this is not an original thesis,[8] but it will also be argued here that priority in terms of both the ideology of the Byzantines and the functioning of their political sphere should be given by historians to the *Roman* component. The theology of the imperial office, which has dazzled the field for too long, should be demoted. We should not be approaching Byzantine politics exclusively or even primarily through religion. Byzantium was in fact the continuation of the Roman *res publica;* and its politics, despite changes in institutions, continued to be dominated by the ideological modes and orders of the republican tradition. This was Beck's great insight, but he found few followers,[9] and his alternate reading of the evidence has not been taken up by the field as an analytical or historical framework. Part of the problem is that he did not so much develop his thesis as sketch it in a few scattered articles and chapters, providing little documentation.[10] In my view the greatest weakness of his work, which ensured that few would grasp what he was saying, is that he did not explicitly challenge dominant views in the field, though he understood their flaws, and thus failed to explain the significance of what he was saying for what other scholars were thinking about the topic. As a result, he was folded into the background as yet another generic restatement of what everyone already knew. It thus became possible to tame Beck by citing him along with scholars who held more or less the opposite view, as if they were all saying the same thing. This creates a false image of unanimity and consensus in the field.

Our understanding of the Byzantine political sphere is missing a crucial element that has a prominent place in almost all the primary sources: I mean the concept of the *politeia,* an ancient translation of the Latin *res publica,* along with its cognates and synonyms (premodern terminology never being uniform in most literary or documentary genres). Beck's version of the republican thesis suffered also because it failed to bring out the meaning and centrality for the Byzantines of this concept, to show how fundamental it was for their political thinking and behavior, though he was aware of its importance. The *politeia* as a political sphere reflected the consensus of the Roman people that operated in a conceptual space that encompassed both the emperor and the community of whom he was the emperor. The importance of this concept should not be underestimated for the Byzantine view of politics, and yet it is entirely missing from our representation of their culture. This book seeks to restore "the mental map by which individuals oriented themselves politically,"[11] first by revealing the logic about politics that pervades Byzantine texts in many genres, especially legal texts, military treatises, historiography, and others. Each of these presents and discusses the same core ideas, albeit from a different viewpoint, which enables us to form a rounded picture and to consider the interests of different parties within it.

After considering first the ideological framework, I will turn to the *politeia* as a historical entity in action (in Chapter 5). Only in the final chapter (Chapter 6) will the interaction of Roman and Christian ideologies be considered, for I will argue that what we have so far taken to be definitive of the political sphere—the theocratic imperial idea—was an attempt by the court to ameliorate rhetorically the vulnerable position in which it found itself always in managing a turbulent republic. Most of the book will, therefore, be devoted to presenting the latter model on its own terms, to see what political phenomena and discourses we can explain by it. Only at the end will I step back to consider the broader context of multiple discourses of power in Byzantium.

While the *politeia* has been effaced in the scholarship, it is pervasive in the sources. For this reason I cite many quotations from the sources and place the Greek in the notes and sometimes in the text. I use the transliterated form *politeia* when discussing the contents of a particular source but sometimes use the form "polity" in my own exposition; I often use the closest direct translation, "republic," for reasons that will become clear. As an English word, "polity" does not carry the baggage of "commonwealth" (complicated by the British Commonwealth and Obolensky's fictitious Byzantine Commonwealth, both worlds apart from what *politeia* meant), nor does *politeia* mean "state," which is how it is often translated, with consequences that are sometimes disastrous.

"Empire" is another confusing term, which has also been inadequately theorized. By "empire" in relation to Byzantium I mean that it was governed by a ruler whom we conventionally call an emperor, in effect a monarch, the *basileus* of the Romans. In other words, in my usage "empire" means "monarchy," and I remain provisionally skeptical of other senses that are attributed to the word by scholars. For example, an alternative would be to call it an empire because it exerted imperial dominion over non-Romans, which at times it did, but this poses the danger of sliding into the concept of the "multiethnic empire," about which I am skeptical in the case of Byzantium. The latter is a misleading concept that intentionally or not disintegrates and elides the (Roman) homogeneity of the vast majority of the population of the "empire." It is unfortunate that we use the same term to refer to such different aspects (namely, having an "emperor" and being a multiethnic empire), which did not always coincide. They did coincide in the early Roman empire, where our terms "imperium" and "imperator" originate, but less so in Byzantium.[12] These are issues that I will explore more fully in the sequel to this study.

As this book will present a Byzantium considerably different from what is found in most surveys and specialized studies, the argument must be presented in steps. Not every lateral problem can be identified and examined at each step, for that would break up the exposition and create many digressions, some of which are separate topics in their own right. I hope that the general concerns of each reader are addressed at a later point in the argument, but I know that it will not be possible to cover everything at first.

It is customary to begin with a review of the scholarship, but in this case that would include most of what has been written by historians about Byzantium in general terms. I would have to write a *History of Byzantine Studies*. While we desperately need that, it cannot be done here or by me. It is at least possible to say this. Most of the misunderstandings about Byzantium that I seek to correct were set in place before the lifetime of any scholar now alive. Scholars today may have their own reasons for repeating them, but they did not invent them. These core notions of ours about Byzantium, however, were not established by rigorous scholarly methods to begin with, were never actually "proven," and have not been subjected to critical scrutiny in modern times. Some, including the denial of the Byzantines' Roman identity, have been handed down to us from ages before the emergence of academic scholarship, and their origins are linked to political and religious interests that we would disown as historians, if only we knew of them. It is my hope that while we have grown comfortable with these notions, we also have no personal stake in them. From many experiences at conferences I gain the sense that the field is ready to begin exploring the Roman dimension of Byzantium, to move past the horror of the Roman name and the "obsession and . . . single-minded focus on Christianity."[13]

In the course of this book, I will be citing exponents of views with which I disagree. Most of these views are so pervasive that they could be illustrated from dozens or hundreds of modern publications. They are positions that everyone in the field has held at one time or another, myself included. I generally try to cite the works of leading scholars in the field, whom I respect immensely. But, as I explained above, they are not the original exponents of these positions, only their modern carriers. Sometimes I cite publications almost at random, since these positions can be found almost everywhere. So if you see your name in the notes, please know that it (usually) could have been anyone else. As I said above, most Byzantinists work on specific issues and produce excellent results. My targets are the broad abstractions that we use to define the culture and its political ideology. No one today is responsible for them, though we have all perpetuated them.

The argument in the book will draw on material from the late fifth century to the twelfth. The starting point is marked by the settling of the emperors in Constantinople and the dynamic resumption of populist republican norms after the intermission of itinerant military rule that started in the third century. The argument could have been based on material from the middle Byzantine period alone, but I wanted to show how these traditions were anchored in Roman late antiquity. As Walter Kaegi pointed out, "the reluctance of many scholars to combine their investigations of the seventh and eighth centuries with researches on the fifth and sixth centuries has contributed to an unnecessary obfuscation of many topics."[14] I am not arguing that the Byzantine republic appeared suddenly in the fifth century and then just as suddenly disappeared when the Crusaders destroyed it. Its history actually extends back into the Roman Republic and forward to 1453, and aspects of that long trajectory will be presented along the way.[15] History did not unfold always according to academic boundaries. But extending the argument fully in those two directions would complicate it unnecessarily; it would require further discussions of its messy rise and fall. There is enough to work with in the period 500–1200.

The argument will inevitably be faulted for not highlighting changes that may have taken place during this period, for presenting a monolithic picture of an unchanging Byzantium. My goal, however, is to define the baseline against which changes can be identified and interpreted. Given past views of the culture as locked in timeless decadence, Byzantinists have understandably embraced the slogan of change, but sometimes it seems to be for its own sake. Byzantium was a remarkably coherent society. We take for granted how easy it is to recognize in the source-record and forget how tied its culture and society were to a specific political order. What I am looking for are precisely the basic parameters of that identity and continuity, and these, I maintain, changed little over time. Lack of change on this fundamental level used to be taken as a sign of permanent decadence, but I take it as proof of dynamic stability and a source of strength.

The Byzantine Republic

CHAPTER 1

Introducing the Byzantine Republic

The term "political ideology" is used regularly in the field of Byzantine Studies and there is a nearly universal consensus about what it was: Byzantine political ideology consisted of the theocratic interpretation of imperial rule found, for example, in imperial panegyrics from Eusebios onward and was echoed in the titles and ceremonies of the court. According to this interpretation, the emperor was appointed to rule by God and had a responsibility to imitate or obey God in his manner of rule. Almost no Byzantinists, however, explain what they mean by the word "ideology" or situate it within a specific theoretical approach.[1] Usually, the term is used to mean just "a basic set of beliefs," on the assumption that most people in the empire held these beliefs and thus tacitly consented to the imperial system. But no one has yet proven *that*, or *in what way*, the population accepted the theocratic notions of court literature, nor has any methodology been devised for generating such proof.

This book is meant as a contribution to the study of Byzantine political ideology. Indeed, it approaches the topic for the first time as an open question and not as a settled set of assumptions on which future research can safely be built. "Ideology" happens to be a potent term with a rich philosophical history, even though most historians use it in a domesticated sense as any set of beliefs that a person or society seems to hold, whether relating to politics, social and economic orders, sex, religion, or some other category.[2] Sometimes beliefs are inferred from historical phenomena (actions or institutions) and sometimes they are quoted from texts, which may or may not adequately explain those historical phenomena (in Byzantine Studies, ideology is largely drawn from texts, and it is rarely brought into the analysis of political history). While

1

they have enriched the term's history and semantic range, modern theoretical schools of thought that have proposed "theories of ideology" are often at odds with each other, and they are not always applicable to the specific problems posed by Byzantine material. My study of this literature has turned up no model whose benefits outweigh its disadvantages. Most theories focus on modern problems, usually relating to class struggle and radical politics, the construction of the Self from a psychoanalytic standpoint, or the thought of a modern thinker, and too much is written in code. In this area, it seems, premodern historians must still fend for themselves.

Words do not have innate meanings, and "ideology" in particular is quite malleable. I will use it in a specific way and ask the reader's indulgence if it does not correspond exactly to the one he or she prefers or is used to. If it still grates, a cumbersome substitute would be "background beliefs, shared between rulers and subjects, about the normative aspects of a given political order, which can be shown to have shaped how the population interacted within the political sphere, especially in times when there was disagreement about the allocation of power." As disagreements over the allocation of power are the stuff of politics, this definition of ideology requires that theory and praxis be studied in tandem. That, then, may serve as a concise definition of ideology. In some respects, it overlaps with prevalent definitions, especially Marxist ones, but in other respects it differs from them.

Specifically, like most historians of Rome and Byzantium today, I do not define ideology explicitly as *false* belief, for example, as a belief whose function was to rationalize social orders and hierarchies by making them appear natural and thus inevitable (or supernatural and thus inevitable), when in fact they were only contingent fictions linked to the interest of specific groups, usually elites. I refrain from this tradition of analysis in part because the beliefs discussed in this book were generated, maintained, and enforced by a broad political consensus. They were about the proper use of state power, the purpose of the imperial position, and who had the right to legitimate the allocation and reallocation of power. It is not clear how a historian can argue that such beliefs were either true or false. It is, by contrast, possible to argue that the theocratic notion that the emperor was appointed to rule by God was false and that it did serve the needs of the court more than those of the population (though not exclusively so, as we will see). According to my definition, however, that theocratic notion might not qualify as an ideology to begin with. Therefore, while some ideologies may well be generally accepted false beliefs that serve the interests of elites (and there are many of those all around us today, and even within us), the ideology that will be presented here will not be of that type.

Another difference between prevalent definitions and my own is that ideologies are not always manufactured by and for the benefit of political elites. I will be arguing that the ideology of the Byzantine political sphere represented a survival of Roman republican notions about the sources, uses, and legitimation of power. A bottom-up model of political authority will be presented to temper, even push back against, the top-down one that prevails in the field. Incidentally, this model will help to explain two unique features of the Byzantine political sphere: why it survived for so long as an integrated, coherent moral and political community (longer than any other monarchy) and why the imperial throne sat atop a political realm that was so turbulent and potentially disloyal. Ordinarily, these two facts would be in tension, but in the Byzantine "monarchical republic" they reinforced each other.

Therefore, ideology will not here be used to refer to "rhetoric" *as opposed to* "reality" or simply to any set of doctrines that can be articulated even if they were not determinative of political practice. *Ideology must help us to understand the actual operations of the political sphere.* The political history of a culture cannot be a refutation of its (alleged) dominant ideology. Not all stated beliefs, then, were equivalent in terms of their existential valence, cognitive and political ontology, or the degree of their popular acceptance and historical impact. The goal of this book will be to identify how people understood their place in society and how they interacted with each other and their political institutions. It will attempt to uncover the Byzantines' basic notions about what kind of political society they lived in, what its moral logic was, what was acceptable and what not; in other words, what "made sense" to them politically and what not.[3] A physicist has compared this to the "mental wallpaper" of a society or "a short-hand for the assumptions we don't get around to articulating,"[4] a neuroscientist to the "most hardwired instincts [that] have usually been left out of the spotlight of inquiry."[5] Ideology is what was taken for granted in the political culture and not only, or not primarily, what was loudly and defensively proclaimed. A fuller treatment of ideology, therefore, might not classify it ontologically as a type of *belief* at all, for beliefs can be easily changed. "Ideology is more personal than belief (since we can simply change our beliefs), less conscious than knowledge or reasons, larger than the individual."[6]

This brings us to the problem of the *sources* and their context-specific limitations. Despite the prevalence of studies with the words "Byzantine political ideology" or "political theory" in their titles, the Byzantines did not theorize their state or society in systematic and comprehensive ways.[7] It is unlikely that any one genre or text perfectly encapsulated the norms of the political sphere, as all were produced within specific historical, political, and discursive contexts and usually served the particular interests of individuals or institutions. Ideologies are matrices of meaning and normativity, but we should not expect to find them laid out in convenient formulas. They are usually implicit rather than explicit, the underlying logic that facilitates the move from premise to conclusion in the act of political reasoning. And what makes the most sense is precisely what needs to be affirmed the least, as it can be taken for granted. Ideology must be excavated; it will not necessarily be written in letters of gold ten feet tall.

The Byzantine sources present us with a wide range of attitudes and even "beliefs" that appear in different settings, were activated in specific contexts, and were relevant primarily, or even exclusively, in those contexts. For example, an innovative political treatise, a *topos* of imperial rhetoric, the standards by which historians evaluated emperors' reigns, a legal preface, the slogans chanted in the streets against an emperor by a rioting populace, and a work of moral advice addressed to an emperor do not all operate on the same level or have equivalent claims on our attention. In general, the argument presented here will avoid the few speculative works of original political thought that were produced during the Byzantine millennium and are now receiving renewed attention, such as the anonymous sixth-century *Dialogue on Political Science,* Thomas Magistros's treatise on kings and their subjects, and Moschopoulos's theory of oaths.[8] Their proposals may have rested on commonly shared assumptions, but we can know this only by comparison with other types of evidence. These texts have to be understood in relation to the political sphere as a whole, but they are idiosyncratic variations of particular aspects of it. They must be brought into the discussion afterward, as they cannot be assumed in advance to reflect the norms of the Byzantine polity.

The orthodox view of Byzantine ideology does not rest on those treatises anyway. Scholars have instead latched on to the formula that the emperor was appointed by God, and pursue it, to the exclusion of all else, through all genres in which it appears. This has resulted in a series of interchangeable views, some more legalistic, other moralizing, or ceremonial, or theological, and so on,[9] and they share an absolute commitment to the nexus of God and emperor. But it is possible that we have been led astray by the court here. The imperial idea is so often recycled because it is impressive, is conveniently discursive, and consists of a handy formula. But that is exactly how it was designed. The formulaic nature of the God-emperor schema makes it easily repeatable, both in Byzantium and in scholarship. This does not mean, however, that we should gullibly view the rest of the culture through it. For instance, no one has yet explained how the alleged belief that the emperor was crowned by God (and all that) shaped subject-ruler interactions in real time, nor have the facts of political history been explained by it. So we need to be skeptical: what is asserted the loudest by those who have the means to broadcast messages is not necessarily an ideology. It was an important part of the culture, no doubt, but in what way exactly remains unclear. We must instead use a variety of sources to "triangulate" their political logic in search of an (often unspoken) ideological core. That is why I will use as wide a variety of sources as possible. The result may not be entirely coherent or orderly, in part because no complex culture such as Byzantium was fully coherent or orderly. But its center held for a long time, and I do not believe that it was located in the theology of the imperial position.

Some aspects of Byzantine ideology are easy to identify. All historians would agree that monarchy was (nearly) universally regarded as the optimal type of regime. In the period studied here, there were no movements to institute a different regime and only two or three theorists (in the early sixth century) favored the Republic. Therefore, in terms of the ontology of the political sphere, it made intuitive "sense" to the Byzantines that one person should be in charge. Yet this does not take us far. Monarchy is a broad category that can be inflected by different ideologies concerning the source and legitimate use of its power and the relationship between ruler and subjects. What type of monarchy, then, was Byzantium? The thesis of this book is that Byzantium was a republican monarchy and not primarily a monarchy by divine right. In the rest of this section,

I will set out some of the reasons that warrant skepticism of the theo-cratic rhetoric. The evidence for them will be presented in the rest of the book.

First, our current version of imperial ideology focuses almost exclu-sively on the emperor and has little to say about the terms that defined his relationship with his subjects. As that relationship is not theorized, it is treated pragmatically as the operation of largely coercive institu-tions. Most studies that purport to talk about "imperial ideology" really mean *ideology about the emperor*,[10] as if he were the only political entity of consequence; they do not mean *ideology about how Byzantine political society was supposed to operate*. The notion that "the person of the emperor [was] the embodiment of Byzantine ideology"[11] is fairly uncontroversial but is doubly wrong: it was not the *person* that mattered as much as the *office*, and the office hardly exhausted the reach and content of Byzantine po-litical ideology. The Byzantines had a sophisticated ideological ontology that placed the office into a particular kind of relation with the rest of society, of which they also had a specific, distinctively Roman view. But this is invisible in most modern accounts, which are biased in favor of the most theological end of court propaganda and tend to omit from their discussion passages in those texts that point toward the republican di-mension of political ideology, or even go so far as to quote passages in which the legitimacy of imperial rule is drawn from the *people* to support a view that it was bestowed by *God*.[12] No scholar is playing fast and loose with the evidence here, in part because no one seems to be aware that there are in fact alternatives in play here. Rather, the theological bias is so ingrained in the field that we assume that all texts must be saying the same thing, namely, what we have all instructed each other to see through sheer repetition. There is a general bias (that also permeates the study of Byzantine religion) in favor of official doctrinal positions as opposed to ideologies that are revealed in social practice or less official sources. That is, in part, why the study of religion in Byzantium is identical with the study of Orthodoxy, and why anthropology has made so little headway: we tend to privilege what the Byzantines professed to believe over what they actually did.

Second, there is a gap between our theories of Byzantine ideology and how the Byzantines actually behaved as historical agents. If the emper-or's legitimacy was theological; if, as Cyril Mango flatly stated, "not only did God ordain the existence of the empire, He also chose each individual emperor, which was why no human rules were formulated for his appointment";[13] and also, if the Byzantines were as orthodox as we have been led to believe, then how was it that they not only criticized their emperors so virulently and so commonly, sang offensive songs about them in public, and plotted against them but also rebelled against them or joined rebellions against them and then killed them or blinded them, without seeming to remember God or his ordinations at such times? Why was tenure of the throne so fragile? This fact is rarely mentioned in studies of the imperial office and system of Byzantium, an omission that enables the illusion of the alleged dominant ideology.[14] It is not surprising, consequently, that no one has yet been able to explain the turbulence of Byzantine politics on the basis of the "imperial ideology." Political history is recounted pragmatically in modern scholarship, in whatever way each scholar thinks the dynamics of power played out each time. But why do we set the allegedly dominant ideology aside when we describe such events? Should it not rather be *precisely* the ideology that helps us to interpret them? "Dynamics of power" and "pragmatism" are culturally specific in most other fields, but not in how we write Byzantine history, because our chosen model of "ideology" has nothing to say about the actual operation of the political sphere, leaving us each at the mercy of his own intuitions about how power worked.

A literary genre that has curiously been omitted from our reconstruction of Byzantine ideology is historiography, which is odd given how crucial it is for the reconstruction of Byzantine history. Yet upon reflection this makes sense, given that the Byzantine historians often present a picture of the polity and emperor that is at odds with what the court genres say, sometimes explicitly so, and their narratives, from which we must infer the "dynamics of power," do not lend themselves to handy formulas; they are in fact quite complex. The exception that proves the rule is the heavy use by scholars of those few historical sources that are close in spirit and intention to panegyrical texts, for example, the *Life of Basileios I (Vita Basilii)*.

Third, given that the Byzantines were Romans (it was intuitively obvious to them, if not to us), no account of their ideology can stand unless it seriously considers the Roman basis of their polity. Statements such as that "Christianity was the all-pervasive ideology of the Byzantine empire, its rituals, doctrines, and structures dominating every aspect of life . . . In being Byzantine, one was first and foremost a Christian"[15] sound increasingly stranger the more time one spends with the primary sources. They are, in fact, products of the echo chamber that is Byzantine Studies, which has rigidly barred entry to the Roman voice for its own ideological reasons. So far only Beck openly resisted this trend and pushed back against the weight of political interests (turned into academic biases) that have denied the Roman identity of Byzantium for so long. This aspect of the argument will, then, be developed in detail. "Rome" was not just a prestigious name used by the emperors for propaganda or diplomacy. It was the matrix that generated the moral logic of the Byzantine polity. What we call Byzantium was nothing other than a Roman *politeia,* a "republic." Two features of its ideology can be stated here to indicate its difference from the imperial-theological model: One, it postulated a theoretically secular political sphere that operated between the emperor and his subjects (secular not in that it excluded religion but in that it was not defined by it, religion being only one part of the polity). This space was obviously not the same as the metaphysical space that mediated the relationship between emperor and God. Two, it authorized a bottom-up model of sovereignty in which the emperor could be and often was held accountable to the rest of the polity.

The identification of Byzantium with a particular type of theocratic order was promoted by Enlightenment thinkers who wanted to use it as a model by which to discuss contemporary problems indirectly. They were not interested in the historical truth about Byzantium; it was only a convenient model, and they were using it for their own political purposes. In recent years there has been a concerted effort to push back against many aspects of that polemical model, but the theocratic ideology abides. It is not easy to understand why this is. We are no longer beholden to the notion that Rome belongs exclusively to western, Latin-based cultures and institutions. Instead, it is possible that the imperial idea is still promoted by scholars precisely because it is alien to modern western ways of thinking about politics. By proclaiming that they are in touch with "other" ways of thinking that are allegedly incommensurate with our own, scholars can establish anthropological credentials and reassure themselves and their audiences that they are respecting the otherness of a foreign culture by not projecting modern norms onto it. It would then be an anthropological failure to make the Byzantines seem too rational, normal, pragmatic, or whatever. This becomes programmatic: "The Byzantines were different from modern western cultures in most respects," begins a recent collection of essays, and its approach is not untypical.[16] Our need to believe such things is probably built into *our* ideology.[17]

An Emperor in Dialogue with the *Politeia:* The *Novels* of Leon VI

I will take as a starting point the collection of 113 laws (technically called *Novels: Nearai* in Greek, *Novellae Constitutiones* in Latin) issued by the emperor Leon VI (886–911) in the very middle of the middle Byzantine period. These texts are not well known outside the subfield of Byzantine legal studies, and there is almost no scholarship devoted to them in English. As it has come down to us, the collection was edited and revised, probably privately, before the production of the earliest surviving manuscript, though the revision aimed only to summarize and condense the contents and eliminate the formal protocols that had in the meantime become redundant. It is likely that the original collection was made or sponsored by Leon himself, who wrote the *Novels* personally in the first years of his reign (between 886 and 889). If they were not originally issued as a single corpus, they quickly became that.[18] We will not be concerned here with how these *Novels* fit into the overall history and shape of Byzantine law, how they were meant to interact with prior legislation, or with their specific provisions, sources, and social impact, topics that have already been discussed by others.[19] Nor is it my purpose to highlight or demote Leon as an original thinker, only to bring out the notions that he seems to have taken for granted regarding his role as lawgiver in relation to the polity that he was governing and his dialectical engagement with its "pre-legal" normative practices.

In the preface to the collection, Leon explains how the laws have fallen into confusion and declares that he cannot overlook matters "on which the tranquility and good order of the *politeia* depend." He therefore decided to "ratify, by the written decisions of our *basileia* [imperial authority], the validity in the *politeia* of those laws that were deemed useful," while others he would "exile from the *politeuma*." Moreover, "given that among the customs that are currently practiced some appeared that were neither irrational nor such that a prudent mind would scorn, we have honored these with the privileges of law, elevating them from the rank of silent custom to the normative honor of a law."[20] In Leon's terminology, laws that are, or become, valid take their place among the elements of the *politeia* through the verb *politeuontai*, which I will be translating "to be part of the *politeia*" or "to take part in the *politeia*." This verb, we will see, was applied generally in Byzantium to subjects and rulers alike, including emperors. The verb *politeuomai* is used, then, at first sight, for anything that plays a legitimate role in the *politeia*; it is a normative term. As we will see in this chapter, it is also a Roman term, a result of the Roman colonization of the meaning of Greek words.[21] But it contains an ambiguity relating to the source of legitimacy: was that source the *basileia* itself or generated by the rest of the polity? Leon's language implies a dialectical process for creating full legitimacy.

The first *Novel* begins by praising the legislative work of Justinian, as an obvious model for that of Leon.[22] Justinian's decision to harmonize the laws was "a most useful and excellent one for the *politeia*" and worked "to the benefit of the subjects," but it was not altogether successful as confusion crept in through the addition of new laws as well as "by customs that were not ratified by law but had as their sole authority the will of the masses."[23] Leon declares his intention to reharmonize the laws in the way that he explains in the preface, but he instructs his magistrates and judges that no custom is to be considered as legally binding unless it bears the stamp of his official approval. In other words, custom has a right to the lawgiver's attention and consideration and poses a normative claim in the polity, but it is not legally binding unless it is formally made into a law by the proper authority, that is, the emperor.[24] The *Novels* adhere to this programmatic statement closely. In one case, a current custom is explicitly called better than an old law and takes its place.[25] In another it is noted that an awkward law had been rejected by "the will of the people" (τῶν ἀνθρώπων ἡ προαίρεσις) and so it had to go: its provisions were already not part of the *politeia* (οὐ πολιτευομένων) and therefore the emperor formally "ostracized them from the *politeia*."[26] It would seem, then, that what Leon calls "the will of the people" had already ensured that this law was not de facto part of the polity before the emperor's intervention, regardless of the fact that it still had *de iure* validity. This raises the question of who really constituted and defined the polity. The polity seems to be constituted by both official and unofficial decisions taken respectively by the emperor and "the people."

This ambiguity in the definition of what counts as "being part of the *politeia*" comes to the fore at the end of *Novel* 21, where the emperor ratifies another custom with this confusing imperative: τοῦτο δὲ πολιτευέσθω . . . καὶ πρὸ δόγματος νόμου πολιτευόμενον ("let that now be part of the *politeia* . . . which was already part of the *politeia* before this legal ratification"). The polity appears here in two guises that are in tension: a prior de facto aspect constituted by popular will, and a posterior *de iure* aspect constituted by imperial ratification. Leon, as emperor, uses the imperative to do something that the people have already done. In *Novel* 20, he recognizes that an attempt by his father Basileios I to revive an older law and annul recent legislation had proven futile, as the people were irrationally clinging to their customs. Rather grudgingly, he endorses their practice. He gives the impression of having been compelled to do so by the customs of the popular polity.

Leon alternately calls the bearers of custom "the people," "the majority," or "the masses" (οἱ ἄνθρωποι, τὸ πλῆθος, ὁ ὄχλος), all ways of rendering the Latin *populus*.[27] He refers to them in a *Novel* as the "crew" or "complement" (πλήρωμα) of the *politeia*, an interesting metaphor, alluding perhaps to the ancient metaphor of the ship of state.[28] In *Novel* 57, Leon ratifies a customary practice, noting that even without ratification it seems adequate "to people these days (τοῖς νῦν)," but still he deems it worthy of official sanction. In some cases he paternalistically revives laws that had fallen into desuetude,[29] so we might speak of a certain sort of "negotiation" taking place between the emperor and his subjects. But this is not exactly how Leon wanted to present it. He waxes paternalistic in *Novel* 59: "The laws ought to be to citizens *(politai)* what a father is to his children, looking, that is, solely to the advantage and security of those who comprise the *politeia (politeuomenoi)*."[30] But the same tension that we observed above applies here too: What kind of father makes rules based on what his children are doing? Who is in charge here? Leon wants his audience to believe that it is he. But he is not taking the lead in most issues.[31] His simile disguises, rather than reveals, what is going on. This is related to the fact that Leon does not appear to have firm standards for which "customs" to ratify and which not. At any rate, one thing is clear: we are operating here in a realm of negotiation that is "down-to-earth,"[32] that exists between the emperor and his subjects and not between the emperor and God.

The *politeia* can be insulted by bad practices,[33] it can be purified,[34] and it must be orderly.[35] "For the good order of the *politeia* nothing is to be preferred over the good order of the laws, for one could fittingly say that the laws are the eyes of the *politeia*."[36] "The laws are the supports and foundations of the *politeia*" and "they are the leaders *(hegemones)* of the *politeia*."[37] Still, the *Novels* suggest, in their totality, that the *politeia* also has a quasi-autonomous and prior existence: it is not completely defined by the legislator, as it seems to operate independently, to a certain degree. First, both customs and laws (old and recent) are judged by whether they are useful and advantageous to the *politeia*, and they are constantly being judged so by both the legislator and the other members of the *politeia*.[38] So the good of the *politeia* is a standard that exists prior to the operation of law, and may be interpreted variously. Unfortunately, Leon does not explain what standards he has been following. There does not seem to be a coherent sense of policy here.[39] Second, the citizens do not always wait for the legislator to tell them their interest. The polity is the abstracted concept of a community that is *constituted* by the citizens (or subjects) of the empire, their values, and their choices, while it is *regulated* or *strengthened* by the imperial laws. The laws do not create the polity. It is not an artificial legal entity arbitrarily projected by the state onto its subjects; rather, its norms shape imperial legislation, without being, in themselves, sources of formal law, as Leon hastens to note. Gilbert Dagron has written that we are observing "a gradual transfer of the norms generated by a society (practices) to the state (i.e., imperial thought and discourse) . . . On the whole Leon merely records the change, as if describing and governing a society comes to the same thing when one is an emperor."[40]

This dynamic of custom and ratification is not as dominant, or even evident, in all legal projects of the middle period. John Haldon has written about how, in the seventh century, "imperial action was not directed at emending laws to conform to reality, but rather at emending reality to conform to the inherited legal-moral apparatus."[41] Haldon is addressing here the question of the relative decline of the *Novella* as a means of legislation after Justinian. Still, Leon VI was acting within an established tradition of Roman jurisprudence which recognized that custom had a claim on the lawgiver. As Jill Harries put it succinctly about late antiquity:

> Emperors were entitled to respond, or not, not only to legal pressures but to social and political pressures as well. This right was in fact essential to the emperor's own legitimacy as a law-giver; he could expect his constitutions to be backed by the consent of society as a whole, the *consensus universorum* . . . The emperors' openness to social change may

have made their legislation more responsive to public needs and changing social mores than it would otherwise have been . . . Historically Roman law has always contained a moral dimension, meaning that it was
responsive to the social mores of the time, and it was an accepted part
of juristic theory that the application of some laws was heavily depen-
dent on social attitudes.[42]

The following legal opinion was enshrined in Justinian's *Digest* and retained in the *Basilika* (the Greek translation officially published under
Leon VI): "Those matters about which there is no written law are to be
governed by custom and usage . . . Ancient custom takes the place of law.
So just as law is put in place, whether it is written or unwritten, so too is
it annulled, either through writing or without it, that is, through lack of
use."[43] As we have seen, this was a principle followed by at least some Byzantine emperors. Leon's son Konstantinos VII would use even stronger
language for "the prior validity of unwritten custom": ὅπερ ἡ συνήθεια
ἀγράφως πρώην ἐκύρωσε (*kyros* here denotes official authority or jurisdiction).[44] In the twelfth century, the historian and legal scholar Ioannes
Zonaras criticized in his *Chronicle* the emperor Basileios II for not ruling
"according to the prevailing custom, which legislative authorities have
deemed fit to ratify as law; instead, he ruled according to his own will."[45]

It is a picture such as the one that Harries paints for late antiquity
that this book will seek to defend regarding the Byzantine polity, and
not only about law but about its very conception and political sphere.
Specifically, the polity was conceived by its rulers and subjects as a unified community founded on shared values, and the legitimacy of the regime was based on its solicitude for the values and welfare of its subjects
in the Roman "republican" tradition. This is of course not a statement
about how individuals or groups actually behaved at all times but rather
about the ideology that underpinned Romanía, the moral and political
framework of their actions. This framework created reciprocal responsibilities between rulers and subjects, and emperors had to take the pulse
of the *politeia* before making decisions. The law itself fell into this arena
of negotiation. Leon personified the laws and treated them as metaphorical subjects to some of whom he would bestow "ranks and titles"
(here legal validity) while others he would "exile" (pref.), as if they were
magistrates.[46] Therefore, in making decisions about both laws and persons, emperors were shaping the *politeia* by contributing to an ongoing

general discussion about its nature and direction, about what would be included and what excluded. The law (as we will see in more detail in Chapter 3) was subject to the prevailing consensus about the common good. We should not obscure this point with reference to putative special-interest groups. When Leon refers to "customs" in a given *Novel* he is usually referring to norms prevailing only in a particular segment of society, the segment to which the provisions of that *Novel* apply (e.g., fishermen). But he does not frame it that way: he needed to invoke "the people" as a whole rather than a special-interest group, because that was how reforms were justified in Roman society. Were we to cynically disperse his *populus* into lobbying groups, we would miss the ideological forest for the special-interest trees.

The moral logic and reasoning behind Leon's *Novels* contain several keys to this ideology. While some emperors may have chosen to dictate their terms to the polity, others, such as Leon, entered into a more dialectical relationship with it. It is from the latter that we must take the lead if we wish to understand the ideological framework of imperial action, the political sphere in which it self-consciously operated. Haldon argues that "the law, whether or not its detailed prescriptions and demands were understood or applied, symbolized the Roman state . . . It existed as the theoretical backdrop to the practical ideology of the state and to the political-cultural beliefs upon which people based their understanding of the world."[47] The terms on which subjects and rulers conceived their mutual relationship are encoded there, and we must attend to them closely. However, there has yet been no study of the Byzantine notion of the *politeia* or of the sphere to which it points. Given its centrality to the political thinking of all Byzantines, emperors and subjects alike, we must now ask, what was this *politeia* to which Leon keeps referring?

The Byzantine Concept of the *Politeia*

Clearly, it is not satisfactory to translate *politeia* as "state," as is commonly done.[48] Most of Leon's uses of the word and its cognates would not make sense if taken in this restrictive sense (we will examine modern notions of "the state" and their problems below). Leon certainly has the whole of Roman society in mind when he refers to the *politeia*, but at the same time he does not want to theorize it as independent of the institutions of the state and his own laws: he has no notion of a "civil society" constituted by private interests that are separate from the state.[49] He believes that a proper *politeia* cannot exist without good laws but at the same time reluctantly grants that some of its elements are operating prior to or without receiving legal sanction. Before we trace the genealogy of this term, let us flesh out its semantic range in this period by examining texts in different genres.

It was probably in the ninth century that a certain Syrianos wrote a military manual later used as a source by Leon VI when he wrote his own *Taktika* at the end of the century.[50] To frame the social context of military science, Syrianos, in the first chapter of his treatise, lists the parts of the *politeia,* though the first page or more of his work has been lost. When the text begins we find "teachers of grammar and rhetoric, physicians, farmers, and those in like professions." He adds priests, lawyers, many types of merchants and craftsmen, and "the unproductive classes," such as the infirm, the old, and children, "who are unable to contribute anything to the needs of the community (τὴν τῶν κοινῶν χρείαν)." All these, he says, "are the parts of the *politeia.*" He considers adding the leisured classes but decides not to because they contribute nothing (and presumably, unlike the infirm, the old, and children, they have no excuse). He imagines the polity through the organic metaphor of the living body: "Just as in the human body you will not find any single part that has no function, so too in the best *politeia* there should be no part that, while it is able to contribute to the welfare of the *politeia,* does nothing." In the second chapter, he lists the functions of each part of the *politeia,* while in the third he explains the moral and professional qualifications of those men who preside over each part: almost all of them are state officials of one kind or another. Again, the polity is imagined as the whole of society under the ideal aspect of the common good, and not independently of the institutions of the state. What we call "the state" is a fully integrated part of the polity, but a part different from the others in that it acts in an official capacity: it regulates the various elements with an eye on the common good and thereby makes the operations of the polity legitimate in its own eyes.

Syrianos's *politeia* cannot be translated as "the state." The translator George Dennis here and only here translates it as "the various classes of citizens." But when translating the headings, he goes with "statecraft" and "the state," though it is the same word. Syrianos has in mind the whole of what we call "society" in all its diversity. When he looks back at it in introducing the military science, he calls it "the multitude of civilians who take part in the *politeia*."[51] We could also go with "populace" here or "unarmed citizens." At the same time, however, he takes this society to be an organic whole integrally linked with and regulated by government institutions. This is also how Leon imagined the relation between the people and the laws: the laws are metaphorical magistrates. This organism has a common good, which Syrianos calls τὰ κοινά, and he evaluates its various limbs based on what they contribute to that common good. As we will see, τὰ κοινά was only a way of designating the *politeia* through the prism of its collective interests. Leon VI had imagined his legislation working in the same way: "It is nobly fitting for those who are willing to devise, through their own efforts, some benefit for use in life, to make it a benefit for all in common (ἐν κοινῷ); this is better than to want to limit it to a small group, and exclude all others from it. It is all the more fitting that the benefaction caused by the laws should be common (κοινήν). Just as with the virtue of a leader, so too with the laws: it is our duty that the good that comes from it should be enjoyed in common (κοινῇ) by all rulers and ruled alike."[52] This principle strongly affirms the superiority of the common good over individual interests.

In other words, for all that Syrianos takes a global view of his society and classifies its constituent parts, he does not have a purely descriptive view of it. The normative concept of "the best *politeia*" is part and parcel of his very concept of a *politeia;* in other words, he believes that a proper *politeia* ought to try to be a good one. This is a global extension of his thinking that each particular part of the *politeia,* whether doctors, lawyers, or magistrates, also ought to strive to be *good* doctors, lawyers, and magistrates.[53] He offers an organic vision of a unified society under the tutelage of the state, in which neither side can exist without the other. It is hard to put this in modern terms because it is based on a unified idea of the common good and not on a balancing of separate interests. As with Leon, Syrianos does not view the elements of the *politeia* as constituting a self-standing world of private interests (a "civil society") over which "the state" is imposed as a regulatory agency. What we call the state is built into the fabric and the very purpose of this collective because the collective is defined by its common good and "the state" is what enables it to achieve it.

Syrianos's classification of the parts of the polity was not official in a legal or other sense. Any writer looking at Byzantine society could produce a different classification, usually one that suited his objectives at that moment. What they do share, however, is a concept of the common good of a unified republic. In the long accession-speech attributed to him by the court poet Corippus, Justin II (in 565) compares the *imperium Romanum* to a single body, only he is really talking about the *res publica*, not the "empire" if by that we mean the provinces, and in fact he calls it the *res publica* in the middle of the speech. Its head is the emperor, the senators are the breast and arms, the lower orders are the feet (he singles out the farmers for special attention), and the treasury is the stomach.[54] The preface to a treatise on agriculture *(Geoponika)* dedicated in the mid-tenth century to Leon's son, Konstantinos VII, states that the emperor knows that "the *politeia* is divided into three parts: the military, the priesthood, and agriculture."[55] This is shorthand for "everyone." The historian Attaleiates in the late eleventh century conceded that craftsmen and workmen (βάναυσοι) also contributed useful things to the *politeia*.[56] Everyone who wanted to attract imperial attention or claim a benefit for his own field or profession would make it one of the key divisions of the *politeia* precisely in order to argue that it was indispensable for the common good. For example, in the preface of his *Taktika* Leon VI states that military science was an essential element of the "affairs of the *politeia*," a phrase that he uses synonymously in the same sentence with "the affairs of the Romans."[57] To give a related example, the preface to a treatise on naval warfare composed in 959 for the *parakoimomenos* Basileios begins by declaring that naval warfare is "as useful for life and constitutes a *politeia*" as nothing else.[58] Hyperbole, to be sure, but that was how the importance of anything was gauged in Byzantium: what did it contribute to the polity? Konstantinos VII was himself praised by his biographer for "adorning and enriching the *politeia* of the Romans with wisdom," given that "there are many noble and praiseworthy sciences, technical arts, and disciplines in our *politeia*."[59] The common good, therefore, was defined always in relation to the polity, and it embraced and governed both state and nonstate activities—all of them that had any social or moral value.

It is in this spirit that we should take the opening lines of the *Eisagoge*, the controversial legal text written possibly by the patriarch Photios in the ninth century: "The *politeia* is constituted of members and limbs, in a like manner to human beings, and the greatest and most necessary parts are the emperor and the patriarch."[60] None of these classificatory systems was either exhaustive or exclusive, as each was designed to promote only the element of the polity that was of immediate concern to the author at that moment (in the case of this text, the patriarchate). They reveal that the polity was a collectivity in terms of whose good every type of profession or person was defined, including the emperor. In fact, treating the emperor as part of the polity was hardly controversial, though the *Eisagoge*'s attempt to postulate an equality between him and the patriarch and to distinguish their jurisdiction was.

The modern study of Byzantine politics and political ideology has largely effaced the concept of the *politeia* and the relationships that it entailed, and has fixed all attention on the person, position, and divine pretensions of the emperor, as though the political sphere in Byzantium began and ended with the *basileia*. Translating *politeia* as "the state" in all instances, even when it clearly has a much broader and deeper meaning, facilitates this narrowing of vision in favor of the emperor (given that he controlled the institutions of governance) and eliminates the existence of a common good that was not entirely under his control, a κοινόν, precisely what Leon was negotiating with in his *Novels*. In practice, of course, the *basileia* and *politeia* were inseparable. One could not have a polity without a state, and the state happened to be monarchical. Therefore, some (not all) of Syrianos's parts of the polity, for example, soldiers, tax-inspectors, and judges, could also be seen as aspects of imperial administration. According to Psellos, when Konstantinos IX ascended the throne, he saw that the *basileia* was a "composite thing" and had to appoint generals to govern one part of it, judges to another, advisors to a third, and so on. "And lest the state (τὸ κράτος) be broken into its parts," he appointed one man to oversee it all, the honorand of the speech, Konstantinos Leichoudes.[61] But in moving from the *politeia* to the "state" via the *basileia,* something has been lost, namely, a global view of society, replaced with a more narrow view, namely, that of "administration." This narrowing was a function of Psellos's genre, panegyric. We should remember this when dealing with the evidence of imperial orations: to shine the spotlight, as they must, on one person, they relegate everything else to the sidelines or see it exclusively from the imperial point of view. Thus it was possible to view the *politeia* from the standpoint of the *basileia* or the *kratos,* but we have to keep in mind that this was a partial view imposed by one genre.

Let us stay with Psellos for a moment. His orations and *Chronographia* are concerned more with the *basileia* than the *politeia,* for obvious reasons of genre, but toward the end of the first edition of the *Chronographia* he offers a fascinating summary of how the *politeia* had declined because of imperial mismanagement, specifically, fiscal mismanagement.[62] Here he uses the terms κράτος ("the state"), τὸ πολιτικὸν σῶμα ("the body politic" or "the civil administration"), τὰ πολιτικὰ πράγματα ("political affairs"), and τὸ σῶμα τῆς πολιτείας ("the body of the *politeia*") interchangeably. He offers a grotesque metaphor of a state budget that had many heads and countless arms and legs, that was swollen in some parts, rotting in others, and growing through successive reigns.[63] In a later section, he compares the *politeia* to an overloaded merchant ship.[64] This was a narrower conception of the *politeia* than what we found in Syrianos and Leon VI, but it was still a valid way of looking at one and the same political sphere. We could say that Psellos was looking at it from above, from inside the palace, rather than building it up from the ground, as Syrianos and others were doing.

So from where had Byzantium inherited a conception of the polity that referred at once to society-at-large, the political sphere, the people in their political capacity, the affairs of the state, and the state itself? The answer is: from ancient Rome, whose direct descendent Byzantium was in an unbroken line of political and ideological continuity. The Byzantine *politeia* was but a translation of Latin *res publica.*

The *Politeia* between Republic and Empire

Calling Byzantium (or any Roman-style empire) a "republic" will strike most readers as counterintuitive. In modern times, increasingly since the eighteenth century, monarchies and republics have been viewed as mutually exclusive types of regimes. This has been reinforced by the modern (not Roman) convention of using the labels "Republic" and "Empire" to distinguish two phases of Roman history. But *res publica* in Roman usage (*politeia* in Byzantine Greek translation) did not refer to the type of regime that governed the polity. It referred rather to certain underlying aspects of a polity that, among other things, legitimated the use of state power in a context of popular sovereignty. In the eyes of the Romans themselves, what we call "the Empire" was just another phase of the history of the Roman *res publica,* for the purpose of state power and the theory of popular sovereignty did not necessarily change in the transition from the regime of the consuls to that of the emperors. This section will try to look past the distracting conventions of modern terminology to unearth Roman and Byzantine notions about the continuity of the *res publica.*

The Greek term *politeia* had a long and complicated history and had come, by late antiquity and into Byzantine times, to mean many different things. For example, it could refer to the regimen or "lifestyle" of a person or group, such as monks, a usage we find in hagiography. It could refer to a city, though this was uncommon.[65] In classical authors, however, it referred primarily to the type of regime by which a city-state was governed, especially the arrangement of its offices. There were various types of *politeiai,* for example monarchy, aristocracy, and democracy.[66] Many of these senses survived in Byzantium. But here we will focus on its dominant meaning in Byzantine political, legal, and historical texts, where *politeia* was the most common way of rendering *res publica.* We encounter a range of additional terms for that concept in the sources, which correspond to different senses of the Latin original (*res publica,* or *res Romana*) and which are attested in official bilingual inscriptions in antiquity: *res publica* could also be τὸ κοινόν, τὰ κοινά, τὰ πολιτικὰ πράγματα, τὰ δημόσια πράγματα, τὰ κοινὰ πράγματα, τὰ τῶν Ῥωμαίων πράγματα, τὰ Ῥωμαϊκά, and other combinations. Some of these were used already in the widely disseminated Greek version of Augustus's *Res Gestae.* That version disregarded terms that resonated in Greek tradition and used odd renditions, possibly to assert a "distinctive Romanness."[67] It was the beginning of a process that ultimately infused Greek terms with a Roman semantic range. By the age of Justinian, *politeia* was the dominant standard translation of *res publica.*[68] Many of these Greek terms used to translate *res publica* had little history in Greek thought before Rome. Byzantium was a Roman and not a Greek culture in this respect. So Byzantine *politeia* might strike us as a Greek term, and it was—except for what it meant. So let us explain why the term *politeia* was being used to mean *res publica* so long after what we call "the Republic" had ended.

In ancient Rome, *res publica* (also in the form *res Romana*) could refer to the Roman state, the public administration, the public property, the political affairs, the collective agency, and the common good of the Roman people: in sum, it had the same semantic range as Byzantine *politeia*.[69] Harriet Flower's definition, based on ancient Roman sources, elucidates the concept that we explicated based on the texts of Syrianos, Leon VI, and others: "the term *res publica* suggests the unity of all citizens in a shared civic community that transcends the social divisions of class, neighborhood, or family. Such a community is fundamentally at odds with the whole concept of political parties that divide citizens into permanent factions or allegiance groups."[70] The *res publica* was owned by the *populus* collectively. Cicero's definition is famous: the *res publica* "is the property of a people. But a people is not just any collection of human beings brought together in any sort of way, but an assemblage of people in large numbers associated in an agreement with respect to justice and a partnership for the common good."[71] We will come back to the implications of this definition, but some terminological observations are first in order. *Res publica* also happened to be how Roman authors such as Cicero translated the prior Greek philosophical term *politeia*, which had many of the same connotations. But there is a key distinction: ancient Greek *politeia* usually referred to the type of regime by which a city-state was governed. While we must allow for cross-contamination between Latin and Greek, especially in theoretical authors such as Cicero,[72] in Roman usage *res publica* referred to the public affairs and state of the Romans regardless of the type of political regime by which they were governed.

Cicero allowed for the possibility of a *res publica* governed well by kings, an aristocracy, or a democracy: "provided the bond holds firm, which in the first place fastened the people to each other in the fellowship of a community, any of these three types may be, not indeed perfect, nor in my view the best, but at least tolerable."[73] Cicero's view of Rome under the kings shows that he recognized the possibility of a monarchical *res publica*,[74] and his Scipio, when pressed to choose one of three simple constitutional forms (rather than the mixed constitution of Rome), opts for monarchy. So Cicero did not view monarchy as incompatible with a *res publica* although he did think that it posed the risk of tyranny and loss of the rule of law.[75] Conversely, Cicero's exaggerated view of the role and power in the *res publica* of the senate (his own preferred leading body of governance) could have easily been said by a Byzantine thinker about his emperor.[76] So according to Cicero the *res publica* was not regime-specific:

monarchies could be republican. This understanding of "republican" survived until early modern times. Some early modern theorists also maintained that republican monarchies were viable.[77] James Hankins has recently exposed the debates of the Renaissance that gradually led to the term *res publica* being associated exclusively with nonmonarchical regimes.[78] This was a function of modern politics. Down to that point, however, the term had more or less retained its original Roman meaning, which was not regime-specific.

Moreover, Schofield has shown that Cicero's discussion of the *res publica* is not primarily about the best regime-type but the grounds for the *legitimacy* of the government (whatever form it may take), and that his argument relies on distinctly Roman concepts that had little precedent in Greek tradition; this is, after all, how Cicero presents his own project.[79] In Greek theory, the best type of *politeia* was cast as a regime of virtue, less so of law, and there was no question of its legitimacy being grounded in popular consensus. While the argument for popular sovereignty in Byzantium will be made in two later chapters of this book, the case I am making here is that the Roman idea of the *res publica* underlay the Byzantine *politeia*: it was, in fact, the same "*politeia* of the Romans" in a later phase of its history. As a sixth-century treatise echoed Cicero (now in Greek), "a *politeia* is a *koinon* [something shared] consisting of many people."[80] Starting in the fourth century (and possibly in the third), the Byzantines had given this republic a name: Romanía. We could, then, call the regime of Byzantium an "imperial republic,"[81] that is, a republic with an emperor (as opposed to an expansionist republic). Preferably, we should call it a republican monarchy, monarchical republic, or just "the Roman Republic in its monarchic phase."[82] A number of scholars have proposed such terms, though sometimes with the usual arbitrary limitations ("until the reign of Diocletian").[83]

But what about the modern distinction between "the Republic" and "the Empire"? This distinction may still make it counterintuitive to call Byzantium a republic. It is, however, largely modern and interferes with our understanding of the original terms. The "Republic" is a modern misnomer. To see this we have to make a distinction between how the Romans, both before and after Augustus, used the term *res publica* and how our scholarship has pressed it into service as a (politicized and moralizing) label for a period of Roman history. Actually, with us it is not so much a label for a period (in the way that Classical and Archaic are) as it is for a particular type of regime, that governed by the consuls. Both Romans and Byzantines alike, however, could and did distinguish between the *res publica* and the way in which the *res publica* was governed (see below). Use of the term "republic" to refer to a period and a form of regime (that of the consuls or the senate) is a feature of the *modern* languages. To quote Flower again: "The Romans themselves did not have a way of labeling their government with terms that specifically designated a republic . . . Moreover, *res publica* was the term still employed to describe the government during the subsequent 'imperial' period, both by emperors and by their critics."[84] What we call "the Republic" was for them but one regime of governance in the long history of the *res publica*. The *res publica* itself was what underlay regime-change. Thus, we can draw a distinction between "republican," which points to the original meanings of *res publica,* and "Republican," which refers to the period and institutions of one phase of Roman history.

In sum, modern scholars say that under Augustus the Republic was abolished and the Empire instituted. An ancient Roman scholar, by contrast, would say that the form of governance of the *res publica* changed from that of the consuls to that of emperors. (Witness, for example, Arcadius Charisius, a jurist of the Tetrarchy: *regimentis rei publicae ad imperatores perpetuos translatis.*)[85]

To be sure, dramatic changes occurred in the transition from the consuls to the monarchy, but this was not taken by the vast majority of Romans to mean that their *res publica* had been abolished. The Romans of the empire used the term for their own society in the same way that their Republican ancestors had done, knowing that Augustus had altered the regime.[86] He controversially claimed to have restored the *res publica,*[87] and contemporaries would have greeted this claim with more or less skepticism depending on how integral they believed a specific type of regime was to the essence of the *res Romana.* Few were as skeptical as the mainstream of modern scholarship has been.

The *res publica* in ancient Rome and the *politeia* in Byzantium did not refer to a type of regime but to a political sphere that legitimated the exercise of power with reference to the common interests and ultimate sovereignty of the Roman people. The *res publica* could be governed by a monarchy. The textual basis for the modern misnomer is a passage in Tacitus, who remarks that by the time of the death of Augustus "there was no one left to remember the *res publica.*"[88] His tone is melodramatic and his purpose is ironic, to remind readers that it is part of the definition of a true *res publica* that it be free—free, at least, for people whose freedom mattered to Tacitus and his readers.[89] But his was a partial and even personal view. He knew that the *res Romana* remained a *res publica,* as is shown by the fact that he often calls it that in writing the history of the empire outside this passage and also in his ambiguous reference to "the old *res publica,*"[90] which implies that the Principate was the new one. He understood that *res publica* did not refer to a type of regime, as when he claimed that under Augustus "the *res publica* was established as neither a kingship nor dictatorship, but under the title of *princeps.*"[91] We will discuss below how this notion was theorized in Greek, in texts available to the Byzantines.

For Tacitus, the old *res publica* was in some respects better than the new one because in it men such as himself were "free," though it is doubtful that it was better for anyone else. Modern scholarship has made his idiosyncratic view of the *res publica* the foundation for its periodization and theorization of Roman history. This theorization has contributed decisively to the negative view of Byzantium that has prevailed for so long. Therefore, what I am advocating is that we listen to our other sources for a change—the vast majority of them, in fact—and consider the less politically partisan notion of a *res publica* held by most Romans of the empire, including the Byzantines. The problem with our partisan terminology is that it requires us to talk about the *Republic* where a handful of sources are only reflecting nostalgia under the monarchy for *freedom (libertas,* ἐλευθερία),[92] and to forget that they have a narrow conception of what freedom entailed. We tend to blur the distinction between "senatorial" interests and "republican ideology" and thereby conclude that the latter was essentially antimonarchical.[93] But the *res publica* was not just about the senate. In many respects, the monarchy served the needs and interests of the *populus* better than the late Republic, as was recognized at the time and afterward. Tacitus is explicit that the provinces preferred the emperor over the senate, which they mistrusted.[94] In the historian Velleius (writing under Tiberius), "Rome has not moved from Republic to Principate, but from Republic to a better Republic."[95] In Eutropius, a fourth-century historian surveying both the Republic and the empire, *res publica* is used overwhelmingly for the empire, by a factor of almost twenty to one. Eutropius praised Augustus for bringing about peace and allowing Rome to flourish. The language is indicative: *Romana res floruit* in the Latin, ἤνθησε γοῦν τὰ τῆς Ῥώμης πράγματα in the Greek translation.[96] At least one modern textbook concurs: "Moralists might continue to hold forth about the 'good old days,' but by most sober historical measures, Rome's best days actually were just about to begin."[97]

The "Republican" bias in scholarship is the assumption that there was no *res publica* after Augustus. This is actually only a terminological confusion on our part. We should not take a few men's nostalgia for "freedom" (in reality, their own privileged position) as a standard for defining what is and what is not a *res publica*. Cicero would probably have agreed with Tacitus's assessment that what we call the Principate was not a "true" *res publica,* but that verdict would largely have been a result of the violent way in which the transition was accomplished and his personal experience of it. Cicero himself lamented that the *res publica* had already been lost *before* the civil wars, but he meant by this a decline in the emergence of virtuous leaders.[98] This is another personal view that should also not be (and has not been) made the basis for modern periodization.

When scholars assert that "Rome remained a *res publica* even under the monarchy in name if not in fact,"[99] they are making a distinction that is based on a moral-political view of Roman history. They are effectively taking the side of a minority of senators under the early Principate who pined for their lost "liberty." But why should their outlook be decisive? The vast majority of other Romans, including the Byzantines, held that they too had a *res publica* insofar as (a) the legitimacy of their government was ultimately based in its accountability to the people, who were its true foundation (Cicero's *res populi*); (b) their society was based on law (his *iuris consensus*); and (c) they were not a random aggregate of peoples but a nation with common values (his *utilitatis communione sociatus*). This book will argue for a republican monarchy in Byzantium but not based on the survival of Republican institutions, on the balance of personal and impersonal relations in the exercise of power, or on the "style" of the regime, which have, at times, been the methodological cues followed by scholars who look for traces of the Republic under the empire.[100] It will be about the ideology of the polity that defined and sustained the political sphere, and our preliminary look at the *Novels* of Leon VI suggests that the search will not be fruitless. It will also be about the behavior of the elements of the republic in the political sphere, which will reveal that this ideology was not limited to a rarefied conceptual level. Byzantium was a Roman republic in practice too.

I will presently turn to ancient and Byzantine sources that demonstrate that the *politeia* was held to have survived the transition from Republic to empire: the *res publica* underlay regime-change. But first it is worth pointing out, by way of concluding the previous discussion, how problematic our periodization of Roman history is. The continuity of the republic is broken up and obscured by the compartmentalization of knowledge into semantic fields: there is a division between Republic and Empire, and then the Empire is broken up into Principate, Dominate, and Byzantium. Flower has warned that while "periodization forms the basis of any interpretation and commentary in a historical context, it should never be simply taken for granted, but should be regularly re-evaluated as the foundation of historical analysis."[101] One problem with this foundation is that it remains deeply imbued with outdated moralizing notions. This has seriously affected the study of Byzantium, which has traditionally been held to occupy the final and lowest place in a narrative of decline. That narrative basically encodes a metanarrative of diminishing "freedom," from Republic to Principate and then on to Byzantium, which Enlightenment historiography believed was supremely unfree in both the political and religious spheres. Gibbon, for example, had made the long-term story of Rome and Byzantium one of declining liberty, and tyranny was apparently strengthened by Orthodoxy.[102] It is this invidious metanarrative, reinforced by an ignorance of the sources, that enables good historians of earlier periods of Roman history to assert roundly that in Byzantium "all pretense of republicanism had vanished . . . no one thought of the emperor as anything other than an autocratic monarch . . . these ideologies argued that legitimate rulers were divinely inspired and divinely chosen."[103] This, we will see, is quite misleading.

One of the most curious aspects of this metanarrative is the way in which names have been invented to give reality to its four periods. The "Republic" was invented when segments of modern political thought decided that republics and monarchies were incompatible. The "Principate"— from Latin *princeps,* one of the many things that Augustus called himself— reflects the emperor's supremacy, while "Dominate" is based on the word *dominus* used by later emperors, a word that was apparently anathema to the more freedom-loving Romans of . . . the Principate. But no Roman used these labels to refer to periods of Roman history or to types of regimes. In reality, the long transition from the Principate to the Dominate involved the creation of a larger bureaucracy and an intensification of cultural changes. These trends were visible already in the Principate and entailed no essential rupture. Changes of titulature and court imagery do not justify the conclusion that Roman history ended at that time. It is common now to doubt that much changed in that transition.[104] As for "Byzantium," which is a modern term based on a *Greek* name used to designate what was in reality a later phase in the history of the Roman state, its function as a term has always been to mark it off as "essentially" different from its predecessor. To question only one criterion, there is nothing in the transition from Dominate to Byzantium that suggests the latter was less "free." But in the morality play of the long decline, Byzantium stands for Christian theocracy and oriental despotism (terms that are still used);[105] it was servile, Greekish, and superstitious; it was governed by eunuchs and palace intrigue; and it was smaller in size. It is precisely on the basis of such moralizing notions, falsehoods, and irrelevant criteria that periods have been divided and "essences" defined, while academic specialization has prevented exchanges that should have exposed this narrative for what it is.

It is doubtful that these labels and periodizations can be defended on the basis of source and facts rather than just the traditions and inertia of scholarship. The familiar narrative is a composite series of moral tales that evolved during the emergence of modern politics. The function of each step was pragmatic, namely, to defend political positions in the present by constructing ancient and medieval models of freedom and despotism. Transposed into professional historiography, they are now only a distorting framework for the long course of Roman history. The belief in "essential ruptures" is generally being questioned. Matthew Canepa has written that, "confronted by the great variety of changes in Roman culture, many have succumbed to a temptation to reify boundaries in the continuum of Roman history by inventing names for them . . . obscuring the Romans' sense of the continuity of their culture."[106] Those Romans included the Byzantines, who had a strong belief in the continuity of Roman history. It is to their evidence that we can now turn.

Probably no one in Byzantium wanted to restore the Republic, but many were interested in the long run of Roman history, which was, after all, their own history, and they were drawn to the period of transition between the Republic and monarchy. It is worth listening to what they had to say about it because it reveals how they understood the underlying continuity in their history. What they believed was continuous was precisely the Roman polity that underlay regime-change. As it turns out, Greek writers of the early empire had given a more developed account of it than the Latin ones, in part because they had no loyalty to the forms of the old Republic and no aversion to monarchy or the word *basileus* ("king"). On the Latin side we generally find vague acknowledgments that the *res publica* had "changed," that there was a current one different from the "old" one (as we saw in Tacitus).[107] But Greek writers such as Plutarch, Appianos, and Kassios Dion (all Romans, albeit Greek-speaking Romans of the empire and therefore proto-Byzantines), made a more subtle observation, that the *politeia* had changed its form of governance from whatever the Republic was (a democracy?) to a monarchy.

Plutarch claims that during the last phase of civil war "there were many who were daring to say, even openly, that the *politeia* was doomed unless it could be preserved by a monarchy."[108] According to Appianos, Augustus "prevailed over the men of his time, took hold of power and made it safe and secure; he preserved the form and name of the *politeia*, but established himself as a monarch over all. And this form of government has lasted until this time, namely under one ruler."[109] Appianos later says that Caesar was assassinated by men who "longed for the ancestral *politeia*,"[110] which presumably refers to its *form*, for later he says that "the *politeia* survived for the Romans through the various civil wars to reach a point of consensus and monarchy."[111] Kassios Dion's narrative of the end of the Republic and the rise of the monarchy is the longest that survives and the most sophisticated from the standpoint of political theory. While for him too the *politeia* of the Romans carried on under the empire, he presents a more complex succession of regimes, from a *demokratia* to a *dynasteia* (the warlords) and finally the *monarchia*. Dion offered the most powerful exposition of "regime-change" at Rome, and was followed by later Byzantine writers, as we will see. His final verdict was that "in this way the *politeia* was reformed for the better and it became more secure; in any case, it would have been impossible for them to be safe under the previous democracy."[112] Augustus, for him, established order and preserved the freedom of Romans by combining democracy with monarchy.[113]

The long course of Roman history was imagined and theorized as the history of one continuous polity punctuated by constitutional changes in the form of its governance. It was possible to do this without openly discussing the transition that took place under Augustus. For example, Dionysios of Halikarnassos made regime-change one of the main themes of his *Roman Antiquities,* only here he used the term *politeia* in the Greek way, to refer to the different types of regimes by which Rome had been governed.[114] His discussion linked up with Greek constitutional theory (e.g., the debate in Herodotos among the Persians). The constitutional debate in Kassios Dion is effectively set in the same tradition, only Dion, a Roman senator, understood *politeia* as the *res publica,* not as its specific regime at any moment.

Turning now to the Byzantine evidence, a range of texts reveal that writers of the middle period viewed the transition from Republic to monarchy in the same way, that is, they regarded "the *politeia* of the Romans" as a continuum stretching from the time of the kings after Romulus down to the Byzantine emperor of their own time; only the type of regime changed (for the better in the establishment of monarchy). They often refer to the Republic as "the time when Rome was ruled by the consuls." Detailed arguments to this effect can be found in writers of the sixth century, especially Zosimos and Ioannes Lydos,[115] but I pass them by to focus on writers of the middle Byzantine period.

- Georgios Synkellos (ca. 800): Caesar, "coming to Rome, dissolved the power of the consuls which had held sway in a direct line from Tarquinius Superbus; he was the first to rule as a monarch over the Romans, becoming more benevolent than any who had ever reigned as king."[116] And: "later Roman emperors were named Caesars after Julius Caesar and Augusti after Augustus. Under him the *res Romana* reached its apogee."[117]
- Georgios Monachos (870s): "The *res Romana* was formerly governed by the consuls for 364 years until Julius Caesar."[118] And, for example, on the emperor Valentinian I (364–375 AD): "he governed the *politeia* well through the venerable authority of the *basileia* of the Romans."[119]

- Michael Psellos (1070s): "The *politeia* of the Romans in its royal form lasted after the founding of Rome for 244 years. It became a tyranny under the last king Tarquinius and was dissolved by most noble men. With the end of the monarchy, or kingship, the state became an aristocracy."[120] And later about Caesar: "he changed the aristocracy of the Romans into a monarchy and the consulship into a *basileia*."[121]

- In the 1070s, Ioannes Xiphilinos made an epitome of Kassios Dion and, when he reached the "constitutional settlement" of 27 BC, he interjected the following in his own voice: "I will now recount each event to the degree that it is necessary, especially from this point on, because our own lives and *politeuma* depend fully on what happened at that time. I say this now no longer as Dion of Prousa, who lived under the emperors Severus and Alexander, but as Ioannes Xiphilinos, the nephew of Ioannes the patriarch, I who am composing this epitome of the many books of Dion under the emperor Michael Doukas."[122]

- Ioannes Zonaras (mid-twelfth century): in the preface to his *Chronicle*, Zonaras lists all the regime changes at Rome that he later discusses in his narrative: "Tarquinius Superbus, having turned the kingship into a tyranny, was deposed . . . then the *pragmata* [= *res publica*] for the Romans turned to an aristocracy and then a democracy, of consuls and dictators, and then the tribunes governed the administration of the *koina* . . . and later from this state of affairs political power was turned for the Romans into a monarchy."[123] In a later book, commenting on the sequence of kingdoms in the book of Daniel, he considers various possibilities relating to different regimes at Rome, first when Rome was governed by the consuls and later when the *pragmata* had become a monarchy. He notes that civil strife did harm to the *politeia*, making the contemporary relevance of all this clear with a νῦν.[124]

Similar expositions are found in later Byzantine sources.[125]

This is not the place to discuss the Byzantines' view of their national past and their identity as Romans. I cite these passages only to show that they perceived the transition from the kings to the Republic and then to the monarchy in terms of regime change within a single *politeia*, the *res publica Romana*, and identified the different phases by their governing offices. Unlike modern scholarship they had no doubt that a continuous history of a single *politeia* extended to their own present, and they could and did trace every step in that history. They thought of the *politeia* as theoretically prior to the specific type of regime that ruled it at any particular time. It remains to show now that their conception of this polity, even in its monarchical phase, was in fact "republican" in the sense explained above.

CHAPTER 2

The Emperor in the Republic

Modern scholarship on Byzantine political ideology has largely missed the centrality of the *politeia,* and later chapters will reveal that we have accordingly missed its implications for how politics were actually conducted in Byzantium. The chief result of this failure is that our understanding of Byzantine ideology and politics is narrowly focused on the emperor as if he were the only relevant political site. The ontology that we have constructed for the political sphere consists of a supernatural entity, God; a historical political agent, the emperor, and his instruments of governance ("the state"); and a mass of "subjects" who seem to have had no identity other than that conferred on them by their religion and the fact that they were subjects of the emperor. The root of this error lies ultimately in our refusal to take their Roman identity seriously. That is why, in the dominant schema, they are defined in relation to the emperor and not, as the Byzantines saw it, the emperor in relation to them. Having no political identity in our eyes, they neither have nor constitute a true *res publica.* To repeat the thesis of this book, Roman identity in Byzantium was not merely assertive but embedded in the configuration of the political sphere. When we get one of them wrong, we invatibly misunderstand the other too.

Modern reconstructions of the Byzantine political sphere focus on only one of its two legitimizing ideologies, the theocratic one, and excludes the republican. These two coexisted although they operated on different levels and in different contexts, an issue we will discuss in Chapter 6. Our fixation on the theocratic model has drawn lines of authority in an exclusively top-down way. But the republican model authorizes a bottom-up perspective according to which the emperor derived his authority from the Roman people and was answerable to them in both theory and fact. This perspective is barred to us if we overlook the republic, or *politeia*. The republic was chronologically prior to the monarchy, and I propose that it also remained theoretically prior to the monarchy under the empire: it was in terms of the *politeia* that the *basileia* was defined and justified, not the reverse. The polity was not autonomous because it was not strictly speaking a law unto itself, as we saw in our reading of Leon's *Novels*. The *politeia* was the source of the regime's legitimacy, but it needed that regime, whether a monarchy or Republic, to represent its own legitimacy to itself. The Roman polity was not a specific type of regime but the political sphere of a people with a populist ideology. Our scholarship has not so far recognized its existence, even though it is pervasive in the Byzantine sources (then again, so is the Roman name, which modern historians have scrupulously avoided).

"Republic" and "State" in Byzantium

Part of the problem is that the modern term "state" has interfered with our ability to see the Romans' *res publica*. Our term "state" organizes relations of power along different criteria and distinctions than does the Roman republican tradition. There is also disagreement about whether the term is even applicable in premodern contexts. Jean-Claude Cheynet has written about Byzantium that "the idea of a state, a heritage of the Roman world, was too incarnated in the emperor to be in itself efficacious . . . In this period, it had largely given place to personal ties."[1] According to this position, the *ancient* Romans had both a state and the concept of a state (though Cheynet does not tell us what that concept was), but the Byzantines, while inheriting that concept, had only an emperor in practice. We have to be careful, however, about what we mean by "the idea of the state" and "the heritage of the Roman world." Jon Lendon, for example, has argued that the ancient Romans too "did not see their empire as an abstraction. To the emperor's subjects all their rulers together were 'the authorities' rather than 'the state.'"[2] I take it he means that they had no "concept of the state" either. So depending on whom we follow, neither the Romans nor the Byzantines had a concept of the state and thought merely in terms of individuals who held power. In the Byzantine case these would have been the emperor and his functionaries.

To be sure, personal ties were important and relations of power were often represented in personal moral terms. But this is not incompatible with the impersonal state. Both of the countries in which I have lived, the United States and Greece, are governed in part by political dynasties that pass power from generation to generation in a hereditary way. Washington is rife with cronyism and nepotism, while in Greece the impersonal *politeia* is exploited by many as a façade for the exchange of personal favors. But that does not mean that the idea is not there. In fact, the impersonal state is ideologically dominant and explains the disaffection of the populace at these phenomena. There is no *ideology* of personal power; it cannot be defended or even articulated in public. Therefore, I resist the idea that an impersonal state cannot have existed wherever we can detect the operation of personal networks.[3] So while personal relationships were hugely important for the functioning of the state apparatus and society *in practice*, the totality of those relations does not amount to the phenomenon of the state.

The same was true of Byzantium. While it is possible to say, as Cheynet did, that the Byzantine state was in reality only a web of personal relations that emanated from the emperor, it is impossible to apply that view consistently in an analysis of how it actually functioned. For example, Haldon and Brubaker have recently written that "the Byzantine bureaucratic system was not an anonymous, independent, and self-regulating administrative structure . . . [but] a patrimonial network of concentric circles of clientage and patronage, concentrated around the imperial court and, more importantly, around the person of the emperors."[4] But not only is their book largely about the continuity of institutions despite changes in personnel, when they summarize their conclusions about how it worked, we find the exact opposite picture, which I think is more correct.

> The government and court, in spite of often dramatic transfers of political power from ruler to ruler and their supporting factions and vested interests, remained stable and continued to function . . . A standing army was maintained through an administrative apparatus whose resources were independent of the imperial household . . . Even in the worst of crises [when an emperor was killed in battle] the state was hardly shaken . . . The state's fiscal and administrative machinery was kept running with barely a murmur of unease . . . Institutional

stability of this sort was deeply rooted, and the state and its apparatus were embedded in the social-political order.[5]

As a modern theorist has noted, "the essence of institutional stability was the transfer of primary allegiance away from the emperor and toward an abstracted conception of the state."[6] Byzantium certainly had institutional stability, and we will see that it too had an abstracted sense not so much of a state as of a republic, the republic of the Romans.

All the negative arguments by Cheynet, Lendon, and Haldon about what the Byzantines *did not have* are framed in problematic terms. First, they fail to discuss or even identify the Roman idea of the *res publica*, whether in the early imperial or Byzantine context. Fergus Millar has correctly observed that we have to focus on the idea of the *res publica* if we are to assess whether the Romans (or their heirs) had an impersonal concept: "the notion of a state as a *res publica*, an impersonal entity logically distinct from the individuals exercising power, was an important legacy of Roman law."[7] Cheynet does not specify what he takes "the heritage of the Roman world" to have been, and Lendon does not explain why he focuses on the concept of "empire" rather than the *res publica*. His choice seems to reflect the modern Republican bias according to which there was no *res publica* after Augustus, regardless of what the Romans of the empire may have thought. "Empire" is ambiguous. It is doubtful that Lendon is referring to the dominion that Romans held over non-Romans. Following convention, he uses "empire" to refer to "the Roman state after Augustus," thereby conflating the state with the emperor and occluding the fact that the basic principles of the *res publica* soldiered on and, as the Greeks too gradually became Romans, even colonized the semantic range of the Greek term *politeia*. Put differently, it would have been more reassuring if the denial that the Romans of the empire had an impersonal "state" was based on a thorough examination of the terms by which they understood their own political sphere and the public interest. But no such examination has been undertaken in these cases.

In denying the existence of an impersonal Roman state, Cheynet and possibly Lendon are echoing a fairly established view among modern theorists according to which the impersonal state emerged in early modernity, whereas before that "public power had been treated in far more personal and charismatic terms."[8] This is sometimes called the "patrimonial state," which is the property of the monarch. If this fiction bears any relation to actual medieval polities, it has little or none to Byzantium. Moreover, not all medieval historians are persuaded that they cannot use the term "state." While there is no universally agreed-upon definition of the state among political scientists, some premodern historians offer general definitions that reflect conventional uses of the term. For example, Susan Reynolds defines the state as "an organization of human society within a fixed territory that more or less successfully claims the control (not the monopoly) of the legitimate use of physical force within that territory." She argues, moreover, that "if one were to deny statehood on this definition to medieval kingdoms or lesser lordships in general . . . on grounds of fluidity etc. one would have to deny it to a good many modern states."[9] Haldon is exceptional among Byzantinists in that he often defines the concept of the state before using it. In his view, a state is a territorial entity with a center that exerts a monopoly on force; it must have an ideological system; and it must reproduce its functions over time.[10] There is no doubt that in these terms Byzantium qualifies as a state, regardless of whether or not the Byzantines had a fixed term for that concept. That Byzantium was a state is accepted by almost all historians, whether intuitively or backed by theoretical definitions. Cheynet is exceptional in doubting it, but perhaps he is doubting only that the Byzantine state was fully impersonal; perhaps he is only stressing the supremacy of the emperor as a personal agent.

So where does this leave us in terms of theory? We seem to face two alternatives: either we view the Byzantine state as an affect of the emperor's personal rule and of his personal relations with his subjects, thereby concluding that the Byzantines had no "impersonal" view of the state (and so no real state at all), or we postulate a Byzantine state in more or less modern terms as separable from the persons who govern it as well as from "the whole society over which its powers are exercised . . . distinct from both the rulers are the ruled," to quote Quentin Skinner, a theorist of the origin of the modern concept of the state.[11] My discussion so far has seemed to argue in favor of the impersonal state, consistent with the long quotation of Haldon and Brubaker given above. But in fact neither alternative adequately represents the Roman *res publica*. The personal definition does not reflect how Romans or Byzantines thought of their polity, which could not be reduced to the *basileia*, as the latter was a function of the *politeia*. As for a fully impersonal definition, while it enables us to talk about the Byzantine state in recognizably modern terms (an often appropriate and useful exercise), it does obscure the republican ideology that governed the operations of that state. That polity was impersonal when viewed in relation to the emperor, as it signified the collective affairs of the Roman people. But it could not be abstracted from their overall moral community and so was not impersonal when viewed in relation to the Roman people, whom modern theory would box into the category of "civil society." The Roman collectivity was not just a civil society; it was a political community. The *res publica* was the *res Romana,* "the property and business of the Roman people." What was the relationship, then, between state and republic?

To better explain the theoretical distinctions at stake, I will use Skinner's history of the origins of the concept of the modern state. I do so here solely for the purposes of conceptual clarity, without requiring that his schema accurately describes historical processes on the ground; my chief concern is to classify the Byzantine polity in relation to the theoretical models used in political science, and also to put it forward as a supplement to their basic repertoire. According to Skinner, then, from the allegedly "personal rule" of the Middle Ages, republican theorists first abstracted the apparatus of rule and separated it from the ruler's person. "They [thought] of the powers of civil government as embodied in a structure of laws and institutions which our rulers and magistrates are entrusted to administer in the name of the common good." But they did not distinguish between the body of the *res publica* (the people) and the state. Terms for the state were "thus conceived as nothing more than a means of expressing the powers of the people in an administratively more convenient form" (the republican "state," moreover, could be monarchical, as we saw). "No effective contrast [was] drawn between the power of the people and the powers of the state." This I will call the republican idea of a state. It was only later, according to Skinner, that absolutist theorists, notably Hobbes, abstracted the state from the people too and from civil society as a whole. As a result of this second move, "the state tends to appear in the modern imagination as a unitary, free-standing agency, one that is forever separated by a kind of impermeable membrane from the society over which it holds sway."[12]

This schema is not necessarily an accurate description of what happened historically. The separation of state and society can be doubted in the modern context too.[13] Moreover, medieval polities prior to the Renaissance "republican" revolution were not as "personal" as many modernist theorists assume. Byzantium, I maintain, meets Skinner's standards of a republican state, which is not surprising, for it was but a living extension of the ancient Roman tradition on which all early modern republican theorists were building. Its misfortune as a political culture has been that its Roman basis has been overlooked in the scholarship because of irrelevant medieval polemics, which has left the emperor in a vacuum, filled only by his own personal presence or enmeshed in platitudinous theological rhetoric. If we restore the *politeia* to the equation, we see this society for what it was: a republic.

While Byzantium certainly was a state and can be discussed as such, "the state" is, for modern theory, something largely abstracted from and imposed upon "civil society." It is a regulatory and protective agency for what is basically a field of private interests. Mediating between them is the "public sphere," which brings private and state interests into discussion, though some things are (at the one end) too private to enter that sphere while other things are (at the other end) too "classified" from the state's point of view (so neither is "public" unless it is exposed). This model may be used up to a point in discussing Byzantium, but it does distort the ideology of the *politeia*. Within a *politeia* one cannot easily isolate the state from the rest of society because, as we saw with Syrianos in Chapter 1, the *politeia* is constituted by everything that contributes to the common good, including the people and the apparatus of the state. One could identify the aspects of governance that were more or less under the emperor's control at any moment. The terms *kratos* (power) and *basileia* (the imperial office or monarchy and its authority, functions, and extensions) could be used to approximate what we mean by the state. After all, the purpose of the *basileia* was to govern and regulate the *politeia*. But there was no concept of a public sphere to mediate between the state and private interests, for the polity was a political sphere oriented toward the collective good of the Roman people. The emperor's function was to promote that good. We see here how the modern concept of the state distorts this culture. Not only do the "common-sense" definitions quoted above (by Reynolds and Haldon) fail to mention the common good, they do not say what the state is good for at all. They focus only on its powers. This is a problem of the sociologist's outside view. As Raymond Geuss has noted, the state thereby becomes "merely an agency operating and exercising powers in a certain way. Part of the object being observed, to be sure, is a set of beliefs about legitimacy held by the members of the state under consideration, but the sociologist may or may not be interested in assessing these beliefs morally."[14]

The state for most modern theorists simply exists, apparently with its own interests. It thereby becomes easy to identify with the emperor personally, who had mastery over it. Thus, with no *res publica,* there are only "subjects," and the emperor becomes the state. Scholars then invoke God to give him some kind of legitimacy and the flavor of a premodern "ideology."

The failure of post-Hobbesian theories of the state to understand republican regimes is most striking in their propensity, in their focus on punitive powers, to define the state in terms of its monopoly of coercive power within a society.[15] While this may have been a feature of the republican state, it is not a *definition* of it; it is only an attribute. Its definition, for any of its subjects, would have been synonymous with its function, namely, to promote the common good of the Romans. A monopoly on certain kinds of power was only one of the *means* that enabled it to perform that function. In sum, while we can say that Byzantium was a state (or had one), modern notions of the state do not help us understand the ideology that governed the Byzantine polity. We need a theory for the office of the emperor different both from that of personal rule (on the one hand) and of the self-subsisting, punitive, and impersonal state (on the other).

The texts presented in Chapter 1 give preliminary plausibility to an alternative thesis according to which the emperor must be understood in relation to the polity of which he was the emperor. As his function was defined by that political community, it was neither personal nor abstracted from it. That polity, moreover, represented a moral consensus, not an abstracted state. Later chapters of this book will fill in other parts of this picture. For now I will focus on the priority of the *politeia* and its theoretical difference from and priority to the *basileia,* which was merely the monarchy that governed the polity after Augustus.

I have discussed several ways in which the republic was experienced as something separate, prior, and in some respects more fundamental than the *basileia.* The evidence presented in the first chapter refutes the idea that the Byzantines regarded what was going on in their "state" as a mere affect of personal relations, or even that their emperors held such a belief while in the process of governing. That the *politeia* and *basileia* were neither extensionally nor conceptually identical emerges clearly from

Leon's *Novels* as well as from many texts that list the parts of the *politeia* in such a way as to suggest that it included the whole of "society" in its political aspect in addition to the instruments of governance (the "state"). The perceived continuity of the polity in the transition from the Republic to the monarchy underscores its theoretical and historical priority and independence from the *basileia*. The sovereign Roman people existed before they had emperors and Leon VI, for one, had no doubt that his chief duty was to promote their welfare.

While the *basileia* had a monopoly on the governance of all Romans, the latter did not identify their state or society with that executive power.[16] In most texts, whatever the genre, it is stated or implied that imperial action took place against the deeper background of a theoretically prior polity. This is exactly how Leon understood his legislative activity. The language of our sources has been overlooked but, when seen in this light, becomes significant. For example, in his *Taktika* Leon states that soldiers fight "on behalf of our *basileia* and the Christ-loving *politeia* of the Romans." They should be assembled by units and reminded "of the rewards and benefactions that come from our *basileia* and the wages that they receive for their loyalty to the *politeia*."[17] Emperors wanted to tie themselves personally to the loyalty that Romans felt toward their *patris,* the republic. This was different from the loyalty that they felt toward individual emperors, as our later discussion of Byzantine rebellions will highlight. The military context is significant here, as Haldon, following Beck, points out: "there is little evidence that soldiers were expected to die for the emperor, rather than for the Christian faith and the Roman state. On the contrary, the emphasis in military harangues and other texts is on survival and on the fact that soldiers fought for their faith and empire, rather than any particular emperor" ("state" and "empire" are here glosses for *politeia*).[18] Soldiers and officials swore oaths to defend the emperor *and* the polity.[19] In the sixth century, the epitomator Jordanes claimed that the rebel Vitalianos was "hostile not to the republic but to the emperor."[20] In one passage of his *Taktika,* Leon VI instructs that soldiers should be promoted who are the most eager to serve "our Roman *politeia*."[21] A tenth-century manual on *Campaign Organization* refers to soldiers who "eagerly endure dangers for our holy emperor and their own fatherland (πατρίς)."[22]

An episode from the late sixth century illustrates that when emperor and God failed to command respect, the authorities fell back on the soldiers' devotion to the polity, that is, to their patriotism as Romans, which was also part of their oath. When the eastern armies mutinied in 588 over a pay reduction, the general Priskos tried to cow them by bringing out from Edessa and parading before them the *mandylion,* the holy relic upon which Christ's image had been impressed, "so that by respect for the holy object, the anger might be humbled." But the men "pelted the ineffable object with stones" and the general had to run away.[23] The task fell to Gregorios, the bishop of Antioch, who spoke to them the following year and did appease them. His speech is recorded by his secretary Euagrios, who wrote his history a few years afterward. Gregorios began by addressing the soldiers as "O men, Romans in both name and deed," and he praised them for defeating the Persians even during their mutiny: "for you have demonstrated that even when you have a grievance toward your generals, there is nothing of greater importance to you than the *politeuma.*"[24] On behalf of the emperor, he then calls on their "loyalty to the *politeia*"[25] and appeals to their ancestors, "those who begat you, who obeyed first the consuls and then the emperors," inspiring them with an *exemplum* from the Republic (Manlius Torquatus). At the end he calls on them as Christians too, but again beseeches them "to consider what is beneficial for ourselves and for the *politeuma.*"[26]

This speech is revealing, given its circumstances. When "loyalty to the emperor" (the modern misunderstanding of what it meant to be a Roman in Byzantium) and the veneration of relics are stripped away, what was left was the ultimate backbone of Roman patriotism and Byzantine solidarity: devotion to a polity, a *patris,* that had endured under both consuls and emperors. Soldiers' loyalty was to the polity, and Gregorios appealed to their Roman patriotism. The stoning of the relic is also revealing: we will see that when push came to shove, the religious ideology that modern scholarship ascribes to the Byzantines did not count for much.

It is a testament to the strength of the Byzantines' republicanism that they continued to juxtapose the *basileia* and *politeia* and generally kept them distinct in their mental map of the political sphere. Psellos wrote that the uncles of Michael V had no serious plans "either for the *basileia* or the state of the *koinon.*"[27] In writing to Robert Guiscard, Michael VII hoped that the Norman's disposition "toward my *basileia* and Romanía" would be passed on to his heirs.[28] Other texts reify the political sphere and make it impossible to conflate with the *basileia.* The *kaisar*

Bardas, for example, "took charge of the *politika* and had his eye on the *basileia.*"[29] The two were evidently not the same. The *politika* was something of which one could take charge, to improve or harm, but it was distinct from the *basileia* and was not linked to any one person; it was impersonal and belonged to all Romans in common. It appears strikingly in the texts when it is placed in the care of the emperor's "right-hand man," often a eunuch. As always in premodern sources, the vocabulary varies but the idea is consistent. In Attaleiates we have Ioannes the Orphanotrophos τὴν τῶν πραγμάτων εἶχεν ὡς μεσοβασιλεὺς διοίκησιν; Theodora entrusted to Leon τὴν διοίκησιν τῶν πραγμάτων; Leichoudes was, under Konstantinos IX, ἀνὴρ μέγιστον διαλάμψας τοῖς βασιλικοῖς καὶ πολιτικοῖς πράγμασιν... μεσάζων ἐν τοῖς βασιλείοις τὴν τῶν ὅλων διοίκησιν; Michael VII appointed Ioannes, bishop of Side, τῶν κοινῶν πραγμάτων διοικητήν—but Nikephoros sidelined Ioannes from τοῦ τὰ κοινὰ διοικεῖν so that he himself εἰς τὴν τῶν κοινῶν πραγμάτων διοίκησιν προστησάμενος; Michael of Nikomedeia was ὁ ἐπὶ τῶν πολιτικῶν πραγμάτων προστάς under Botaneiates.[30] The Latin for all this would be something like Cicero's *ad rem publicam tuendam.*[31]

Emperors were not identified with the political sphere, nor were they always personally dominant in it. Others also played a role in determining its fortunes, for good or ill. A corrupt official was "an outrage and disease for the *politeia* of the Romans."[32] Conversely, the *politeia* was something that the imperial officials of all ranks could "do well by" and "endow with something great—or not."[33] Mauropous praised an acquaintance as the "shinning eye of the *politeia.*"[34] In other words, it was not only the emperors but all their officials and soldiers whose functions were understood in relation to the polity and whose job performance was continually being judged by the standard of the common good. These people served not only the current emperor but the *res Romana* too, and, as we will see, the second was not an empty notion: these men often had to choose, sometimes fatally, between the two. Psellos served many emperors in his time, some of them with less than total devotion. He did, however, often stress that he was a Roman patriot at heart.[35] This quality became critical when a regime was collapsing and choices had to be made between rivals for the throne.[36] But even in stable times, Psellos knew that a good politician had to mediate between the monarchy and the rest of the polity. When he refused the office of *protoasekretis* under Konstantinos IX, Psellos defended his actions at the emperor's side: "I collaborated with him in many matters regarding the public interest (τὰ κοινά), proposed to him the most perfect *politeia,* and adapted him to all those things in which monarchy reveals itself, at least as it seemed to me."[37] In a number of writings Psellos developed the ideal of the "political man," who was less a perfect courtier than an enlightened public servant who could mediate between rival claims for the good of all.[38] The retired functionary Ioannes Zonaras thought of public affairs as being "in the middle" of things.[39] That space was not owned by any one person.

Emperors were nominally in charge of the public space of the *politeia* but only as its custodians, not its owners. Some were more than nominally in charge and took a personal interest in its "administration" and "management," probably the best way to translate the terms *dioikesis* and *epimeleia,*[40] which are pervasive in all sources that refer to politics. The *dioikesis* was always *of something,* either of the κοινά, the κοινὰ πράγματα, the κράτος, and so on,[41] in the same way that the emperor was always understood to be the emperor *of the Romans* and not simply emperor in his own right.[42] In a *Novel,* Leon III called himself the "guardian" or "steward of the *politeia.*"[43] Psellos has a nice image for Ioannes Orphanotrophos, who governed the empire under his brother Michael IV: "he took it upon himself to pull the Roman axle," as if the polity were a chariot.[44] These metaphors were attempts to reify a political sphere that belonged to all Romans collectively. That is essentially what Konstantinos XI Palaiologos signified when he refused to surrender the City in 1453. Among the last words of this last Roman emperor were, "I do not have the right to give you the City, nor does anyone else of those who live in it. By a collective decision (κοινῇ γνώμῃ), we will all willingly die and not try to save our lives."[45] Cicero would have recognized in this the *consensus universorum.*

Public versus Private in the Exercise of Power

It was a basic principle of Roman law, operative in Byzantium, that "all human goods are either public (δημόσια) or private. The public ones belong to no one but the community; the private ones belong to each person separately."[46] There were, accordingly, distinctions between "public and private law. Public law is that which respects the establishment of the *res Romana,* private that which respects individuals' interests."[47]

For example, "public rituals are performed on behalf of the people at public expense," while "private rituals are performed for individual men, families, and households."[48] Public authority stemmed from the office, not the man personally.[49] As we have seen, since the days of the Republic and Augustus (in the Greek version of his *Res Gestae*), as also in Byzantium, one way to translate *res publica* was τὰ δημόσια πράγματα or simply τὰ πράγματα, which could be expanded to Ῥωμαϊκὰ πράγματα and then abbreviated as τὰ Ῥωμαϊκά. Contrary to what is routinely asserted by modernist theorists regarding the personal nature of premodern polities,[50] nothing could be more "public" in the Roman tradition than the *res publica,* which could not belong to the emperor privately. Not even the infrastructure of the *basileia*—for example, the palace—belonged to him, and we will see both emperors and authors conceding the point. One of the two main imperial treasuries was even called τὸ δημόσιον, reinforcing the point.[51] This was one of the reasons why there existed no right of succession to the throne: what was not owned privately could not be bequeathed.[52] As we will see, such transference could be accomplished only by popular acclamation (and the people could take back those rights through "de-acclamation"). We will discuss the sovereignty and its transference in Chapters 4 and 5, when we turn to the political consequences in historical time of the regime's republican basis. My purpose here is to outline the normative republican ideology about public issues. When we finally get a study of the imperial office that examines what the emperors actually did and the purpose and limits of their power, it will show that they generally did behave in accordance with an ideology of custodianship: they were the stewards of a polity that did not belong to them. They had opportunity to abuse their power, but this had consequences. In Byzantium, they were often bloody.

As we will see in the following section, emperors took every possible opportunity to proclaim that they ruled solely for the benefit of their subjects. They also periodically reminded their subjects that imperial assets were destined for public use, not the "private" use by emperors. In 566, Justin II explained that "the taxes paid by our subjects are used and expended partly for themselves and partly indirectly on their account, for we do not derive any benefit from them and are only charged with their administration."[53] Tiberios II (578–582 AD) noted in a *Novel* that "it is fitting to consider that the assets of imperial properties are not ours alone but are the common property *(koina)* of our *politeuma.*"[54] In his

Novel of 934 barring office-holders and other powerful interests from acquiring protected lands, Romanos I noted that violators were to "pay the
price of the acquisition to the treasury, not for the profit of or contribution to the treasury—for how could we, in our endeavors to restrain the
insatiable covetousness of others, shamelessly issue this ruling for our
own gain (οἰκεῖον κέρδος) and show ourselves to be guilty of acting not
for the common good (κοινὴν ὠφέλειαν) but for our own?—but for the
care of the poor."[55] Even in this case, the emperor does not mean his own
private benefit but that of the *basileia* (itself a public good); the money will
rather be given over directly to public use. In one of his *Novels* (996 AD),
Basileios II also "presents himself as a custodian of the fisc's property
rights and as the legally empowered authority to protect them."[56] His relation to the fisc here was only one aspect of a broadly conceived ideology
of stewardship with respect to the entire polity. The person was not identified with the office, and the office was defined in relation to the common good. In the thirteenth century, Nikephoros Blemmydes likewise
"reasoned that the emperor held nothing in private because he was not a
private individual, but administered public wealth (τὰ κοινὰ) for the benefit of the community (τὸ κοινόν)."[57]

Contemporary historians criticized emperors for wasting public funds
on private purposes. Euagrios (late sixth century), who believed that Justinian was a bad emperor, criticized his building of many churches and
reminded those who would do the same to pay for them "from their own
resources."[58] Presumably he means from existing imperial funds, that is,
no new taxes, but he may be referring to private assets. Skylitzes criticized Michael IV for spending "public and common funds" in order to
perform pious deeds and earn forgiveness for the crimes by which he had
ascended the throne: "he was buying his own repentance with the money
of others," said Skylitzes, meaning the money of the Romans.[59] Psellos
criticized Konstantinos IX for spending money from the imperial treasury on his passion for Skleraina and later for wasting more on his Alan
mistress, and he also criticized Zoe and Theodora for emptying the treasury to give presents to their favorites.[60] In these cases, rulers were being
accused of spending public money in ways that did not benefit the Roman people.

Other genres reflect this ideology too. I will present an example from
the ninth century and then turn to the historians of the Komnenoi regime in the twelfth century. The *Hortatory Chapters Addressed to Leon VI*

belongs to the genre that scholars call Mirrors of Princes. One of the main features of this genre, of which many specimens survive, was to remind emperors that their sole duty was to promote the public good and not to rule for their private benefit. Ruling for the benefit of the ruler rather than the ruled was the definition of tyranny in all these texts.[61] In this text addressed to Leon VI, the emperor is reminded not to place too much value on material wealth. "Besides, your property is not really your own but belongs to your fellow slaves [i.e., of God], especially the poor and outsiders. So take care to emerge as a benefactor when it comes to the *koina*."[62] To be sure, behind this exhortation lies the notion that all wealth belongs to God (though it is not stated explicitly), but this only reinforces the role of steward that the republican tradition imposed on the emperor. Roman and Christian notions here converged. The same point is later made differently: "The palace belongs to you today but tomorrow it will not; and after tomorrow it will belong to someone else, and the day after that to the one after him, so that it never belongs to anyone. For even though it changes hands often, it has no true owner."[63] From the vantage-point of eternity this, of course, could ultimately be said about any type of property, but it serves to reinforce a political axiom here.

For robust nontheological expressions of this view, we turn to the era of the Komnenoi, whose dynastic manner of rule disturbed traditional assumptions and so exposed what had previously been taken for granted. Modern historians have shown how the regime of the Komnenoi pushed the empire in the direction of personal or family rule, where blood mattered more than office.[64] Contemporaries noted the erosion of the distinction between public and imperial and between owner and custodian of the republic. It was not that they suddenly rediscovered republican values,[65] but they perceived that previously dominant values were being undermined by the Komnenian style of rule, and deplored it. Already at the beginning of the reign of Alexios I (1081–1118), Ioannes Oxeites, bishop of Antioch, complained to the emperor that "your relatives are proving to be a great pestilence upon both the *basileia* and all the rest of us ... they are more concerned with making a profit for themselves than with the common interest (κοινῇ)." Ioannes advises Alexios to "do everything with the advice of the best men in the army, the Church, and all the other people [i.e., the *politeia*] ... and place your deliberations in the middle (εἰς μέσον)."[66]

That was the very term that Zonaras had used to refer to his political career,[67] and it was he who articulated a republican critique of the new regime. Zonaras praises Alexios's moral qualities but adds that more is to be expected from a ruler, who

> must also care for justice, provide for his subjects, and maintain the ancient principles of the *politeuma*. But Alexios' agenda was to alter the ancient forms of the *politeia* . . . He approached political affairs not as if they were common (κοινά) or public (δημόσια), and he did not regard himself to be their steward (οἰκονόμος) but their master (δεσπότης). He thought that the palace was his own private house and called it that . . . He did not give to each his own based on merit but rather gave over public money to his relatives and servants by the cartload.[68]

The critique works only if Zonaras expected his readership to sympathize with the republican values he outlines. Zonaras criticized a number of other emperors for spending public funds for their own private purposes.[69] He happened to believe that recent history had witnessed a revolutionary transformation. Writing about the foundation of Constantinople, he notes the prediction of the astrologer Valens that the new capital would last for 696 years.

> But these have now long since passed, so that we must either regard his prediction as false and his art as flawed or we must suppose that he meant the years during which the forms of the *politeia* would be maintained along with the proper protocols, when the senate would be honored, its citizens would flourish, when there would be a lawful supervision (ἔννομος ἐπιστασία),[70] and the regime would be a *basileia* rather than a tyranny, when the rulers would consider that common things (κοινά) were their own and use them for their private pleasures.[71]

Niketas Choniates leveled similar criticisms against Manuel Komnenos. Rulers, he says, "love to squander the public money (τὰ δημόσια) as if it were their own private patrimony and treat free men as their slaves."[72]

The Komnenoi, of course, did not come to power with the intention of implementing a radical, antirepublican agenda, and we must take Zonaras's criticisms with a grain of salt, as he seems to have belonged to the very classes that lost power when the family took over. The Komnenoi did not abolish the *politeia;* at least they, and probably most of their subjects, did not think so. Their system of governance, more personal though it was, developed in response to a series of crises and can be credited with saving the *politeia* from foreign enemies. The terms of Zonaras's critique, however, reveal what he and others believed the consensus was regarding the responsibilities of the emperor toward the public trust and the distinction between private and public interests. In his analysis of Zonaras's critique, Paul Magdalino has shown that the Komnenoi and their spokesmen did not uphold a different model of either the *basileia* or the *politeia* but rather defended the regime on traditional grounds (for all that they glossed over the changes that had taken place).[73] There was, then, no ideological rift: the Komnenoi were basically claiming to be Roman emperors no different than their predecessors. Moreover, Dimiter Angelov has shown that many authors of the Palaiologan period likewise evaluated their emperors on how conscientiously they maintained the integrity of the public interest, which was entrusted to them by their subjects and did not belong to them personally.[74]

This view of imperial "custodianship" goes back to the earliest days of the empire. Tiberius I once declared that the soldiers belonged not to himself but to the public (δημόσιοι), and Marcus Aurelius professed that the fisc belonged to the senate and people: "moreover, it is your house in which we live."[75] We might be tempted to dismiss this as mere rhetoric or as "high-flown theory,"[76] but in reality it was a deeply rooted republican ideology that was inseparable from the *res Romana* at any point in history. To be sure, the statements made by these and other emperors do not clarify the facts of power, which is what many historians are really after, whence the dismissive language. But we should be more careful. We cannot write off as rhetorical fluff or as a republican "remnant" an ideology that seemed to be thriving—that is, shaping fundamental assumptions about the exercise of power—a thousand and more years after the end of the Republic. The list of Byzantine beliefs and practices that would have to be written off in this way as mere remnants would be quite long.[77] The alternative is to group them together and realize that the Byzantine polity was really shaped by a republican Roman ideology all along. This ideology governed how subjects evaluated their rulers and consequently how they behaved in critical circumstances, which were more frequent in Byzantine history than many realize. In moments of crisis, those underlying assumptions came to the fore.

(Also, if we were to dismiss as "mere rhetoric" ideologies that allegedly do not bear on the cold hard facts of imperial power, then the first to go should be the idea that the emperor was appointed to rule by God and had a duty to imitate Christ.)

The distinction between private and public interest is reflected in how writers evaluated office-holders of all ranks, including emperors. Ammianus criticizes Valentinian for putting family over the common good when he chose his brother Valens as his partner in empire, but approves his decision later not to march to Valens's aid against the rebel Procopius because the latter was an enemy only of his brother whereas the Alamanni were the enemies of the entire Roman world.[78] Prokopios says that Belisarios was "reviled by all the Romans for sacrificing the most critical needs of the *politeia* to his domestic affairs."[79] The emperor Konstantinos X forced his wife Eudokia to swear that she would not remarry after his death (in 1067), but then she, the senate, and the patriarch

> agreed that forethought on behalf of the whole should be their guiding criterion: it was reasonable for the common good to be preferred over the private wish of one man who was about to die. It was not possible to allow a private wish to override the public good. Thus it was recognized that not to have an emperor because one man was too jealous to allow his widow to be with another man would harm the common good and contribute to the destruction of the Roman empire. This view of the matter prevailed.[80]

In the late twelfth century, Eustathios of Thessalonike castigated the governor of his city, David Komnenos, during the Norman siege of 1185 for "neglecting and despising the common good and looking only to his own welfare, like an open traitor." When his personal position became precarious, he continued to "replace the private disaster which menaced him with one which would affect our whole community."[81]

Attaleiates, in the late eleventh century, criticized the entire imperial high command in his effort to explain the collapse of his times.

> As for the Romans of our times, their leaders and emperors commit the worst crimes and God-detested deeds under the pretext of the public interest (προφάσει δημοσιακῆς ὠφελείας). The commander of the army cares not one whit for the war nor does what is right and proper by his fatherland (τῇ πατρίδι), and even shows contempt for the glory of victory; instead, he bends his whole self to the making of profit, converting his

command into a mercantile venture, and so he brings no prosperity or glory to his own people (τοῦ ἰδίου ἔθνους).[82]

The ideological supremacy of the "public interest" is evident here especially, as it seems that these emperors and generals took care to invoke it even when, in this historian's opinion, they were really serving their private interests. In Byzantium, all state action had to be justified on the grounds of the public interest, in relation to the fatherland and the Roman people, even if only as a pretext. The Romans of old, by contrast, Attaleiates points out, "did not strive for money and acquisition of wealth but simply for renown, the demonstration of their manliness, and their country's safety and splendor."[83]

The texts we have surveyed reflect a strong devotion to the common good and the public interest. Obviously, there would have been strong disagreements about what it was exactly and how to best support it—that was the stuff of politics—but what matters for us here is that imperial policy had to be justified by reference to it and that it was perceived to be separate from the private interests of both the emperor and his officials. To give two examples of the appeal to the public good, when the patriarch Nikolaos Mystikos (in the early tenth century) was trying to persuade a secular official not to implement an administrative change in the Church under wartime pressure, he argues first based on what would please God and concludes with this: "Surely the *koinon* will derive no profit whatever either from clerics being enlisted in the army or from the poor of the Church being reduced to slavery."[84] The translators again render *koinon* as "state," but that makes less sense: the reforms in question were being considered precisely to benefit the state. Nikolaos was appealing to a broader and higher standard, that of the *politeia* and the common good.

When he took the throne in 1057, Isaakios Komnenos decided that the state budget was too bloated and so he made cutbacks, especially in payments to title-holders. This caused widespread disaffection. Psellos, who supported these cuts, would have us believe that eventually they were accepted "because the public interest [or treasury: ὁ δημόσιος] was a sufficient justification of them against those who wanted to criticize this policy."[85] If we can trust Psellos, this would count as an instance of political maturity in Byzantium, private interests being sacrificed for the public good in a moment of crisis. But it does not matter whether Psellos is telling the truth: what counts are the terms in which he chose to frame his defense of the policy. The only terms by which political action could be justified in Byzantium were these. Here we are accessing what I have defined as ideology.

Romanía appears in our texts as an impersonal entity whose needs justify imperial actions. In a grant of exemptions to a monastery, Alexios I even refers to imperial officials who might draft sailors into service "because of the pressing needs of Romanía (κατά τινα ἀναγκαιοτάτην χρείαν τῆς Ῥωμανίας)."[86] The nation-state is here personalized. Likewise in foreign policy. Alexios promised the Venetians whatever they wanted in exchange for help against the Normans, "so long as it was not against the interests of the Roman state."[87] This echoes the ancient Roman *rei publicae causa*.[88] In the preface of the *De administrando imperio*, Konstantinos VII explains that he wants to teach his son how "not to stumble concerning the best counsels and the common interests (τὸ κοινῇ συμφέρον): first, in what each nation has power to advantage the Romans and in what to hurt."[89] We lack a study of how Byzantines parsed the morality of their foreign policy, trapped between "reasons of state" and Christian ethics. How often did the public interest trump other considerations? Was the moral logic of the public interest different from that of private life? There is reason to think so, but we need a full study. For example, imperial officials seem to have taken part in pagan rituals and even sacrifices, or recognized them as valid, in order to seal necessary alliances with barbarian peoples.[90] This violated the religious norms of the republic to safeguard its foreign interests. There is, moreover, a passage in Psellos's *Chronographia* that raises this issue explicitly in relation to the blinding of Romanos IV Diogenes by the Doukas faction to which Psellos now belonged. He there admits that this was a horrible crime but believed that it had to be done: "an action which should not have happened, but—to repeat what I just said in only a slightly different way—which *had to happen at all costs:* the former on account of piety and religious scruple against cruelty, the latter on account of the state of τὰ πράγματα and the precariousness of the moment."[91]

In discussing the emergence of the impersonal state in early modernity, Harvey Mansfield explains how "doing something morally distasteful for the state acquires a moral exemption because such actions are no longer selfish. They are, of course, generalized selfishness and specious too, since the state does in fact belong to somebody."[92] Psellos wants us to believe that the *pragmata* to which he refers, the common interests that required Romanos to be blinded, belonged to the Romans, who needed to get past the civil war and put Asia Minor in order; but of course, the beneficiaries were the Doukai, who controlled the state at that moment. The use of modern executive power presents exactly the same ambiguities. "Ideology" is located precisely in the invocation of the common good to justify actions that benefit private interests, which had no standing on their own. They were but historical facts but needed ideological cover to become acceptable political reality.

We have gone further than necessary. All this section aimed to show is that the Byzantines conceived their *politeia* in a normative sense as a collective but impersonal entity whose needs trumped private interests, even, or especially, those of the emperor. It is not hard to detect this ideology if one but spends a moderate amount of time in the company of Byzantine sources. The problem for the field has been how to get around it. Gilbert Dagron, for instance, recognized that "the empire existed independently of the emperor who came to power and who attempted to found a dynasty. It existed in the Roman form of a vast administrative and juridical construction which the sovereign dominated and whose cohesion he ensured without ever becoming entirely identified with it." A distinction was drawn, "as sharply as today, between the imperial office and its holder."[93] But Dagron's study is not devoted to this topic, being rather about the esoteric question of whether the emperor felt guilty for usurping some sacerdotal functions. As a result, he reads the imperial office almost exclusively in relation to Old Testament models rather than Roman ones.[94]

Paul Magdalino also produced an accurate and eloquent formulation of the basic point:

There can be no doubt that the Byzantines believed in and experienced the state as an impersonal, public affair—a *politeia*. The fiscal system, the standing army and the law courts formed an institutional ensemble which was more than the sum of the personal ties that held it together. The dignities and salaries bestowed by the emperor were perceived as rights which men deserved by their merits and forfeited only by committing capital crimes. The hierarchy of dignitaries could flatter themselves that they were not imperial but public servants, not courtiers but senators, whose individual and collective honor was guaranteed by a traditional order *(taxis)* and established procedure *(katastasis)* to which the emperor was as committed as they were.[95]

Unfortunately, Magdalino then goes on to undermine this picture by claiming that it all "existed only in the minds and words of intellectuals steeped in ancient history." This is a reflex instinct in the field of Byzantine Studies: anything that seems too classical or too Roman must be downplayed, marginalized, or otherwise qualified. It does not matter whether it is the picture that actually emerges from the sources, that these principles were avowed by the emperors themselves, or that these intellectuals were the judges, generals, and bishops through whom the emperors actually governed. Magdalino again points to personal relations: "it is difficult to distinguish between the public office and the private patronage." But this applies to all polities, modern ones too. Private interests and personal ties were as important in Byzantium as they are today, and historians are right to focus on them. Nevertheless, the Byzantines understood that such things did not constitute their republic, which represented the common affairs and interests of all the Romans.

The Monarchy Served the Republic

Paul Veyne once argued, with reference to the early Roman empire, that "the state was the emperor," that it was his property, and that "he could say, *'L'État, c'est moi.'*"[96] But no emperor, Roman or Byzantine, ever said or implied anything like that, or suggested that he ruled for any purpose or reason other than to benefit his fellow Romans, and benefit them materially at that, for the most part. This is precisely what we expect to find in a republican regime, in which the *politeia* is understood to be the people's business, and Veyne seems to have come around on that point in a later book.[97] This accountability to a sovereign *populus* is not what we expect to find in regimes where there is no idea of a unified polity based on consensus or where power is bestowed by God for the monarch to do God's will, or just his own. That was how the ancient Greeks imagined Persian despotism: if the ruler acted badly, he was not answerable to anyone else.[98] To be sure, the Byzantine emperor was expected to do God's work, but it is no coincidence that the will of the Byzantine God was that the emperor work hard to benefit the republic. It was, in fact, a requirement of all Roman offices under the early empire, even the most local, municipal ones, that a magistrate was "under a moral constraint to act for the good of the urban community . . . Public servants were required to swear an oath in public that they would act for the good of the town."[99]

The emperor was not different in this regard: his *basileia* was defined as a service to the entire Roman polity, and that polity was the community of the Romans.

Historically all kings have been expected to benefit their subjects in some way, but this does not mean that their kingdoms were republics. To understand clearly what was distinctive about Roman rulers, it is worth digressing on the Hellenistic kings whom Rome replaced, because they offer striking models of nonrepublican rule (also because they are often upheld as precedents for the Byzantine emperors, in my view a thoroughly mistaken assumption). The Hellenistic kingdoms can be said to have been states, or to have subsumed many subordinate states, but they were not unified *politeiai* in any sense. The kings could not (and did not) claim to be acting primarily or exclusively in the interest of "a people." They were not defined in terms of the specific polities over which they ruled, because they did not rule over specific polities constituted to promote the interests of a *populus*: their kingdoms were ad hoc collections of territories, peoples, and cities, encompassing different types of political and legal entities.[100] The latter were liable to break off, or be stolen by other kings, and seek their fortunes elsewhere. The component parts of each kingdom interacted as separate legal entities, sometimes presenting a bewildering picture. With the partial exception of the kings of Macedonia,[101] the Hellenistic kings were not kings "of" anything in particular, whether a people or territory; they were just called "kings" without any qualification (e.g., *basileus Seleukos*), and they entered into personal treaties with cities, peoples, and other kingdoms. Service to these kings was understood in personal terms, as a tie to a person and not an impersonal polity: the king's men were his "friends."[102] Succession was largely dynastic and the apparatus of the state was a patrimony. The kings too could move from one kingdom to another, or opportunistically carve out new realms for themselves. Subjects understood the king to be acting primarily in his own interest, in many cases as an exploiter. Royal patronage had its advantages, but the king was at best expected to merely honor treaties and do his subjects some "favors" or be "well-disposed toward them," not to work all night in order to benefit his people.[103] They were not "his people" to begin with. There was no concept of service to a *politeia* because there was no *politeia*, no republic.

These multiethnic kingdoms had little coherence beyond being held together by the power of the king, and they usually had no collective identity beyond that. Excepting perhaps the Macedonians in Macedonia, there was no notion of a polity uniting all subjects in terms of identity, history, legal status, religion, and custom. With the partial exception of Egypt, administration, law, taxation, and military service were generally not uniform and, in any case, were understood not as the collective self-rule of a people but as the instruments of royal power. There was no uniform law of persons: the kings were often not even citizens in many of the cities that they ruled. Their legitimacy, therefore, was not derived from a consenting polity, but through inheritance, right of conquest (usually inherited), military prowess, and divine qualities, favor, or ancestry.[104]

This is not at all the picture presented by the Byzantine empire, which was the *politeia* of the Romans. Many scholars have defined Byzantium as an extension of Hellenistic civilization, a move that implicitly detaches it from the Roman tradition. However, in Byzantium as before, "the Romans never conceived of the *res publica* as culturally Greek, no matter how much Greek cultural forms served to express Roman ideas." Even Roman Hellenism "was colored by distinctly Roman moral debates which find no parallels in the earlier dynastic Hellenism of Ptolemies, Attalids, or Seleucids."[105] The emperor's rule was a form of service and unthinkable apart from that function. A range of texts from different centuries and genres confirms this. I will cite only a few here to illustrate the emphasis with which the idea was affirmed, or taken for granted, by emperors and authors who differed greatly in their outlook on other matters, especially religion. But what they did have in common was membership in the Roman polity. In the early fourth century, the emperor Galerius explained that the persecution of the Christians was intended for "the advantage and benefit of the republic (*pro rei publicae* / τοῖς δημοσίοις) . . . in accordance with the ancient laws and public order of the Romans."[106] Eusebios likewise took it for granted in his *Life of Constantine* that the job of an emperor in peace was "to restore the *koina*"— echoing here Augustus's restoration of the republic—"to promote the interest of each person, and to arrange laws for the advantage of the *politeia* of those whom he governed."[107] The *politeia* is again defined in terms of the ruled; it is not "the state." A century later Eunapios, apologist of the last pagan emperor Julian, wrote that his hero seized power "not because he lusted after kingship . . . or sought vulgar popularity, but because he knew that this was to the advantage of the *koina*."[108] When Anastasios I was elected emperor in 491 and was thanking the crowds in the hippodrome, he made sure to acknowledge, "I am not unaware how great a burden of responsibility has been placed upon me for the common safety (κοινὴ σωτηρία) of all," and "I entreat God the Almighty that you will find me working as hard at public affairs (τὰ πράγματα) as you had hoped when you universally elected me now (ἐν ταύτῃ τῇ κοινῇ ἐκλογῇ)."[109] The preface of Theophanes Continuatus (mid-tenth century), addressed to Konstantinos VII, says that "an emperor is required to practice things that bring advantage to the *politeia* in combination with literary culture."[110]

The idea that the emperor was supposed to work hard for the benefit of his subjects, that this was the basic function of his position, is expressed in more texts than can be cited here. In fact, it is the explicit or underlying assumption of all narratives, speeches, pronouncements, and documents relating to the *basileia*. It was something that the emperors themselves readily acknowledged and never doubted. Each emperor also tried hard to ensure that his subjects knew that he understood this clearly, as if it were a kind of "contract" between them, and to persuade them that he lived up to the image that they had of an ideal emperor. We must not, however, allow the banality and repetitious nature of this doctrine to lull us as it was meant to lull them. We will see later that this public relations effort was of critical importance and could not be allowed to fail, for Byzantine public opinion was harsh and unforgiving and the consequences of failure could be catastrophic for a reign. The emperors themselves willingly defined their position in relation to the *politeia*. I have decided to present some representative texts here from the spheres of law, administration, and warfare, though there are other moments and genres that could be used to prove the same points.[111]

In the prefaces to their laws, emperors insisted that they were motivated purely by the desire to benefit, aid, care for, and plan ahead for their subjects and that their goal was to preserve, improve, order, and protect the *politeia* in order to make it more just, prosperous, compassionate, free, and/or equal.[112] "The public interest," "the public good," "the common good *(koinon)*," "the benefit of our subjects," "the good of the *dêmosion* and the *politeia*," and many other variations of the same are constantly invoked in decrees and legal texts, and it seems that this public interest is always what pleases God too, on the occasions when he is mentioned.[113] In sum, emperors made it clear that the main purpose of their office was to benefit their subjects, and that this was the reason that justified all the legislation they issued.[114] These subjects, moreover, were not imagined, as in our scholarship, to be an agglomeration of random ethnicities cowed by force, but, as Cicero had defined it, a polity of a unified people with a natural order that had to be preserved. In the preface to his codification of the laws, the *Ekloge,* Leon III declared that he wanted the kingdom to be peaceful and the *politeuma* stable.[115] Either he or Leon V declared in a *Novel* that the Roman *politeia* should be peaceful and without disturbance.[116] Psellos praised Konstantinos IX for "preserving the perfection of the *politeia.*"[117]

In the preface of his *Taktika,* which was in form a long edict on military matters, Leon VI declares,

> It is not imperial pageantry and authority, not the power and extent of that authority, not the display and enjoyment of all that, nor any of those things sought after and esteemed by men that brings such joy to Our Majesty as does the peace and prosperity of our subjects and the setting aright and the constant improvement of our public affairs (πολιτικὰ πράγματα).[118]

In later sections of the preface he alternates between *politika pragmata, politeia,* and "the *pragmata* of the Romans." What he is saying effectively is, "It's not about me; it's about you." The same idea runs through his *Novels,* as we saw in the first chapter.

Turning to administration, the message was that some emperors never slept, so hard did they labor on their subjects' behalf. The idea was a trope of the imperial idea and was broadcast in legal prefaces, especially by Justinian, who even described himself in a public inscription as "the Sleepless Emperor." Prokopios tried to turn this around to make him appear sinister, but it was a banal image.[119] Later emperors who did not sleep included Leon III (on behalf of *to koinon*), Basileios I (on behalf of his subjects and *ta koina*), and Nikephoros III Botaneiates (over *ta pragmata*).[120] Psellos wrote of Isaakios I that "his eye is sleepless and not one of you has seen him indulging in any pleasure during the entire length of his reign, or feasting extravagantly, or celebrating conspicuously, or taking any rest in sleep, or sparing his body in his labors."[121] This was generally expected of all emperors, and they accepted it as part of the job.[122] But the rhetoric was not confined to them: the same seems to have been expected of all imperial functionaries, though they appear less frequently in the surviving literature, for obvious reasons. But whenever one of them turned to write about his own kind, we find again the rhetoric of working hard through the night.[123] The emperor was, in this sense, only a more exalted functionary of the republic.

War was another sphere in which labors on behalf of the polity could be performed. Herakleios "risked his life on behalf of his *politeia*."[124] Emperors who campaigned in person made sure that their subjects knew on whose behalf they were fighting and incurring personal dangers. In his epitaph, Basileios II boasts, "I kept vigilant through the whole span of my life, guarding the children of New Rome."[125] Psellos praised Isaakios as "a great benefit for the Romans" who "would be willing to die ten thousand times in order to increase the Roman empire."[126] The same author argues speciously that the family name of that most unmilitary emperor Konstantinos IX Monomachos "designated the one who would face danger in advance and alone for the state (κράτος), a worthy fighter beyond everyone else, fighting in single-combat for the common fame of our people (ὑπὲρ τῆς κοινῆς τοῦ γένους εὐκλείας)."[127] Many more cases could be cited, but let us consider the tragic one of Romanos IV. In a *silention* (possibly of 1071) he states twice that he is incurring the risks of war on behalf of all his subjects: "I don a helmet instead of a crown . . . and march out ahead of the phalanx so that I may be struck and you may live in peace."[128] Before he departed on campaign, Psellos addressed him in an oration: "you take thought for us, and wear yourself down with every form of labor and solicitude."[129] After he was cruelly blinded by the Doukas regime, his defender Attaleiates bursts out against Michael VII:

> What do you have to say, O emperor, you and those who crafted this unholy decision along with you? The eyes of a man who had done no wrong but risked his life for the welfare of the Romans and who had fought with a powerful army against the most warlike nations when he could have waited it all out in the palace without any danger and shrugged off the toils and horrors of the military life?[130]

The common good was something to which everyone was supposed to contribute in proportion to his ability (as we saw in the analysis of Syrianos above). Emperors, given their extraordinary powers, were naturally held to the highest standard. They in turn evaluated their subjects' contributions. When they wished to reward or benefit, even humble contributions were honored.[131] When emperors grew angry, sectors of the polity were declared to be useless. Witness Nikephoros Phokas, a general who hated the tax-collectors who oppressed soldiers: "they have no utility for the *koinon*," he exaggerated.[132]

It was by the same standard that the emperors themselves were evaluated by their subjects, both during and after their reigns. Opinions differed about the particulars of each case, but there was consensus about the standard. This did not change in the later period.[133] A comic anecdote from the early thirteenth century strikingly reveals what subjects expected from their emperors and how emperors wanted to be perceived. It belongs to a subgenre of imperial imagery, namely, the encounter with a common person that showcases an emperor's personal interest in his problems. These vignettes highlighted imperial virtues and so set the tone for subjects' perceptions. A certain simpleton was going around saying that soon there would be a good emperor. This came to the ears of the emperor, Theodoros Laskaris, and he had the man brought to him.

> "And what am I?" he said. "Do I not look like a good emperor to you?"
>
> "What have you ever given to me that would make me think you are good?"
>
> "Did I not give myself to you every day, fighting to the death on your behalf and all our people?"
>
> "The sun shines and so heats us and gives us light, but we are not thankful to it. It fulfills the function that has been set for it. And you are doing what you ought to do, toiling and laboring, as you say, on behalf of your compatriots."
>
> "So . . . if I give you some gifts, will I be good then?"
>
> "Yes, of course."
>
> And so he gave him clothes and money.[134]

The humor in the story stems from the contrast between the emperor's abstract sense of duty toward an entire nation and a simpleton's expectation of personal favors ("what have you done for *me*?").

It was even possible to advocate the view that the emperor was basically a magistrate, though this type of argument is found mostly in polemical texts. In his work *On Kingship* addressed to Arkadios (a foundational text of the genre of Mirrors of Princes), Synesios called for an emperor who was "a servant of the *politeia* (λειτουργὸν τῆς πολιτείας)."[135] In exhorting Arkadios to take charge of the army, Synesios advocates a return to Roman tradition (Ῥωμαίων τὰ πάτρια), not, however, the traditions that entered the *politeia* recently but those of the founders of the empire.[136] He is reacting specifically to the pomp and ceremony that made it difficult for emperors to get their hands dirty with the business of governing and warfare as well as to the hiring of mercenaries. Synesios's speech is read by some scholars as expressing conventional notions, while others believe that it was so inflammatory as to have been undeliverable and so circulated in a small circle of sympathizers.[137] Both readings are correct: the speech takes polemical positions but grounds them in traditional ideals. However controversial its specific views, it definitely held the moral high ground when it claimed that the emperor was a servant of the *politeia*.

Prokopios also considered emperors to be basically magistrates. At one point, in criticizing Justinian's extraordinary rituals of submission, he refers to a time when the emperor could be ranked "among the rest of the magistrates."[138] Psellos was not reacting against excessive pomp but only to incompetence when he declared that Konstantinos IX did not understand "the nature of the *basileia,* that is a form of service to benefit one's subjects (λειτουργία τίς ἐστι λυσιτελὴς εἰς τὸ ὑπήκοον) and it requires alertness of mind to properly administrate political affairs."[139] This is the view of the office that Psellos maintains throughout his history and the standard by which he judges all emperors.[140] Many Palaiologan texts also reflect the assumption that emperors were basically executive officials who wielded power that had been delegated to them by the republic.[141]

One might suppose, with Magdalino, that all these writers were classically educated and therefore out of touch with Byzantine realities. But this postulates unnecessary polarities and conflates their education, which was Greek and theoretical, with the ideology of the polity, which was Roman and built into political practice. The emperors themselves, as we have seen repeatedly, defined their own position within a republican framework—"I rule for your benefit, not mine." A theoretical education merely enabled the likes of Psellos to articulate precisely this republican aspect of the Byzantine polity and make it the basis for a critique and reform. But it was also visible elsewhere. Dagron has observed that the coronation of the emperor

> occupies a surprising place within the structure of the *Book of Ceremonies,* that is, at the head of a section devoted to civil ceremonies—as opposed to religious ceremonies—and the promotions of dignitaries. The

emperor and the Augusta were thus placed at the top of a hierarchy which descended to the level of the office head and *protospatharios*, making the *basileus* a sort of top civil servant.[142]

What is more surprising is that Dagron regards this as surprising, but this is because he regards the emperor in Byzantium as mostly a religious figure. We will return to this problem in Chapter 6, for we have only begun to consider the implications of viewing Byzantium as a Roman republic.

CHAPTER 3

Extralegal Authority in a Lawful Polity

This chapter will examine the role of law and its limits in defining the Roman-Byzantine concept and operation of the republic. There was a consensus that a true *politeia* has to be ruled by law, but how could this be reconciled with the existence of a monarch who could issue, change, annul, or ignore the laws? This created an apparent contradiction: was the emperor subject to or above the law? Both opinions were expressed, which had led to an impasse among modern legal scholars. Part of the problem, it will be argued, is that we have failed to define both the law and the emperor in relation to the republic, which was prior to and more important than either. Moreover, the emperor was not the only one who could "legitimately" act beyond the laws: the people could do so too, especially when they decided to depose an emperor, for the republic was theirs, after all.

The Ideal of the "Lawful Polity"

In 484, Verina, widow of the emperor Leon I (457–474) and mother-in-law of the reigning emperor Zenon (474–491), was persuaded by the rebel general Illos, who held her in his power at Tarsos, to proclaim a certain Leontios emperor. This was only one moment in a series of shifting alliances, but we will focus on the letter that Verina sent to the people of Antioch proclaiming her support for Leontios. It read as follows:

"Ailia Verina, perpetual Augusta, to our citizens of Antioch. Know that the imperial authority, after the death of the blessed Leon, is ours. We made Strakodisseos emperor, who was afterwards called Zenon, to benefit our subjects and all the military units. But now we see that the *politeia,* and along with it our subjects, being ruined by his greed, and so we have deemed it necessary to crown a pious emperor for you who is adorned with justice so that he may save the affairs of the Roman *politeia,* induce our enemies to be at peace, and make secure all the subjects in accordance with the laws. We have crowned Leontios the most pious, who will deem you all worthy of his care and providence." And the entire populace of Antioch immediately rose up as one and cried out, "God is Great! and Lord have mercy, do what is good and best for us."[1]

This letter reflects a number of fundamental assumptions about the workings of the *politeia* and the relationship between emperors and subjects. Verina had to persuade her subjects to accept her decision, and to that end she needed to deploy precisely the arguments that most closely corresponded to the prevalent ideology concerning the use and purpose of imperial power. She had to create a new consensus by identifying and appealing to the expectations that her subjects had of her. In this regard, her position was no different than that of any emperor ruling in peace. These, then, are the assumptions reflected in her letter: Communication is imagined as taking place between imperial authority and an undifferentiated body of citizens (the *politai* of Antioch). It is deemed successful when it is greeted by a universal consensus among them, who are here called "the entire populace" (δῆμος = *populus*). We may be skeptical of whether that actually happened, though it certainly may have. What is more important is that this was how imperial communication was represented as successful. In other words, imperial legitimacy was established by universal popular consent. The sole motive that Verina alleges for both the elevation of Zenon and his deposition (and the elevation of Leontios) is her desire to benefit the *politeia,* called here both *res publica* and *res Romana.* Therefore, for imperial decisions to be ratified by the universal consent of the *populus,* the only allowable motive for imperial action was the good of the *res publica.* As far as ideological parameters go, these were universal in Byzantium too, as we have seen. Also, an emperor could be deposed for failing to do right by the *politeia.* Verina specifies that her choice, Leontios, will govern according to the laws. This a key criterion that we will discuss in this and the following section. Finally, moral qualities and religion are invoked only to distinguish potentially "good" emperors from past "bad" ones (piety versus greed). There is nothing theological in the relationship between the Augusta and her subjects; it does not operate in the space between emperor and God.

There was nothing radical, revolutionary, or even unusual in how this communication was framed, either as a piece of imperial rhetoric or as an event in Roman history. Leon VI's *Novels,* examined in Chapter 1, aimed to meet the same standards of rhetorical appeal, though he was elevating and demoting laws rather than candidates for the throne. It would have been difficult for Verina to frame her appeal in different terms; she had to express shared assumptions about the exercise of Roman power that were already hardwired into both emperors and subjects. Of course, we do not need to believe that all the characters in this drama were personally motivated by these notions, no more than any politicians do what they do solely for the good of their constituents. What we are interested in is the constitution of the political sphere, what emperors had to do to be recognizable as legitimate emperors in the first place.

I selected Verina's letter to the Antiochenes for discussion from among countless similar moments because her attempt to depose Zenon on the grounds that he had failed the *res publica* happened around the same time that Priskos of Panion published his *History* (probably in the late 470s).[2] The work survives in fragments, of which the longest and most famous recounts an embassy to Attila in 449 that Priskos accompanied. The group traveled from Constantinople to the borders of the Hun empire and then north, well outside what the Romans would have deemed the civilized world, to the court of Attila. Against the backdrop of diplomatic negotiations, Priskos, a literary historian, narrates an encounter that he had there with a Greek-speaking Roman expatriate (a *Graikos,* yet another Hellenized Latin word). If not outright invented by Priskos, the encounter was elaborated by him to become a debate on the fundamental principles, merits, and flaws of the Roman *politeia*.[3] The fugitive incarnated the possibility, conditions, and consequences of opting out of the *politeia,* while Priskos's decision to situate the debate at the camp of Attila made the presence of alternatives palpable. It might have seemed ludicrous to even raise the question in Constantinople, much less debate it.

This Graikos had done well among the Huns. He explains to Priskos that he had been captured in a raid but had served his owner well in a war and had purchased his freedom from the spoils. Obviously, he feels compelled to explain why he had then chosen to remain among the Huns and launches into a tirade against Roman life: people are not allowed to bear arms for their own defense and the generals are no good; taxes are heavy; there is corruption everywhere; and the laws are not applied equally, as the rich manage to get off, trials last too long, and one has to pay the judges. In his response, Priskos does not argue that these things do not happen. Part of the reason he included the exchange in his *History* was to air these criticisms through someone else's mouth. Instead, he takes the discussion to a deeper level, to the principles on which "the *politeia* of the Romans" was founded. These, he proposes, were wise, as they required the separation of military, judicial, and agricultural functions, each of which made its own contribution to the workings of the whole. Each of these classes "guarded" or "supervised" a different aspect of the *politeia*. The condensation of the passage by the Byzantine excerptor makes it difficult to follow parts of the exposition, but it seems that Priskos defended the justice of the entire system along the lines of Sokrates's argument in the *Republic*, which links justice to separation of functions. Priskos is concerned to defend the justice of the fundamental principles even if he knows that they are not always implemented in the best way. He goes so far as to assert that "the laws apply to all, and even the emperor obeys them."[4] We will see below that this was a difficult point.

Priskos then turns the tables on the Graikos by bringing the discussion to his own circumstances among the Huns. "As for your freedom, you should give thanks to Chance." Anything could have happened to him in captivity or in the battle where he earned his freedom. He got lucky. Life among the Huns is apparently governed by luck, the arbitrary whim of a despot, which could be a metaphor for Attila. With the Romans, by contrast, there are laws about how one can treat slaves and "there are many sanctioned ways of giving freedom among them." At this point, "my acquaintance wept and said that the laws were fair and the *politeia* of the Romans was good, but that the authorities were ruining it by not taking the same thought for it as had those of old."[5] Priskos then says that their discussion was interrupted, signifying that the question in some respects remains open. Clearly he intended his readers to think about the ways in which the functioning and maintenance of the *politeia* could be improved. He virtually lays out an agenda for reform through the mouth of the Graikos. Generally, the Graikos attacks the way the *politeia* operates in practice while Priskos defends the principles behind many of its arrangements, conceding that they do not always work the way they were supposed to.

What conclusions can we draw from this passage? One is that the concept of the *politeia* of the Romans was an ideal abstraction compared to which current practice could be found wanting. Individual Romans could invoke the principles of the *politeia* to advocate reform, but the same could be done by emperors, as we saw with Leon VI in Chapter 1. Moreover, the *politeia* is not constituted by government action or the imperial system; instead, it is something prior to them, constituted by the whole of society whose elements have entered into relations of mutual codependence according to shared principles of justice. These principles are expressed and manifested in the laws and Priskos wants to subordinate the emperors to them. We shall examine in the next section how this particular question was approached in Byzantium.

The terms of the discussion in Priskos's encounter with the Graikos have one more substantive consequence: it seems unlikely that there could be a *politeia* among the Huns. Their world was governed by chance, or the whim of a despot, not by established laws and customs to which all adhere. Perhaps the Graikos weeps at the end because he recognizes the precarious situation that he finds himself in. The advantages of a *politeia* emerge strongly even from what Priskos does *not* say. There can be no *res publica* of the Huns, not so much because of who the Huns were (Priskos depicts them as rather civilized, in their own way), but because of the stringent requirements needed to have a *res publica,* as Cicero and others had explained them and as the Byzantines understood them. Having any kind of state or social and political power structure did not mean that you also had a lawful polity. While the word *politeia* could sometimes be used to mean "state" and applied to any foreign power, Byzantine writers could also be clear when they meant "a polity in the Roman manner," that is, a lawfully constituted one.[6] Let us consider two examples.

Prokopios devotes one of the many ethnographic digressions in his *Wars* (550 AD) to the Ephthalitai Huns, who lived in Central Asia to the northeast of the Persians.

> They are not nomads like the other Hunnic peoples, but for a long period have been established in a rich land . . . They are the only Huns who have white bodies and faces that are not ugly. It is also true that their manner of living is unlike that of their kinsmen, nor do they live a savage life as they do; but they are ruled by one king, and since they possess an *ennomos politeia,* they observe right and justice in their dealings

both with one another and with their neighbors, in no degree less than the Romans and the Persians.[7]

Ennomos politeia ("lawful polity") was one way to differentiate a *res publica* along Roman lines from any other type of power formation. It is a technical term that we will encounter often below. Prokopios is here suggesting that the Ephthalitai, Romans, and Persians each had their own *res publica,* and bases this verdict on the relations of justice that they maintain among and between them and also on their level of what we loosely call civilization. Roman imperial authorities of his time recognized the Persian empire as a state on a par with Rome and treated it more or less as an equal.[8] Prokopios's successor and continuer, Agathias (writing in ca. 580), admitted that he did not know any other *politeia* that had changed so many "formations" and "shapes" as had the Persian one over the long course of its history,[9] but he still treated it as a peer polity. The historian Theophylaktos, writing in the seventh century, grants the dignity of the name *politeia* only to the Romans and the Persians.[10]

Agathias devoted a digression to the society of the Franks, focusing precisely on the nature of their *politeia* in relation to Roman norms.

> The Franks are not nomads, as some barbarians are, but their *politeia* and laws are modeled on the Roman pattern, apart from which they uphold similar standards with regard to contracts, marriage and religious observance. They are in fact all Christians and adhere to the strictest orthodoxy. They also have magistrates in their cities and priests and celebrate the feasts in the same way as we do; and, for a barbarian people, strike me as extremely well-bred and civilized and as practically the same as us except for their uncouth style of dress and peculiar language. I admire them for their other attributes and especially for the spirit of justice and harmony which prevails amongst them.[11]

Repeatedly we find that not every state or people qualify as a *politeia*. Roman standards are used as a benchmark in comparisons with other peoples. Again we encounter the claim that polities cannot be constituted by nomadic peoples. Polities require laws and the social bonds of religion and public administration: the rulers of lawful polities must adhere to a common set of standards ratified by the public consensus of a people, and not simply follow their whim. The Franks differ in their language and dress because they are a different people from the Romans, a different national culture, but according to this fictional presentation by Agathias they fulfill the formal requirements of a proper polity.

These historians, who were also political theorists, were not talking about foreign polities for their own sake. They crafted these digressions primarily as indirect reflections on the state of the Roman polity, much as Priskos employed an anonymous stranger to vent serious criticisms of Roman public policy. This subversive effect is triggered in part by the preposterous claims that they make about Ephthalite and Frankish society, which should alert most readers.[12] But in the process they reveal the general qualities that they thought should be found in any proper *politeia*. I note also that their conception was fundamentally secular. Religion is important because it is part of the national culture, but the polity itself is a function of relations of justice. The Persians were not Christians, but they had a polity; nor had the founders of the Roman *res publica* itself been Christians.

A Roman polity was supposed to have a lawful order. Laws aimed to promote community values and protect the common good from private interests. This was a standard by which barbarians could be distinguished. Orosius (early fifth century) relates a revealing apocryphal anecdote. Athaulf, the successor of Alaric as king of the Goths, had considered obliterating the Roman name and simply replacing *Romania* with *Gothia* but changed his mind when he considered that the Goths could simply not obey any law and "he believed it wrong to deprive a polity of laws (without which a polity is not a polity at all)."[13]

In Chapter 1, we looked at how Byzantine historians imagined the transition of their polity from monarchy to Republic and then back to monarchy. Some of them viewed that history from a legal aspect. Ioannes Lydos (in the sixth century) insisted that a proper *politeia* had to be an *ennomos politeia* or else it was just a tyranny. He wrote the history of the Roman republic from this standpoint, but his history too, like the digressions in the historians, was polemical. What he wanted to argue was that Justinian was a tyrant and that the Roman polity had declined from the time of the consuls, who, along with the laws, had once been the bulwarks of its freedom.[14] The opposite of lawful freedom was subjection to the whim of a despot such as Justinian (or Attila). The same notion pervades Prokopios's *Secret History*, a text possibly known to Lydos. Prokopios focuses on Justinian's systematic abuse of the legal system, his failure to adhere to the old good laws, and his passage of bad new ones to serve his temporary advantage. One of the goals of the *Secret History* was to show precisely that whim had now *become* law. It was his constant innovation in the field of law that made Justinian a tyrant in Prokopios's eyes. The opposite of a *politeia* was slavery, the loss of the freedom that was guaranteed by the laws. It was precisely this that people such as Theodora could not understand or respect. Prokopios presents her as having a thoroughly personal view of power; she had no idea what an impersonal *politeia* was: "The *politeia* was thereby reduced to a slave-pen and she was our teacher in servility."[15] All this was a targeted response to Justinian's own proclamations, in which the emperor boasted that he had restored freedom to the Romans and also recognized that the basis of the *politeia* was law.[16]

The complaints of Lydos and Prokopios were exaggerated, of course, as were the complaints of Zonaras and Choniates against the Komnenoi (which we examined in Chapter 2). The republic of the Romans had not been irrevocably destroyed by Justinian any more than it was later by the Komnenoi. These authors were participating in a tradition of Roman polemic. Cicero, for example, famously believed that the "true *res publica*" had been destroyed long before his own time. His makes his speaker Scipio Aemilianus (second century BC) say that "it is not by some accident—no, it is because of our own moral failings—that we are left with the name of the *res publica*, having long since lost its substance."[17] Prokopios, Lydos, and Zonaras were saying the same thing. The republic was always being destroyed and restored. Augustus restored it after Cicero, and Justin II restored it after Justinian.[18] The republic was restored after civil wars or when new emperors wanted to signal a change of direction.[19] This was a persistent rhythm in Roman political rhetoric, indeed constitutive of it.

To focus on the question of law, I draw attention to an anonymous and obscure three-page history of Roman law written possibly in the late eleventh century. "One must know," this text says, "that in the first beginning and genesis of Rome, when Romulus ruled, the *politeia* was without law . . . When the *populus* again took power, it relied on a vague kind of law and on custom rather than functioning as a *politeia* according to the laws." Eventually, however, they formed the committee of the Ten Men "to lay the foundations of the Roman *politeia* in the laws."[20] The treatise contains some bizarre misunderstandings of early Roman history (such as that the *reges* ruled beneath the *basileus*), but it proposes an interesting model by which the polity became lawful: no law under the kings, customary law at first in the early Republic, and proper laws later on. The second phase has theoretical affinities with Leon VI's view of how customs can constitute a polity before receiving official ratification from him, a curious form of unofficial *ennomos politeia,* such as this text proposes for the early Republic. All this, however, raises the question of the status of the lawful polity under the imperial monarchy. Unfortunately, the text is confused at this point. It claims that "in time the *politeia* grew and the number of cases and trials grew as well . . . And so under Caesar Augustus the divisions of the *populus* began to pass legislation, both the commoners and the more select, along with the generals, the wise men, and the *praetors.*" It is not clear what the author was thinking of here. At any rate, like most Romans he did not believe that there was any conflict between having an emperor and a lawful polity. How, then, did the Byzantines imagine that a supreme monarch could rule an *ennomos politeia* without its lapsing into a tyranny of whim? Was there not a fundamental tension between autocracy and the rule of law?

The Emperor and the Law: A Contradiction Resolved

At first sight, as well as a second and third, Byzantium was a lawful polity. It had a substantial corpus of law that had been issued, compiled, and revised by legitimate authorities, and it was not questioned that a proper polity had to be governed on the basis of law, not the arbitrary whim of the powerful; that officials had to obey the laws and not pursue private interests;[21] and that the laws should be applied equally and fairly to all. To be sure, reality did not always or fully conform to this picture. It was possible for individuals to break the law and not be punished and for officials to abuse their power. We do not really know to what degree the laws were enforced by the authorities, applied in the courts, or known to the populace. We cannot then measure the gap between theory and practice. We will never know how Byzantium would measure up by the standards of modern societies (which are riding low at the moment). What matters for our purpose is that subjects understood or hoped that theirs was a lawful polity and that the laws were meant to be binding on rulers as well as the ruled. Their awareness and exploitation of this premise are more evident in early Byzantine Egypt, where documentary evidence survives. As Joëlle Beaucamp has observed:

Mentions of the laws occur frequently in petitions and other types of documents related to proceedings before the authorities. These texts express general comments on the benefits provided by the laws . . . They ask the authorities to enforce the law bearing on the case submitted to them . . . These statements could be considered mere *topoi*, traditionally conveyed by the genre of the petition. However, the term "law" here indicates a higher order, and a public one: this order is connected with the authorities and sometimes explicitly with the emperor.[22]

The *ennomos politeia* was an unquestioned principle. Leon VI, as we saw, believed that popular customs required ratification by formal authority (i.e., his own). But the real problem and source of anxiety and political reflection was the imperial position itself. How could a polity be lawful when it was governed by an emperor who could ignore or cancel a law and was not subject to legal or political oversight? This was the threat of tyranny that lurked in every monarchy, and it preoccupied Cicero in his *Republic*. The *res publica* could be jeopardized even under a wise and good king, "for the property of the public (which is, as I said, the definition of a republic) was managed by one man's nod and wish."[23] A thin line separated good kings and despots.[24] In fact, imperial history seems to oscillate between the two.

There have been many discussions of the relation between the emperor and the law. I am not interested here in how legal policies were formulated; how laws were issued, interpreted, enforced, and subsequently compiled; or how law intersected with imperial propaganda, serving as a vehicle for court rhetoric and to project the emperor as a bulwark of the lawful order. I am referring more specifically to the question of whether the emperor was subject to or above the laws. An emperor who is subject to the laws would approximate the model of the servant of the republic sketched in Chapter 2, while an emperor who exists—more importantly, who is held to exist—above the laws would seem, at least at first sight, to challenge that model. Good emperors were presented as submissive to the authority of the laws, which called for a certain humility on their part, even if only a show of it, while bad emperors tended to act as they wished without regard to the law. At least this is how they were depicted by their partisans and enemies, respectively, which suggests that the model of the emperor who submits to the law held the moral high ground and, therefore, was ideologically dominant.

As we saw above in Priskos, the notion that the emperor did (or should?) obey the laws just like any other magistrate was firmly linked to the republican premises of the regime. But the way Priskos invokes this principle in defending the *politeia* as an ideal model betrays his insecurity: rather than asserting a point of fact, it is more like he is reminding readers of the preconditions of a lawful polity, having acknowledged that not all is as it should be in real life. How could one ensure that emperors governed lawfully? The context of his claim makes it programmatic, and not necessarily descriptive. But if the right people could be made to accept it, especially the emperors themselves, it could became real. The evidence suggests that these "reminders" by theorists did make it through to the emperors, at least on a rhetorical level. Synesios promulgated a definition that became a commonplace, namely, that the legitimate king makes the law his will while the tyrant makes his whim the law.[25] This was adopted verbatim by other theorists, such as Ioannes Lydos in the sixth century, but also by emperors, such as Konstantinos IX in the eleventh, in a *Novel* establishing a school of law and the office of *nomophylax* ("guardian of the laws").[26] The text was written by Ioannes Mauropous, reminding us that the emperors had to speak through theorists and orators. But we should not view the latter as imposing their views on otherwise reluctant authoritarian emperors. Emperors *wanted* to be seen by their subjects as governing lawfully in the same way that they wanted to be seen as governing solely in their subjects' interests (in fact, we will see that they *had* to be seen this way if they wanted to keep their thrones and, often, their lives). A lawful polity had need of lawful supervision, and this is precisely what many writers and emperors in their legislation took to be the essence of the imperial position: it was an *ennomos epistasia*, a lawful oversight that was "a common good for all the subjects."[27]

An edict issued in 429 by Theodosios II and Valentinianus III, which was summarized in the Byzantine *Basilika*, went even further and proclaimed this:

> It is a statement worthy of the majesty of a reigning prince for him to profess to be subject to the laws; for our authority is dependent upon that of the law. And it is the greatest attribute of imperial power for the sovereign to be subject to the laws, and we forbid to others what we do not suffer ourselves to do by the terms of the present edict.[28]

Unfortunately, we lack the context behind this pronouncement, which would have clarified why the emperors made it.[29] There was certainly some advantage in it. It is likely that they were receiving too many requests for exemptions from general laws and were, with this pronouncement, ostentatiously shutting that door even for themselves. No one could complain now. The emperors simply proclaimed that they were as subject to the laws as anyone else and accepted that the authority of their position stemmed from the law, which no one could deny without challenging the very foundations of the *ennomos politeia*.

If we left matters there, the view that the Byzantine polity was republican in nature would gain another pillar of support. The emperors professed that they were subject to impersonal public institutions no less than were their subjects. In fact, no matter what alternative or rival evidence we might encounter, we have enough here to conclude that there was at least a will to believe in a republican monarchy.

But when the matter was looked at from a different point of view, it was possible to conclude that the emperor in fact stood above the law, leading to a fundamental tension in legal theory about the imperial position. This has caused a conflicted discussion in modern scholarship, which oscillates between the two views. I will first explain the rationale for the view that the emperor stood above the law and then argue that the two views, for all that they were in tension, were ultimately reconcilable—but only if we accept the priority and supremacy of the *politeia*. Without that, the Roman view of the emperor is contradictory, leaving modern scholars no choice but to accept the more cynical, authoritarian view (lest they appear to be idealists).

The emperor was the supreme legislative authority and also the highest court of appeal. He could alter the law if he thought that was best for the polity; in fact, he had a responsibility to do so when current law no longer served the polity's needs. Justinian's *Novels* recognize that the laws have to be continually adapted to changing circumstances, the *varia rerum natura*,[30] and this was also the premise behind the *Novels* of Leon VI three and half centuries later. We saw in Chapter 1 that Leon ratified and annulled laws just as if he were promoting and retiring magistrates. Moreover, as legal theory had long understood, laws are often too general and inflexible when it comes to particular cases premised on unique circumstances. Exceptions had to be made in the name of justice, but these could be made only by the judgment of men acting in real time.[31] Law emanated from the emperor, so how could he be subject to it? This tension gave rise in Greek theory to the idea of the king as a "living" or "animate" law (ἔμψυχος νόμος), a living, walking, and speaking source of law. This concept was invoked by many Byzantine emperors, though what exactly they meant by it on each occasion is opaque.[32] In a public oration, Themistios, a propagandist for Constantius II and Theodosius I, deduced from this concept that emperors were above the laws.[33] And we find the opinion in the *Digest* that "the *princeps* is not bound by the laws" (carried over into the *Basilika*).[34] Moreover, some historians have argued that it served the emperors' interests to maintain a level of legal ambiguity in order to assert their relevance and authority as ultimate arbiters.[35]

The idea that a governing authority could make an exception to a given rule in order to serve a higher purpose in a specific instance or to prevent an unusual case from warping the spirit of the general rule was called *oikonomia* in Byzantium. It was an option that called for prudent management, a higher sense of justice, and moral consensus as well as pragmatism and an acknowledgment that not all ends could be served at once. *Oikonomia* was invoked most commonly in the application of canon law but was, in itself, a broad concept. God's interventions in history were regarded as "economical" in this sense, and provincial judges were not expected to literally and strictly apply the law in all cases.[36] In one of his *Novels,* Leon VI noted that an emperor can "practice οἰκονομία, but this is not contrary to the law. For those who are entrusted by God with the management (οἰκονομία) of worldly affairs are permitted to manage them (οἰκονομεῖν) at a level above the law that governs subjects."[37] In the twelfth century, when the canonist Theodoros Balsamon noted that "the emperor is not subject to the laws or to the canons," he cited the prerogative of "imperial *oikonomia*."[38]

Given that there was no higher legal authority, as the *Digest* put it, "what pleases the *princeps* has the force of law."[39] The Greek translation in the *Basilika* went further in saying that "what pleases the *basileus* is a law."[40] This necessarily applied whether the emperor issued a formal general law, made a legal decision in a particular case, granted an exemption in writing, or simply verbally ordered one of his officials or subjects to do something. This ambiguity opened them to criticism. Ammianus, for example, complained that whatever the Caesar Gallus said held the force of law. This made him a tyrant.[41] But the same effect could be achieved through written legislation, as Prokopios complained about Justinian. It was he who, more than any other emperor, governed by issuing laws that explained and specified what he wanted done.[42] Though much evidence has been lost, it seems that later emperors governed by issuing orders in different ways.[43] Those orders had "the force of law" even if they were not formally laws. But if the emperor's will was the law, it makes little sense to ask whether he was above the law or subject to it. Only one emperor in our period (Nikephoros III Botaneiates) passed a law that was meant to apply primarily to other emperors. It was never enforced, as far as we know, and certainly did not set a trend.[44]

The sources, therefore, are contradictory. Was the emperor subject to the law or above the laws? Was his authority grounded in law or the reverse? The Romans devised no legal doctrine to solve this conundrum.[45] What emperors, theorists, and subjects did instead was break through it with a formula that was essentially an expression of republican will that would echo in the Byzantine legal tradition: "While we are not bound by the laws, still we abide by them."[46] The emperors were making a personal pledge to voluntarily abide by the laws even though they had the option of not doing so. This combined the republican servant with the "animate law" and explained celebrated acts of extravagant obedience to specific laws, such as by Trajan and Julian.[47] As Charles Pazdernik has observed:

> Roman imperial ideology never repudiated the principle that a good emperor should not appear to be above the law and that he should do nothing contrary to the laws; an emperor who failed to evince a correct understanding of his role within the state was susceptible of being branded a tyrant, an outcome that might not only authorize insurrection but also represent the settled judgment of history. Although the observance of such strictures was in large measure a matter of decorum and modes of imperial self-presentation, part of political theater rather than an insurmountable limitation on power, emperors well understood the value of conserving respect for the law and appearance of lawfulness as a critical underpinning of their authority.[48]

We will study the form that those insurrections could take, when emperors failed to strike the right tone, in Chapters 4 and 5.

A certain amount of theater was imposed by the republican foundations of the regime. But imperial law-abidingness was not only a matter of appearance, for the integrity of the legal order had to be maintained for emperors to govern at all, as the patriarch Nikolaos noted.[49] Too much interference could undermine the entire system, though interference was as likely or more to originate from subjects seeking favors as from the imperial will. In 491, Anastasios instructed his judges not to accept "any rescript, pragmatic sanction, or imperial notation that is contrary to the general law or adverse to the public interest (*generali iuri vel utilitati publicae adversa*) . . . nor to hesitate to follow in every respect the general imperial constitutions."[50] In effect, the emperor was asserting the moral and legal supremacy of general laws over specific enactments that he or his predecessors might have passed in individual cases. This was meant to protect the integrity of the *ennomos politeia* against subjects who would twist imperial power for their own ends. In 1158, Manuel I issued a similar directive.[51] Emperors relied on their legal advisors to keep them within the bounds of precedent and legality,[52] and there is at least one case (from the eleventh century) where a high court judge rejected an emperor's understanding of a law, explaining sarcastically that *if* the emperor were simply exercising his legislative power in the matter, then his decision must stand, of course, but *if* it were being offered on the basis of that existing law, then "your holy Majesty has an obligation to actually know the law in question" (according to Spyros Troianos, the judge "put him in his place").[53]

The Roman legal tradition, therefore, remained something separate from the imperial will and operated, for the most part, independently of the monarch and sometimes even to check him.[54] More importantly, power was not taken to be legitimate unless it was perceived to be lawful. Dagron has astutely pointed out that "it was not power that was legitimate; but whoever appropriated power could be made legitimate by choosing to respect the law . . . Legitimacy was achieved through a conversion to legality."[55] Also, in refuting the notion that the emperor was the owner of all land in the empire, G. C. Maniatis argues that "Byzantine historians held that confiscations were an infringement on the rights of property owners and not an exercise of the emperor's lawful rights." Illegal confiscations were probably rare, but they do highlight a potential for abuse.[56] "The middle Byzantine idea of justice," Angeliki Laiou explained in a paper on economic ideology, "included the concern that the possessions of all subjects (especially the weaker ones) should be safeguarded and that a proper and orderly society should not be disturbed by encroachment on the rights and possessions of others."[57] Both subjects and emperors agreed that the *politeia* had to be *ennomos,* and this consensus constrained and shaped everyone's actions and expectations to such a degree that emperors routinely declared that they would abide by the laws themselves even though they did not have to.

From a practical point of view, this solution or compromise is not as bad as it might seem at first, especially if we factor in the extreme punishments that emperors could suffer if their rule was perceived as lawless. But from the legal point of view this situation has led to something of an impasse in the field. Were the Byzantines so fundamentally confused about the relationship between legal authority and imperial power that they could break the stalemate only through an act of republican will? It is insufficient to weigh the sources for and against and declare that "overall" the Byzantines believed that emperors were subject to the law.[58] They were not struggling with two contradictory views of imperial power, the one republican and the other despotic. The two views were in fact complementary but appear to be contradictory because we have examined this issue as a technical legal question without considering the broader context of the polity that framed the issue in the first place. It is when we remove the *politeia* from the equation, as most scholarship does, that the emperor is left in splendid isolation, with the problematic results that we have seen. We are then faced with the artificial challenge of assembling contradictory pronouncements and weighing their relative value or frequency in an attempt to discover which one was true, or true most of the time, or "overall," or to look for a formula that resolves the basic problem: was the emperor the source of the law's authority or the reverse? To escape from this dilemma, then, we have to convert the question of the emperor's standing in the law, which was secondary, to the question of his standing in the polity, which was primary.

The ultimate standard was not the law itself but the common good of the republic: *salus rei publicae suprema lex.*[59] The emperor's job was to promote it and the law was an instrument that expressed that good and protected it from private interests. Particular laws on a matter could not provide the final standard: they were only temporary regulatory mechanisms to protect common values. The same principle governed the enforcement of ecclesiastical law too.[60] The ultimate standard was what emperors called "the benefit of all" or the like, or what Cicero had called, in his definition of the *res publica,* a *utilitatis communione sociatus.*[61]

The legal doctrine that the emperor was not bound by the laws evolved out of the *lex de imperio* which, for the first three centuries of the Roman empire's existence, formally authorized each emperor to rule. P. A. Brunt identified the clause in the only surviving such *lex* (that of Vespasian), which eventually gave rise to the doctrine we are discussing: "Whatever [the emperor] considers to be in accordance with the advantage of the *res publica* and the dignity of divine, human, public, and private interests he shall have the right and the power to do and to execute."[62] In sum, the emperor was bound to obey the laws unless the common good required him not to: these contingencies were complementary. In a general sense, for example, Constantine and Licinius declared that justice and fairness should prevail over the strict letter of the law.[63]

A law could become disadvantageous or obsolete, and too many laws could create confusion. This much we saw in the *Novels* of Leon VI, who believed he was restoring and improving the *politeia* through his reforms. Mere legality was not equivalent to the public good. This emerges clearly, for example, in Prokopios's *Secret History,* which denounces Justinian as a tyrant on the grounds that he ruined the Roman polity. Yet Justinian was not always acting illegally: many of his crimes were backed up with an appropriate ad hoc law.[64] His was in many ways a lawful tyranny, but Prokopios was judging the emperor and his laws by a higher standard: the good of the *politeia.* Moreover, and this is the crucial point, *never in the Roman and Byzantine tradition was the view accepted that the emperor could act beyond the law for any reason other than to benefit the Roman people.* In other words, the overriding criterion was not that of the written law; it was the good of the republic. Both the written law and the extralegal acts of the emperors were evaluated by that standard. The one was not always better than the other: a written law could be a bad law, whereas a technically illegal imperial act could be universally praised for its justice. In this sense, both the law and the emperor were equally servants of the republic, being a fixed and an "animate" source of justice, respectively, and expected to work together for the good of all Romans. The Arab philosopher Ibn Rushd (Averroes) accordingly "distinguished between cities that are ruled according to fixed and immutable laws, as is the case with the Islamic law, and cities whose laws change according to what is most expedient, as is the case with many of the laws in Byzantium."[65]

The motives and circumstances of such extralegal actions, we will see, were closely watched and evaluated by public opinion. As Harries has argued, "consensus precluded arbitrary decisions by the ruler."[66] Perhaps it did not so much preclude them as make them extremely risky. Subjects sometimes had to exercise independent moral judgment and evaluate whether imperial orders should be followed or not. We will examine cases of this "right to resistance" when we turn to the republican dimensions of political action in Byzantium. For now it should suffice to point out that the basic principle was understood. Kekaumenos, a modest but hardly unintelligent writer of the late eleventh century, acknowledged that

> some say that the emperor is not subject to the law, but is a law, and I say this too. In all that he does and legislates he does well and we should obey him, but if he should say, "drink poison," by no means do it. If he says, "jump in the sea and swim across it," don't do this either. So know from this that the emperor is a man and is subject to the laws of religion.[67]

Religion was, of course, an essential element of the Byzantines' conception of the common good, though neither of Kekaumenos's examples is specifically religious, far less stems from a particular religion. His "laws of religion" point to a vague conception of natural law. Religious controversies proper also occasioned theories of resistance to the imperial will, but the principles to which they gave rise were, again, based on general moral considerations. Witness Nikolaos, a deposed patriarch in the early tenth century, writing to the pope about how he personally pleaded with Leon VI not to take a fourth wife:

> "The emperor," they say, "is an unwritten law," not so that he may break laws and do whatever he pleases, but so that he may be such in his unauthorized actions as a written law would be.[68]

That is, in both following and not following existing law, the emperor ought to be aiming at the good of his subjects in sustaining the *ennomos politeia*. Later in the same letter, Nikolaos develops a theory of resistance:

> The imperial dignity is indeed a great matter, and it is right to obey emperors and not to resist their edicts, but only in those edicts that display the dignity of the imperial rule. Does he order us to do justly? These are truly imperial edicts, and these we must not resist. Does the emperor order us to take arms against the enemy? Does he decide that we must contribute something to the public interest (τὴν τῶν κοινῶν λυσιτέλειαν)? His decision must then be obeyed eagerly. Does he order

us to do whatever else may bring strength and honor to his rule and to
his subjects? We must then do his bidding at once. These things are the
emperor's duties ... On the other hand, does he ... bid us renounce our
piety toward God? But this is not an emperor's duty: so that we must
not obey, and must ignore his order as the impious edict of an impious
man. Does he bid us to slander, to slay another by guile, to corrupt another's marriage, or wrongfully take another's goods? This, however, is
not a work of an imperial government, but rather of a footpad, a slan-
derer, an adulterer, a thief ... It is evil, it is most evil doctrine to say
that "because he is an emperor" he is permitted to sin in a way that no
one would permit his subjects to do.[69]

Byzantine history abounds in instances of men and women who refused
to obey an emperor's orders, mostly on religious grounds.[70]

In considering extralegal imperial acts, we should not dwell only on
their negative aspect, on arbitrary "tyrannical" acts. Extralegal interventions could be justified for the positive reasons cited by Nikolaos, and the
items that he lists could be used against his specific position. For instance, Leon VI could argue that his fourth marriage fulfilled one of
these conditions, such as "contributing something to the public interest,"
perhaps by ensuring dynastic stability and legitimacy. There was room
for disagreement here and therefore for politics and the struggle to build
consensus. But either way emperors had to make the case before their
subjects. A mother complained to Julian that he had only banished and
not executed the rapist of her daughter. Julian appealed to a higher law:
"The laws may reproach my clemency, but a merciful emperor may rise
above other laws."[71] Theodoros the Stoudite argued vehemently against
a marriage of Konstantinos VI that, he claimed, was not *oikonomia* but
paranomia—just illegality.[72] Irregular unions were criticized again in the
eleventh century,[73] and in 1043 the people (ὁ δῆμος=*populus*) rose up and
threatened to kill the emperor during a procession in the belief that he
intended to marry his mistress.[74] The people had opinions about these
matters, or could be persuaded to have them.

In sum, legality was not as important as legitimacy, and legitimacy
was maintained when emperors cultivated the perception that they were
governing in the interests of all the Romans. One way to do this, and
probably the easiest, was to actually govern in the interests of all the Romans. Ultimately, legitimacy was the only thing that mattered, and

legitimacy, we will see, meant popularity. Whether one adhered to the law was secondary, but it was probably safest too.

Extralegal authority was always a gamble. Psellos says that Basileios II ruled not according to the laws but to the dictates of his own mind, yet Psellos approved the results, and so, it seems, did most Byzantines.[75] Michael III, on the other hand, was demonized after his murder by the descendants of his killer, Basileios I. The facts of the case may be beyond our reach, but the way in which the criticisms were couched indicates how their authors and audience, including an emperor (Konstantinos VII), understood the relationship between the emperor and the norms of the republic. Michael is said to have engaged in various vile practices and to have put people to death without proper trials, simply on a whim.[76] In sum, he offended against "religious scruples and against the laws of the *politeia* and those of nature."[77] "He was behaving and taking part in the *politeia* in a way that was opposite to the very norms of that *politeia*."[78] Michael was therefore killed for his infractions, or so these texts would have us believe. This brings us to the question of how the emperor was kept in check within the polity in the first place, I mean in practical terms, a discussion I will defer to Chapter 4.

In closing this section, I would like to present how two Byzantine legal scholars theorized or imagined illegal or extralegal behavior by emperors. In the early thirteenth century, the bishop of Ohrid Demetrios Chomatenos opined that it was no sin on the part of Theodoros Laskaris to have executed a robber without trial so long as it was done "for the promotion of the common good (ὑπὲρ ὠφελείας τοῦ κοινοῦ)."[79] But pardons too could be "illegal." In his *History*, Attaleiates, a high-ranking judge, presents a scenario regarding the Norman mercenary Rouselios who had proven his mettle against the Turks overrunning Asia Minor but who had then rebelled against the emperor. By law, Rouselios had to be condemned, but the interests of the empire called for him to be sent out against the Turks. Attaleiates devised a theoretical scenario that allowed him to have it both ways, combining legality and extralegal imperial intervention. Here is how he thought this could play out (it did not happen in the end, but that allows us to see how a Byzantine judge *imagined* the intervention of imperial authority outside the strict letter of the law):

The emperor had no intention to bring the captive before his presence and into his sight, nor did he reach a decision worthy of imperial benevolence and magnanimity, which would have been to bring legal proceedings against him, and, after the verdict had been reached, to condemn him to death, all in order to be able, at that point, to temper his righteous wrath with gentleness and compassion and thus to preserve for the Roman empire a soldier and commander of his caliber, who was capable of healing many of the wounds festering in the east. Thus the latter would admit an immense gratitude towards the emperor for his salvation and express endless thanks.[80]

Attaleiates's ideal was strict legality tempered by the ability to make exceptions for the common good. This was how most Byzantines viewed the extraordinary powers and position of their emperor, and they reserved the right to judge him on how well he used those powers. The emperor's relationship to the law was not a legal question; it was a political one, to be dealt with politically. But how could the polity enforce its norms, and its verdicts, on the emperor?

Autonomy in Heteronomy

In his discussion of the dynamic between emperor and law in the sources for the early Palaiologan period, Dimiter Angelov points out that panegyrical orations tended to proclaim the emperor as above the laws, whereas works in other genres, sometimes written by the same authors, explained the strict requirements for extralegal acts to be legitimate, for example, the practice of recognized virtues such as philanthropy, and that the rights of subjects ought not to be violated.[81] This division of labor between genres makes sense, as the purpose of panegyrics was to highlight the emperor's personal virtue, and this was showcased sharply in morally autonomous acts. By contrast, the Mirrors of Princes tended to present the emperor as a mere office-holder who ought to obey the law.[82] Obeying the law was in itself a praiseworthy choice and corresponded to the imperial virtues of legality and (republican) humility. It is therefore possible to cite panegyrical orations that also take that approach, starting from Pliny on Trajan and going strong in the thirteenth century.[83] The different genres that we have relied on so far to reconstruct the parameters of the Byzantine republic reflect a single underlying ideology, inflected differently in each genre: legal sources presented the functions of the imperial office just as emperors wanted their subjects to perceive them; panegyrical orations aimed to prove that each occupant of the throne was personally fit for the office; Mirrors of Princes were an externalized form of self-reflection through which emperors acknowledged their duties and recognized the difference between kingship and tyranny; and historiography was the genre in which each emperor was judged by the standards that were proclaimed in the other genres. Religious arguments and rhetoric were deployed in all genres (albeit less so in historiography) to support the message, whether to buttress the emperor's authority or call him to order.

Not just the literary works themselves but the ceremonial and social contexts in which they were performed, presented, and circulated served to remind emperors of the moral and political purpose of their office: emperors were expected to work hard on behalf of their subjects, not to abuse their power by transgressing against their subjects' rights; they were to practice virtue, ensure justice, and pursue only the common good when issuing legislation or acting in extraordinary ways. The emperor was constantly surrounded by the rhetoric of the polity's moral consensus and was asked to internalize it and speak it himself in his official pronouncements. In none of these genres is the emperor represented as he is in so many modern studies: in splendid isolation, he (or his extended celestial court) engaged only in a metaphysical relationship with God. As Paul Magdalino has written, "I do not accept that imperial panegyric was primarily a court as opposed to a civic genre: it celebrates the emperor on behalf of, and as the head of, the whole *politeia*."[84] Prokopios of Gaza put it as follows in a speech that he delivered locally to honor the emperor Anastasios: "Since the city realizes that there is not time for each man to speak for himself, the community, by the agreement of all (κοινῇ ψήφῳ), is content with the voice of the orator. For he is chosen for his ability to speak on behalf of the city, and with one voice he expresses the thought of all."[85] In an oration for Eudokia (1068 AD), Psellos says that he will "express through my words the voices of the *politai*," a claim that he repeated the following year in an address to Romanos IV.[86]

Many of our studies treat Byzantium as an affect of the court, and from a certain historical perspective that is valid, but at the same time we have to restore the Byzantines' understanding that the emperor made sense only in terms of the polity of the Romans. The idea, for instance, that the emperor had to abide by the laws even though he was not required to was formulated in a specific way: κατὰ νόμους πολιτεύεται, or "he takes part in the *politeia* according to the laws."[87] This verb did not mean only to "take part in politics" or "be politically active," as it is often translated. It meant that one was part of the polity, whether actively or passively, or even that one was "alive." The Paulician heretics under the emperor Nikephoros I, for example, "were allowed to live in the *politeia* without fear," an awkward translation, but it avoids the technically misleading "given leave to enjoy the rights of citizenship."[88] This "political" identity of the Byzantines was primary, even in their private lives. In law, when one spouse was captured by barbarians, the other remained "in the *politeia*," which can mean that he or she retain political rights, that is, was free.[89] The canonist Balsamon proclaimed that all Romans "are required to πολιτεύεσθαι according to the laws" and that "Roman men must know the law" (unless they are peasants, in which case allowances may be made).[90] As all classes of society constituted the *politeia*, their primary mode of existence in the language of the Byzantines was as *politeuomenoi*.[91] Leon Paraspondylos, the empress Theodora's chief administrator, "made the law his will. He also created an orderly and lawful environment for the *politeia*,"[92] that is, for the way in which all other Romans went about their lives.

The phrase, then, that the emperor "takes part in the *politeia* according to the laws" folded him into the general community of all Romans and placed him on the same level, in this sense, as everyone else. The *Hortatory Chapters Addressed to Leon VI* even argue, in addressing the emperor, that the memory of his reign will be honored "if you follow the good laws of your predecessors and maintain them inviolate as you take part in the *politeia* (πολιτεύεσθαι) . . . Because if you do not take part in the *politeia* (πολιτεύσῃ) according to the laws of those who reigned before you, others later may not follow *your* decrees. And so one set of laws will follow another and this will make life tumultuous and confusing, which has caused whole nations to slide into destruction."[93]

Therefore, the dominant ideological framework was republican in this sense. But our texts, whether legal or hortatory, also imply that emperors had a choice of whether to obey the laws or not, and exhortation was necessary because they had the power to do as they wished. The collective polity could, through its spokesmen (jurists, orators, moral advisors), remind and persuade emperors to abide by the consensus, but was this not a form of wishful thinking? Every one of these texts betrays an anxiety that tyranny is but a small step away and only the monarch's will can prevent it. Worse, did the circulation of these Mirrors not provide republican "cover" or even "alibis" for emperors to pursue absolutist policies? After all, they refer to no enforcement mechanism and rely for their success solely on personal conversion.[94] "Please be nice to us" is no foundation for a republic. Attaleiates spelled this out in his legal treatise. Citing the precept that the emperor is not subject to the laws, he adds this clarification: "that is to say, he is not punished if he transgresses against them."[95]

Even historians who view the emperors as "absolute" monarchs concede that their power was severely limited in practice, given premodern technology and communications; they had to rule through bureaucracies and elites whose ways of doing things were not easy to change and whose support was sometimes crucial;[96] and, to become a tyrant, one had to break free of the ideology of lawful, republican rule that surrounded and smothered the office in honeyed words. Answering petitions and appeals; receiving embassies; attending court, church, and city ceremonies; and receiving reports from heads of departments kept emperors busy with routine work. To be a tyrant one had to find both the time and energy to go against the grain, to bend these people and institutions to one's will, which could not have been easy. It was probably much more work to be a tyrant than a proper republican emperor, which required only that one go with the current, that is, accept the republican consensus.

Yet when all is said and done, a heart of radical autonomy beat within the republican ideology of strict heteronomy. The ruler of this polity, the person who was supposed to protect it and promote its common good and who stood "at the center of a system of shared cultural values,"[97] also stood above those laws. It was, perversely, only by an act of his own will that he submitted to those laws. It was only by an act of will that he bent his will to the laws. He was authorized to act in ways available to no other Roman and had immense power compared to them. His position was not exactly a magistracy, though it was possible to think of it as such; nor was it really possible to distinguish clearly between the private and public aspects of his life and power, as many Byzantines claimed to do. To think that this position was a bulwark and support of a republican political order was an act of faith. *Everything* in Byzantium conformed to that political order *except* for the most important and powerful thing.

Giorgio Agamben has written a provocative treatise on "the state of exception," the emergency suspension of the normal operation of law in order to meet a crisis. While he theorizes this as a feature of modern liberal regimes that is tending to become the rule rather than the exception, he discusses also its Roman precedents, including, though only tangentially, the person of the emperor. He quotes previous theorists according to whom the state of exception constitutes a "point of imbalance between public law and political fact . . . the intersection of the legal and the political," and concludes that it "appears as the legal form of what cannot have legal form . . . a no-man's-land between public law and political fact."[98] This state of exception, a form of which was the position of the Roman emperor, "is not a special kind of law (like the law of war); rather, insofar as it is a suspension of the juridical order itself, it defines law's threshold or limit concept."[99] Whoever holds power at that point may or may not choose to apply laws and uphold common values. The emperor's awkward position ("I am not bound by laws, but will obey them anyway—except when I don't") gives rise to a

> division between those who seek to include the state of exception within the sphere of the juridical order and those who consider it something external, that is, an essentially political, or in any case extrajuridical, phenomenon. Among the former, some understand it to be an integral part of positive law because the necessity that grounds it acts as an autonomous source of law, while others conceive of it as the state's subjective (natural or constitutional) right to its own preservation.[100]

These alternatives correspond exactly to the bifurcation we observed in the legal sources.

The monarchy had its roots in the chaos of the Republic and the monarch was a way to save the polity from its own systemic flaws, but it provided "an anomic foundation of the juridical order. The identification between sovereign and law represents, that is, the first attempt to assert the anomie of the sovereign and, at the same time, his essential link to the juridical order."[101] Agamben warns, in relation to the present but in terms that Romans of the age of Caesar would readily grasp, that "this transformation of a provisional and exceptional measure into a technique of government threatens radically to alter—in fact, has already palpably altered—the structure and meaning of the traditional distinction between constitutional forms"[102]—in the Roman case the sense that the *res publica* was the *res populi* and not the property of any one man.

How, then, can one maintain that Byzantium was a republic when it was governed by such a permanent state of exception? The answer is twofold. First, the ideological norms of the republic were accepted by most of the emperors, or by all the emperors most of the time. The imperial office was constituted as part of, and in relation to, the polity in the particular Roman ways we have explored. These norms were not so much *limitations* on the office as they were its *purpose*.[103] We should not be starting from a model of absolute monarchy, which is nowhere reflected in the evidence, and then look for its limitations. Rather, we should understand the office primarily the way all Byzantines did, in relation to a lawful polity, and then ask how and under what circumstances it could distort that relation. After all, Agamben's analysis applies primarily to modern democratic regimes, many of which are now in a permanent state of exception. We all want to believe that we live in societies governed by law but at the same time our very laws grant institutions and authorities the power to do as they please with impunity in certain respects, to say nothing of the fact that people in power are able to act outside the law and are almost never brought to justice. Some would argue that these contemporary societies are no longer lawful polities and so no longer qualify as democracies, republics, or whatever.

The real question, however, is, what consequences do those who govern in a state of exception face when they violate the norms of that republic? This brings us to the second point, the subject of Chapter 4. *The power of the emperor was not the only state of exception in the polity.* In fact, the rest of the polity could suspend its own lawful participation and take matters into its own hands against the emperors. This too led to the establishment of an extrajuridical state of affairs but one that was, like the imperial office itself, also within the norms of the polity, given that the polity was understood as the property of the people. The people could take back what was theirs to begin with. In other words, what we need to reconsider is the question of who the sovereign was. Most Byzantinists assume that this was the emperor, but perhaps we have been confusing power—and that only under certain circumstances—with sovereignty. The history of Byzantium oscillated between two states of exception: governance by an emperor and the tumult of regime-change. The laws governed only the states in between (though this was a big "only"). Therefore, when Attaleiates said that the emperor is not punished when he breaks the law, he was speaking only as a jurist, not the historian that he would become. The emperor may not have been subject to what an American politician once confusingly called "a controlling legal authority," but he

was subject to political fact, and that fact in Byzantium could also operate outside the law, more specifically the law against treason. The *populus*
could act outside that law (and any other law) when it so chose, because
it ultimately was the source of all authority in the Byzantine political
sphere. The authority of the people could trump the legal enactments of
the emperors. And not only of the *populus:* rebels too could appeal to the
higher law of the common good of the republic when they set aside the
laws of treason and their own oaths of loyalty.

Let us close with the genre with which we began. The deacon Agapetos
addressed a series of moral maxims to Justinian among which was the
following: "Impose on yourself the necessity of keeping the laws, since
you have on earth no one able to compel you."[104] But a later maxim is
ominous: "Consider yourself to rule safely when you rule willing subjects.
For the unwilling subject rebels when he has the opportunity. But he
who is ruled by the bonds of goodwill is firm in his obedience to his
ruler."[105] In other contexts, such language has been read as a combination
of "an implicit threat of violence and a deferential tone of address."[106]

CHAPTER 4

The Sovereignty of the People in Theory

This chapter will argue that the people, the δῆμος of the Romans, the old *populus,* were sovereign in Byzantium. This was not a mere antiquarian fiction, as many scholars of Rome and Byzantium have thought, but an ideological and historical fact understood by the people themselves and accepted by almost all emperors, at least those who wanted to keep their throne. As has recently been written about the old Republic itself, the evidence for popular sovereignty "does exist, but it has to be rescued and interpreted with a conscious effort to remember not just the great and powerful but the Roman People too."[1] It is time to put some blood back into the Byzantine republic, and not just the metaphorical kind. This effort will make good on the promise of Chapter 1 to provide a bottom-up model of the Byzantine polity that will act as a counterweight to the top-down one that currently prevails. Examining some key events, this chapter will tease out broader implications for how the various elements of the republic behaved—that is, what they took for granted regarding the political action—and how that action was represented in our sources.

This chapter transitions between the more theoretical discussion so far and the more historical chapters to follow. It aims to provide a model of sovereignty that fits the facts of Byzantine history as well as the way in which our texts describe transfers of power, especially violent ones. Violent transitions better indicate which element of the republic had the ideologically uncontested right to reassign the legitimate exercise of power. These were also moments when the operation of the law was usually suspended, and not only of the law relating to the person of the emperor (including the validity of oaths of allegiance and lawful deference to his authority). They were general "states of exception" that witnessed the breakdown of the legal order. That order may have periodically crumbled, but not so the more fundamental right of the people to determine who was entitled to reconstitute it. This state of emergency was the polar opposite to that represented by imperial authority itself when it acted outside the law. The political history of Byzantium oscillated between the two.

The Rise and Fall of Michael V

Before presenting a model for republican sovereignty, I will examine the end of a brief reign that dramatically illustrates the points made above. Many scholars present this event as aberrant and limited in significance to its own time, but I believe that it reveals tensions and assumptions that were always present in the Byzantine political sphere, even if only in a latent state. Chapter 5, which will focus on the historical manifestations of popular sovereignty in Byzantium, will show that they were in fact part of a long-standing pattern of behavior, the very matrix, in fact, of Byzantine politics.

My launching-point will be the fall of the emperor Michael V in 1042.[2] This event is well known, as are its alarming implications for the balance of power in Constantinople, but it is usually treated as distinctive to the politics of the mid-eleventh century and associated with an alleged "rise of the urban classes." This rise is usually defined on the basis of this event, making the argument circular. Other periods of Byzantine history when the people (and sometimes the senate) took a prominent role in imperial politics, especially the seventh and eighth centuries, are also treated as atypical by scholars who focus on those periods. They are included in accounts of their individual contexts but not integrated into general accounts of the Byzantine political sphere. The effect, if not the intention, is to marginalize popular actions as idiosyncratic. A whole series of similar events are thereby bracketed off and marginalized.[3] In fact, whatever may have been happening both socially and economically in eleventh-century Constantinople, the *political* matrix of the events of 1042 was not atypical. The event in question differed from others in its class only in that it was narrated in dramatic detail by three contemporaries (or close enough): Psellos, Attaleiates, and Skylitzes. I could have used for this purpose the Nika riots that almost toppled Justinian in 532, as they reveal the same underlying assumptions about who had the right to do what, were it not for its outcome: Justinian was unique in using violence against his people on such a scale, which contributed to his reputation as a tyrant. As we move through the events in the life and brief reign of Michael V, I will highlight the norms that we can see operating throughout most of Byzantine history. They corresponded closely to the norms behind Verina's letter to the people of Antioch in 484, examined in Chapter 3.

Michael V came to power at the nexus of two dynastic interests. He was the nephew of the previous emperor, Michael IV the Paphlagonian (1034–1041), who had, in turn, been elevated to the throne by marriage to Zoe, heiress of the long-lived Macedonian dynasty. Before the death of his uncle Michael IV, who was well regarded as an emperor, the future Michael V had been elevated to the subordinate imperial rank of *kaisar* and formally adopted by Zoe as her son. Both changes in his status occurred at a public (δημοτελῆς) ceremony at the Blachernai church that was attended by all office-holders as well. Our source, Psellos, states that he was acclaimed by all in attendance and that further ceremonies took place relating to the creation of a *kaisar,* but he does not divulge details, as they would have been well known to his readers.[4] When Michael IV died, Zoe found herself in sole possession of the *basileia.* Skylitzes records that she realized that she was not up to the task of governing the *koina* and, after three days, decided to elevate Michael, who was energetic when it came to public affairs *(ta pragmata).*[5] This, Psellos adds, calmed the City down, which was in suspense about the future. We note again that the imperial office was regarded as the highest form of public administration and its potential holder is evaluated by that criterion alone. The *kaisar* was raised to the rank of *basileus* with the usual procession, coronation, "and all the rest that follows." Psellos again does not divulge the details, which certainly included acclamation by the people.[6] We should note two things about the narrative so far: first, Zoe's choice was ostensibly guided primarily by the criterion of competence in the administration of the public interests, and, second, we are told that the City was watching, obviously interested in the politics of the palace.

Michael V swore oaths to honor Zoe and respect her imperial privileges. As an Augusta, she was regarded as the heir to the throne (it was through her that both Michaels had come to it), "and she was universally popular, being a woman . . . and she had also won over everyone's heart through her generous gifts."[7] Michael V may not have had much choice in the matter of this oath: as we will see, perceptions of public opinion exerted almost overwhelming pressure on imperial action. We will presently see what an asset it was to be popular and how critical a factor public opinion was for holding the throne. The new emperor began to cultivate public opinion himself, winning over the people of the City, "not only the elite but the commoners and the craftsmen too," granting them "freedoms."[8] They became so devoted to him that he began to think that he could oust Zoe. According to Skylitzes, Michael "tested the citizens first, to see what opinion they had of him." On the Sunday after Easter "he attempted to ascertain what public opinion was" during the procession.[9] The festivities were splendid, so that night he exiled Zoe to an island and had her tonsured. Psellos says that Michael informed the senate that she had plotted against him and then "attempted to persuade the demotic crowd." Finding that his words were being echoed back to him by his supporters, he "dissolved that assembly."[10] But shortly thereafter "the entire City, and I do mean everyone regardless of sex, fortune, and age . . . roused itself and began to move in small groups, becoming tumultuous." They began to speak against him; public opinion turned foul. By the second day, it was clear that this was a popular movement to depose him.[11]

Attaleiates and Skylitzes, by contrast, have Michael send a herald to the forum of Constantine to read a document out to the people explaining his action; Skylitzes places this before any discontent, but Attaleiates, more plausibly, in the midst of it, as an attempt to win back public opinion. Either way, the crowd would have none of it, threw stones, and rioted. They began to chant slogans against him and "the entire people with one voice" shouted the rallying cry "Dig up his bones," which had long been a signal for deposing an emperor.[12] This was signaled also by the chant "Unworthy (ἀνάξιος)," that is, of the throne.[13] We will hear more of this term. Michael had few options left. He recalled Zoe and presented her to the people in the hippodrome, next to the palace.[14] But this made them all the more angry. They forced the patriarch to side with them, and then pulled Zoe's sister Theodora out of her convent to join their cause, though she was unwilling. The people had by now taken over the entire City, besieging the palace and breaking in, so Michael fled to the monastery of Stoudios, where by order of the two sisters he was blinded. Imperial power was restored through popular action to the two sisters.

Our sources agree that this was a genuinely popular revolt in which all classes of the City participated, including even women. It was not orchestrated by anyone in particular—the sisters were only caught up in it—and our authors provide gripping narratives of "mob" action, reactions, planning, and dynamics. Also fundamental to the narrative is the role of public opinion: most emperors, no less than modern politicians, were extremely keen to monitor it and shape it, if possible, in their favor. We will see that they were not always successful, and when a roar of "Unworthy!" reached the emperors' ears through the palace windows, their days were usually numbered. In this polity, emperors were answerable to the people, in a directly physical way if it came to it. And here is the key point that we must observe: the people seem to have acted in full cognizance of their right to take down an unworthy ruler. Nor do our authors, who belonged to the upper levels of society, question that right. Dimitris Krallis has demonstrated this in connection with Atteleiates's narrative, which draws on a "republican" background.[15] There was no notion that the *populus* was acting illegally, or above its station, or against an authority constituted by God. To the contrary, Psellos and Attaleiates state that the people acted as if impelled by God[16] (despite the fact that they plundered monasteries and churches, which, both historians believed, were too wealthy to begin with). This was effectively another way of saying that their actions were legitimate.[17] Apparently no one, at least in retrospect, thought it relevant that the people were violating the loyalty oaths they had sworn to that emperor or disregarding the idea that the emperor was appointed to rule by God.

The moment the "entire people" reached a point of consensus against an emperor, he was legitimate no longer. It was they, after all, who had made him legitimate in the first place, by acclamations at his accession. Psellos expressed this symmetry (and paradox) by referring to the *mysterion* of the *basileia* into which Michael V was inducted at the start of his reign and then later again to "the great and most public *mysterion*" that brought him down, that is, the action by the *dêmos* (the word is δημοσιώτατον).[18] When the sources refer to the crowd's "disapprobation" of an emperor (δυσφημία), they mean the technical opposite of their original "acclamation" (εὐφημία) of him. As Beck demonstrated, this was how they indicated that he was no longer worthy of the throne in their eyes.[19] We will see many examples of this in Chapter 5.

Rebellion against a lawfully constituted emperor was called a "tyranny" in Byzantium, assuming the person speaking sided with the existing ruler. This was exclusively a function of perspective: during rebellions, both sides considered themselves to be lawful and the opposing side to consist of tyrants. Which label would finally prevail was determined by success or failure. In this case, the people were acting in a "tyrannical" capacity, but because the *populus* was also the ultimate arbiter of imperial elections and the source of legitimacy, its consensus instantly made *Michael* into the "tyrant." Psellos expressed this nicely in a paradox: "the common crowd was a counter-tyrant to him who had already become tyrant (τὸ δ᾽ ἀγοραῖον γένος... ἀντιτυραννῆσον τῷ τυραννεύσαντι)."[20] The case of Michael V is more complicated, of course, because he had moved against Zoe, who was more legitimate than him. That already made him a tyrant in the eyes of the people. A duly constituted emperor had violated his oaths and acted in a "state of exception" against Zoe. The people then did exactly the same when they intervened to (re-)create the order that they wanted. They too violated their oaths (to Michael) and instituted their own state of exception. But they did not simply restore the dynastic status quo before Michael V. Theodora was dragged from her convent to Hagia Sophia, where "she was acclaimed empress... not only by the entire *dêmos* but by all the notables as well."[21] She had enjoyed imperial honors before, but now the people exercised their right to endow her with full imperial rank. Zoe now had to cope with this situation, which was not to her liking, for she and her sister had not been on good terms. Skylitzes says that she wanted to push Theodora out "but was prevented by the crowd, which demanded that she rule in conjunction with her."[22] It was the people, then, who defined how the *basileia* would be reconstituted for the near future, against the wishes of their protégé Zoe, and no one challenged their right to do so.

When the people acted "unanimously" they were set in a realm beyond obedience or deference to lawful authority precisely because they *were* the polity and could, in a moment of crisis, directly decide what they wanted. This was the premise behind their acclamation of new emperors, after all. Their consensus overrode law and prior commitments: oaths were ignored and past acclamations canceled. Put differently, when the people acted as a single agent in a political capacity, Byzantium would enter the second type of its "states of exception." We can be cynical and suspect that special interests lay behind popular actions, and sometimes they did. But this is true of political agents at all times. What matters is the ideological framework that defined such actions, what created legitimacy in the eyes of the republic.

A Model of Sovereignty

As we will see, the events recounted above were only the tip of the iceberg when it came to popular interventions in Byzantine politics. Still, they give preliminary support to the conclusion that the people's right to make and unmake emperors was not questioned, and was slighted at the emperors' peril. This we must now combine with the other conclusions that we have drawn, namely, that the main justification that emperors gave for their rule and specific policies was that they benefited the Roman people (and thereby pleased God); that the emperors were not seen as the proprietors of power but were understood to hold it in trust from the Roman people; and that the state apparatus was a function of the "public interest" and existed to promote the common good. In the following section, we will see that emperors were legitimate only when they had been acclaimed by the people, that is, when their "election" had been ratified by universal consensus in a popular assembly. All this, then, makes Byzantium an excellent candidate for being a republic. A more explicit theory of sovereignty may help to clarify the fundamental issues.

The term "sovereignty" is used by scholars in many contexts and senses. We must make a preliminary distinction at the start. I am not interested here in sovereignty as a factor in international relations, that is, in whether one state respects (or not) the "autonomy" of another or recognizes its rights on the world stage,[23] but in how a politically unified society, in our case Byzantium, grounded the legitimacy of its political institutions on the domestic political stage. In this sense, the term is used often by modern historians but in a loose sense. In the Byzantine case, sovereignty is typically ascribed to the emperor on the grounds that he wielded all lawful power, at least when the regime was stable and our sources give the impression that he was generally "in charge." This is a loose meaning of sovereignty in part because it overlooks what happened when the regime was not stable, was being toppled, challenged, or in transition, at which point more fundamental factors came to the fore; in sum, because it does not look at the grounds of the regime's legitimacy but only at the wielders of power.[24] I know of only one attempt, by Beck, to ascertain more precisely who was sovereign in Byzantium, and he concluded that the people were sovereign. Beck was a historian looking at the relations of legitimacy between the elements of the Byzantine polity, not for the most visible power-holder.

To be sure, the Byzantines never developed a constitutional theory that explicitly addressed this question. If asked who had the final say in the polity, most of them would probably think of the emperor or God, but that would not be a precise way to frame the question. The question before us is not how the polity was governed in times of peace. Certainly the people were expected to serve the emperor, and this relationship was reinforced by discursive, legal, and political practices; but at the same time the emperor was also supposed, in turn, to serve the people, a relationship that was expressed and codified in different discourses and practices. These relationships were complementary and yet also asymmetrical, so they cannot be homologically compared. The two parties were also unequal in a basic sense, which is that within the ideology of the *res publica* legitimacy flowed from the people to the holders of power and never the reverse; indeed, we cannot imagine what the reverse might look like in a Roman context. Moreover, in their ideal form they operated like this only in periods of political stability, which is to say not all the time in Byzantium. The right questions to ask would be: Did emperors have the right to rule without popular consent? Did they have the right to act against the interests of their subjects? And, if the people decided that an emperor was no longer acting in their interests, did they have the right to depose him? These questions point us in the right direction.

Carl Schmitt provides a similar way to frame the issue. According to Schmitt, the sovereign is the one who decides when there is a state of emergency, which Agamben called a "state of exception." He who can invoke extraordinary circumstances in order to implement emergency measures, above and beyond the framework of normality defined by the laws, is the true master of the political sphere.[25] We have seen that the emperor could operate outside that framework but it was understood that he could do so only in order to promote the good of his subjects. The people, on the other hand, could and did suspend the rule of law in order to rid themselves of an emperor whom they did not like and, within that state of exception, appoint whomever they wanted as his replacement. The suspension of law at those moments went beyond the repudiation of the current emperor and, therefore, the breaking of all oaths of loyalty to him. It also often entailed the looting of mansions, churches, and monasteries, the burning down of government buildings, freeing the prisoners in the *praitorion,* and lynching unpopular high officials. All this was done with impunity in part because the next emperor could not retroactively treat the events that brought him to the throne as illegal, but in part also because they occurred precisely when the order of law was suspended; that is, there was no legitimate "lawful order." We have seen enough instances of that already to provide prima facie support for the general thesis, and Chapter 5 will further flesh out its history.

In short, for our present purposes, we must not confuse sovereignty with the government, that is, the wielding of official power that is delegated to the emperors by the people. The distinction was made clear by modern theorists of republicanism, and the one whose theory fits Byzantium best is, ironically and deliciously, Rousseau. He would be horrified to hear that, given what he believed about Byzantium,[26] but he and his age really knew little about it. The thinkers of the Enlightenment tended to treat it as a mirror in which to reflect and abjure those aspects of their own societies that they wanted to abolish. Their idea of "Byzantium" was a useful polemical tool, not a scholarly construct. What makes Rousseau useful is that he theorized the Roman republican tradition. It just so happens, though he did not know it, that Byzantium was a later phase of that tradition.

At the beginning of his *Social Contract*, Rousseau echoes Cicero's definition of the *res publica* when he claims that

> there will always be a great difference between subjugating a multitude and ruling a society. When scattered men, regardless of their number, are successively enslaved to a single man, I see in this nothing but a master and slaves, I do not see in it a people and its chief; it is, if you will, an aggregation, but not an association; there is here neither public good, nor body politic . . . A people is a people before giving itself to a king.[27]

That "aggregation" is what Roman writers like Priskos believed, say, the empire of Attila was; it was not a proper *politeia*. By contrast, Romanía was unified by a broad consensus of which religion was only one aspect. Rousseau reveals himself a classical rather than a modern thinker when he says that the most important laws in such a polity are not those that are written down but are "in the hearts of the citizens; which is the State's genuine constitution . . . I speak of morals, customs, and above all of opinion."[28] The moral consensus of Romanía was such a constitution; it was not something set down in writing. Its modes and orders are more visible to the historian, who studies the society in action, and less so to the legal scholar, at least insofar as the latter deals primarily with legal texts. It is even less visible to scholars who limit themselves to court propaganda. Below we will also consider the supreme role of "opinion" in shaping the exercise of power in Byzantium, though the episodes presented above have often touched on it.

Rousseau explains that republics are not defined by a particular type of government. "I call republic any state ruled by laws, whatever may be the form of administration: for then the public interest alone governs and the *res publica* counts for something. Every legitimate government is republican." He adds in a crucial note on the last word: "By this word I understand not only aristocracy or a democracy, but in general any government guided by the general will, which is the law. To be legitimate, the government must not be confused with the sovereign, but be its minister: then monarchy itself is a republic."[29] As we have noted, the fact of monarchy should not hinder us from viewing Byzantium as a republic. This has crucial implications for the position of the ruler: "Those who contend that the act by which a people subjects itself to chiefs is not a contract are perfectly right. It is absolutely nothing but a commission, an office in which they, as mere officers of the sovereign, exercise in its name the power it has vested in them."[30] The sovereign and his government were not homologous entities, such as could enter into a contract with each other. Powers were delegated, but not unconditionally, and in the previous section we witnessed a moment when the sovereign took power back from his government, an eventuality that Rousseau theorized in formal terms: "The instant the people is legitimately assembled as a sovereign body, all jurisdiction of the government ceases." With the exception of assemblies to ratify imperial elections, Byzantium lacked "legitimate" popular assemblies, if that refers to formally convoked institutions on the Swiss model that Rousseau envisaged. Popular action was usually "extralegal," but that did not make it "illegitimate"; quite the contrary. It was a state of de facto suspension of the laws during which the true sovereign, the people, exercised raw political authority. To return to Rousseau, "these intervals of suspension [of the powers of the government], when the prince [king] recognizes or has to recognize an actual superior have always been threatening to it, and these assemblies of the people which are the shield of the body politic and the curb of the government have at all times been the dread of chiefs."[31] Let us here imagine a Byzantine emperor hearing two or three hundred thousand mouths chant "Unworthy!" outside his palace windows.

Rousseau's distinction between government and sovereign, his explication of the moral or customary grounds of a Roman *res publica,* and his model for how the sovereignty may still be popular when the government is monarchical make his thought an antidote to the Hobbesian notions that permeate the concept of "the state" that many historians intuitively use. We saw above Hobbes's view of the state as conceptually separable from the people over which it ruled.[32] Hobbes did not allow for a separation between the sovereign and the government. In the *Leviathan,* the people by themselves have no sovereign authority; in agreeing among themselves to entrust it to the monarch they basically bring it into being, but never own it. They therefore have no right to take it back or transfer it: "they that are subjects to a monarch, cannot without his leave cast off monarchy, and return to the confusion of a disunited multitude; nor transfer their person from him that beareth it, to another man, or other assembly of men."[33] Clearly, the Byzantines were not Hobbesians. Their *politeia* was not dissolved when an emperor was taken down and the crown transferred, nor did the people become a "disunited multitude." They were the sovereign *populus Romanus.* But Hobbes, unlike Rousseau, had no conception of the *mores* that can create a people apart from their monarch: he thought in terms of abstract relations of power, legally defined. He was also far from the Roman way of thinking when he said this about the monarch: "whatever he do, it can be no injury to any of his subjects; nor ought he to be by any of them accused of injustice."[34] Hobbes basically *defined* this to be the case. In his view, subjects are not allowed to question or abuse the monarch.[35] In the Byzantine tradition, by contrast, there was hardly a single emperor not accused of injustice, and we will consider in Chapter 5 the many ways in which the populace abused emperors. Hobbes alludes to Roman alternatives to his theory when he says that elective kings and kings with limited power "are not sovereigns, but ministers of the sovereign," because "if it be known who have the power to give the sovereignty after his death, it is known also that the sovereignty was in them before . . . The sovereignty therefore was always in that assembly which had the right to limit him."[36] In other words, Hobbes recognized that in Roman tradition the sovereign power resided in the people, though he did not elaborate on what this might have meant for Roman *imperial* history, that is, Byzantium.[37] In his view, efforts to "licentiously control the action of sovereigns" were illegitimate by definition and stemmed from reading too much Greek and Roman literature.[38]

It is perhaps not as well known as it should be that in the early empire power was formally transferred from the senate and people to each emperor upon his accession. Imperial authority was grounded in a specific enactment (or a set of them) called a *lex de imperio* that stipulated an emperor's exact powers in terms of the offices and conventions of the Republic. Only that of Vespasian now survives, but a new one was passed for each emperor, its wording repeating that of his predecessors, until at least the early third century. It seems that comitial assemblies—now "harmless ceremonies"—ratified these *leges*.[39] We might be tempted to dismiss this as a legal fiction, but we first have to be clear where the fiction resides. Certainly, by this point the people and senate had little choice in the matter, so these were not free assemblies in any modern sense (however, it is likely that our own elections are also fictions in that sense).[40] But the origin of the monarchy had a strong populist rationale, and legitimacy. As T. P. Wiseman has written, Caesar's powers

> were all voted on by the Roman People, and there is no reason to imagine that the People were bribed or coerced. Caesar's power was not usurped, but granted constitutionally by the only authority competent to do so. Of course senior *optimates* thought the republic was dead, because their own freedom of action was curtailed. Curtailing their freedom of action was what the Roman People wanted.[41]

Moreover, the very fact that these popular assemblies were deemed necessary in the first place during the early empire to grant legitimacy to the imperial regime indicates that legitimacy was indeed grounded in popular consent: this, at least, was no fiction. As Brunt noted in his study of the *lex de imperio*, "any autocrat had to bear in mind what his subjects would tolerate,"[42] and it was republican ideology, prior to political fact, which dictated what was tolerable and what not. The way in which the succession to imperial power played out historically in Byzantium, in both stable and tumultuous instances, reveals that what we might be tempted to dismiss as a fiction was actually a deep-seated aspect of the polity's ideology.

"From the start," wrote J. B. Campbell, the empire "had been an absolute monarchy in a framework of constitutional formality and legality."[43]

Moreover, as imperial power was understood legally as well as morally in relation to the *res publica* and its owner, the *populus*, it can be said that "formal sovereignty still resided" with the people: "What is at issue here is the formal structure of the *res publica* and the relations of its component parts, not the question of the real location of political power."[44] Paul Veyne begins a recent magisterial survey of the Roman empire by noting that "the regime of the Caesars was very different from the monarchies with which we are most familiar." Specifically, the emperor "did not occupy the throne as a proprietor, but as someone mandated by the collectivity, charged by it to direct the republic." Veyne repeatedly calls this a fiction but also concedes that its existence prevented the authority of the position from being usurped by the person: it could only be delegated by the people. The emperor ruled in theory as the servant of the republic, "not for his own glory, in the fashion of a king, but for the glory of the Romans."[45] This, of course, explains much about the relationship between the emperor and the polity that we have already seen in the Byzantine case, and Veyne adds that the doctrine of popular sovereignty lasted to the end of Byzantium. Still, it is strange how few historians have been willing to admit this, to say nothing of making it the basis for their research into Byzantine history.

The notion that the basis of the emperor's *imperium* was a law enacted by the people, through which they transferred to him their *imperium* and *potestas*, is mentioned as the *lex regia* in the *Digest*, the *Institutes*, and by Justinian himself in the constitution *Deo Auctore* and his *Novels*.[46] It passed into the Greek tradition in the form of this definition: βασιλεύς ἐστι ὁ τὸ κράτος τοῦ ἄρχειν παρὰ τοῦ δήμου λαβών.[47] Justinian, of course, also claimed to be ruling under the authority of God, and in Chapter 6 we will examine the uneasy fusion of these two notions of imperial authority that ran on different tracks. From the references to the *lex regia* in the *Corpus*, it seems that by the age of Justinian the process was imagined as a once-and-for-all transfer of *imperium* from the people to the office of the emperor,[48] as the custom of passing a new *lex de imperio* with each accession ceased in the disturbances of the third century and the ensuing period of military rule (after ca. 235).

In accordance with his model of the *res publica*, Cicero imagined that the early kings of Rome were formally elected by the people, while those who were not sought popular acclamation afterward; in any case, to be legitimate they had to govern on the people's behalf.[49] The fundamental logic was well understood in Byzantium. The twelfth-century verse chronicler Konstantinos Manasses has all the Romans gather and vote to abolish the monarchy and institute the consuls at the founding of the Republic.[50] This is the inverse of the *lex regia* but perfectly complements it. It was possible under the Komnenoi to believe that the Roman *populus* had such sovereign powers. Beyond such specific instances, however, it was a commonplace in the Mirrors that the foundations of an emperor's rule lay in popular consent. In the 1080s, Theophylaktos, already or soon to be the archbishop of Bulgaria, addressed a potential heir to the throne in a work which explained that the term *basileia* comes from βάσις οὖσα λαοῦ, "the foundation of the people" (you have a *demokratia*, by contrast, "when the entire people make an active contribution to the administration of the *politeia*").[51] The key difference between a tyrant and a lawful *basileus* is that the tyrant does not receive the reins of power from the people but grabs them for himself by force.[52] The *basileus*, by contrast, receives power "by the good will of the multitude and the consent of the people."[53] Theophylaktos delineates the different characters and reigns of the tyrant and the legitimate king, and the first item that he mentions for each is how he came to power. He does this not because his descriptions have a chronological format but because this criterion cuts to the heart of their legitimacy. In the case of the legitimate king, he leaves no doubt about the source of his position: "the entire multitude makes him its leader."[54]

Interesting while these texts are, and perhaps idiosyncratic,[55] popular sovereignty in Byzantium cannot be established by piling up quotations that gesture in that direction. It would, after all, be much easier to prove through a preponderance of citations that the legitimacy of the emperor was a function of divine favor, and that Byzantium was therefore a theocracy. It is rather from the patterns of political action, in conjunction with their discursive representation, that we must infer underlying assumptions about relations of power and legitimacy. We must also look more closely at how emperors were made and how they were taken down, as so many of them were. It is in these events that we will find the blood with which to reanimate popular sovereignty.

Popular Acclamations and Imperial Accession

To become emperor of the Romans in Byzantium one had first to be *elected* (i.e., chosen) for the office and then *elevated* to it. *Elevation* almost always took place in a public ceremony of universal acclamation: "every imperial appointment was supposed to issue from an instant popular demand."[56] Legitimacy was derived from universal consensus to every emperor's accession, the *consensus universorum* or *consensus omnium,* basically a monarchical variation of Cicero's definition of *res publica.*[57] As one text put it, "the crowds applauded . . . all had one voice, one mind: one name pleased all the people."[58] The *election,* by contrast, depended on the contingent facts of power at that moment in the empire's political history. It could be orchestrated by a ruling emperor for an heir, in the expectation that it would be ratified by universal consensus at a public ceremony. Or an army would march on the capital and its general presented himself as a candidate for the throne: if he took the City he was almost certain to be acclaimed (in part because it was difficult to take the City without the support of its population); if he did not take the City, the matter was uncertain.[59] Or, in the absence of an heir or a claimant, the right to elect an emperor was delegated, through a variety of procedures that seem to have differed each time, to some element of the polity (usually the senate, or the empress or a committee), but the ensuing candidate again had to secure universal acclamation.

These moves and machinations were the stuff of politics. They did not change the fact that the result of this process was regarded as legitimate because it reflected the universal will of the Roman people. The people were rarely active in the election of emperors, but they were necessary to legitimate their accession. This crucial distinction is not always made in the scholarship, which tends to focus more on the election (as revealing the facts of power) than the elevation (which is usually seen as an empty ceremony). But that ceremony reveals that the facts of power played out within an ideology of popular consent and ratification, if not popular choice. Our elections are not altogether different: few of us see the fund-raisers and other "meet-and-greets" by which the plutocracy decides in advance who the candidates are going to be and who is excluded. These facts of power are not, strictly speaking, democratic, and violate the spirit of democracy. Yet they are ratified retroactively by a popular vote in "free" elections, without which the whole setup would be illegitimate. In Byzantium, as in ancient and modern republics, the people were the ultimate source of political legitimacy, though they regularly ceded choices of personnel to elite groups.

How was the will of the Romans represented as universal? The formula used in modern scholarship, and in some ancient and Byzantine sources, is that new emperors had to obtain the support of "the Senate, army, and people."[60] Two qualifications are in order. First, we are not concerned with whether each of these elements played an active role in the selection of the new emperor, though at times each of them did. Their main role, which they normally had to play in unison, was to legitimate the choice or refuse to do so. Second, the exact manner in which consensus was orchestrated ceremonially changed from one accession to another, in terms of setting, the order of events, the emphasis, the prominence of persons and groups, and also in how it was described in different sources. The protocol was flexible and the organizers had a range of options and precedents from which to choose based on their particular circumstances, challenges, and tastes.[61] We should not expect uniformity. This is also true of the sources that report these events. Each lists the elements of the polity that were present at imperial elevations in its own way, trying to approximate comprehensiveness but not reflecting a fixed formula. The formula of senate, army, and people was not quite as fixed as many scholars think. So, in various combinations, we have references to the imperial family, different army units, the palace guard, palace officials, the top magistrates, the racing factions, the representatives of the racing factions, the people collectively, merchants, the senate, "the laws," "the entire world," the patriarch, and the clergy. Different sources even reported the same event differently, listing different elements of the republic as participating.[62]

This has two consequences. First, we cannot use these impressionistic lists to track the changing "constitutional requirements" by which a new emperor was made legitimate in each period;[63] after all, there was no formal constitution that defined any of these relationships. Second, we cannot necessarily use these lists to track the changing social history of Byzantium, on the assumption that specified groups must have been especially prominent in imperial politics at that time.[64] Our authors were not following set constitutional formulae, which did not exist, nor were they necessarily reflecting social relations. Hans-Georg Beck was in fact among those historians who anachronistically tried to extract a formal constitution from the messy election processes that our sources describe, and cast it in terms of different "organs" of the state (typically the senate, people, and army). His view of this constitution and its legal dimension was too formal, but only quasi-institutional, and lacked a theory of ideology.[65] What our sources were trying to do, each in its own way, was to say "everyone in the polity," or else they mention one element of the polity as a kind of shorthand (usually the senate, the army, or the people).

Certainly, Byzantium did have a social history. Different elements of the polity (the army, the senatorial "aristocracy," the higher clergy, or trade groups) had moments of greater or lesser prominence in the political and economic life of the republic, and their role in the making and unmaking of emperors may have reflected these fluctuations. The people, as we will see, usually did not take the lead at such moments, although their consent was necessary to legitimate the outcome. A separate study will discuss the nature of the aristocracy of this Byzantine "republic of the Romans" and the extent to which the people and the leading elements (political, military, or ecclesiastical) understood themselves as belonging to a relatively undifferentiated national group. The point being made here is different: the texts that report the participation of specific groups at these acclamations are not covertly writing social history. They are usually trying to emphasize the diversity of the support enjoyed by a new emperor. The idea was that a variety of different social groups represented more of the republic. The historian Theophylaktos Simokattes tells us that in 574, when Justin II began to lose his mind, he summoned the senate, top clergy, and patriarch to the palace to announce that he was elevating Tiberios II to the rank of *kaisar*. Addressing Tiberios, Justin said, "As you behold these men here, you behold the entire *politeia*."[66] We have to accept that each source presents a limited view of events. Other contemporary sources state that additional elements of the republic were present on that occasion than just the senate and top clergy,[67] and when much later sources narrated the event in hindsight they took it for granted that Justin had summoned the people, senate, priests, and magistrates.[68] Then, to make the transition from *kaisar* under Justin to *basileus* in his own right, Tiberios II was likely later acclaimed formally by the people, though our sources say little about it.[69]

As we saw also with Michael V (who was toppled by the people in 1042), heirs could be elevated by a reigning emperor or empress to a lesser imperial rank (e.g., *kaisar*) in a more "private" court ceremony that included magistrates, top clergy, palace guard units, and representatives of the people. Subsequently, when they came into power in their own right, they would be acclaimed by the full people in the hippodrome or some other public ceremony. Our sources sometimes only allude to that event in passing, but it could not be avoided. Even if a new emperor or his handlers did not stage a public ceremony specifically for that purpose, he was bound to appear before the people as soon as his imperial sponsor died, whether at the funeral, the games, or in Hagia Sophia. All public appearances required that the people acclaim the emperor, not just at the start of a new reign but every time. Large crowds gathering to approve of an emperor constituted an ongoing ratification of his right to rule;[70] it "iterated the binding links of imperial ideology."[71] An emperor *always* had to meet with universal approval whenever he interacted with his subjects. When this did not happen, when the mood of public opinion turned against an emperor, then the republic entered a crisis phase that triggered events such as we will discuss in Chapter 5 (e.g., the fall of Michael V examined at the beginning of this chapter). In times when the regime was unpopular, emperors might want to avoid large crowds because it could all go wrong quickly. A segment of the people might boo and jeer, and there was no way to predict how events might unfold then. Public appearances could quickly become a referendum on the regime. Most of the time things went well, producing what historians call "ceremony." At other times, the result was "history."

Our sources for Byzantine political history, in the periods when we have them, tend to focus on moments of conflict rather than the routine acclamations of emperors who enjoyed public support. That is why we have few details about the making of new emperors. We happen to have one account, for Anastasios (in 491), that is detailed. It was retained, presumably as a still-relevant model, in the tenth-century *Book of Ceremonies*.[72] This account reveals that republican principles were firmly at work in these events, and it complements the detailed accounts of the fall of Michael V that we examined at the beginning of this chapter, forming convenient book-ends at the start and end of two dissimilar reigns, separated by over 500 years. The comparison reveals that the people of the City retained their fundamental political rights and ideology throughout the period examined in this book.

On the night that Zenon died (9 April 491), the senate, the magistrates, and the patriarch met in the palace while the people and soldiers assembled in the hippodrome. The magistrates told the empress Ariadne to appear in the hippodrome and address the people, which she did, along with the magistrates and the patriarch. In the ensuing exchange, the populace demanded an emperor who was Orthodox and a

Roman (an allusion, in the first place, to the raging theological controversy and, in the second, to the quasi-barbarian ethnicity of the Isaurian Zenon). Ariadne informed the populace that she had already instructed the magistrates and the senate (not the patriarch, we note) to select a Christian Roman man as the next emperor, who would be virtuous. She insists that the process would not be influenced by friendship, hatred, ulterior motives, kinship, or any other personal factor in the selection. We see here clearly how the offices of the polity and the imperial government were conceptualized impersonally: just as the choice of the emperor was, in theory, to be decided impersonally, the emperor himself was expected to rule in the same way. The people take the opportunity now to tell Ariadne to get rid of the prefect of the City, who was a "thief," and she tells them that she already had the same purpose in mind and appointed a new prefect, Ioulianos (later to be dismissed because of popular pressure when his unpopular measures provoked a riot).[73]

The empress and magistrates retire into the palace, and the latter meet to deliberate, but they cannot agree. One of them proposes that the selection be made by the empress, and she then selects Anastasios. Soldiers are sent to his house to bring him to the palace. The funeral of Zenon takes place the following day. On the day after that the magistrates and senators demand that Anastasios swear an oath not to hold a grievance against anyone (that is, to set aside his private life and take on a public role),[74] and that he govern the *politeia* to the best of his ability. He is led to the hippodrome where, to condense a long series of investitures, he is acclaimed by the people as Augustus. Among the ensuing exchanges, the people ask that he appoint only pure magistrates to govern while he stresses that he had been unwilling to accept this position but is persuaded now by their universal consensus. "I am not unaware how great a burden of responsibility has been placed upon me for the common safety of all," and "I entreat God the Almighty that you will find me working as hard at public affairs (τὰ πράγματα) as you had hoped when you universally elected me now (ἐν ταύτῃ τῇ κοινῇ ἐκλογῇ)." Both sides repeatedly express a hope that the Romans will now flourish. Anastasios then goes inside.[75]

This was a more orderly process than many subsequent acclamations. Yet it has not necessarily been whitewashed in the telling. While it is preserved in a ceremonial manual, the latter includes accounts of messy accessions, such as that of Justin I, which is noted as being "disorderly."[76]

The account of Anastasios's election reveals the dissention in the council of magistrates, also the fact that he was at home. Unlike most acclamations, where the choice of emperor was a fait accompli, there was no way in this instance that he could have known for certain that he would be selected. The magistrates did not pretend to disagree simply to have a pretext to turn the matter over to Ariadne. They did not rubber-stamp a predetermined choice. More importantly, the process was inscribed within a republican ideological framework. Anastasios was *made* an Augustus by the fact that the people and the army acclaimed him as such; his right to rule rested on that universal consensus and every step in the process was cleared carefully with the assembled multitudes. He swore an oath to govern the polity conscientiously and promised to work hard on behalf of his subjects. His *basileia,* as a form of service, could have no other purpose, and to this extent the appointment of an emperor did not differ from the appointment of any other magistrate, who also had to swear an oath to fulfill his duties for the good of the polity.[77] During the whole process, the people made their own demands, both ideological (they want a purely Roman emperor this time) and relating to specific personnel ("We don't like the prefect; get rid of him"). Ariadne conceded both points. They also made it clear that Anastasios would be held up to high moral, political, and religious standards, and we will see that he was later found wanting by some of his subjects. When that happened, they tried to depose him, but he survived, unlike many of his successors. The people never forgot that, having made an emperor, they could also unmake him.

The business of imperial accession, then, entailed negotiation with the people, usually in the hippodrome. For example, in the "disorderly" events that led to the accession of Justin I (518), the people assembled in the hippodrome and acclaimed the senate, authorizing it to select a new emperor. One faction of the guard tried to have its own candidate acclaimed, but he was shouted down by the Blues (the fans of a hippodrome racing team), who threw stones at him (he later became a bishop). A second faction had a go with their own candidate, only to have him removed by the first faction. Finally, the senate declared its support for Justin, who was acceptable to all. The politics may have been messy, but the principle governing it, as stated by the leader of one of the factions, was beyond question: "Our lord, being a man, has died. We must now take counsel in common to find the man who will be pleasing to God and advantageous for the *politeia.*"[78]

As noted above, the accession of an emperor was a complex process, and so efforts to isolate the one "constitutional" element that had the formal power to bestow imperial power, or the precise moment at which a man became emperor, are risky. The question has been discussed more extensively in connection with the early Roman empire, but these discussions are often at cross-purposes, as one historian is looking for the facts of power and another for the ideology that was then used to legitimate them; also, different scholars employ different notions of "ideology" and "propaganda."[79] Be that as it may, in his *Res Gestae* Augustus proclaimed that his powers were bestowed upon him by the senate and people, and for centuries thereafter emperors were formally invested with magisterial powers by laws enacted in popular assemblies (the *leges de imperio*). The political system went through the motions of popular sovereignty, and the emperors claimed to have been called to power by the people.[80] We can treat all this as "fiction" or "propaganda" if we like, but we must also recognize that it was a deeply embedded ideology; that is, this was the only acceptable framework for the legitimation of imperial power in Byzantium, and it fundamentally shaped how it could be used. Matters became more complicated in late antiquity, when the idea of divine election moved to the foreground and became a potential alternative source for legitimacy. We will discuss this in Chapter 6.

A word is necessary here on "late antiquity," because Roman historians are likely to be misled about the significance of this now much-studied era for the formation of Byzantium. Specifically, historians who are familiar with the model of the Principate look at the roaming and militaristic emperors of the third century and afterward; they observe the rise in claims to divine election; are told by Byzantinists that the empire now had a thoroughly Christian ideology and was "not really Roman"; and so reasonably conclude that Byzantium, which they assume was the product and extension of late antiquity, must also have been a military dictatorship whose "ideology" was that of divine election. Some even call it still an oriental despotism. I propose, by contrast, that those roughly 200 years in late antiquity were, politically speaking, a deviation from the populist norms of the Roman *res publica,* and so the broader conclusions that are often drawn from it about "Byzantium" are distorted. With the reestablishment of the court in New Rome ca. 400 and the tight relationship that it developed with the populace, we witness both a return to civilian (Roman) modes and an intensification of republican principles. This emerges clearly from the account of Anastasios's accession and from what we know about Constantinopolitan politics in later centuries. It is late antiquity that is aberrant, for all that it has come to seem normative in scholarship of the past decades.

In terms of the political history of the empire, we could define late antiquity as the period between the end of the *leges de imperio* in the early third century and the reestablishment of republican norms at New Rome in the fifth century. During this period, emperors tended to roam with their armies and were usually selected and acclaimed by the armies. But when even these military emperors had to deal with the Roman *populus,* they too encountered what have been called "quasi-republican forms of behavior,"[81] and their military-style acclamations tried hard to preserve the theory of election by the Roman people, the people under arms in this case.[82] Tetrarchic capitals in the provinces were likewise meant to facilitate interaction between the emperor and what has been labeled the "local *populus Romanus,*"[83] though we have no narrative sources about those interactions. It is not my purpose to trace the history of this theme from Rome to Constantinople through "late antiquity," only to explain the principles governing the political sphere once Constantinople had settled into its modes and orders. That is the main reason why this study begins with ca. 500. The theory of imperial legitimacy that I have laid out for Byzantium proper was also operative during the phase of the itinerant armies, but it was inflected and limited in specifically military ways.

For our period (let us say, after Anastasios), it seems clear that *as a matter of principle* an emperor was held to be legitimate only when he had received the universal consent of the Roman people.[84] The converse was also true: popular disapprobation could unmake an emperor. At such moments all the associated accoutrements of accession and power, including crowns, vestments, oaths, relics and icons, and claims to divine sanction, were worthless compared to the power and rights of the *populus.* We will come back to "deacclamation," the flip-side of accession. Here I want to present a sampling of passages that bear on the issue of how the Byzantines thought of legitimacy, especially when there was a choice to be made. They tried, where possible, to keep God involved, but the bedrock of legitimacy was republican. In some of these incidents, populist principles were clearly being invoked to cover up a coup by a faction. Far from being evidence against my argument, this is in fact the strongest possible confirmation for it: the reassignment of power in Byzantium *could be justified solely on populist grounds,* regardless of the facts of power in each case. This is what an "ideology" does.

- When Justinian died in 565, the Senators approached Justin and, according to Corippus, addressed him with these words: "While life remained in your father [actually his uncle], the people knew that the Roman empire was upheld by your counsels, and your efforts, and we agree with the people."[85] The fact that the Senators, or Corippus, felt compelled to speak these words is all the more significant in proportion to the people's limited say in the selection itself. The Senators' rationalizing plea was, of course, confirmed by universal acclamation.

- When Romanos II died in 963, he was succeeded by his sons Basileios II and Konstantinos VIII, who were minors. At that time, the general Nikephoros Phokas returned to Constantinople in triumph. Fearing plots against his life by the eunuch Ioseph Bringas, Nikephoros approached the patriarch Polyeuktos, who summoned the senate to the palace and, among other things, advised them as follows: "Since we are Romans, and regulate our lives according to divine commands, we should maintain the young children of the emperor Romanos . . . inasmuch as they were proclaimed emperors by us and all the people."[86] He proposed that Nikephoros be placed in charge of the army but only after "he was bound with oaths that he would not plan anything undesirable against the state and the Senate."

- In recounting the role of the patriarch Michael Keroularios in the struggle between Michael VI and the rebel Isaakios Komnenos in 1057, Psellos says that the patriarch was basically powerless to change the outcome: "If he had supported him who was only formally emperor [Michael], resisting the one who already had power in his hands [Isaakios], he would still not have blocked the latter from becoming emperor, as he was beloved by the entire people (ὅλῳ τῷ πλήθει ποθούμενον)."[87] We know from historical sources that Keroularios sent Michael VI the command to step down "because this was what the multitude were demanding."[88] Psellos then explicitly says that thereby "the rebellion *(tyrannis)* was transformed into a lawful power *(ennomos arche)*."[89]

- Romanos IV Diogenes was captured by the Seljuks at the battle of Mantzikert in 1071. After a brief captivity, the sultan let him go, but the Doukas faction in Constantinople seized power. "Diogenes proceeded as far as the theme of the Armeniakoi where he learned the news about himself, namely, that he had been declared deposed by the people of the City and the palace."[90] Everyone understood that this was a palace coup, but a coup had no chance of being regarded as legitimate unless it was presented as a popular decision.

- In 1195, Isaakios II Angelos was deposed by his brother Alexios III. "The magistrates of the *politeia* had already acclaimed him, and his entrance had been prepared in advance by his wife Euphrosyne. As for the Senate, at least a part of it happily accepted what had happened. When the *dêmos* heard the announcement, they engaged in no seditious behavior: from the start all of them were calm and applauded the news, neither protesting nor becoming inflamed with righteous anger at the fact that the army had removed from them their customary right to appoint the emperor."[91] This passage speaks for itself. It is especially revealing in that its author, Niketas Choniates, was contemptuous of the people of Constantinople and would not have written this were it not a generally understood truth in his time.[92]

I add a report regarding the succession of Michael III in 842, though it is unlikely to be factual in the way in which it is reported. The leading character, Manuel, had possibly already died, and his biographers seem to have extended his life for their own reasons and made him a star in the succession to showcase his popularity. This was a case where the people are presented as disinclined to extend the career of the ruling (Amorian) dynasty.

- Manuel gathered the people and the soldiers in the hippodrome and, after reminding them of his previous benefactions to them, asked them to swear an oath that they would do as he asked. They hoped that he was about to propose himself for the throne, and so did what he asked. He then proclaimed Michael III and Theodora (his mother) as emperors. "They were greatly disappointed ... but obeyed his command, and so the succession was ensured."[93]

This story circulated in historical texts, which means that it was plausible to a readership that had witnessed other transitions of power, and there is nothing in it that is impossible given what we have seen already. In Chapter 5, we will discuss instances when the palace negotiated with the people regarding the succession. The story about Manuel works because it is based on a cardinal truth of Byzantine politics: popularity with the people was the most crucial factor in moments of potential instability. Manuel could have taken the throne for himself through his sheer popularity with a *populus* that was empowered to acclaim him. Conversely, the dynasty could not take popular support for granted and had to elicit consensus from the people even through such tricks. This shows us clearly who *had* legitimating power and who *needed to obtain* it.

While we are for the moment not constrained by historicity, we may mention also the sixth-century *Julian Romance,* written in Syriac in Edessa. It is a romance about the emperors Julian and Jovian. While little in it is historical and most of its storylines are exaggerated for literary effect, one of them concerns the attempts by would-be emperors to gain the throne through popular acclamation. "Julian proceeds to Rome to receive his acclamation, but is refused by the citizens when he denies the religious toleration they request and imprisons the elites of the city."[94] He then goes to Constantinople, where he is opposed by one Maximos, who tells his fellow citizens to refuse him and tries to assassinate him, but fails. "Maximos' example does not convince the inhabitants of Constantinople, since [Julian] is acclaimed there and 'called the king of the Romans.'"[95] The text seems to have a bias against Constantinople, as only acclamation in Rome makes one a proper emperor; nevertheless, it "emphasizes the contractual nature of Roman authority."[96] One character advises the emperor that he should not step outside the law because he would then become a tyrant.

The most common term by which Byzantine sources refer to a formal act of political assent is ψῆφος, which can also be translated as a "vote." Here is the hypothetical scenario by which Pacatus expressed the consensus that made an emperor legitimate, in this case Theodosius I:

> Let us imagine that we are enquiring in some kind of world assembly about which man should shoulder such a burden and take charge of the destiny of the *res Romana* as it faltered. Would not *he* [i.e., Theodosius] be chosen by all the votes of all men in tribes and centuries [the now obsolete Republican voting assemblies]?[97]

After the mid-fifth century, this image of a universal assembly would not have been hypothetical, at least in Constantinople, most of whose population, a few hundred thousand people at times, turned out to "vote" in the imperial acclamations. There are many examples of the language of "election" in the later sources, alluding to the ancient voting assemblies.[98] It was so ingrained that it was even used to describe how conspiracies were hatched, that is, when the source is not hostile to the conspiracy. In fact, a conspiracy *had* to be cast in the language of imperial election in order to be presented as legitimate even to itself, for a conspiracy was but a step in the making of what would hopefully be a new emperor.[99] With no fixed points of reference other than popular will, the political field of the republic was split between actual emperors and potential emperors, the balance of power shifting between them according to the vagaries of history, among which their popularity with the people was a key factor. Chapter 5 will describe the tense situation in which this equation placed everyone, rulers and subjects alike.

It was this republican schema of legitimation that prevented the formal establishment of a dynastic model. Though scholarship has generally missed the republican aspect, it is well understood that there was no rightful dynastic claim to the throne: "The imperial office never became legally hereditary . . . : in theory always, and on occasion in practice, the empire was elective."[100] Spokesmen for regimes that had attained de facto dynastic succession still projected an ideology of meritocracy and popular choice.[101] Hereditary "right" was basically only one among many arguments that could be used to support a candidacy, a condition that precludes this from being considered a hereditary monarchy.[102] In practice, an emperor who was not unpopular could arrange for the elevation of his heir, but this was "the unpredictable pursuit of an individual destiny, an extension to the family of a personal adventure."[103] Temporary dynasties could be permitted, but they should also be terminated by popular opinion and interventions. Foreign observers commented on this dynastic instability in Byzantium and the tenuous hold that emperors had on the throne. Arab writers commented that there was no hereditary right among the Romans or rule for the succession and that weak emperors would be deposed.[104] A Chinese traveler of the seventh to eighth century noted that Romans chose the most capable man as their king but deposed him if he failed, and a Khazar in the ninth century wondered why they chose emperors from different families.[105]

The most interesting foreign evidence is found in the account of ibn Shahram's embassy to Basileios II and his court in 981–982. His masters, the Buyids in Baghdad, were sheltering the defeated Byzantine rebel Bardas

Skleros. The emperor was negotiating over his extradiction, but was also afraid of his own top general, Bardas Phokas, who had just defeated Skleros. We have a fairly detailed account of ibn Shahram's meetings with all the powerful men at the court. At one point the Buyid ambassador tells the emperor that "the continuance of the [Roman] state does not imply your [personal] continued existence, for the Rumi people are indifferent as to who is the emperor over them." Unfortunately, the original Arabic text seems to be corrupt at this point, so this is partially a reconstruction. The young emperor returns to this point later in the discussion, when he admits that he has to tread carefully: "It is not in my power to resist the general body [that is, of the Romans], which might regard me as their betrayer and undoer."[106] Therefore, if we believe this otherwise reliable report, what we have here is not "foreign" testimony after all, but a Byzantine emperor's admission of his own *systemic* vulnerability. It matches what we can infer from the Byzantine evidence.

Dynastic succession was in fact more common in Byzantium than these testimonies suggest. But we should not view dynastic succession as antithetical to the people's right to assign or reassign power, any more than we do in modern republics that also have political dynasties. In many cases, the survival of a dynasty was due to the people's intervention to save it in the face of usurpers or interlopers who would abolish it (perhaps to institute their own). The popular uprising against Michael V in 1042 was an instance of this, and Konstantinos VII and his grandchildren Basileios II and Konstantinos VIII were partially protected by popular support from the ambitions of strongmen who temporarily seized the throne.

All these phenomena were based on one fact: the succession was not a legal issue; it was a political one. It could not be decided by legal fact because it was not something the emperor was authorized to decide in his capacity as legislator. The assignment of power was a matter for the entire *politeia*. Legal enactments, after all, could be rejected by the people in a tumult, and they could be altered by imperial fiat. In other words, a succession law was vulnerable to both of the two states of exception to which the Byzantine polity was prone, namely, to extralegal acts by both the emperor and the people. We return, then, to Rousseau's view of republican sovereignty which perfectly reflects Byzantine norms: "When it happens that the people institutes a hereditary government, either monarchical in one family, or aristocratic in one order of citizens, this is not an

engagement it enters into; it is a provisional form it gives to the administration, until such time as it pleases to order it differently."[107]

The establishment of the Palaiologos family on the throne of Byzantium in the dying days of the republic drew criticism from intellectuals
who "viewed the emperor as the holder of an elective public office which
the current dynasty had illegitimately turned into a hereditary one."[108]

There are now sufficient grounds to conclude that the Byzantine political sphere was defined in large part by a distinctly Roman and republican ideology. It is no longer possible to say dismissively that all these
Roman notions survived only "in an antiquarian and vestigial sense."[109]
They were very much alive. The *basileia* belonged to the *politeia,* not to the
person who happened to occupy the throne, and the *politeia* belonged to
all members of the republic, including the people. The emperor's sole responsibility was to labor on behalf of the polity, and he was morally and
politically accountable to his subjects. The people may not have had much
say in determining who was thrust before them as a candidate for the
throne, but their consent was absolutely necessary for his accession and
reign to be legitimate. There was no source of authority that could override the will of the people in this matter. They were, as Cliff Ando called
them, the "shareholders in the *res publica* and in their corporate capacity
still sovereign in the state."[110]

Not only did imperial legitimacy have popular roots, it was contingent
upon the people's continued good will. Popular opinion, as we will see in
Chapter 5, could not be taken for granted even when it had formally approved an emperor at a ceremony of accession; it had to be cultivated
continuously. In this respect, Byzantium was the exact opposite of an
oriental despotism or a monarchy by divine right. This will emerge clearly
when we consider the fate of emperors who lost the people's favor. What
happened to them demonstrates that this republicanism was not a fiction or merely propaganda deployed by the monarchy to mobilize popular support. It corresponded to what people believed was within their
rights and power. Episodes of popular intervention "illustrate how conscious all sections of Constantinopolitan society were of their constitutional role in the making and unmaking of emperors, and not just of emperors."[111] No emperor or author ever denied that the collective will of the
Roman people had the right to exert itself in this way, even when it was
doing so regularly and bloodily.

In fact, the popular role in the political sphere was even greater than has been indicated by the argument presented so far. The argument has shown only that the people played a crucial role in the elevation and sometimes the deposition of an emperor. I will argue in Chapter 5 that the people were at almost all times a foremost factor in the political life of the Byzantine republic: the emperor had to cultivate public opinion and keep it on his side, because the moment it began to slip from his grasp, which happened often, there were many rivals present who would use it to raise themselves to the throne. In this sense, politics in Byzantium was always popular. One's hold on the throne was always a function of public opinion. This explains more about the picture that Byzantine political history presents than does the rhetorical fiction of divine favor.

Power was never theorized as absolute. Its republican framework did not so much *limit* the exercise of power, as many historians claim today, as it actually *defined its purpose;* it set the conditions under which the people were prepared to accept what was happening politically, and this is what imposed restrictions on the exercise of power. It was upon this basis that the superstructure of theocratic rhetoric was imposed, not as an alternative, as we will see, but as a partner: its purpose was to counter the extreme vulnerability of the emperor in the face of the volatility and supremacy of "public opinion" and the absence of any absolute source of political legitimacy, for the political sphere of Byzantium was always negotiable. It is to this aspect, in its historical dimension, that we now turn.

The Sovereignty of the People in Practice

At this stage in the argument our portrait of the Byzantine Republic contains *only* the following elements: (a) a concept (the *politeia*) that posits republican norms for the operation of the public sphere; (b) programmatic acknowledgments by the emperors themselves that the purpose of their office was to promote the welfare of their subjects and the good of the republic; (c) ritual participation of the people (in fact, the entire *politeia,* through its representatives) in the acclamation of a new emperor, in order to confer legitimacy upon him according to those republican norms (but rarely in his election); and (d) a few moments of "mob action," when the people took the political sphere into their own hands outside the framework of formal institutions. In fact, the only institution in which the people had the right to participate were those acclamations, which, many scholars believe, were an antiquated shadow of Roman practices.

Even this is saying a lot already, and provides the basis for a reevaluation of the Byzantine political sphere. The argument for republicanism, however, can be taken much further. We must first set aside the field's fixation on the formal institutions of the state, for, with the partial exception of the acclamations of new emperors, these were almost all part of the *basileia* itself, that is, they were aspects of the exercise of imperial authority (judicial, military, fiscal, etc.). But the *basileia* and the *politeia* were not interchangeable. The republicanism of Byzantium was a function not so much of institutions as of the ideological context in which those institutions operated. For instance, there was no structure of public law that defined the purpose and scope of the exercise of monarchical power within the republic; that was something that emperors and subjects knew and negotiated between them by virtue of being shareholders in the republic. It was not any written "constitution" that educated emperors as to the purpose of their power, yet they consistently proclaimed that it was to serve the republic. No institutions set formal limits on the emperors, yet they crossed the limits of consensus at their peril. There were no laws that regulated the manner of the succession, and here the people had the final say. In sum, the real power of the people was extralegal and outside the operation of institutions. In fact, when the people intervened, that often took the form of a suspension of legal authority, during which some even took the opportunity to commit criminal acts. But the purpose of these noninstitutional interventions was to institute a new legal authority, or to restore one that was in jeopardy. Byzantium oscillated between the "animate law" of the emperor, a state of permanent exception that was stable only insofar as the emperor chose to respect the norms of the republic, and the extralegal sovereignty of the people, which, in the absence of fixed institutions, was often asserted in a violent and revolutionary way. Precisely because it could make and unmake imperial legitimacy, it operated beyond the sphere of imperial law.

Patterns of Popular Intervention

This chapter will give historical weight to the theoretical argument by considering a range of environments in which the people asserted sovereign rights. The downfall of Michael V was not an aberration. The people intervened regularly in many types of controversies—political, religious, and dynastic—even if only to register their discontent, and emperors had to pay heed if they wished to stay on the throne. The following selection of episodes aims to show how the narrative of popular intervention played out and what its underlying premises were. I have restricted the selection here to instances when the people were the primary agent of discontent. I have avoided those in which the racing factions (also called the *demes*) dominated the action, in order to stay clear of the debate over their role and the degree to which they represented the people.[1] I have also deferred to a later section of this chapter discussion of cases where there was a conspiracy or rebel army in motion, even if the people played a decisive role in the resolution of the crisis; such events will require us to nuance the argument for popular sovereignty. When the people flexed their collective muscle, they could either depose an emperor or block a rebel from seizing the throne. The deciding factor was the relative "popularity" of the two men, so this will lead to a discussion of public opinion in Byzantium.

My purpose is to restore the *political* dimension of these interventions, to show that they were not just riots by the restless masses ("the mob") over nonpolitical issues, such as entertainments. I wish also to draw attention to how emperors responded to these interventions: with few exceptions, they submitted to the demands of the people, or had no choice in the matter, or humbly asked for forgiveness, to play for time or reestablish their legitimacy. This is what we would expect in a republican monarchy. It is not what we would expect if the throne was understood to be based on absolute, especially theocratic, principles. Only one emperor ever struck back successfully against a concerted uprising, Justinian.[2] We begin with Anastasios, the circumstances and terms of whose accession we witnessed in Chapter 4.

- In 511, a doctrinal controversy pitted the emperor Anastasios against the patriarch Makedonios. A source favorable to Makedonios, Theodoros Anagnostes, who may have been present, claims that a vast multitude (πλῆθος ἄπειρον), including women, children, and abbots, surged to the patriarch's defense and insulted the emperor, calling him a Manichaean and "unworthy of the *basileia*." Theodoros would have us believe that because of this protest Anastasios changed his mind "out of his fear of the crowd" and invited Makedonios back to the palace; along the way, the patriarch was even acclaimed by the guard.[3] Certainly, the populace was divided on this issue and the protests did not topple the regime, but this source wants its readers to believe that Anastasios was *de iure* illegitimate in the eyes of the community, or potentially so, for as long as he did not respect their wishes. Religious protest was here expressing itself in the form of republican politics. Anastasios eventually deposed the patriarch for calling him a heretic and allegedly plotting against him. But before doing so, he summoned the captains of the guard and the *patrikioi* of the court and required them to swear an oath of loyalty to him and the *politeia*, gave largess to the army, and set guards at the gates and harbors.[4]
- In 512, Anastasios's reign was rocked by another popular protest over a religious question. The protesters were chanting, "A new

emperor for Romanía (ἄλλον βασιλέα τῇ ῾Ρωμανίᾳ)," and they declared for Areobindos after burning the house of the unpopular ex-prefect Marinos. Areobindos fled but Anastasios appeared in the hippodrome without his crown and offered to abdicate, which calmed the crowd.[5] When the people told him to put his crown back on, they were symbolically reinvesting him with imperial authority, which they had originally given to him in 491.[6] A contrite appearance in the hippodrome and a desire to open negotiations were a standard imperial response to such situations, as we saw with Michael V (in 1042) and will see often in this chapter.

- In 532, the people of the City attempted to take down the regime of the emperor Justinian in one of the most violent uprisings in Roman history, the Nika riots. To be sure, it was sparked by a confrontation between the factions and the urban authorities, but it soon acquired a general character as the populace joined in with its grievances against the regime, setting fire to the *praitorion* (which quickly spread). It should be noted that most or all of the senate eventually joined the uprising but had not orchestrated it, and the rival emperors proclaimed by the crowd, first Probos who fled (the crowd had chanted Πρόβον βασιλέα τῇ ῾Ρωμανίᾳ), then Hypatios (also a nephew of Anastasios) were unwilling, though Hypatios warmed to it. It was the people, on their own initiative, who proclaimed him emperor in the hippodrome, which indicates that they believed that they had the right to do this. No source counters this belief.[7] Justinian made concessions to pacify the crowd, dismissing unpopular officials whose deposition had been demanded and appearing in the hippodrome to negotiate with the populace. When all seemed lost, he considered flight until, according to Prokopios, he was emboldened to fight back by his wife Theodora, whom the historian generally presents as an enemy of the modes and orders of the free Roman *politeia*.[8] At any rate, this was the only insurrection of the people in Byzantine history that failed.

- In 577, pagans from eastern cities were put on trial in Constantinople for performing nefarious rites, but, it was believed, they were let go because the judges had been bribed. The people began to murmur and protest and soon gather in large numbers, chanting, "Dig up the judges' bones!" and "Dig up the pagans' bones!" A hundred thousand people rallied to these cries. They smashed the palace in which the trials had been held, broke open the prisons and set the prisoners free, and destroyed the records in the *praitorion*. The emperor (Tiberios II) managed to calm their spirits; one account notes that the protesters had been denouncing him as well. He then punished some of the alleged ringleaders of the riot, but also retried and convicted the pagans who had originally been acquitted, leading to an antipagan purge.[9]

- In 598, the general Kommentiolos was defeated in battle by the Avars and took many casualties. It was believed that he had deliberately led his soldiers to their deaths to punish them for reasons that are given variously in different accounts, including even that the emperor Maurikios had instructed him to do so. The armies in Thrace sent letters demanding that he be investigated. A fierce riot broke out in the City, which forced the emperor to appoint a commission to investigate (the charge was refuted and the general was reappointed).[10]

- At the lowest point in the war with Persia, probably in the late 610s, Herakleios proposed in despair to move the capital to Carthage, but "the citizens opposed this as best they could" and the patriarch made him swear on the altar that he would not leave the City.[11]

- In 641, after the death of Herakleios, his widow (and niece), Martina, who was unpopular, assembled the patriarch, the magistrates, and the people of Constantinople; announced Herakleios's will that his sons Konstantinos and Herakleios (Heraklonas) be proclaimed co-emperors; and asked that she, as Augusta, be given the senior imperial rank. But some of the people cried out to her that she should be content with the rank of mother of the emperors. Nor was she to receive foreign embassies: "May God forbid that the Roman *politeia* should come to such a pass." They then acclaimed the emperors, but not her.[12] We cannot know who said what at that meeting or how the people collectively expressed their opinion. Possibly some of the notables were doing the speaking, though not necessarily: the people may well have had their own spokesmen. What matters, however, is that "the people" collectively are depicted as having the final say, regardless of who was actually doing the talking. Only they had the authority to ratify such decisions. Martina withdrew her claim.

- According to Peter Hatlie, "mass popular manifestations against Church and government continued to occur periodically over the course of the [seventh] century, including protests against the reduction in bread rations early in the century, the denunciations of patriarch Pyrrhos by 'Senate and City' at mid-century, and the odium vented against Konstas II and Justinian II prior to their respective dethronements in 668 and 695. All of these demonstrations in Constantinople's streets, hippodrome, and Great Church took place, remarkably, without any reported participation by monks on an individual or group basis" (he cites sources for all of this).[13]

• In 1044, Konstantinos IX was on his way to church in a grand procession when someone called out, "We do not want Skleraina [his mistress] as an empress, nor do we want our mothers, Zoe and Theodora who were born in the purple, to die for her sake." Whereupon the people rioted and came close to killing the emperor. They calmed down only when the empresses appeared, and the emperor fled back to the palace. This was a follow-up to the deposition of Michael V in 1042.[14]

• In 1197, Alexios III Angelos imposed a "German tax," basically protection money to stave off a western attack. He assembled all the people of the City, the senate, the clergy, and the trades, probably in the hippodrome, and asked for a contribution from each.

> But soon he saw that he was accomplishing nothing and that his words were only empty talk. The majority deemed these burdensome and unwonted injunctions to be wholly intolerable and became clamorous and seditious. The emperor, blamed by some for squandering the public wealth (τὰ κοινὰ) and distributing the provinces to his kinsmen, all of whom were worthless and benighted, quickly discarded the proposal, as much as saying that it was not he who had introduced the scheme.[15]

• In early 1204, the people of the City realized that Alexios IV was only a puppet of the Latins. The narrative of events from Choniates, who was an eyewitness and participant, deserves to be quoted at length:

> The City's populace (τὸ δημῶδες τῆς πόλεως), acquitting themselves like men, pressed the emperor to take part with the soldiers in the struggle against the enemy [i.e., the Latins], as they were patriots (πατριώταις) . . . But Isaakios [his father] encouraged him to ignore the idle talk of the vulgar populace and to bestow the highest honors

on those who had restored him to his country [the Latins] . . . Some
who associated with the Latins as comrades ignored the people's
deliberations as old wives' gossip, being quicker to avoid battle with
the Latins than an army of deer with a roaring lion . . . The City
populace, finding no fellow combatant and ally to draw the sword
against the Latins, began to rise up in rebellion and, like a boiling
kettle, to blow off steam of abuse against the emperors . . . A great
and tumultuous concourse of people gathered in the Great Church;
the senate, the assembly of bishops, and the venerable clergy were
compelled to convene there and deliberate together as to who should
succeed as emperor . . . The multitude, simpleminded and volatile,
asserted that they no longer wished to be ruled by the Angelos
family, and that the assembly would not disband unless an emperor
to their liking was first chosen.[16]

The preceding list is a selection of episodes when the people of Constantinople took the initiative to defend and enforce their views when it
came to religious, political, fiscal, and dynastic matters, or when they dis-
liked an emperor and wanted to get rid of him. Again, I have listed here
only episodes in which the role of the people was primary; when we turn
to the rebellions in which their role was secondary but still decisive, we
will then no longer be able to avoid the role of "public opinion," that
which all sides in political disputes were trying to monitor closely, cater
to, and win over.

Even in this small set of episodes we can discern some recurring patterns of behavior. The people typically chant slogans about Romanía or
against the emperor and his officials, they disrupt the operations of the
praitorion, and they assemble in the hippodrome. It is noteworthy that
the slogan "Dig up his bones!" and the attack on the *praitorion* (the hub
of imperial law-and-order enforcement) are attested as early as the sixth
century. We saw both in the events that led to the fall of Michael V (in
1042). As the people of the City were presumably not reading histories of
earlier eras, this means that they had their own traditions—rituals even,
perhaps even "institutions"—for instigating a popular uprising, traditions
that remained relatively stable over the course of many centuries. We
will encounter and discuss some of these again below.

It is also important to note that the people asserted their will in all matters that interested them, secular as well as religious. In the following

detailed analysis I will concentrate on the former, mostly on civil wars and the succession problem where the people played (and were typically asked to play) a decisive role. But they were not passive when it came to religious issues, and did not wait to be told what to do.[17] At the end of his landmark study of popular participation in religious controversies, Tim Gregory tries to explain why the emperors paid any attention to public opinion at all. He prefers to cite pragmatic factors (especially their desire to stay on the throne), but when he has to explain what created the causal link between appeasing the people and staying on the throne in the first place, he ultimately invokes the surviving "spark of the old Roman 'democratic' tradition," the idea "that power came ultimately from the governed."[18] Gregory is understandably reluctant to fall back on this, because it makes historians seem "idealistic" and a bit wooly headed. Hence the qualifiers, such as the word "spark" and the scare quotes around "democratic." But if there is no other way to explain the dynamic, we should abolish the qualifiers and the bad conscience that comes with them. It was no spark. As the rest of this chapter will show, it was a conflagration that could erupt and consume emperors at any time.

Public Opinion and Contests for Power: A Theory of Civil War

There has always been a tension between our understanding of the ideology of the imperial office, which is grounded in absolute theological principles, and the messy and unpredictable realities of Byzantine political history. What is most troubling is the gap between the alleged belief of the Byzantines that their emperor was appointed to rule by God and the ease and frequency with which they rebelled against him. All emperors asserted that they were appointed to rule by God in some way, but this divine favor did not protect them from plots, rebellions, and popular uprisings. It is of course possible that someone thinking of rebelling decided against it because of religious scruples, but there is little evidence of that in the sources (in part because sources tend not to record events that failed to happen). The boundary between rebels and legitimate emperors was always porous. Byzantine political history is marked throughout by plots and conspiracies leading to the "regular imperial assassinations that have to be seen as qualifying any absolutist political theory in Byzantium."[19]

When scholars try to account for this gap, they resort to language that they otherwise never use when setting forth the principles of Byzantine political theory in the abstract. Gregory made use of "Roman democracy," in the passage quoted above. Paul Lemerle had this to say about Byzantine rebels (note, again, the use of scare quotes and conditional qualifiers):

> Usurpation had a significance and almost a function that was political. It was less an illegal act than the first act in the process of legitimation . . . Between the basileus and the usurper there is more parallelism than opposition. Hence the existence of two different notions of legitimacy, one "dynastic" and the other one might call (in the Roman sense) "republican." These are not truly in conflict, but rather reinforce each other.[20]

In fact, they often were in conflict, and there was then no question about which was dominant. In an ideal form of this conflict, the sitting emperor or rebel has only a dynastic "right," such as it was, whereas his opponent has the "republic" behind him. There is no doubt who will prevail here. As we have seen, dynastic claims were not a right but only one among many rhetorical arguments that an emperor (or potential emperor) could make. In the real world, only the right balance of power could make an emperor safe, and one of the key factors in that equation was what our sources call public opinion. We saw this strikingly in the case of Michael V. The narrative of his downfall was cast in the language of "popularity": how Zoe had it, how Michael tried to gain it, and how he lost it—along with his throne and eyes.

While we have many studies of plots and rebellions in Byzantium, little attention has been paid to the role in them of public opinion. By this I mean not only the opinion of the social and political elite regarding the state of the empire and the merits or flaws of the current emperor but the opinions of the majority of the population about such things. In the first instance, this would be the people of Constantinople, though a case will be made later in this chapter for the importance of the provincials as well. This omission is partly a result of the fact that historians consider politics as a business taking place among the elite, or between the elite and the emperor, with the people as passive bystanders. J.-C. Cheynet's classic study of contests for power between 963 and 1210 casts them entirely as a function of elite competition. He devotes only three pages to the people, which summarize the elite's condescending attitudes toward them, and he seems to suggest that the people lacked a collective identity. As for what rebels might have done to garner public support, he has two brief paragraphs on the dissemination of oracles.[21] Yet in one place he tantalizingly refers to "the versatility of public opinion and the fragility of imperial power,"[22] which is perfectly stated albeit undeveloped. That is the theme that we will take up here, to complement Cheynet's otherwise thorough analysis.

The omission of public opinion from modern analyses stems in part from the assumption made by some theorists that past cultures operated according to norms and categories that were incommensurate with our own, and that we should therefore not use allegedly "modern" terms such as religion, art, the state, sovereignty, the nation, public opinion, atheism, and a host of others, in relation to them. Paul Veyne made an extreme case with regard to public opinion in the Roman empire (including Byzantium):

> There did not then exist the phenomenon of public opinion, which cannot coexist for long with absolute right, or consequently with . . . a sovereign who is a god or who reigns by divine right. For public opinion does not consist in rebelling, suffering silently or being discontented, but in *claiming* that one has the right to be discontented and that the monarch, even when his ministers may have misled him, can nevertheless be at fault . . . Today public opinion passes judgment on the government; then, the people loved their sovereign and right-thinking persons praised submission as the duty of every loyal subject . . . People did not have political opinions and political discussion was unknown.[23]

Few today would agree with this extreme formulation, but still no one has shown just how wrong it is in the case of Byzantium or refuted it by studying the political opinions, discussions, and *political claims* of the Byzantines at the times when they were not being submissive or much in love with their ruler.[24] There is also a body of theory which claims that "public opinion" is a function of modern bourgeois society.[25] In some circles this is an axiom,[26] and has probably blocked further inquiry. I remain skeptical of such arguments when their proponents do not know the sources for premodern societies at first hand and when the concept that is being upheld as exclusively modern is also defined in precisely such a way as to apply only to modernity, thus, through reverse-engineering, producing a form of tautology (for example, by defining the nation through *one process* by which it may emerge, industrialization, rather than by its properties as a form of collective identity and organization). Sweeping negative arguments collapse in the face of positive evidence, so let us consider that evidence.

I will start with an episode that belongs in the footnotes of history (if that) but which powerfully illustrates what could happen when Constantinopolitan public opinion *positively refused to become involved* in a political contest. In 1056, upon the death of Theodora and the accession of Michael VI, Theodosios Monomachos, a cousin of the late emperor Konstantinos IX who believed that he had a claim to the throne, gathered his dependents and processed through the City, protesting against the regime and declaring his candidacy for the throne. He went to the *praitorion* and freed the prisoners (a ritual action, as we saw), but he found the palace armed against him. He then went to Hagia Sophia, hoping that the patriarch and the people would acclaim him, but he found that closed too. The more people found out what was happening, the emptier the streets became. Abandoned by all, Theodosios finally sat before the church with his son and was eventually exiled to Pergamos.[27] He had badly misjudged his popularity. The people's role here was decisive through inaction. Theodosios was counting on them to get involved. The historian Zonaras adds that the "popular masses" later made up a ditty for him, "Stupid Monomachos, did whatever jumped into his head."[28]

What did Theodosios think would happen? What he hoped for, at least, was a popular uprising that would lift him to the throne. It was not beyond the realm of possibility, but it all hinged on how unpopular the current regime was and how "the people" perceived him personally. Let us see how differently it *might* have gone by looking at other episodes when political figures made a bid for popular support against unpopular regimes.

- In 695, the general Leontios, fearing for his life under Justinian II, went to the *praitorion,* where he released and armed the prisoners. He then ran to the forum of Constantine with his men calling on the people to assemble at Hagia Sophia and sending heralds to the different parts of the City to proclaim the news. When the people assembled, the patriarch Kallinikos supported Leontios, whereupon the people insulted Justinian (ἐδυσφήμει) and cried out, "Dig up his bones!" a form of curse that signaled popular rejection of someone's authority, in this case the emperor's (we heard it also in 579 and 1042). The people rushed to the hippodrome, and on the next day, Justinian was brought out and his nose was cut off; they demanded that he be killed, but Leontios spared him. The people acclaimed Leontios emperor.[29] He had apparently known that public opinion was hostile to Justinian, but he took a huge risk in running to the forum. All depended on what the people would do when matters came to a head. In fact, even after Leontios's acclamation and "against his wishes," the people still rounded up some of Justinian's associates, dragged them to the forum Tauri, and burned them.

- In 1181, the princess Maria, daughter of the recently deceased Manuel I Komnenos, plotted on behalf of Andronikos Komnenos against the courtier Alexios Komnenos (a *protosebastos* in rank), who had taken up with Manuel's second wife, Maria of Antioch, in order to control the child-emperor, Alexios II. Her designs exposed, she fled to Hagia Sophia seeking sanctuary, but the people rallied to her cause, especially the very poor, among whom she was popular. When the *protosebastos* threatened to evict her from the church, she placed guards at the entrance and fortified it. Soon, military units went over to her side and began to curse the *protosebastos* and the empress. They did this at the Milion and in the hippodrome until the populace rose up in open rebellion. This led to bloodshed and, eventually, the downfall of the *protosebastos* and the rise of Andronikos Komnenos.[30] Choniates's narrative suggests that "this was not a spontaneous riot, but it took several days of propaganda and organization before the people rose in open revolt, even though they were solidly hostile to the current government."[31]

- In 1185, having killed the man whom Andronikos I Komnenos had sent against him and fearing for his life, Isaakios Angelos fled through the City to Hagia Sophia, shouting out what he had done and waving his sword. The people turned out in the thousands and decided to protect him and his family against Andronikos. By morning, the people had decided that Isaakios should rule and that Andronikos, who was now unpopular, should be dethroned.[32] The latter tried to bring the people to their senses with a brief letter that was presumably read out to them, but to no avail. The people acclaimed Isaakios, freed the prisoners from the *praitorion,* began to insult

Andronikos, and besieged the palace. Andronikos fled, was captured, and days later was turned over to the crowd, who tore him to pieces.[33] There is no hint in our main source, Niketas Choniates, that this was anything but a popular action. It is an unquestioned and even unspoken axiom of his narrative that the emperor is who the people say he is, and we saw above Choniates's view of the events of 1203–1204, which proved the same.

Theodosios Monomachos was hoping for that kind of popular support in 1056, if perhaps less bloody. He was trying to stimulate a spontaneous acclamation. Generals such as Leontios and aristocrats (such as the Monomachoi and Angeloi) may have belonged to the elite, but at the most crucial moment of their political career they had to take a leap of faith and bet everything on their assessment of popular opinion. They could not guarantee whether anyone other than their own dependents would turn out in support. Sometimes they did not, as in the following cases.

- Alexios Komnenos, before he became emperor, once made a bid on behalf of Konstantios Doukas, the brother or son of the deposed Michael VII, in 1078. He placed the purple sandals on Konstantios's feet and processed him through the City to the palace. "But the *dêmos*, with one voice, loudly shouted that they did not want to be ruled by him." Konstantios begged Alexios to stop helping him.[34] Alexios then failed to persuade Nikephoros III Botaneiates in the palace to recognize Konstantios as his heir.
- After the success of Isaakios Angelos in 1185 (see the episode above), his predecessor's son, Isaakios Komnenos, tried the same tactic in Hagia Sophia but failed.[35]

One could not easily force public opinion under such circumstances. Just as the people could turn out in numbers to end a dynasty (in 695, 1042, and 1185), so too could they rally to defend it when it was popular and they perceived it as being under threat.

- In 642–643, the general Valentinos sought to seize the imperial power from Konstas II, possibly by trying to persuade the senate to acclaim him, "but when the people of Constantinople heard, they arose against him, and straightaway he put off the [imperial] robes." After a negotiation, he was placed in command of the armies.[36] But in 644–645, with 3,000 soldiers that he had in the City, he made another attempt on the throne. The chronicle attributed to Sebeos reports that when one of his men struck the patriarch,

> the crowd was aroused, and they fell on him. They forcibly dragged him by the foot into the middle of the City and burned him with fire. Valentinos was informed, and trembling gripped him. Immediately the crowd descended on him, and dragging him out of his house cut off his head . . . They confirmed Konstas on the throne of the kingdom.[37]

• In 944, a sick Romanos I Lakapenos was arrested and exiled by his sons Stephanos and Konstantinos. But when word got out that the position and even the life of the heir of the Macedonian dynasty, Konstantinos VII, were being threatened (he had been sidelined by Romanos I for over twenty years, but not harmed), "the entire people" gathered at the palace gates and demanded to see him, whereupon the Lakapenoi had to display him and restore him to his position. Soon afterward he sent them packing to join their father in exile.[38] No one objected.

We have so far considered events that took place within the City where the people enjoyed a crushing numerical advantage. These events can be seen as elections of a sort, irregular ones to be sure, but the people had the opportunity to make a choice and they did so with decisive consequences. We have still not found any case where our source, or any of the parties involved, considered the people's intervention to be illegitimate, in violation of the political norms of the *politeia*. And we have also found few cases where the people's intervention was not decisive in settling the issue. The political history of Byzantium was that of a monarchy punctuated by revolutionary popular interventions.

The episodes presented so far took place within the City. What happened, however, when a rebel army approached the City? At such times the people were often not passive spectators of the struggle for power. In other fields of research it would be redundant to point out that civil wars count as political history, yet Byzantinists are capable of seeing them exclusively in religious terms, as being theological disputes over who had God's favor.[39] But that question was settled afterward. While the war was raging, the question of who had the *people* on his side was more pressing.

• The narrative axis in our sources for the rebellion of Thomas the Slav and his siege of Constantinople (821–823) is the relative popularity of the rebel versus that of his opponent, Michael II. In recounting the origin of the rebellion, Theophanes Continuatus emphasizes that Thomas believed that Michael II was universally hated (ὑπὸ πάντων μισούμενος) because of his rumored affiliation with a heretical group, his manner of speech, and low moral qualities; by contrast, Thomas thought that he himself would be far more popular because of his more agreeable personality (among other reasons). "He thought that the people of the City would throw open the gates for him as soon as they saw him there, simply out of their hatred for Michael. But he failed in this hope; in fact, he was even insulted and covered in ridicule," at which point he resorted to arms, to no avail in the end.[40] Thomas may have been wrong, but this passage is indicative of the thought-process of the Byzantine rebels. They were but a step away from having focus-group testing or "exploratory committees" for their bid for the throne.

- In 963, when Nikephoros Phokas was marching on the capital demanding to be acclaimed as emperor, the most powerful man in the capital, Ioseph Bringas, ruling on behalf of the young Basileios II and Konstantinos VIII, found himself in a dangerous position "because he was by no means beloved of the citizens on account of being so unapproachable . . . He was totally incapable of flattering and swaying public opinion in adverse circumstances. It would have been necessary to massage the crowd's attitude with soft and flattering speeches, while he tended rather to prickle and aggravate them." He gave soldiers to two of his men and they tried to put down the growing turmoil in the capital, "but the people became enraged and resorted to force, and resisted them in close combat, and forced them into open flight." His political enemy, Basileios the *parakoimomenos* (imperial chamberlain), began to use violence against Bringas's civilian supporters, and the City descended into mayhem. Basileios also arranged for part of the fleet to go over to Nikephoros, "with the approval of the people and the Senate," though how exactly this was secured is unclear. "While this was going on . . . in the main thoroughfares, the marketplaces, and the back streets they were acclaiming Nikephoros the conqueror." Bringas then surrendered and "the entire city population" received Nikephoros upon his arrival.[41] The account preserved in the *Book of Ceremonies* (probably at Basileios's instigation) gives the people an even more prominent role in settling the conflict in Phokas's favor.[42]

- When the armies of Leon Tornikes approached in 1047, "multitudes in the City" were unsure about whether the ailing Konstantinos IX was still alive or whether they should go out and join the rebel. This forced the emperor to come out repeatedly and spend time with them.[43] Tornikes's hope was that "the people of the City would be angry with the emperor as he did not treat them the way they thought he should."[44] When he drew up his battle line before the walls, his men began to remind those who were standing on them of the evil they had endured under Konstantinos and promised that they would be free of it if only they opened the gates. They would then have a "lenient and useful emperor, who would treat them compassionately and augment the Roman power with wars and trophies against the barbarians."[45] This was timely political rhetoric—the Byzantine version of public relations, a stump speech—for the emperor had just that year settled Pecheneg tribes on the Roman side of the Danube against the objections of many who advocated a hawkish policy.[46] It also happened at that time that the City was denuded of a garrison, which meant that this public relations effort was being addressed to the citizens who had been drafted for the defense. Psellos, a witness, notes that these makeshift soldiers were no good and that "the entire City was thinking of going over to the rebel."[47] After suffering a military defeat, Konstantinos "turned his attention to the populace of the City and tried to win back their favor." Tornikes likewise had his prisoners implore the same "multitude" for mercy and condemn the evil deeds of the emperor.[48] Despite the military context, what was going on here was a political struggle over public opinion, which the emperor ultimately won by waiting out the patience of the rebel's forces.
- Let us also consider the battle for public opinion—or rather, how it was invoked by all sides to legitimate their actions—in the struggle that ensued after the armies of Michael VI were defeated by the rebel Isaakios Komnenos in 1057. Michael VI first thought of flight but was restrained by his counselors: "Maybe he would survive if he could secure the support of the citizens, so he tried to address them and to win them over with gifts and bounties."[49] Acting through envoys, he agreed to make Isaakios his partner but asked to postpone that action on the pretext that "I am afraid of the multitude of the *dêmos* and the senatorial order, as I am not certain that they will approve

the plan."[50] In fact, he was highly unpopular. His own envoys went back to Isaakios, who was now much closer to the City, and assured him "that the entire urban multitude was on his side; that he need only approach the City and they would expel the old man, receiving *him* with triumphal songs and hymns."[51] Michael then tried to "reinforce the citizens' support for himself with gifts, money, excessive honors and whatever else flatters and artfully wins over a people, securing their support and loyalty."[52] But both people and senate began to turn against him anyway, and the multitudes gathered in Hagia Sophia. Psellos goes on at length about how they included every social class, profession, age, and sex.[53] Finally, the patriarch Keroularios declared Michael VI deposed and commanded him to step down "because this was what the multitude were demanding."[54] The patriarch was hiding his own plot behind these words, but it speaks volumes about the ideological basis of the Byzantine polity that he would phrase it that way. In the end, "it was only after being bruised and shaken by the citizens that Michael did eventually reluctantly withdraw from the throne."[55]

- When Nikephoros Bryennios rebelled in 1078, he "trusted that the citizens [of Constantinople] were furious with and deeply hated (δι' ὀργῆς καὶ μίσους) the emperor [Michael VII] and the *logothetes* [Nikephoritzes] and would go over to his side when his brother [Ioannes] arrived at the head of a large army in formation, and that they would receive him into the City having come to an agreement with him." The rebel's brother tried similar rhetorical tactics to those of Leon Tornikes thirty years earlier, but failed, especially when his men set a suburb on fire, which alienated the populace.[56] When Bryennios was later brought before his more successful rival Nikephoros III Botaneiates, the latter reflected back on this moment and castigated him for not being deemed worthy (ἄξιος) of the throne by the people and being dishonored by their insults,[57] as if he were talking about a popularity contest (which he himself had won).

- Regarding Michael VII, Attaleiates says that by 1078 "public opinion (κοινὴ γλῶσσα) was displeased with his ignorance and unbridled arrogance and believed that he was at fault for the evils that were pouring in from all sides."[58] An emperor in such a position rarely lasted for long. Now, the final section of the *History* of Attaleiates is basically a panegyric for Michael's enemy and successor Botaneiates and we should not take everything in it at face value. Even so it offers strong evidence for the way in which a successful usurpation could be cast after the fact as the people's choice (which is not to say that it was not that in fact, too), just as Botaneiates had presented the failure of Bryennios as the people's choice (see the previous episode). Attaleiates tells us that when Michael VII was at the Blachernai palace with the entire senate, the people in Hagia Sophia began to acclaim Botaneiates, who was superpopular. "They cast off all fear of the emperor and conducted themselves as if they were a democracy (δημοκρατία)."[59] The battle for public opinion was on again, just as in the other cases we have seen. Both Michael VII and the alternative rebel Bryennios now sent their proclamations to be read to the people, but the latter responded with insults because they wanted Botaneiates: "the will and momentum of the people were with him."[60] The rebel's reception in Constantinople occurred in the midst of massive popular demonstrations in his favor.[61]

Much of the evidence I have discussed so far in this chapter comes from the eleventh century. Some historians have concluded that the power of the people of Constantinople in this period resulted from contingent and temporary factors that do not apply to the rest of Byzantine history,[62] and certainly there were fluctuations in the dynamics of imperial politics, especially in this turbulent period of transition between two dynasties and two modes of governance (the Macedonian and the Komnenian). But there are overwhelming objections to the view that eleventh-century politics belong to a different category from the rest of Byzantine history. First of all, the sources for that century happen to be fuller than for other periods. For the others we rely on brief entries or sources that are more interested in the personal virtues or vices of the rulers than the workings of the public sphere. Second, we have seen the people flex their political muscles also in the sixth to seventh century and in the twelfth to early thirteenth century in ways that reveal the same forms and underlying assumptions as the eleventh, for example, the cry "Dig up his bones!" and the freeing of prisoners from the *praitorion*.[63] "Dig up the bones of x" basically meant "Down with x."[64] Another "technical" term in this context was the cry of *Anaxios!* ("Unworthy!"), by which the people withdrew their favor from a particular emperor. This term, which was used throughout our period, was the inverse and cancelation of *Axios!,* which the people chanted at an emperor's acclamation.[65] There are deep structural and symbolic continuities here between the late fifth and thirteenth centuries. There is no good reason to believe the eleventh was aberrant, except in that it is better documented.

Thomas the Slav's belief in the efficacy of public opinion to decide such contests takes us to the 820s, and it seems that the same dynamic governed the three marches up to the walls by Vitalianos in 513–515 (against Anastasios). The sources that we have for Vitalianos's rebellion are meager,[66] but his strategy seems to have aimed at securing popular support in an effort to take the City. That, then, was a basic structural feature of the political sphere, starting already in 500 AD. As the events of 1203–1204 reveal, it even survived the Komnenian revolution in governance. It was not a "marginal" phenomenon, as some have called it.[67]

We may therefore reconsider events that occurred in the more poorly documented periods and the politics of the populace when a rebel army was before the gates.

- In 705 Justinian II returned from exile to reclaim his throne with Bulgar support. Nikephoros says that "for three days he encamped by the walls of Blachernai and demanded that the inhabitants of the City (τοὺς τῆς πόλεως) receive him as emperor; but they dismissed him with foul insults. However, he crept with a few men at night into the aqueduct of the City and in this way captured Constantinople."[68] Unfortunately, we cannot reconstruct the nature or the parties to the negotiations that took place on the walls, nor do we know much about public opinion at that time (Zonaras later embellished his sources and made the scene more graphic).[69] How did Justinian retake the City from an apparently hostile populace? At this point we must remember that all this is being reported secondhand from an original source that was hostile to Justinian and trying to make him seem illegitimate.[70] Theophanes has the same narrative but adds that Justinian won the City with the familiar shout of "Dig up his bones!"[71] This rallied the people to take down the emperor Tiberios III Apsimar. But why did they join Justinian this time?
- In 717, two years after his forced abdication, Anastasios II tried, with Bulgar support, to regain Constantinople. According to Theophanes, he marched on Constantinople but "the City did not accept him" and he was surrendered.[72] According to Nikephoros, he wrote

letters to some key players, hoping that they would open the City for him, but they were betrayed; he gathered his army but did not make it quite as far as the City, only to Herakleia. The emperor, Leon III, made promises to the Bulgars, and they surrendered him.[73] Zonaras, again, has a more dramatic and more populist narrative: Anastasios "thought that he would be accepted by the populace. But the people would not accept him."[74] It is possible that Zonaras, writing in the mid-twelfth century, was modeling his version of these events on the more familiar template of the eleventh century, but he may not have been entirely wrong to do so.

Twenty years ago Lynda Garland drew the following conclusions from her survey of popular power (focusing on the eleventh and twelfth centuries though, I believe, applicable generally).[75] According to the image in our sources, the people of the City were present everywhere, except in the palace, and were ready to comment on all types of events. They were well informed about current events, and cynical and discerning about the actions of their rulers, while their own actions were often informed by a sense of justice. They were on the alert for opportunities to intervene in the politics of the City and could mobilize within hours. They tended to act as one group and were rarely split on opposite sides; minority groups were rarely successful. The people felt that they had the right to choose emperors and did not seem to be afraid of the emperor or the imperial government. It was impossible to appeal their verdict. "As a result, emperors, however powerful or autocratic, continually had to maintain an awareness of popular feeling . . . and ensure that they propitiated the people . . . and consulted them or informed them about events of national importance." Policies were in fact adjusted to cater to public opinion, which we have seen repeatedly.

In the contests for power that punctuated Byzantine political life, the elites on which modern scholarship has lavished all its attention were fully aware of the crucial role that popular interventions could play, and gave every sign of accepting the legitimacy of those interventions. After all, "to exercise power in the name of another party is always to run the risk that the formal titleholder will attempt to reclaim its substance as well as its form."[76] This is exactly what we would expect in a monarchical republic. The theory of the *politeia* corresponded to the practice of politics.

I therefore propose a new theory of civil war in Byzantium. The many civil wars that wracked the empire did not represent a failure or necessarily even a weakness of its political framework. They represented only failures on the part of sitting emperors to maintain control and, chiefly, their own popularity. Wars were at one extreme of a spectrum of challenges to a sitting emperor's authority. They gave the population of the empire, and especially of the capital, a choice between two (or more) candidates. To be blunt, civil wars and other challenges were a form of election. "Contestation" was at the heart of politics in Romanía, because there was no absolute right to hold power beyond what the elements of the republic in their collective judgment would allow, and their sufferance was always temporary. "Civil war," then, was the empire's answer to the elections of the Republic: rival potential leaders competing for the favor of the populace. It was one way by which the empire managed its politics. This interpretation of Byzantine civil war explains the following striking fact: no state in history ever had more civil wars that changed nothing about the structure or the ideology of the polity. Byzantine civil wars were usually only about personnel. Let us not forget that the politics of the old Republic in its final century had themselves included a hefty dose of periodic civil war and urban violence, which culminated in the republican monarchy of the "Empire" (in fact, we know so much about the late Republic because the Byzantines, fascinated by Roman civil war, preserved many records about that very period).[77]

Above and beyond their military aspects, then, civil wars were essentially political contests over public opinion and hinged on perceptions of popularity and unpopularity. Most were over within a few months. Despite the damage that they did, they also ensured that Byzantium was ruled by generally capable and popular rulers. At the heart of it all lay "public opinion," or what all the people believed about their rulers. Contrary to what Veyne asserted, people did have political opinions, political discussion seems to have been rampant, and public opinion passed judgment on the government, all the time. But the implications of this for our understanding of the Byzantine political sphere have yet to be worked out. That cannot be done, I believe, in one monograph, much less in a few pages, but some preliminary observations can be made.

The Politics of Popularity

According to the evidence presented so far, a familiar model of the Byzantine political sphere is no longer tenable. That is a model which, following the conventions of panegyric, regards the emperor as the essence of the political sphere. All were subject to his transcendent authority and "politics" happened only within the tiny circles of the elite. In this model the people were spectators, with no institutions through which to pursue their political interests. "Imperial attitudes toward the 'mob' of the City were limited to the provision of charity and good works and monetary distributions on public festivals . . . the populace played an important, if passive, ceremonial role."[78] On occasion, they did riot, but these were violent, isolated incidents with no ideological significance.

This model must be replaced, not just tweaked. There was no imperial legitimacy without popular consent. Only that authorized an emperor to govern in the name of the Roman people as "the emperor of the Romans" (not as "the Roman emperor," which is a modern term). Moreover, popular consent could be retracted at any time until concessions were made or a more acceptable rival emerged. All depended on how popular the emperor was with his subjects in relation to potential rivals. Rebelling in Byzantium in large part meant assessing that balance. Only in a political culture whose foundations were populist could a man aspire to the throne or be considered a viable competitor by others, simply on the basis of his popularity. Lactantius imagined how Galerius and Diocletian planned to handle the problem posed by the popularity of Constantine (then still a private citizen, but a potential rival).[79] Justinian's courtiers were terrified of the popularity of Belisarios.[80] Michael IV allegedly feared the popularity of Michael Keroularios (before he became patriarch).[81] Manuel I sent Axouch to a monastery because he too feared his popularity.[82] Popularity can become a political problem of this magnitude only in a republican monarchy. For that reason it was risky to be more popular than the emperor, but it also fueled ambitions.

This has dramatic consequences for the politicization of society, at least in the capital (though a case will be made below for provincial society too). There was no point of absolute stability in imperial politics. Imperial authority could always be recalled and reassigned, sometimes quickly, which meant that all subjects were constantly assessing their options, deciding whether they liked the emperor and comparing him to other leading men of the day. Emperors, for their part, governed and lived in a state of permanent probation, and hence of anxiety and insecurity. They had to maintain their popularity at all times. The history of Byzantine politics is the story of how well they did this. Potential usurpers were always assessing their own relative popularity compared to that of the sitting emperor.

We urgently need focused studies of Byzantine public opinion, for which there is ample material. To my knowledge, there is only one monograph that even tangentially touches on the topic, a little-cited dissertation in French by Nike-Catherine Koutrakou.[83] Without discussing the dynamics of rebellion or its ideological implications, Koutrakou shows how concerned emperors were to gain and keep public opinion on their side: "to assure the approbation of public opinion was a constant preoccupation of the imperial government."[84] She surveys the vocabulary of popularity and unpopularity, and the terms by which our sources refer to the public. While it is difficult to make inferences about the specific audiences to which emperors addressed their propaganda in order to sway public opinion, it is crucial that "the public, in the Byzantine mentality, remained impersonal."[85] It is modern historians who have tried to make it both personal and limited to the elite. Byzantine politicians, by contrast, imagined that their actions were being closely watched and evaluated by an undifferentiated, impersonal, and national audience. Let me give one striking example. Niketas Choniates reports that when Alexios I Komnenos was dying and was being pressured by his wife to exclude their son Ioannes from the succession, he responded by saying that if he did that he would become a laughingstock to τὸ Πανρώμαιον, the entirety of Roman society. This is the impersonal collectivity of the Roman people to whose opinion all successful emperors were sensitive.[86]

We need studies of what qualities made a man popular or unpopular in Byzantium and in which contexts those qualities were perceived and discussed. Historical sources often mention that this or that emperor "tried to win over the good opinion of his subjects."[87] How was this done? We must be careful here not to despise our subjects if what we see does not strike us as especially profound. To put matters in perspective, let us not forget the reasons for which modern voters seem to prefer one politician over another. With that in mind, we should not disdain the vapid moralizing of the Byzantine public-relations system. The qualities urged by the so-called Mirrors of Princes may have been precisely those that enhanced an emperor's image among his subjects. We have seen how the author of one of them, Agapetos, delivers a veiled threat: "Consider yourself to rule safely when you rule willing subjects. For the unwilling subject rebels when he has the opportunity. But he who is ruled by the bonds of goodwill is firm in his obedience to his ruler."[88] A later text in that tradition notes that "subjects are severe judges of their ruler's actions."[89] These texts, then, can be seen as survival manuals, at least in the field of public opinion. When Tiberios II raised Maurikios to the throne in 582, he instructed him to foster goodwill in his subjects, not fear, and to welcome criticism.[90] It was grimly ironic of his historian, Theophylaktos, to place this passage at the beginning of his narrative, given what happened to Maurikios at its end, in 602. In a letter to the empress Eirene, Theodoros the Stoudite praises her good measures, fiscal policies, religious qualities, and philanthropy, and notes that she thereby "preserves the integrity of the kingdom for yourself and your subjects willingly consent to your rule."[91] More irony this time, but unintended: Eirene was deposed by her chief finance minister (in 802).

Emperors tried to win over public opinion generally but also for specific policies.[92] Subjects' loyalty could not be taken for granted. The Byzantines were predisposed to be critical of their rulers. There are cases when we see emperors engaged in "damage-control," as their unpopularity in some area became a liability. Often this entailed caving to public opinion. Konstantinos X Doukas, a civilian emperor, was even forced to march out of the capital a short distance because *everyone* was openly reviling him for not marching out against the barbarians due to his stinginess."[93] His response may have made him look weak or calculating—the dilemma of every politician, ancient, medieval, or modern, in a republic: is he doing what he thinks people want him to out of fear or what he thinks is right? Friends would see matters differently than enemies, the stuff of politics. We are far here from the model of the "absolute ruler unconstrained by either law or public opinion."[94]

Consider Leon V (813–820). The continuer of Theophanes, a mostly hostile source, says that his virtues were actually the product of his desire to fawn upon the *politeia* and to shamefully purchase his subjects' favor, that is, to cater to public opinion.[95] The same source admits of Theophilos (829–842) that he was believed, at least in theory, to be a fiery lover of justice, though the author believes that he only pretended to be that in order to counter any rebellion against him.[96] There are worse things, of course, than an emperor who is only pretending to be just. It is interesting to see that, at least according to these cynical observers, the moral context of the republic could make some emperors more decent than they would otherwise have been.

There are many angles from which the phenomenon of public opinion in Byzantium can be examined. Here I will look at one, namely, that unpopularity could become a death sentence, and I choose this in order to highlight the lethal urgency of the challenge faced by all emperors and politicians in contrast to the more complacent model of governance that we have constructed by relying too much on the "imperial idea." Conspiracies, rebellions, and usurpations—in sum, all violent regime-change—were commonly justified by reference to negative public opinion. We do not need to accept the historical reliability of every single one of these accounts, some of which were written after the fact, but a persistent pattern indicates how Byzantines thought, talked, and educated each other and their rulers about imperial politics. Konstas II, for example, was murdered (in Sicily, in 668) because he was hated (ἐμισήθη) by the people of Constantinople.[97] We have already seen what happened to the most hated Justinian II, Michael V, and Andronikos I. These claims about the power of popularity to effect regime-change pass into our modern narratives even in the absence of a theory of the imperial position that would explain them.[98] Thus historians take the republic for granted in practice without acknowledging it in theory.

In 803, many joined the rebellion of Bardanes against Nikephoros I because they hated (ἐμίσει) him on account of the taxes.[99] Nikephoros II Phokas also became "hated by all,"[100] which certainly facilitated popular acceptance of his murder. Isaakios Komnenos was removed from power in 1059 in a bloodless coup: Psellos tells us that he too "was detested (ἀπεχθάνεται) by the people of the City and not a small part of the army," Zonaras that he was hated (μισητός) by the people, senate, and army.[101] In 1061, Konstantinos X Doukas was relieved to discover that the plot he had just survived originated "in a few people only; it was not a universal consensus and movement that had launched the attack. This revived his spirits."[102] Michael VII, as we saw, faced many rebellions, more than we can discuss. Suffice it to say that public opinion, Attaleiates's κοινὴ γλῶσσα, "was displeased with his ignorance and unbridled arrogance and believed that he was at fault for the evils that were pouring in from all sides."[103] No regime could survive for long under such conditions, and neither did his. Conversely, popularity could propel one to the very top: "To the people of Constantinople [Andronikos Komnenos] was a god on earth, second only to the one in heaven ... He brought the entire City over to his side ... in almost no time those of high and low estate and those in between were all sailing to join him ... He rose to supreme power through the strength of the populace."[104] His opponents at that time, namely, the regency of Alexios II, were "hated" for having deposed a popular patriarch, Theodosios.[105] Another historical irony, given how Andronikos ended up (in pieces, in the hippodrome).

We need a study of Byzantine "hatred," as a political term. Consider the reasons given for the murder of Michael III by Basileios I in 867. The murder itself had a number of motives, of course, ambition being at the top of the list, but note how Basileios's rise was presented, long after the fact, in sources favorable to him. Michael had just adopted Basileios when he

> began to be reviled and booed by the Senate and the *politeuma* and by almost all who were in positions of the administration and in charge of public affairs; and also by the armies and the entire populace of the City. The emperor learned these things through some associates ... Discovering not only his own negligence with regard to public matters but also his laziness, total lack of suitability, and foolishness, and fearing an uprising or rebellion on the part of the multitude (ἐπανάστασιν ἢ ἀπόστασιν παρὰ τοῦ πλήθους), he decided to take on a partner in the management of public affairs and power.[106]

In other words, the rise of Basileios corresponded to, in fact was the expression of, popular will. The text is explicit that his elevation was "according to the wish of those in office and the entire populace and the armies and generals and all the multitudes who were subject to the empire in all lands and cities."[107] This was, of course, the ideology of *consensus omnium,* here in favor of Basileios and hostile to Michael. It was effectively the ceremony of popular acclamation projected onto political history. When Michael worsened, Basileios tried to persuade him to set aside his evil ways: "for we are hated (μισούμεθα)," he said, "by the entire City and Senate, the bishops of God regard as accursed, and everyone is saying terrible things about us and insulting us."[108] We are meant to infer from this that Basileios had no choice but to kill him. It was that or be destroyed with him in a general uprising. Such was the logic of the biography issued at the command of Basileios's grandson, Konstantinos

VII, which was meant to whitewash his career. A defense lawyer would argue that "public opinion made him do it."

It was perilous to be regarded as unpopular, for emperors as well as for magistrates. Subordinates often had to take the fall when an emperor's policies became unpopular and he had to sacrifice some leading officials to the crowd. Conversely, popularity was a leading qualification for a career in public service—unless it worried an emperor. Psellos, who stressed how his own qualities as a charmer facilitated his rise at the court, has also left us with the most detailed discussions of the "political type" of man, by which he meant mostly the emperor's right-hand man rather than the emperor himself.[109] Psellos elevates the ability to ingratiate oneself with others, in fact with a diverse and manifold constituency, to a leading quality of statecraft. For instance, he praises the ex–prime minister and later patriarch Konstantinos Leichoudes for being able to adapt himself to different circumstances so that he was beloved by both the army and the political class.[110] He even cast the ancient Roman king Tullus Hostilius as a *popularis*: "He was very popular with the people (δημοτικώτατος) from the very beginning and made all of the citizens his friends,"[111] following the more martial Romulus and pious Numa (Psellos was writing these portraits as pedagogical models for Michael VII). Even the puppet Alexios Komnenos, harbored by William II of Sicily, "boasted that the entirety of Romaïs [= Romanía] was on his side and truly loved him," hoping to become emperor in Constantinople by the strength of Norman arms.[112] It was as if he were thinking of a popularity contest, not a military invasion. We note again that he has an undifferentiated, national Roman audience in mind.

Both rulers and potential usurpers looked to their subjects and monitored their popularity to assess their chances of staying on, or gaining, the throne. This made "the people," "the entire *dêmos*," "the populace of the City," or "Romanía," a central element of the politics of the republic, perhaps even its center of gravity. The historical sources leave us with a sense of the ubiquity of the people, who, "except for within the palace, always seem to be present in the City to witness and comment on significant current events of every sort."[113] We need to factor this element into our understanding of Byzantine politics. As Susan Reynolds has argued regarding the West, "we need to pay more attention than we customarily do to lay political ideas. Medieval political thought is generally studied only, or largely, through the works of systematic and academic writers . . .

Political thought is not, however, the prerogative of political philosophers, jurists, or theologians."[114]

Part of the challenge is that we still lack a proper study of Byzantine popular culture.[115] I do not mean folklore, which has tended to serve nationalist agendas, but something more like a *People's History of Byzantium*. We have seen repeatedly that the people were not powerless just because there were no formal institutions to channel their agency other than their acclamation of the emperor. Yet "the people" have been largely written out of our histories, which focus on formal institutions and "official ideologies" and cast popular interventions as aberrant instances of "mob riots." The people of Byzantium, like the Roman *plebs,* were "not some *Lumpenproletariat* but a class possessed of an ancient tradition."[116] Jerry Toner's *Popular Culture in Ancient Rome* resonates with what I have argued about Byzantium, the direct heir and continuation of his Rome. He says that "the non-elite had a strong sense of social justice that operated as . . . a 'moral economy' to ensure that the elite fulfilled their social obligations to the people . . . Popular culture in ancient Rome was not just about folklore; it was about how people sometimes mocked, subverted and insulted their superiors; how they manipulated the elite to get something of their own way; and how they saw through the ideologies by which the powerful sought to dominate them."[117] It was the people themselves who enforced the populist ideology of the republic, even under the emperors. At such moments the republican proclamations of the emperors came home to roost. "Once an ideal had been established, every emperor could be judged against it. And knowing what the attributes of an ideal emperor were gave ordinary Romans a way of thinking about the degree to which the reality fell short."[118] "Stonings served as the ultimate in popular justice."[119] Social superiors, including the emperors, were abused and made the targets of popular wit, and it was considered good form for them to take it in stride.[120]

Toner presents a vigorous culture of public opinion and intense political discussion.[121] Other historians have tried to uncover the threatening dynamics of popular mobilization in ancient Rome, which elite authors sought to demean.[122] There might well be enough evidence for us to understand such groups in more detail in Byzantium, below the macro level at which they have been described here. But even at that level, I would propose that this aspect of popular culture was stronger in Byzantium than it had been in the early imperial period and late antiquity. This would reverse the familiar (and worn) metanarrative according to which Byzantium took a step in the direction of increased autocracy and despotism. Byzantium was probably more republican than its predecessors, the Principate and the Dominate.

Throughout our period the people of Constantinople (and probably of the provinces too) regularly mocked emperors either by staging vicious parodic skits or by singing insulting ditties and songs, often with a sexual content. A number of them survive, and more are alluded to in historiographical sources. Maurikios (582–602) was heading to his downfall when the people staged shows to mock him and sang verses about his sexual life and repressive regime. We have also abusive verses addressed to Phokas (602–610), Konstantinos V (741–775), Ioannes I Tzimiskes (969–976), and Theophano (a highly inventive sexual parody), Alexios I Komnenos (1081–1118), and others, in addition to references in the histories that this was done during disturbances.[123] Someone even trained a parrot to insult the empress Euphrosyne, "You whore, pay a fair price!"[124] This is what emperors had to bear patiently, in addition to a range of nicknames, most of which were not flattering: Thick Neck, Apostate, Butcher, Dikoros (eyes of different color), Big Beard, Nose-Cut-Off, Dung-Name, Khazar, Stutterer, Drunkard, Wise, Born-in-the-Purple, Pretty Boy, Caulker, The Old Man, and Discount-Fare (Parapinakis). Some were in use during the reign. In addition to being frequently disloyal, the Byzantines also had one of the most irreverent imperial cultures.

These forms of abuse provide snippet views of the popular response to the "imperial idea," the street's answer to the splendors of the palace. James Scott, an anthropologist who has written an influential study of subversive, often hidden, popular modes of discourse, has argued that

> what may develop under such circumstances is virtually a dual culture: the official culture filled with bright euphemisms, silences, and platitudes and an unofficial culture that has its own history, its own literature and poetry, its own biting slang, its own music and poetry, its own humor, its own knowledge of shortages, corruption, and inequalities that may, once again, be widely known but that may not be introduced into public discourse.[125]

Byzantine high officials, both popular and unpopular, were also targeted, as were failed usurpers. "The Constantinopolitans, at all social levels, had a distinct predilection for ridicule ... [which] was an important factor in the political life of the capital, often serving as the public expression of the people's opinions."[126] We saw above how the people made up a ditty about Theodosios Monomachos after his exile, which Zonaras quotes; it stresses his delusional failure to mobilize public opinion. This reflects a vibrant culture of popular political engagement. But one rarely finds references to these songs in most modern histories of the reigns in question, as if they had nothing to do with politics, the latter being the business of the elite and palace. Given the evidence presented in this chapter, I believe that emperors monitored such things closely. It was perhaps a small step from a sexual slogan to *Anaxios!* and Dig up his bones! "Emperors and their subjects feared each other."[127] Moreover, there was never a point in the history of the Byzantine empire when subjects did not know that their emperors were vulnerable to mass action. Sitting on the throne was always as Tiberius I had first described it: holding the wolf by the ears.[128]

Popular songs have rightly been seen as the flip-side of acclamations, and their history was continuous from Rome to Byzantium. M. S. Williams argues that they

> produced a collective "unity and energy" that could be directed toward political and social ends. As such, they represented a potential threat to anyone in authority and, in any case, could certainly not be ignored by those who claimed implicitly or explicitly to govern on behalf of the people . . . A crowd that acted together, and in the process showed its strength, was not to be argued with, and it represented much that mattered in Roman politics and religion: unity, common identity, consensus, and, ultimately, authority and legitimacy.[129]

There was no one site associated with the performance of this popular culture, which stemmed from the inchoate and probably untraceable roots of public opinion. But there were venues where emperors tried to channel this potentially destructive force and corral it in a supportive direction, especially the hippodrome, the forum of Constantine, and Hagia Sophia (which often acted as much as a public forum as a church). We have seen how those same places could also become focal points in revolutionary moments as well. The people deposed unpopular emperors at the same places where they had collectively acclaimed them, chants of *Anaxios!* now canceling out the former *Axios!* The hippodrome was mostly where emperors tried to win public opinion to their side. It was also where the people made their grievances known, about an unpopular official or policy. This dynamic was in place in early imperial Rome, but it seems to have been more prominent in late antiquity.[130] Some historians have seen these encounters as surrogates of the lost voting rights of the Roman *populus*.[131] Van Nuffelen has rightly objected to those who view acclamations as staged and empty gestures of loyalty to the emperors: "no formal distinction can be drawn between shouts of support and insults: both were voiced in similar ways and identical contexts."[132] They were full of risk for both sides.

"With the emperor in his box, surrounded by representatives of all ranks and classes seated in due order, the circus was indeed a microcosm of the Roman state"[133]—or, rather, of the Roman *politeia*. Yet we must not make the (persistent) mistake of confusing ceremonial orders with *ideology*, for the former reflect only an *interested* arrangement of social orders that obtained under contingent political circumstances, usually in a bracketed ceremonial context. If we want to view the hippodrome as a microcosm of Romanía we can do so, but we must remember that its orderly ceremonial norms reflected an imperial view of the social order, a form of wishful thinking. Yet the hippodrome also witnessed anger, turmoil, negotiations, and violence, and such moments reflected rather the instability and fragility of the imperial order. Centuries later, the place was still haunted by the dead of Justinian's massacre: stories had emerged about where the emperor had buried their bodies by the hippodrome itself.[134]

I would like to close this section with a passage from Niketas Choniates that is often used to illustrate the condescending views that the elite had of the Constantinopolitan "mob," but is actually quite revealing from the viewpoint of popular sovereignty. Choniates had, of course, witnessed the people effect many regime-changes in his lifetime. Referring to the events of 1181, when the people rallied behind Maria Komnene in her struggle against the *protosebastos* Alexios, and ultimately elevated Andronikos to the throne,[135] he had this to say:

> The entire populace of any other city might be found to rejoice in irrationality and be unstoppable once it has set its mind to something. But that of the City of Constantine is the most disorderly of them all, rejoicing in its impulsiveness and *crooked in its ways*,[136] insofar as people of different backgrounds take part in its public life and it varies its way of thinking, one could say, according to the diversity of their trades. But

given that the worst cause always wins and that one can scarcely find a ripe grape among the many sour ones, for this reason the populace neither proceeds to its objectives with reason nor gives adequate forethought to their execution; rather, rumor alone impels it to sedition, and it rages more destructively than fire ... Reasonably it has been accused of being afflicted with inconstancy of character and fickleness. The inhabitants of the City of Constantine have never been known to do what was best for themselves nor have they obeyed others who were proposing to benefit the common interest ... Their indifference to the authorities has been maintained as an evil innate to them. The same man whom today they legally declare to be a magistrate, the next day they will insult as a malefactor, revealing in both instances that they do not know what they are doing and that they are ignorant of good judgment and moderate temperament.[137]

All this really means is that members of the social and political elite such as Choniates and the imperial authorities could neither predict nor control the behavior of the populace in the way that they would like. The populace's "lack of reason," however, may just mean that they had their own reasons for doing what they did, reasons that were opaque to the elite.[138] This is another glimpse into our *People's History of Byzantium*. Choniates is frustrated that he and his class were at the mercy of the people's political choices. He does not deny that they had the right to intervene in whatever way they saw fit; he is merely complaining about the way that they did so: they ought to have been more "reasonable." He does not even say that they should know their place and stay out of politics. But popular fickleness is a political problem only within republican (or democratic) systems, not in absolute monarchies. Choniates seems to accept that, within this system of governance, the people's shouts of *Axios!* and *Anaxios!* shaped the course of the empire's political history, reflecting the changing popularity of imperial officials. Maybe he wished it were otherwise, but let us not rush to judgment even on that. In his account of the fateful year 1203–1204, Choniates seems to praise the populace who took charge at a time when the political elite was failing: it was they who, more than anyone else, took to heart the defense of national interests in the face of Latin aggression and the collusion of their own elite with the foreigners.[139] Choniates's own sympathies and views were not any more fixed and stable than those of the populace he scorned (teams of modern scholars have failed to pin him down).

In sum, the limitations on the emperor's power were not theological or legal: they were political-ideological and stemmed from the populist basis of the republic. Emperors had to govern within the boundaries of what their subjects considered acceptable or risk the consequences. *Legitimacy meant popularity*. This was imperial governance by public opinion. Each emperor faced this challenge in a different way, and there was no formula that guaranteed success.

Expanding the Political Sphere beyond Constantinople

Was the republic limited to Constantinople? It is assumed that "the political process was effectively concentrated in Constantinople."[140] As Magdalino has succinctly put it, Byzantium = Constantinople.[141] Even Beck, who advocated a republican Byzantium, excluded the provinces from his argument.[142] But there are reasons to revise this approach. We have encountered texts that seemed to refer to a pan-Roman political collective. This section will accordingly outline an argument that would bring provincial Romans into the workings of the republic.

Before presenting the argument, I would like to draw attention back to the first sentence of the passage from Choniates that was just quoted. What he says is that the people in *all* Byzantine cities were irrational and ungovernable, but that those of the capital were the worst. Correcting for his biased language, that the provincials exerted their will in politics is a possibility worth considering. But we face a methodological problem. Our sources were written either in the capital or with a Constantinopolitan bias. Their authors were men who had reached high office and believed that the writing of history concerned the most momentous events that transpired at the center of power. They were no more interested in provincial politics than they were in recording the daily experiences of ordinary men and women, unless of course those somehow impacted the capital. But this does not mean that there were no provincial politics any more than it means that average men and women had no day-to-day experiences. By provincial politics, moreover, I do not mean politics about matters of purely local significance but the same kind of "taking part in the *politeia*" (πολιτεύεσθαι) that I have proposed for Constantinople, a participation in empirewide political processes. How, in the absence of sources comparable to those that we have for the capital (which are themselves rarely detailed), can we make the case that the political sphere spread across the empire, even if admittedly thinner in some places than others? Was the republic confined to the City? Did provincial public opinion count for anything? Did provincial perceptions of the popularity of political figures affect politics at the center?

We could make a general argument and say that, Constantinopolitan snobbery notwithstanding, the *politeia* was always understood to be the "*politeia* of the Romans," that is, of *all* the Romans, just as the emperor was the emperor of all the Romans, not merely those of the capital. The community of Romanía was not limited to one city. This approach, however, faces two problems. First, its premises will not be accepted by everyone. Many historians believe that the Byzantines were not Romans at all, despite what they themselves claimed, or that they were Roman only insofar as they were the subjects of the "Roman emperor," and therefore that those who were closer to him had a greater role to play in the game of being Roman in Byzantium, whatever exactly that was. To respond to these objections would require another volume. While that is being written alongside the present book and will address the question of how the Byzantines themselves perceived the homogeneity and national scope of their Roman identity as well as the multiple channels and connections that linked the capital and provinces into a single society, it would be best to avoid this line of interpretation here. The second problem is more pragmatic. Even if we grant that Romanía was a homogeneous political field that encompassed all the Romans, including those of the provinces, that does not change the fact that some of them were so situated as to be more active in it than others. The concept of the *politeia* cannot preclude the possibility, indeed the likelihood, that most Romans took little part and had little say in it. They basically had to abide by the decisions that were made elsewhere, even if by the *populus* of the capital.[143]

In assessing the provincial role in the politics of Byzantium, we must first specify what we are looking for. According to the Byzantine meaning of the verb *politeuomai*, any activity that brought one into contact with the common interests; any public act or social role; any interaction with the institutions of governance, whether fiscal, judicial, administrative, or military; or simply living passively in accordance with the laws could be understood as "taking part in the *politeia*." In this respect, provincial Romans were on the same footing as those of the capital. However, we are looking for participation of a kind that goes to the heart of the society's republican ideology, namely, that only popular consent could make those institutions of governance legitimate. We have seen the ways in which the people of the capital performed this function. What about provincial Romans?

Let us recall a crucial fact about provincial life. Many of the rebels who aimed for the throne of Byzantium began their rebellions in the provinces and fought their way to the capital, consolidating support and resources along the way. Many succeeded, including Phokas, Herakleios, Tiberios III, Justinian II (in 705), Leon III, Konstantinos V (against Artabasdos, in 741), Nikephoros II Phokas, Isaakios I Komnenos, Nikephoros III Botaneiates, Alexios I Komnenos, and (in part) Andronikos I Komnenos. But we should not limit the argument to those who succeeded, for, until they were defeated, all rebels went through the same motions. Considering only fully fledged military rebellions, fewer than one in five defeated a sitting emperor,[144] but this is still a far higher ratio of success than, say, modern congressional elections in the United States (where it is typical for over 90% of incumbents to win). If we include the dozens of major revolts that failed, we have an average of about one per decade over the course of the empire's history.[145] What did all this mean for the political life of the provincials? Well, the first thing that we must do is put ourselves in the position of the rebel and the people in the territory he controlled. We must stop regarding the ruler in Constantinople as "the emperor" and his rival as "the rebel," because in his own mind, and in his territory, the rebel was "the emperor." It was the one ruling in Constantinople who was illegitimate. Who determined this balance of legitimacy and illegitimacy? On the basis of what source of legitimacy did the rebel claim that an emperor duly acclaimed in the capital was now illegitimate and had to be replaced? Ultimately it was based on the fact that he himself had been acclaimed by the Romans in his territory, all of them provincials.

The ceremonies by which power was legitimated in Constantinople were performed repeatedly in the provinces. The rebel-emperor was acclaimed, held court, and took on all the insignia, functions, and powers of a Roman emperor. He appointed men to high office, governed his subjects, issued coins in his own name,[146] and led his armies. The celebrations and hierarchies of his regime as well as the principles that gave him legitimacy mirrored those of Constantinople. Provincials temporarily had their own little New Romes.[147] This could be done almost anywhere. It means that, at least to a certain degree, all the politics of popularity and public opinion was replicated in the areas affected by the rebellion. The rebel, assuming that he was not thrust unwillingly into claiming the throne, had gauged popular sentiment. We saw above that many rebels believed that their opponent's lack of popularity would help them secure the throne, and it would have been foolish to rebel against a popular emperor. But this did not apply only to public opinion in Constantinople. It was an opinion often formed by the rebel and his top men in the provinces where they were stationed, and perhaps formed there in the first instance. Provincial opinion would, then, have played a huge role in shaping the assignment of power in Byzantium, given how many rebellions there were. And not only that: imperial policies at the center would always be contending with the *possibility* of provincial rebellions, trying to forestall them by gaining good will for the regime, that is, by playing the game of public opinion. This, in turn, meant that provincial Romans lived—and *knew* that they lived—in a charged political environment that could suddenly require them to make the same choices about the assignment of power as Constantinopolitans did. Governed by rebels or potential rebels, they were always considering their options. They did not live apolitical lives.

Some qualifications are in order. Until we reach the 1070s, our sources tell us next to nothing about what happened within a rebel's territory. Their focus is on his dealings with the emperor in Constantinople and on what happened when he reached the walls of the City, if he made it that far. In other words, we do not have detailed accounts of provincial politics under a rebel regime comparable to the accounts that we have about Constantinople at times of political strife. Therefore, we cannot measure the balance of coercion and consent in the acclamation and legitimation of provincial rebel-emperors. The latter were almost all military governors and had armies, and they could and did use those armies to intimidate the local population and secure an acclamation. Some of them may have been acclaimed only by their army, at least at first, whereas in Constantinople armies were not normally used to extract popular consent in this way. But it is possible also that rebels were pushed to claim the throne by disgruntled local populations acting in the same sovereign spirit as their Constantinopolitan counterparts. The latter too tried to push unwilling candidates to the throne, as when they chanted "Probos for Romanía!" in 532, in the Nika riots (Probos had prudently fled).

In his study of the rebellions between 963 and 1210, Cheynet some-times notes that a revolt was "supported" or "opposed" by the population of this or that city or region, but because of the terse nature of the sources it is difficult to know what this meant for the balance of power between the rebel and those provincials. Popular discontent may have been a huge factor, and we need not suppose that people had to be co-erced into joining a rebel who was promising better things any more than Constantinopolitans were, especially since he was *there* and, being ac-claimed an emperor, immediately had the authority to deliver on his promises. We hear of cases where the people of provincial cities rose up and killed their unpopular local governors, usually because of fiscal op-pression, even in the absence of any rebellion going on.[148] This indicates that they could take matters into their own hands. In the right circum-stances, such a climate of "hatred" could have benefited an ambitious man planning to rebel. This is explicitly said about the people of Nikop-olis in 1040. They had already torn their tax collector limb from limb when the Bulgarian revolt occurred, and they joined it, "not so much out of affection for Deleanos [the Bulgarian rebel] as on account of the Or-phanotrophos's greed and insatiate desire for riches [this was Ioannes, the emperor's brother]."[149] In 1066, the people of Larissa, acting in con-cert with notables representing local interests, rose up against Konstan-tinos X to protest burdensome tax increases. They forced Nikoulitzas Delphinas to take command of the rebellion, though he was unwilling. He managed to quiet them down, but only after extracting concessions from the emperor.[150]

We have a detailed account of the brief Larissa rebellion in Kekau-menos, who based it on a firsthand report written by Nikoulitzas him-self and given to Kekaumenos's grandfather. It highlights the difficult decisions that all parties had to make under these circumstances. Kekau-menos, who is rare among Byzantine writers on imperial politics in that he had a provincial perspective, includes the story under the rubric of advice regarding what to do when you find yourself caught up in a rebel-lion. As we have seen, this was a common enough experience in the prov-inces, especially in the 1070s, when he was writing. His advice (to his sons) is that you should stay loyal to the emperor in Constantinople, but the fact that he has to advocate this reveals how precarious the issue re-ally was. He suggests that if you have no choice, you should *pretend* to join the cause and try later to bring the rebels back to the fold, and this is what Nikoulitzas claimed to have done (but we cannot know how truthful his self-serving version was). It is clear from his account, however, that the people of Larissa had made the choice to rebel before they approached him and that their grievances were financial. In fact, Kekaumenos elsewhere advises provincial officials to prevent tax-collectors from being oppressive because that type of behavior caused rebellions.[151] At one point in his narrative, Kekaumenos-Nikoulitzas also says that "there is an ancient law of strategy that he who comes of his own free will to an emperor, a rebel, or a general, should not be held against his will but should be allowed to return to his home freely." The purpose of this "gentleman's agreement" seems to have been to preserve the integrity of the consensus that both emperors and rebels (who were also emperors in their own eyes) required for legitimacy.

The fact that a story such as this is recorded only in Kekaumenos and none of the historians raises the suspicion that the historians may have omitted many similar events, even at the level of the brief notice that they usually reserve for them. There is a reason why we know more about the provincials' experience of rebellions in the second half of the eleventh century. Apart from Kekaumenos, who presents a partial view from the provinces, we have two histories that offer more detail about rebellions than had previous histories: Attaleiates, because he was writing both under and for a successful usurper, Nikephoros III Botaneiates, whose main opponents were other rebels; and Nikephoros Bryennios, who was basically writing a heroic account of his grandfather's failed rebellion. They do not provide us with the kind of detail that we would like to have, but we can gain a glimpse of the underlying dynamics. The people in provincial cities had to use their judgment and exercise their political will in making the fundamental choice whether to resist or join the rebellion. During the rebellion of Tornikes in 1047, "people who lived in the countryside gathered for themselves as many supplies as they could find under the circumstances and crowded the gates of the City."[152] But all the cities of Macedonia had, in one way or another, gone over to his side. The exception was Raidestos, which remained loyal to Konstantinos IX. When Tornikes retreated from the capital he attacked it with siege-engines, but "the inhabitants resisted him valiantly."[153] Attaleiates owned property at Raidestos and provides a fascinating glimpse of politics there, when the city went over to Bryennios during his revolt in 1077: "the citizens" were apparently persuaded to join, not coerced.[154] A major factor in their decision was certainly the hugely unpopular grain monopoly that the regime instituted in Raidestos.[155] As Bryennios marched toward Constantinople, some cities went over to him willingly, while others did not. Going over to him, of course, meant acclaiming him emperor, in effect proclaiming the unpopular Michael VII Doukas deposed.[156] When the rebel Basilakes was defeated in 1078, he fled to the citadel of Thessalonike, but the people of that city turned against him and sided with Botaneiates's general Alexios Komnenos.[157] When Alexios marched against Botaneiates, all the cities in Thrace went over to him—but not Orestias.[158] It is interesting to see how individual cities made different decisions for or against the rebel or the emperor in Constantinople.

Attention has been paid by historians to Alexios's attempt to persuade the city of Amaseia to side with the emperor he was then working for (Michael VII) and help to pay the ransom that would release the rebel Latin general Rouselios from Turkish captivity. Alexios convened an "assembly" (ἐκκλησία) of the people of the city and asked the leading men to contribute funds. The parallel accounts in Bryennios and Anna reveal that this was a popular assembly, and that Alexios turned to address the notables more specifically when he had to ask for money. The πλῆθος (or the λαός) were present but were not eager to side with Alexios, and he had to persuade them to do so. He did so in part by turning the crowd against the minority that, he alleged, were benefiting from Rouselios's rebellion and exposing the people of Amaseia to danger and reprisals.[159] It is probably impossible to extract from this story concrete information about any institutions of self-governance that Amaseia may have had, far less to situate them in some *longue durée* history of town councils from Justinian to the alleged feudalization of Byzantium. I find it hard to believe that a place such as Amaseia, a thematic capital, would not have had institutions of self-governance when even villages in Byzantium had the means to represent themselves as legal collectives.[160] The search for institutional history would divert us from our goal here, which is to find that provincial cities did have hard choices to make in the context of provincial rebellions; that these decisions were not made solely by the elite; and that, at least in this case, persuasion had to act upon public opinion in order to secure a decision one way or the other.

Constantinople was far and away the most important site in Romanía for the exercise of popular power. The empire-wide *politeia* of the Romans was represented by the Romans of the capital, insofar as "the public of the capital was a representative microcosm of the public of the empire."[161] But Romans in the provinces also had occasion to make their voices heard in the periodic struggles that reassigned the right to wield power. We do not have sources that discuss their actions as we do for Constantinople. But we have to think about what provincial rebellions entailed for those people, whether they directly instigated them or were caught up in them, and to a certain degree we have to use our imagination. I suspect that the same processes played out there that we see in Constantinople when it came to the repudiation of the current emperor and the acclamation of a new one. I doubt that the equation Byzantium = Constantinople would hold up as firmly. Just because we do not have those literary narratives does not mean that the events did not happen.

Looking at events before the 1070s, the people of Amorion seem to have made their own decisions in the complicated series of invasions and re-bellions in the late 710s.[162] Even after Thomas the Slav was defeated before Constantinople, some cities would still not accept Michael II, whom they hated—but most did.[163] At the very same time, Euphemios, emperor of the Romans in Sicily (so a rebel), approached Syracuse, "came to within bow-shot of the city, and addressed the citizens, endeavoring to win them over to his side with his words."[164] Such wall-top diplomacy periodically played out before Constantinople, as we have seen, and before other cit-ies caught up in such wars.[165] Nikolaos, the bishop of Nikaia, persuaded the people of his city to accept Andronikos Komnenos, but the city of Prousa resisted him.[166] In the chaos of the final years of the twelfth cen-tury and for most of the thirteenth, most cities frequently had to fend for themselves. But it was not an experience for which they were entirely unprepared.

We should also not draw too fine a distinction between civilian locals and the Byzantine army in the provinces. To a great degree, "the armies were very much rooted in local society, recruited regionally from peasant communities and officered to a great extent by local men."[167] Haldon has argued that many of the soldiers involved in provincial rebellions must be seen "first as individuals produced by their social and cultural envi-ronment" and secondarily as units with separate corporate identities.[168] The thematic armies were, then, partially representative of the interests of the provincial population. Rebellions and civil wars "had clearly local-ized roots, in respect of the sources of discontent."[169] We should not for-get that the army held a special place when the component parts of the *politeia* were listed by Byzantine authors, along with the Church, merchants, "the people," and other putative representatives of the whole. At other times, however, army and people are blurred in the ambiguous term *laos,* which makes it difficult to visualize who was assembled at the hippodrome, for instance. At any rate, the army, being the Roman people in arms, had just as much a right to participate in the political process as the people of Constantinople. They too were a part of the *politeia* with a recognized right to be heard and to intervene, the same as the people,[170] though they never managed to impose an unpopular emperor against the people's will, at least not for long.

Some conclusions have already emerged from this discussion. First, the right to declare emperors deposed and acclaim new ones was not limited to the people of Constantinople. It was exercised by Romans along the main Balkan and Anatolian routes too. Every emperor aimed at universal consensus, and so would expect to be acclaimed in every part of the empire, whether the wave of recognition flowed out from the capital (if he was elected there) or from a province to the capital, as he marched on it. Second, the evidence does not support the view that provincial politics consisted solely of elite activity, anymore than it did in Constantinople. Even though we cannot reconstruct these histories, the burden of proof lies on those who would deny that "the people" in provincial cities played a crucial and often a leading role in shaping local decisions and, by extension, imperial history. The Constantinopolitan dynamics of public opinion and popularity played out in similar ways there.

These conflicts were not about deep ideological differences; there were no "political parties" in the modern sense. They were certainly about local interests, usually fiscal, and about personnel: Who was the best man to rule the republic in the interest of its citizens? The right of the people to make this determination was not questioned. "Few people were executed for treason" after rebellions, for the goal was to "diffuse tension, restore order, . . . bring as many people as possible back into the imperial fold, and convince them to support the emperor"—or the *new* emperor, I add.[171] Most military rebellions were over within a year, and there was no attempt to collectively punish all the supporters of a failed emperor in such a way as to assert the absolute supremacy of the imperial office over the *politeia* (the Nika riots being the only exception, and a partial one too). Emperors would rather appease and co-opt their rival's supporters, which again illustrates their concern to win over public opinion. Punishing large segments of society would quickly make the regime unpopular. Only ringleaders were denounced and later remembered as traitors and sinners against God's anointed, not the populace that may have backed them. In fact, it was entirely in the interests of the regime that survived the challenge to suppress the memory of popular support for the rebellion and to cast it as the act of one or a few deranged men, because otherwise the narrative would effectively call the regime's own legitimacy into question. The need to retain the perception of public support affected how the history of the rebellions was later told. Later narratives tended to focus on a few leading elements rather than the masses that supported them.

An Extralegal Sovereignty and the Politicization of the Populace

During the past century scholars have occasionally been willing to assert that Byzantium was a mixed type of regime with roots in Roman republicanism. In 1924, Charles Diehl could write that "on connaît la formule fameuse: S.P.Q.R. Il semble bien, que, de la fin du VIe à la fin du IXe siècle, le *Senatus populusque Byzantinus* ait été semblablement un réalité."[172] The challenge was to identify the institutions by which popular power was expressed, apart from the acclamation of the new emperor (which was, and still is, regarded as an empty formality). G. Manojlović, who had a view similar to that of Diehl, unfortunately fixated on the hippodrome factions, misunderstanding their nature and confusing them *(dêmoi)* with the *dêmos (populus)*. Still, he grasped that the Roman people had a crucial "constitutional" role to play of which they themselves were aware.[173] In this he was a forerunner of Beck. But Beck, and the small number of scholars who might be said to be his school in this matter, thought in too-formal constitutionalist terms. State institutions, however, the building blocks of constitutional theory, belonged in Byzantium to the monarchy. The question should rather have been, What was the relationship between the emperor and the *politeia*? This was an extralegal relationship governed not by institutions but by the underlying ideology of Roman republicanism, the matrix of politics. To see this we have to think beyond the level of institutions.

> The political field is not defined by institutional and territorial boundaries, but rather is constituted by groups who are engaged in political activity . . . It may well be that in the study of such activities we encounter

institutions. But these institutions should be regarded as instances of political processes—a particular set of formalized relationships that emerge from, are constituted by, and continue to be altered through political activity.[174]

Augustus may have arrogated most power to himself in a way that violated the uncodified norms of the *mos maiorum,* but when he claimed, over and over again, that his power derived from the senate and the people, who had given it to him, he indicated his acceptance of a basic republican principle. This principle, as an ideology operative in the field of *legitimation,* remained alive throughout all the centuries of Byzantium, and was even strengthened after the mid-fifth century. The emperors themselves did more than anyone to strengthen it.

The framework of the republican monarchy was stable, but every few years "the people" (whether in the capital or the provinces) made a choice, or faced a choice, regarding the transfer of power. There was no institutional framework to accommodate these struggles for power, nor could there have been. The state institutions had long since been dominated by the *basileia,* the monarchy. But the monarchy was only one aspect of the *politeia* and had to draw its legitimacy from it. The *politeia* was the ideological context in which its institutions operated. This meant that struggles over the (re)assignment of the *basileia* had, by necessity, to take place outside the institutions of the government, so they were often violent. That was the result of having a strong monarchy whose legitimacy derived from popular consent and "election" by the people (or their representatives), that is, a republican monarchy. Acclamations were the interface between the ideology of the republic and the institutions of the monarchy, as were (but in the opposite direction) cries of disapprobation.

The emperors were not exercising a fully legal authority to begin with. Their power had an ambiguous relation to law, to put it mildly. What was less ambiguous was their relation to the republic. "The language of accountability became a part of the continual dialogue between the emperors and the once-sovereign *populus.* Those who are accountable are also subject to criticism from those to whom they answer . . . citizens were encouraged to hold their government to account."[175] Thus, as I argued in Chapter 3, the history of the empire oscillated between two "states of exception" that operated potentially beyond the law: that of the emperor, answerable to the republic, and that of the rest of the polity, answerable only to itself. The first, if managed well, resulted in fairly long periods of political and social stability which can give the illusion that the emperor had the final word. For most practical purposes he did, so our histories focus on emperors and their policies. The second often featured outbursts of violence and lawlessness, for all practical purposes the suspension of law. They punctuated the text of Roman history, making reigns and dynasties longer or shorter, introducing more or less abrupt transitions between them. Yet these episodes appear more prominently in the sources than in modern histories. Byzantine narratives are more about people, both individuals and "the people," while our own depend to a far greater degree on stable institutions, however "punctuated" their stability.

In times of revolution, the *ennomos politeia* was suspended. Some of the looting and settling of scores that occurred then was opportunistic.[176] According to Leon the Deacon, Ioannes Tzimiskes murdered Nikephoros II and took control of matters so quickly that he managed to proclaim a decree threatening anyone who looted with the death penalty. Leon comments that "usually, at the time of such changes, the idle and indigent members of the populace used to turn to looting property and destroying houses, and even sometimes to murdering their fellow citizens."[177] It is possible that elements of the populace were inclined to join in usurpations or support coups because it gave them the opportunity to plunder the mansions of the wealthy with impunity. Something like that is suggested in Choniates's account of the uprising of 1201 and the failed coup of Ioannes "the Fat."[178]

But this cynical interpretation goes only so far. At such times, most of the violence was either symbolic or reflected the Sovereign People's sense of justice (whether it was done by the people or on their behalf). Freeing prisoners from the *praitorion,* for instance, that revolutionary cliché, effectively canceled the emperor's authority to execute the law, and probably freed his "political" prisoners too. In 511 the violence targeted the house of an unpopular minister; in 963 the houses of Bringas and his supporters; in 1042 all who were perceived to have benefited unjustly from the regime of Michael V, including churches and monasteries. In 1057, Theodosios, patriarch of Antioch, "was the first to cry out the acclamation of approval [of Isaakios I Komnenos] and to permit the razing and pillaging of the houses of those high officials who were not pleased with what was happening; and he did it inside that sacred and famous church!"[179] In 1181, they targeted the house of the City prefect, among others. In a study of *Why People Obey the Law,* Tom Taylor argued that people do not obey the law only out of rational calculation (i.e., to avoid penalties or because it is in their interest) but also because they think it is the right thing to do. But they are more likely to think that if they perceive that the authorities are legitimate. They are, in other words, concerned with fairness. This may be why there was a breakdown of law when the regime was rejected as illegitimate and why the violence tended to target those who had unfairly benefited from the regime. Legality in Byzantium was proportional to the legitimacy of the regime in power, and legitimacy was here measured by a kind of "street justice" or "People's Court."

Choniates offers an image that stands for the suspension of the *ennomos politeia:* the looters took away from the prefect's house the public law codes, "which contained those measures which pertained to the common good of everyone, or at least the majority; but these were powerless now before the craving for private gain."[180] This was his view of the matter, of course, coming only a page after his diatribe against the fickle populace of Constantinople that we examined earlier in this chapter. But it is still a potent image for the suspension of law that occurred when the populace took matters into its own hands. Power devolved to the extralegal authority of the true sovereign, to be bestowed upon the next favorite of public opinion.

Such scenes transpired not only in Constantinople but probably also in the provinces, first in the town where the rebel was proclaimed and then along his route toward the capital, as each town decided whether to accept or reject his "rolling revolution" sweeping through the empire; and finally in the capital too, if he managed to reach it and dethrone his enemy. If a rebellion began and ended in the capital, the unrest was confined there. But given the frequency of revolts and uprisings, and the need for the population to make choices about the new assignment of power, many Byzantines would have been personally familiar with the dilemmas involved. They would have had an acute sense of the role that they could play in the legitimation or transference of imperial power. In sum, we must abandon the emperor-centric view of these "subjects," which treats them as largely docile in the face of imperial authority and which goes so far, in fact, as to define their identity as Romans as a function of their "loyalty" to the emperor.[181] We must replace it with a model that recognizes that this loyalty was always conditional and that these "citizens of the Roman republic" (as they are as often called in the sources) were at all times evaluating their options and so exercising their political judgment and, when it came to it, their will. Many of them may not have wanted to be in that situation. But they too had little choice in the matter.

We should not regard violent transfers of imperial authority as aberrant moments in an otherwise stable system. The emperors tried hard to develop and project a rhetoric of stability, as we will see in Chapter 6, but it never succeeded in making their throne secure. The Byzantines lived in a constant state of alert. The events of the Arab Spring and the uprisings taking place around the world, including the West, afford a live appreciation of the people's predicament: theoretically sovereign and extremely politicized (despite the efforts of the elite to cow them or lull them into indifference), albeit with few institutions to express their will (as the sham of our democratic elections is being increasingly exposed). The events in Egypt would have been all too familiar to a Byzantine, including mass demonstrations that paralyze the capital followed by an alliance between the people and army to topple a tyranny. In the case of Byzantium we need to situate such events against a long history of uprisings and rebellions. Not only those that succeeded should matter to us, for the failed ones entailed the same fundamental choices. In fact, we must factor in as well all the times when the people decided *not* to act, for these were political decisions too, for all that their number is unknowable. Imagining them can give us a sense of the extent of the Byzantines' politicization. This was the terror of public opinion in the eyes of the elite. It was at times unpredictable and it could throw everything into question, opening opportunities for some while ending careers (and even lives) for others. This also requires us to revisit the tenor of popular acclamations. In modern histories they are treated as owed to the ruling class, provided by docile and passive subjects who fully accepted the "imperial idea." Their value, however, must be reassessed in light of the ease with which the people could reverse them and bring everything tumbling down about the ears of the elite. No tyranny, not even a modern one, can long withstand massive popular resistance and demonstrations. An acclamation was real political capital, but for how long would it pay dividends before it was reassigned? Even today, the photograph of a mass political rally in favor of a candidate for office can look indistinguishable from that of a mass protest poised to bring down a regime.

The state of emergency that the people could institute created "a point of imbalance between public law and political fact."[182] In Byzantium it actually took the form of, and was not only closely related to, "civil war, insurrection, and resistance."[183] This was the truth behind Mommsen's famous definition of the imperial constitution as an autocracy tempered by the legal right of revolution, though it was not exactly a constitution, or an autocracy, nor was revolution strictly speaking legal.[184] Whether it was begun by a provincial general or the people of Constantinople, the cry of *Anaxios!* gave legitimacy to the revolution and signaled the suspension of lawful order. Only the true sovereign remains legitimate when the lawful order is suspended, and only he—or, in this case, *they*—may reconstitute it.

CHAPTER 6

The Secular Republic and the Theocratic "Imperial Idea"

This study has so far presented a model for the ideology and practice of politics in Byzantium that omits what scholars conventionally call the "imperial idea," namely, the theory that the emperor was appointed to rule by the Christian God. The exact formulation of this idea varies in the sources and modern scholarship, though the range of variation is small compared to the vast gulf that separates it from the model that I have presented. At issue are two substantially different ways of perceiving imperial power. Various consequences flowed out from the imperial idea, including that the emperor was authorized, or required, to carry out God's will; that he was viewed by subjects with awe as a religious figure; and that his dealings with his subjects were defined religiously. Versions of this idea are found in almost all the scholarship on Byzantium. Its recitation is formulaic and repetitive. There is an unwritten rule that scholars must offer it homage before moving on to the particular topic of their books and articles. It is treated as an Archimedean point, a fixed center around which the Byzantine world revolved and from which we can leverage its subordinate aspects. It is given such weight and authority that the Roman aspects of the culture seem like quaint antiquarian survivals by comparison, and are often called that. In fact, the alleged divine right of the Byzantine emperors is given such weight that some scholars separate the "Roman" and the "Byzantine" periods based on it alone.[1]

This chapter will turn that picture on its head. It is striking that there is almost no recent scholarship devoted to a critical examination of the imperial idea itself, its sources, social context, and historical implications. The works that established it in Byzantine Studies are dated and problematic. So without having been scrutinized, the imperial idea has become

165

a doctrine, recycled endlessly as a self-evident truth. It accompanies the implicit (though sometimes explicit) denial of the Byzantines' Roman identity and the persistent failure to realize that they lived in what can only be called a republic.

The Contours and Limits of the "Imperial Idea"

Ritual incantation of the imperial idea is part of being a Byzantinist, so I do not mean to single out the scholars I will be citing here, whose names I will normally not mention in the text. The same formula can be cited from hundreds of publications in every language of scholarship. I will, however, draw attention to an influential article from 1962 by Paul Alexander, which is cited more than the rest and is reprinted as a "classic." In my view this article is a Compendium of Errors, but we will get to that later.

> In the Byzantine view the emperor was the only legitimate ruler of their entire Christian world in his capacity as God's image and representative on earth. As God's viceroy he was charged with the maintenance of peace in the Christian world, with the Christian mission to the "barbarians," and with the preservation of law ... The emperor was selected by God and, as was seen above, at the end of time the last Byzantine emperor would bring about the transition from the earthly to the heavenly kingdom.[2]

That, according to the current paradigm of Byzantine Studies, is how the Byzantines viewed their emperor. The word "theocracy" is thrown around a lot in the field as is "absolutism" and the like (the debate now is whether to use "theocratic" or "theocentric").[3] When the Byzantine emperor is introduced and defined in most books and articles it is first, and often exclusively, in relation to God, not the *politeia* that he governed. In many studies the *politeia* is altogether absent, not just as an important concept but as a crucial element of Byzantine political ontology. So when we set the "idea," whose elements are drawn from a particular set of texts (mostly panegyrical and a few apocalyptic fantasies), next to the model of Byzantine politics that I presented in the previous chapters, we encounter an almost unbridgeable gap. The Roman monarchical republic cannot have been the same as the Orthodox imperial theocracy. The two cannot be referring to the same society—and yet they are. It is this gap that I will try to close in the present chapter.

A few remarks must first be made about the history of the imperial idea in modern scholarship. First, the studies that ostensibly established it are outdated and now problematic, but they are still cited as authoritative. For example, we saw above that a study of the fall of the Roman empire, published in 2005, claims that in Byzantium "all pretense of republicanism had vanished . . . no one thought of the emperor as anything other than an autocratic monarch . . . legitimate rulers were divinely inspired and divinely chosen."[4] The work cited in support of this is Fr. Francis Dvornik's *Early Christian and Byzantine Political Philosophy: Origins and Background* (1966). A point worth making about Dvornik's massive survey, apart from its religious slant, is that it has chapters on Egypt, Mesopotamia, the Hittites, and the Old Testament, but nothing on Roman political thought and practice, as if those were irrelevant to the study of Byzantium. Dvornik is cited in another book (2008) as proof of the claim that "the ideology of the late Roman empire had become thoroughly Christian."[5] Another book from 2011 cites for Byzantine political ideology Dvornik, Alexander, and Baynes's 1933 article on Eusebios.[6]

Eusebios was the bishop of Kaisareia in Palestine who lived through the Great Persecution of Diocletian and Constantine's conversion to Christianity. He was the first Christian writer we have who tried to make sense of those events and explain in Christian terms what it might mean to have a Christian emperor. He worked out something like the imperial idea outlined above and used it to praise Constantine. As a result, he is treated in the field as if he were the author of a kind of "Byzantine Constitution." Almost every scholar who wants to illustrate what the Byzantines thought about politics or the emperor trots out some quotations from Eusebios.

> Insofar as there was an official political theory underpinning the Byzantine state, it consisted of the Christianized-ruler theory worked out for Constantine the Great by Eusebius of Caesarea, according to which the empire was the microcosm of heaven and the emperor placed there by God to ensure the maintenance of true religion.[7]

This is followed on the next page by a quotation from another historian that "Byzantium is rightly described as a theocracy."[8]

Among its other aims, this chapter will put Eusebios in his proper place, by drawing on studies of him and his context that are more recent than 1933. For now I will continue sketching the contours of the "imperial idea." A third point is that much of its appeal lies in the opportunity it presents to combine the study of texts and images. Emperors were represented in many media of Byzantine art, and texts that reflect versions of the imperial idea offer a tempting key by which to unlock their meaning. So art historians get to use texts and, conversely, historians get to create the impression of cultural depth by reproducing visual illustrations to accompany their texts. The foundational study here dates to 1936, and is cited as authoritative still.[9] Moreover, the texts and the art can in turn be embedded in the context of court ceremonies, which provide a living image of the imperial idea. Keeping in mind that most of this material was generated by the court, when assembled it presents what appears to be a unified picture of the culture, the elusive goal of historians who struggle to synthesize thought (myth) and ritual.[10] In Byzantium they come together for us seamlessly and effortlessly. The foundational studies here by Alföldi and Treitinger again date to the 1930s.[11]

In short, if we want to understand why we think what we do about the Byzantine emperor, we need to first understand the political issues that scholars were grappling with in the 1930s and how Byzantium was caught up in them. The 1930s was not a decade like any other when it came to thinking about absolute power, to put it mildly. However, I am not going to carry out such an analysis. My focus here will be on Byzantium. I will be offering an alternative way to understand the "imperial idea" which will expose what the pioneers of the field chose to valorize and what to omit, and what they thought "counted" as political ideology. Scholars in the 1930s were drawn to theocratic ideas, for example, but did not know how to contextualize them. They also did not believe that the actual behavior and decisions of anyone outside the court were relevant. That is one of the main problems of viewing Byzantium through the imperial idea. For the imperial idea is not meant in scholarship to be merely a codification of what the Byzantines thought about the emperor in the abstract; it is offered also as an explanation of why the regime was obeyed at all. Any account of an ideology that is also a comprehensive account of a people's political ontology must, after all, be able to explain their political behavior. Otherwise it is a castle in the sky (which is what I think the Byzantine court was in fact constructing).

Byzantine scholarship is therefore bifurcated. On the one hand, its concept of political ideology is irredeemably theological. On the other hand, studies of the institutions through which the emperor actually governed are pragmatic in their approach and do not rely on the imperial idea to explain much. They invoke it to give flavor to the context, for it is *de rigueur,* but their analyses of political fact are based on commonsense (and secular) notions of power. These studies are good but do not theorize Byzantine politics either at all or in terms of Byzantine concepts, and it is easy to see why: the ideology of the imperial idea operates in a theological space between God and the emperor, whereas the institutions operated in a historical space between the emperor and his subjects. One can bridge the gap by arguing that the emperor derived his legitimacy from his relationship with God and that the Byzantines accepted this and so consented to the operation of the institutions. In other words, the gap is closed through the concepts of *belief* and *obedience:* "the emperor is God's representative on earth and obedience is expected from the people for that reason alone."[12]

But this theory fails the most basic test of verification: the Byzantines, including both elites and the people of Constantinople, seem to have had little compunction about rebelling against, deposing, and even killing their divinely appointed ruler; they did so regularly. Moreover, we do not have access to their beliefs, and if one were to question whether they did "believe" in the imperial idea—whatever exactly that may have meant—it is not clear what evidence can be provided to salvage the theory. So the ideology does not explain Byzantine history, while our writing of that history is undertheorized. The imperial idea is tidy, but exists in a self-contained bubble; meanwhile, our historians are at the mercy of whatever "makes sense" to them intuitively in dealing with the facts of power and contestation.

At issue is the concept of "belief." Did anyone actually "believe" the imperial idea, and what does that mean? Given what we know of Byzantine history, it cannot have entailed much of a commitment on anyone's part. At one end of the spectrum, we might propose that it was an airy bit of court rhetoric that no one really took seriously. But this too does not explain its ubiquity and the solemnity with which it was regarded. I have no doubt that, on some level, most Byzantines did accept the imperial idea. The problem is in identifying that level. We should probably not be thinking of a single spectrum of belief in the first place, with one end representing sincere and wholehearted conviction and the other "mere rhetoric" or cynicism. Nor will I be suggesting that we place the ideology of the republic at the former end and the imperial idea at the latter. It seems more likely that the Byzantines' thinking operated *simultaneously* along different axes that did not always intersect, and so they were able to maintain conflicting modalities of thought, each operating in different contexts even when they were theoretically opposed. I think this is true of human beings generally and consistent with findings in neuroscience and evolutionary psychology.[13]

Consider, for example, the statement of then-candidate George W. Bush (in 2000): "I believe that God wants me to become President, but if that doesn't happen, it's OK." In one and the same breath he managed to articulate a theory of divine election *and* a commitment to a democratic process able, apparently, to overrule the divine will.[14] Bush was no more interested than most people in ensuring that his beliefs were consistent; he was only saying what made sense to the double-aspected profile of his audience: evangelicals who were also voters. Certainly he "believed" in God, and probably also believed that he was destined to win the presidency, but most of his supporters would have balked at the idea that those beliefs, if it came down to it, should override the established political process for electing a president (and in fact he did lose the election). Politicians in republics or democracies arouse opposition when they invoke God to justify their specific policies (as with Blair and the Iraq War). But they are perceived positively when they call on God in vague and abstract terms.

It was not much different in Byzantium, also a republic. "God-talk" could be used as a political argument only up to a point, and within specific contexts. Modern scholarship is full of absolute, totalizing, and unreflexive claims about the Byzantines' political theology, as if it encoded metaphysical truths, when in fact, like all historical artifacts, it was a highly contingent stance that should be bracketed as operating in specific contexts. When it seeped out of them and into contexts governed by a different set of rules, say, when emperors carried the imperial idea into places where it was not supposed to operate, the disjunction was painfully evident. When Isaakios II Angelos was reproached for removing church treasures, he grew impatient and said that all things are permitted to emperors because there was nothing that could logically distinguish them from God.[15] This was taking the imperial idea to its breaking point. Choniates mocked him for thinking that God would guarantee and underwrite his ambitions.[16] So too Psellos mocked Romanos III for believing that, since God had given him the throne, he would support him in his various endeavors, military and dynastic. Psellos also tried to talk sense into Konstantinos IX, who concluded that, as he was protected by God, he did not need guards (this led to attempts on his life).[17] These emperors are presented as delusional, but one could also say that they were merely taking the imperial idea to its logical conclusion, that is, to the point of real "belief."

What good was God if he could not be used to support specific policies? Interestingly, the one thing that God definitely wanted, in texts that express the imperial idea, was that the emperor work hard to benefit his subjects, that is, one of the core principles of the republic.[18] On this level, then, the imperial idea was but a theological expression of republican obligations. But what did God give in return? This is more difficult to measure.

One historian has recently claimed that "since the emperor's power was thought to come from God, it was impious for anyone to oppose the legitimate emperor of the day."[19] This is a logical inference from the texts he is discussing, imperial panegyrics. But if he accepts that conclusion, he must also accept what logically follows, namely, that the empire was often full of impious people, even the majority of the populace. But he would be unwilling to say that. Why not? Were rebels not defined as impious through the logic of the imperial idea? There is, however, an additional extratextual fact in play here, namely, that being "the legitimate emperor" was a function of what the republic wanted and not, in practice, of what God said (who, we must not forget, was a theological, not a historical entity). There was always someone doubting the emperor. We *need* the republic in order to explain what people were doing, because the "imperial idea" does not. But what then of divine right? What historical valence does it actually have?

Seen macroscopically, the culture does not evince much belief in divine right. This has always been known, if not explained. The same scholar can say that "one man," that is, Eusebios, had "set the pattern of Byzantine political thought for the rest of the empire's existence," and also that "theory and practice were widely at odds when it came to the role of the voiceless majority in Byzantine political life."[20] We must conclude from this, then, that what is called Byzantine political thought had little to do with political practice, which is a peculiar state for a field to be in. And while it is readily conceded that reality was different from Eusebian theory, no alternative theory is given to explain that reality other than "the ambition of individuals,"[21] as if that were some timeless category that did not operate within specific cultural constraints. As I said above, we have left the reality untheorized in terms of distinctively Byzantine concepts. So, while it is easy to see that "the theory effectively masked the real state of affairs" and that emperors were in fact vulnerable,[22] are we not then required to go beyond the rhetoric and try to uncover the actual dynamics that governed "the real state of affairs"? Appeals to "murder and intrigue" reveal precisely what is missing. Such concessions to reality are pervasive in the scholarship. But if our theory fails to explain reality in terms that the Byzantines might understand, what good is it? We need a different model, which is what I have proposed in the theory of the Byzantine republic. That theory explains the Byzantines' actions as historical agents better than the religious ideas that most scholars formulaically recite in their introductions and then discard in their analyses in favor of "murder and intrigue."

The imperial idea can never explain the workings of power because it was always an ex post facto theological interpretation: it followed history and did not create it.[23] History was created by the republic and then interpreted by theology. If an emperor was secure on the throne, that is, if he was popular, then by that very fact he could also be said to be favored by God. If his position was precarious, that must conversely have meant that God was retracting his favor. But what made the emperor's position precarious in the first place? Usually that meant that he was unpopular with his subjects. The republic was taking matters into its own hands, and whoever it chose as a successor, if indeed it came to that, would then be seen as God's favorite. An imperiled emperor would be a fool to cite the imperial idea and expect it to earn him any support under such circumstances. In this sense, the dynamics of the republic claimed causal primacy, for the theology was in times of crisis disconnected from the gears of history. It was just a way of interpreting after the fact what the republic had done; thus, it was a rhetorical superstructure.[24] As we will see, moreover, the Byzantines were reluctant to bring these two ways of thinking about the political sphere into conjunction and dialectical exchange. They tended to remain separate and incommensurate, in their own literary and social niches.

In his panegyric for Justinian, the *Buildings,* Prokopios claimed that the rebels in the Nika riots had risen up against not just the emperor but also against God, for they burned down the church of Hagia Sophia.[25] Of course, that is not how they would have seen it: in their minds, they were rising up against a hated tyrant and exercising their right to proclaim a new emperor. *For Romanía!* they chanted.[26] The problem is that they lost, and so were branded as unholy rebels. Conversely, when the populace rose up in 1042 against Michael V, they won, and so our sources were quick to discern divine agency behind their actions, even though they looted monasteries during the commotion.

That still leaves us, however, with the problem of explaining the ubiquity and popularity of the imperial idea in Byzantium, even if it meant little in terms of explaining the actual dynamics that propelled the facts of history. It is time to relativize the Archimedean point and show that it can leverage much less of the Byzantine world than has been traditionally assumed.

The Rise and Function of the Imperial Idea

So why did the emperors, and not only they but the entire republic, accept the imperial idea as an ideal for the exercise of power? The full answer is likely to be manifold, and we should look at the question from many angles. For example, as emperors held authority over all aspects of life and were the ultimate arbiters of all disputes, they quickly came to play an important role in the governance of the Christian community, even before Constantine. Starting in the fourth century, they would regulate aspects of ecclesiastical administration, finance, and law in the appointment of bishops, the convening of Church Councils, and the implementation of the canons. The pagan emperors had functioned in a sacerdotal capacity and their Christian heirs needed comparable authority to govern what was quickly becoming a global Christian community. This posed certain theoretical problems that go under the name of "Caesaropapism": Christian emperors required some kind of religious authority no less than pagan ones. We should not see this as a function of Christianization but in terms of the authority needed by emperors to govern their subjects' religious lives. Cameron has demonstrated that emperors down to at least Anastasios retained the title of *pontifex* and "it was in this capacity that they legislated about church affairs."[27] As emperors did not hold pontifical office, but at the same time had to be superior to the highest level of bishop, the imperial idea offered a nicely vague affirmation of their supreme standing in the Christian community. It set the emperor off and elevated him above the many other pontiffs his empire now contained.

Another explanation for the imperial idea that will be developed at greater length in this section is that it attempted to shore up a fragile monarchy that was liable to be toppled at any point in the permanent revolution that was Byzantine politics.[28] It was precisely the instability created by the republican foundations of the regime that led the court to invent for itself a theoretical principle of legitimacy that lay beyond the reach of the constituent parts of the republic, precisely because it lay outside of history. According to this argument, the court was trying to ameliorate a desperate and precarious situation, for as we have seen, there was a constant willingness on the part of subjects to question the legitimacy of the current emperor. We might call this "aggressive self-assertion as a cover for deep insecurities."[29] In other words, the conventional view of the imperial idea as a self-standing and supreme principle of legitimacy is exactly wrong; it was instead a defensive response to a far more powerful ideological force, a force that regularly *did* shape history.

I hasten here to head off a potential misunderstanding: Byzantium was not torn between republican and theocratic forces, far less factions or parties. As we saw, *both* the court *and* the populace accepted the republican framework of the polity, and we will see that *both* had an interest in maintaining the imperial idea on the rhetorical-religious level. To put it differently, the emperors were republicans and the people were believers in Christian monarchy. And no one had an interest in exposing the systemic weakness of the imperial regime. The people too wanted a strong emperor, so long as he was to their liking. "Obey the emperor—until you decide to overthrow him!" could not be a doctrine of power for either rulers or subjects. The reason why these two forces—republican and theocratic, the one ideological and the other rhetorical—peacefully coexisted is because they operated on quite different levels to perform complementary types of work: the one rhetorically ameliorated the reality created by the other. To see this we need to survey the origin of the imperial idea in late antiquity in order to explain its function and thereby restrict its operational and ontological scope. It was never an "ideology" (as defined in Chapter 1) by which the Roman polity ever governed itself. It was a mode of rhetorical damage control that emerged during the third century and was retained thereafter in part because Byzantine politics was essentially a state of perpetual potential revolution, especially when it became more republican after the emperors settled in Constantinople. In order to explain the origin of the imperial idea as a reaction to increasing instability, this section will focus initially on material from the third and fourth centuries, when the distinctively Byzantine balance between theocratic and republican was forged.

A striking impression that emerges from J. R. Fears's survey of the idea of divine election in antiquity is that it was usually invoked to bolster an authority that was at risk of being perceived as illegitimate, for example, after a civil war or a dramatic change of rule.[30] "The need for supernatural legitimation grew less" as the violence was forgotten after Augustus.[31] But a significant shift occurred in the disastrous third century, when the imperial order experienced a sustained crisis of legitimacy. From the beginning of the third century to the end of the fourth, the emperors were mostly with the armies in the field and not in regular contact with the senate and the people of Rome, and this destabilized the normal processes of legitimation. To be sure, in Roman tradition the armies could act as representative bodies of the republic and thereby legitimate an accession, but too many armies were doing this simultaneously during the third century. In this sense, stability was not restored to the republic until the emperors settled back down in New Rome and gradually drew the entire republic back into the process of legitimation (by 491, as we saw in the election of Anastasios). In the meantime, however, emperors had developed various notions of divine election. Previously that had been one strategy among others and perhaps deployed only in literary texts rather than official proclamations.[32] Many historians have ably charted the course of the late third-century developments. "As the empire's crisis deepened in the middle years of the third century, emperors resorted more fully to rhetoric, becoming unconquerable generals whose actions in war demonstrated the support and manifested the will of a single greatest god."[33] This intensified after other rhetorical strategies had failed and began in force with Aurelian (270–275). Many scholars have shown how divine election mutated from pagan to Christian versions, passing from Aurelian's association with Sol Invictus to the personal identification of Diocletian and Maximian with their patron deities, Jupiter and Hercules, then to Maxentius's association with Mars, and finally to

Constantine, who experimented with Apollo and Sol Invictus before turning to the Christian God (whoever he thought that was).[34] Ray Van Dam has provocatively reinterpreted Constantine's religious shifts not as a discovery and acceptance of Christianity but as ongoing strategic moves designed to set off first himself and then his emerging dynasty from the specific theological self-presentation of his political rivals, the Tetrarchy and its heirs.[35]

Certain conclusions emerge that are not apparent in decontextualized recitations of the imperial idea. First, the imperial idea originated as a response to a systemic crisis in legitimacy that was caused by a combination of military defeat and instability and the departure of the emperors from Rome. At Rome the senate and people could endow them with legitimacy, that is, "the conditions any ruler must satisfy in order for subjects to feel they are being governed by proper authority."[36] Accordingly, "divine election was an ideology of crisis."[37] But as a rhetorical strategy it was retained even after the emperors returned to the capital (New Rome), where it fused with the modes and orders of republican ideology. Therefore, the imperial idea's origin in crisis supports the case that even in Byzantine times it functioned to ameliorate the monarchy's systemic instability. The theocratic idea was pioneered by emperors who needed to place themselves beyond the reach of the armies' whim. When some soldiers attempted a revolution, Aurelian told them that they were deluding themselves if they thought that the fate of emperors was in their hands; for God had given him the purple (he held it up in his right hand) and had appointed the time for him to reign.[38] Moreover, the imperial idea was not distinctively Christian. What we find in Eusebios is only one possible variation of a notion with which pagan and Christian emperors had been experimenting for decades.[39] There was no essential difference when it came to their function in the political sphere. The fixation on Eusebios and his elevation as some kind of Founder of Byzantium has obscured the unoriginality of the basic ideas involved and has reinforced the artificial divide that historians like to postulate between Rome and theocratic Byzantium. In fact, the "imperial idea" was fashioned by self-conscious Roman patriots such as Aurelian, Diocletian, and Constantine. It was a Roman response to crisis that only acquired a Christian face under Constantine. In more recent times, historians are less likely to believe that something fundamental changed in the transition: "Christianity only slightly altered the source of the emperor's sacred quality."[40]

Constantine, after all, was adept at "intertwining Roman and Christian threads," making each appear as the other.[41]

We need to stop relying on interpretations of Eusebios from 1933, far less make them central to modern readings of the Byzantine political sphere. Once certain ideas become ingrained in a field it is difficult to see what they are based on, and recent studies have challenged the image of Eusebios as "Constantine's theological hair-dresser."[42] For example, A. Johnson has argued that Eusebios did not identify with the Roman imperial order or give it a special place in his view of history. The "political theology" that has so preoccupied historians is not found in his early works and was a late attempt to explain what a Christian monarch could be.[43] Eusebios in fact developed his imperial theology gradually: at first he too had attributed Constantine's rise to the army, then to the army and God, then finally to just God, and in part this shift was a result of his attempt to ameliorate the ugly reality of what was in fact a military coup.[44] Right from the start, then, the Eusebian idea was only another way of coping with the realities of Roman imperial politics, realities that were not predetermined by the idea itself. More troubling is the powerful warning issued by Ray Van Dam against reading Eusebios's political theology as normative: his writings about Constantine were a way by which he tried to prop up his subordinationist (non-Nicaean) theology. This entailed blurring distinctions between Jesus and Constantine as agents of God on earth. Whereas "Constantine appropriated Jesus' life to serve his political goals, Eusebios appropriated Constantine's life to serve his theological objectives."[45] Byzantines who read his works closely would have questioned their orthodoxy, and in fact it does seem that Eusebios's Constantinian writings were not popular in Byzantium, which was skeptical of them.[46] All told, there are many reasons to stop treating Eusebios as the Founding Father of Byzantine thought.

The military emperors of the third century developed the notion of divine election partly to insulate the imperial office from the chaos that was election by mutinous armies. In practice, the armies were then playing the major role in most transitions, unless an emperor had managed to impose his will on them and steer the succession. The emperors who created the most stable frameworks for this were also those who invested themselves with various forms of divine authority, that is, Diocletian and Constantine, though it is impossible to ascertain now by what mechanisms and to what degree these "theocratic" ideas influenced the armies' decisions. We do not know how Roman armies made decisions. It is likely that they were impressed only by success, and the theocratic-imperial idea was a way for the emperors to retain and project an aura of success. This led to an overdetermination of imperial legitimacy. On the one hand, according to the norms of the republic, emperors derived legitimacy through acclamation by the army (the Roman people at arms), while, on the other hand, according to the rhetoric that hovered over these transactions, they were also somehow appointed to rule by some deity. It is interesting that no one sought to reconcile these two positions theoretically. They both "worked" in their respective spheres, and apparently that was sufficient.

The theocratic and the republican ideas continued to operate on parallel tracks even after the emperors settled down in New Rome and were appointed by the populace (or by the army and the populace, or the representatives of the republic). As argued above, the monarchy was more republican in the middle Byzantine period than the military emperors had been in late antiquity. But no unified theoretical model emerged to reconcile the two incommensurate sources of imperial authority. One might have argued, for instance, that the will of God was manifested in the people's choice (*vox populi vox dei*), but the Byzantines did not develop a theory as to how this worked, or why God was working through such instruments. There was no theology of history and no Old Testament model that might help correlate the two.[47] At most our sources lump the two options together, without telling us how they were related. At his accession, Anastasios thanked the many constituent elements of the republic for elevating him to the throne and then added a genitive absolute clause on the "good will of the Holy Trinity."[48] At his accession, Justin I claimed to have received the monarchy "by the judgment of almighty God and your universal vote."[49] In his laws, Justinian claimed both that the Roman *politeia* had been entrusted to him by God *and* that imperial authority stemmed from the *lex regia*.[50] The sixth-century anonymous *Dialogue on Political Science* says that imperial authority "is given by God and offered by the citizens," though elsewhere it mentions only the citizens or only God.[51] To close with a random example from the middle period, Nikephoros III Botaneiates reproached the rebel Bryennios for flouting the grace of God that had made him, Botaneiates, emperor and then implies that Bryennios should have learned the will of God from the fact that the people of Constantinople rejected him when his armies approached the walls.[52] The conjunction is too vague: we do not learn how one source of authority operated through the other (in whichever direction). How would one know whether the will of God had changed independently of what the people were saying? Did it mean that the people were basically infallible in their political choices? Did it mean that God worked through rebellions in which oaths to him were broken—so long, that is, as the rebel was successful? "No text gives explicit details concerning the process by which the divine will manifested itself or was communicated,"[53] and we can see why, given the challenges that such a text would have overcome in order to bridge these two incommensurate modes of thought.

This is a real problem. The Byzantines thought a lot about God and had developed a fairly elaborate theory about his nature and role in history. Yet they never explained why he would choose to have his deputy on earth appointed in such a way. Arguably no one constructing a theocratic-imperial regime would choose to premise everything on the operation of populist-republican principles. It is clear that we are dealing here with a political sphere whose fundamental and preexisting ideological framework was republican, onto which had been superimposed a theocratic rhetoric. The first had to do with the premises that shaped the behavior of all the agents involved (their intuitive understanding of how power worked between rulers and ruled), the second with how they liked to imagine their political order in its optimum state once the dust had settled. It is not as though the imperial idea in any way challenged or questioned what the people had done in their acclamations and de-acclamations: to the contrary, it gave their actions divine validity. The *populus* too wanted its choices to be cast as divinely approved, so long, that is, as the divine will operated in retrospect.

Some scholars have recognized this "dual track" of legitimacy in the Byzantine imperial tradition,[54] but its existence has made attempts to explain the culture problematic. Some scholars first explain how the emperors were created by human "electors" and then separately discuss the imperial idea, without showing how the two were related.[55] This can have peculiar effects. Consider the work of Aikaterine Christophilopoulou. In her magisterial survey of the election and appointment of the emperors, she almost forgets the imperial idea, adding it as an afterthought albeit calling it "an essential element." But if it was such an essential element, why does it not feature in her long analysis of the institutions and events? Even when she does mention it, she treats it basically as mere public relations.[56] On the other hand, in a general book on the Byzantine state, she offers a top-down approach that defines the imperial position in terms of the usual theocratic notions.[57] Because she does not mention the *politeia* and begins from the Archimedean point of absolute imperial power, she can take the idea that the emperor had to rule on behalf of his subjects as a *limitation* on his power rather than as its very definition and purpose. This is a common mistake produced by the illusory isolation in which the imperial idea places the emperor from the rest of the republic.

Other scholars seem to want to invent their own "grand unified theories," for example, by having recourse to the western trope *vox populi vox Dei*. But this does not appear in Byzantine sources,[58] and the problem with this approach is deeper still. Creating theories that bridge the republic and God blurs the fact that they operated on different historical, rhetorical, and indeed cognitive levels; they should not be interconverted and homogenized. However, few historians even do that because most omit or are not aware of the republican dimension, or think that it was too attenuated in late antiquity and even more so in Byzantium. This is true of Sabine MacCormack's otherwise brilliant evocation of the rhetorical ideals associated with imperial ceremonies, in *Art and Ceremony in Late Antiquity*. She accepts the theological rhetoric of the texts as the deep-seated ideology of her subjects (a move facilitated by the "religious turn" taking place at that time in the study of late antiquity). Therefore, while her texts often allude to the ideology of the republic, she focuses almost exclusively on the religious dimension. She even dismisses the role of the people as a "quasi-fiction"[59] (as if the imperial idea were not a *complete* fiction) and perpetuates the mistake of seeing Byzantium as more theocratic than the empire of late antiquity (so she is surprised that "the element of the emperor's election by the people was never dropped").[60] But sometimes she does see the imperial idea as a way to ameliorate the tensions caused by the ways in which the Roman empire operated. For example, she suggests that the imperial idea enabled the various holders of power to project a consensus after a contentious election.[61] This is a good suggestion. The imperial idea was a rhetorical space in which all relevant parties could, without loss of face, signal their willingness to support the regime—until they chose not to. Again, the republic produced the results and the imperial idea then tried to contain the damage, hide tensions, and put the best face on what had happened.

Some of the texts asserting the imperial idea are so defensive that we can apply to them the adage "Never believe anything until it is officially denied." For example, one panegyrist claimed, "*No* random agreement of men, nor some unexpected burst of popularity, made you emperor."[62] "Do *not* think that the soldiers were the masters of such a momentous appointment; rather, the election comes down from above," claimed another.[63] "God is giving you this rank, *not* I."[64] "The emperor does *not* receive his crown from men, or through men, but from God."[65] One emperor made these denials himself, stressing that it was *not* the hands of the many, or weapons, or speeches that had made him emperor, but the Lord's right hand.[66] This, then, qualifies as a rhetorical *topos*. In its own way, it aimed to bridge the theoretical gap between the republican and the theocratic claims to power that emperors enjoyed, albeit in different contexts. If we want to convert these statements into history, we have to realize that they are revealing a deep anxiety about the relationship between the two: the theocratic was always in danger of being undermined by the republican, in practice as well as in theory (hence the constant denials). The latter were trying to counter precisely what everyone was thinking had happened. When G. W. Bush stridently proclaimed that the Iraq war had "*not* been in vain," his statement in fact reveals that large parts of the elite and the population at large had come to believe exactly that. "The affirmation of any authority tends to become shriller the more seriously that authority is contested."[67] Panegyrical orations, studied within their immediate historical context, can often be seen as short-term crisis-management. Sometimes they failed to rally support.[68]

Let us step back and put our conclusions into perspective. Byzantium was a republican and not a "constitutional" monarchy. While there were no regular legal mechanisms by which the people could exercise power, there were also no formal agreements that could shield an emperor from the anger of the people or other elements of the republic when they had recourse to extralegal measures. Revolution was the permanent but irregular mechanism by which the republic acted against individual emperors. Politics in Byzantium oscillated between monarchical "normalcy" and republican revolution, and in each state everyone had their eyes fixed on the other. The best protection against rebellion was popularity.

The dynastic principle could never take permanent hold because it could always be undone by a reassertion of the republican option. As Tacitus famously declared,[69] the secret was out soon after Augustus that emperors could be made anywhere, and eventually that they could be undone on a whim. It was in these circumstances that emperors at the end of the third and the beginning of the fourth century formulated theological notions of their imperial status whose function was to elevate the institution out of the radical insecurity in which it was mired and enable the emperors to govern with authority. The imperial idea did not guarantee protection, of course, but it may have raised the bar for those considering rebellion. It is hard, however, to measure the degree of its success: we know little about why subjects rebelled against emperors when they did; it is impossible to know why they did not when they did not. So we cannot measure the effectiveness of the imperial idea at stabilizing the institution compared to other variables (for example, Diocletian and Constantine also protected the empire against foreign enemies and were generally popular emperors).

The Roman tradition authorized the use of power solely in the interests of the republic. But from the start of the empire, imperial power was irregular and hard to define. Eventually it also became precarious, once the secret was out, and it is "unwise to speak openly of the executive as an errand boy, for to hurt the executive's pride would diminish his utility."[70] This is what happened in the crisis of empire, when emperors were elevated to satisfy the whims of some provincial army, and then just as quickly deposed. This was the context in which both Aurelian and Diocletian matured. But all Romans wanted a useful, stable, and powerful executive, though they also claimed the right to have a say in the transition of power. The imperial idea and its associated ceremonial apparatus were parts of an attempt to recast the emperor as the executive of a more stable, exalted, and indeed divine power: "ceremonial gives euphemization an air of plausibility."[71] Still, the imperial idea never displaced the republican foundations of Roman politics in Byzantium, nor is there any evidence that it was supposed to do so.

Most Byzantines held both sets of beliefs, albeit in different contexts. They believed that the emperor was appointed to rule by God *and* that they themselves had the right to depose him *without* impiety. Oaths of loyalty were sacrosanct *and* were ignored when the emperor was a "tyrant," that is, unpopular. They believed that the emperor ruled by divine grace *and* that he was appointed by the people: even though they had no way to explain why divine grace would ever choose to operate in that way, they wanted their choice to be cast as the choice of God. The Byzantines were religiously proud of their monarchs, taking an active part in their exaltation, *and* were ready to believe the worst about them, reviling them in the streets, rioting, and fomenting rebellions. They had, then, at least two modes of "belief," which seem not to have been in communication with each other. Like all people, the Byzantines could switch between codes and "beliefs" in different contexts, depending on a complex array of social norms, situational constraints, and psychological needs, few of which we can recapture.

In psychology and cognitive science it is understood that human beings can simultaneously believe contradictory things, each one becoming operative in a context in which it is psychologically or socially advantageous, without feeling the need to compare them and be puzzled about their inconsistency. This is not some kind of disorder but a description of how most people (and cultures) tend to operate most of the time. The imperial idea, for example, seems to have been switched on when the Byzantines compared themselves to foreigners or when they felt confidence in the regime, that is, when legitimacy had been created by the elements of the republic. It was switched off when they wanted to evaluate him and consider their options, again as members of the republic. Its purpose was to facilitate certain relationships and provide a template for them that the court and the people found advantageous—under certain circumstances. When circumstances changed and the people acted on a different set of assumptions, it is not necessary that they also felt the need to articulate them. That is in part why we have an overtheorized ideal and an undertheorized reality.

The patriarch Photios (ninth century) provides us with many examples of this situational logic, which suggest that we should turn to a modular and situational model for thinking about the secular and the religious in Byzantine politics. For example, Photios presented barbarians as savage heathens when he wanted to rally his flock during one of their attacks, but as pious noble pagans worthy of emulation when he wanted to shame his flock for not being religious enough.[72] Different contexts and different rhetorical goals elicited contradictory positions. Well, in a short treatise cast in the form of a letter, Photios presented a radically *secular* argument for the origin of states that deviated in substantial ways from the imperial idea expressed in panegyrical texts, which viewed the empire of the Romans as a divine instrument for the salvation of mankind. Here Photios states bluntly that

> our Savior and God had no intention to establish political regimes or any of their orders. For he knew, he knew well, that human beings would be able to provide these things for themselves from their own experience, that necessity would easily furnish them with instruction on a daily basis, and that the errors of those who came before would prevent future generations from making the same mistakes ... The Savior's intention was only a concern for the salvation of souls.[73]

What is going on? What caused this Byzantine patriarch to renounce the Christian claim to the Roman empire and cast it as the work of men improving through trial and error? The Christian interpretation of the Roman empire is here shown to have flourished only in the limited space of rhetorical and ceremonial contexts. Outside of that bubble there were competing claims and interpretations. This is exactly the predicament Photios found himself in: he had been asked to refute the arguments of the emperor Julian, among which was that Christianity had contributed nothing to political theory or the foundation of states, including the Roman one, which, Julian insisted, had been founded by pagans.[74] That is why Photios falls back on "the salvation of souls" and attributes the foundation of states to the uninspired fumbling of mere human beings. He turns to sarcasm when he adds that Jesus also did not lay down prescriptions for military tactics, market inspectors, and judges.[75] He mocks and trivializes what he cannot have, like Aesop's fox. In other circumstances, he could project a thoroughly theological interpretation of every aspect of the imperial regime. We see here, however, that a secular view of the origin of states was also not beyond him, so long as it was required by the rhetorical context. Here is another example: in the 1080s, "some Byzantines were suggesting that God was only interested in men's souls, and that their political affairs were a matter of fortune."[76] Their modes of thinking were situational, and this should caution us against treating the imperial idea as anyone's settled belief on the nature of imperial politics. There were many ways of thinking available.

The Secular Republic

Byzantine art historians, whose material is mostly of a religious nature, have been more willing in recent years to question the image of a monolithically pious culture. Anthony Cutler has noted that "only in a mythical Byzantium, always supposed to be universally and unwaveringly devout, is the notion of a biblical parody inconceivable."[77] In *Other Icons,* Henry and Eunice Maguire peer "behind the façade of golden solemnity that the Byzantines so successfully created for themselves, to reveal another world. This other world of Byzantium delighted in novelty and contradiction, glorified blood and violence, looked with fascination on nudity and on abandoned movement."[78] Alicia Walker observes that her field has often played up the Christian elements in Byzantine art and missed the exotic ones, and she postulates the existence of "a sophisticated and informed audience, who would have thought beyond the visual platitudes of official imagery and its message of unchanging universal dominion secured through divine endorsement."[79]

By contrast, Byzantine social, political, and intellectual historians have been reluctant to assume that audiences could have seen past the platitudes, even though such scholars have access to a broad array of sources that are not dominated by religious concerns. An exception was Hans-Georg Beck, who wrote a book on Byzantine eroticism arguing that anything that the Church Fathers might have said about the topic is largely irrelevant for understanding how the culture worked.[80] As we have seen, Beck also pioneered "Roman" ways of looking at Byzantine politics. It is odd that neither of the avenues he opened up has been explored further. Why do we have no other books on Byzantine sexuality? There is more than enough material. About the imperial idea, Beck said that it is difficult to form an impression of its power over people's minds because modern scholarship is too trusting of it. But many of its own spokesmen in Byzantium can be shown to have been skeptical of it (especially when they later turned historian, such as Psellos and Choniates). "The people paid far less attention to such philosophical-theological speculations than most scholars believe today."[81]

There is plenty of material generally to illustrate secular ways of thinking in Byzantium, but scholarship has erected barriers between us and it. Let us go back to Paul Alexander's classic article from 1962 on the "Strength of Empire" as seen by the Byzantines, a work that is cited often and still reprinted. This article contains many spectacularly wrong statements, which in some cases go wrong because Alexander was willing to draw general negative conclusions from limited evidence.[82] Along these lines he also produced a thesis that has proven influential: "The Byzantines attributed the greatness of their empire and capital to their supernatural defenders and therefore had little incentive to develop either a historical analysis of their greatness or a secular theory of their political development."[83] We should not try to save this claim by taking "analysis" and "theory" in a special sense. What Alexander was saying, and what he was subsequently taken to have been saying, was no less than that the Byzantines were incapable or uninterested in thinking in secular terms. This theory has echoed through the decades since. To quote some passages from the leading historians: "In every aspect of their public and private existence, what the Byzantines did was explained in terms of divine providence and justified by recourse to God's will and design."[84] Another scholar invokes anthropological studies of Africa to classify the Byzantines as people "who do not share western concepts of causation" and who, while possibly able to think rationally, preferred to attribute events to demons or to God.[85] More can be cited.[86] These notions are then picked up by nonexperts and recast as follows: "The Byzantines lived their spiritual life with an intensity hardly matched in the history of Christendom."[87]

These statements do not seem to me to do justice to Byzantine society, and even less to its intellectuals, who are the ones mostly targeted here. It sounds as if a set of clichés is being recycled without ever having been tested fully against the evidence. Susan Reynolds, a leading medievalist, has argued for instance that the established notion that people in the Middle Ages were incapable of atheism is not true of medieval mentalities but may count as a type of modern scholarly *mentalité*.[88] The ability to see only one type of evidence is a prejudice. Byzantine authors had a lot to say about their state and the reasons for its success. Some of it was religious and some of it secular, depending on the genre, the needs of the text, and the author's outlook at that moment. We cannot always explain modal switches, but we have to recognize their existence. In one passage, for example, Justinian says that "we do *not* place our trust in weapons, soldiers, our military leaders, or our talents, but rest all our hopes in the providence of the Supreme Trinity."[89] But in another place he states categorically that "sound government depends on two things, arms and laws," while in a third he argues historically that the foundations of the Roman empire were laid by the laws and arms of the praetors.[90] I would again draw attention to the defensive rhetoric of the pietistic version: *not* our weapons or soldiers, which reveals that he expected most of his readers to think precisely of weapons and armies. That is how the paradox gains its force, for Justinian's reign was defined more than any other by laws and arms. If he were to take his claim to its conclusion and disband the armies, trusting in prayer alone, his subjects would think that he had gone mad. As it stands, it has only rhetorical value: I *really* trust in God, so much so that I am prepared to say something that we all know is insane (but I will keep my armies and laws).

In most Byzantine scholarship, however, rhetorical-religious modalities are regarded as essential and primary and taken at face value as definitive of the culture as a whole, while secular ones are relegated to the margins, subsumed under the religious ones, or labeled nonexistent. As Haldon has argued,

> It was only in and through the vocabulary of Christianity, which described the "symbolic universe" of the East Roman world, that Justinian and his contemporaries were able to apprehend their world and act in and upon it . . . Politics are thus always "religious," and religion is always "political" . . . it is all too easy to impose a division between "religious" and "political" or "secular" in modern terms.[91]

Yet our scholarship has its own bifurcated modal logic. When it is defining the *essential* parameters of Byzantine thought it sticks closely to "the vocabulary of Christianity," but when it is trying to explain how the politics worked, it often implies that the Byzantines were acting on the basis of secular assumptions.

For example, Haldon and Brubaker's monumental history of Byzantium in the Iconoclast era defines imperial authority (conventionally) as a theological matter and suggests that Byzantines understood events exclusively in religious terms.[92] Their analysis of the rise of Leon III thus comes as a surprise: "he may have owed his throne largely to the fact that he could present himself effectively as an able general capable of dealing with the Arab threat."[93] The authors have given us no prior warning that there was a forum of public opinion in which such "presentations" were made or any sense of the ideological receptivity of the elite or populace to them. The reader here has to imagine a whole arena of public and private debate, of religious and secular considerations jostling for attention. Are we just meant to assume that secular factors were in play anyway because, come on, they were only people after all? The field has it both ways: it plays up its anthropological credentials by making the Byzantines seem religiously alien to allegedly "modern" mentalities, all the while assuming that those mentalities were in play as a matter of course; no need to bring them into the theory.[94]

Historians take the secular side for granted and highlight the religious aspects in their programmatic statements. But this gives a lopsided view of the culture, because the imperial idea only makes sense within the context of an otherwise secular political sphere, a sphere where Leon's military capabilities (as opposed to those of potential competitors) could seem to be a strong argument for making him emperor to "electors" who had pragmatic choices to make within a distinctively republican political arena.

No book exemplifies these challenges better than G. Dagron's otherwise brilliant *Emperor and Priest,* which many regard as the last word on the position of the emperor. In part this is due to the deceptively comprehensive and ambitious subtitle of the English edition (*The Imperial Office in Byzantium;* the original subtitle was much more accurate: *A Study of Byzantine Caesaropapism*). What Dagron does is trace the history of a single issue, the lingering suspicion that the emperor was some kind of sacral figure. His exposition is superb, but it has to be put in perspective. Few Byzantines, perhaps only a handful, can be shown to have been concerned with this issue, and there are many moments that he wants to press into the service of this theme that do not seem to belong (for example, whenever an emperor shows humility or repentance he takes this as a sign of his bad conscience before the clergy over the "secret" of his sacerdotal qualities). Sometimes Dagron gives the impression that he is tapping into deep levels of the Byzantine mind, but at other times he admits that he is dealing with only a handful of texts.[95] The book is accordingly dominated by a discussion of Old Testament parallels and models. Dagron is candid, albeit in passing, about what he has elided: "the empire existed independently of the emperors . . . in the Roman form of a vast administrative and juridical construction which the sovereign dominated and whose cohesion he ensured without ever becoming entirely identified with it."[96] While he knows that there was a "vast" Roman side to the emperor, he does not deal with it. His book has nothing to say about what emperors did for most of the time or how they were evaluated by their subjects. As a result of this occlusion he can conclude that the emperors, being nothing if they were not the providential mediators between people and God, could be resisted *solely* regarding the sacerdotal aspects of their office;[97] presumably, they were *politically* beyond reach. In reality, however, I do not know of *any* time when an emperor was in danger because of his sacerdotal pretensions. Dagron avoids historical sources, concentrating on a few ceremonies that *may* have revealed the emperor in the guise of a "king of the sacrifices" (or the like).

So while we still lack a study of the imperial office in Byzantium, the impression has been reinforced that the emperor must be studied primarily as a religious figure, in relation to the Church. Even before Dagron's book, in *Art and Ceremony in Late Antiquity* MacCormack had cited evidence for the emperor's sacerdotal functions in order to conclude that "it is misleading to distinguish between the secular and the ecclesiastical spheres in early Byzantium, for the distinction cannot be firmly anchored in the evidence."[98] This depends on what "firmly" means. In this case it seems to mean "in every possible case with no instance of ambiguity," which is too high a standard. Besides, even evidence that shows that the emperor was both a religious and a secular ruler does not necessarily mean that general distinctions *could not ever be* made; rather, it means only that in the case of the emperor they *were not always made* because he combined both types of authority. In fact, the distinction between the secular and the ecclesiastical can be "anchored in the evidence" quite well. I offer by way of illustration a site where Roman-political and Christian-ecclesiastical were clearly distinguished by the Byzantines, namely, in their evaluation of emperors.

Evaluations of the job performance of numerous emperors distinguished between the secular and the ecclesiastical spheres, especially when there were noteworthy deviations between the two from the author's standpoint (whether their verdicts were correct or not is beside the point; the first one is especially fantastic). Constantius II was an Arian heretic but was well intentioned toward his subjects, just in his verdicts, restrained in his life style, and careful in making appointments to offices.[99] Julian was condemned for his apostasy by many Christian writers, yet they conceded that he exhibited good qualities as a ruler and was "necessary to the republic."[100] Anastasios was also good at the "management of public affairs" (διοίκησις of the πολιτικὰ πράγματα), but not good when it came to his religious beliefs (δόξα εἰς τὸ θεῖον).[101] Leon V was "impious in religious matters" but "a very competent administrator of public affairs" and "a great provider to the Roman republic."[102] Theophilos was condemned as an iconoclast heretic and persecutor but praised for his justice as a ruler and his magnificent buildings.[103] After his death, his widow Theodora tried to secure his absolution by reminding the monks whom he had persecuted that "you all know what a just judge he was and how well he governed everything (πάντα καλῶς διοικῶν), but he had this one heresy, which he renounced as he was dying."[104] The *kaisar* Bardas was energetic in handling the affairs of state, but no one would call him good for the Church.[105] Interestingly, the emperor Trajan was upheld in Byzantium as a model emperor without being overtly Christianized.[106]

The view that there *could be no* distinction between secular and religious matters in Byzantium requires that the Byzantines could not tell the difference between religious matters and nonreligious matters, which is implausible. Their view of what was and was not religious certainly shifted over time, or may have been debated at any one time, but the same is true today. It does not mean that they could not tell the difference, by and large, in the context of their own lives. To be sure, it would also be implausible to maintain that there was a categorical distinction between the two, that they were kept strictly and absolutely separate. No one is arguing for "separation," which is a normative ideal, not a conceptual distinction. There is no reason to believe that average Byzantines could not make such a distinction. It was not some esoteric doctrine available only to those with an education. It is likely that it was basic to the ongoing popular assessment of each emperor. At this point we must revisit the Roman *politeia* and remember some basic facts about its relation to the Christian community and the Church.

The Roman polity was only accidentally Christian, and this too created a conceptual asymmetry between the two communities, Roman and Christian: they could at most overlap but were not identical because they were different *kinds* of communities, defined by different sets of criteria. Early Christian writers, including Eusebios and Church Fathers such as Gregorios of Nazianzos, had written about Romans and Christians belonging to different *politeiai* and having different sets of laws (human and divine).[107] "It is only from the early fourth century that we can describe Christianity as Roman religion."[108] But even then the transition was rough and left permanent scars. Diocletian and the Tetrarchy had tried in the Great Persecution to make their religion normative for all Romans throughout the empire, to link it, that is, to the very definition of what it meant to be a Roman.[109] They failed. Galerius was the first emperor to make Christianity an acceptable religious option for a Roman, and this union was taken further by Constantine, possibly following the philosophy of his court professor Lactantius. The latter's *Divine Institutes* were a massive effort to harmonize the Roman and Christian *res publicae*,[110] an effort that was not easy or ever entirely successful. I will argue in a separate study that Christian and Roman remained conceptually distinct categories in Byzantium. For all that they often overlapped in practice, there were too many recurring and permanent reminders of their difference for the Byzantines ever to forget it. Anyone who knew any history or ever went to church knew that the Romans were once not Christians. And while most Romans in Byzantium were Christians, not all Christians were Romans.

Mention of the two sets of laws, the two *politeiai,* points to what today is called the problem of Church-State relations. This is a huge issue which I do not intend to enter here.[111] We lack a basic study of the question for Byzantium,[112] and there does not appear to be an ongoing discussion either. In this sense, Dagron's *Emperor and Priest* has blocked further discussion here by derailing the question: rather than examine how institutions functioned in practice, or the debates over where the line lay between sacred and secular, Dagron diverted the field onto the esoteric topic of the emperor's sacred persona. His conclusions are themselves so esoteric that many scholars would rather just avoid the question than get tangled up in them. I know this because I am among them. But the fact remains that we have so many texts which state that *this* is secular and *that* belongs to the Church. I will mention a few more to counter the assumption that "the distinction cannot be firmly anchored in the evidence."

The distinction is sometimes made casually, because it was usually taken for granted. It did not require great conceptual leaps. To give some examples at random, Constantine distinguished between strife within the Church and in the "outside" world.[113] Photios says that the historian Sergios covered the events both of the *politeia* and of the *ekklesia*.[114] Writers also distinguished between different types of authority—secular and ecclesiastical—and their respective bearers; this was a distinction based in the law.[115] Sacred law, that is, the canons of the Church Councils, was theoretically distinct from imperial law, even when the emperors chose to ratify the former and so endow it with imperial authority; Leon VI calls them *to hieron* and *to politikon*.[116] Psellos regularly distinguished between political (πολιτικώτερα) and spiritual (πνευματικώτερα) ways of life.[117] In his *Defense of Eunuchs*, Theophylaktos of Ohrid (or his rhetorical persona) brands as "secular" (κοσμικὴν) and as "inspired by the rulers of this world" the laws of the ancient emperors that outlawed the making of eunuchs. Their goal was to increase the population of the *politeia* and have more soldiers. Constantine, by contrast, annulled laws that penalized the childless and promoted religious values.[118] The argument draws a strong contrast between secular motives and pagan emperors (on the one hand) and religious motives and Christian emperors (on the other).

The distinction between sacred and secular was always at hand and used in different ways depending on the argument that each author was making. The debate over the proper relation between the two, especially at the level of State and Church, generally rose to the surface only when it was being contested. There was a vigorous exchange of ideas about this in Byzantium, because every claim was an implicit or explicit challenge to someone else's view or practice.[119] Ioannes of Damascus argued that emperors should be obeyed when it came to "those matters which pertain to our daily lives, for example taxes," but not when it came to doctrine.[120] Theodoros the Stoudite told Leon V to keep for himself "the ordering of the *politeia* and the armies, but leave the Church alone."[121] Many more such statements can be cited from clerics who felt they were on the losing side of some imperial intervention.

So while there was no single doctrine immutably fixing the exact limits of the sacred and the secular, there was an ongoing debate about the issue, which reveals that it was always perceived as a problem. But such a problem could have existed only if the theoretical distinction between the two was *fundamental* to the culture as a whole; the problem would not have existed if the distinction were nonexistent, as so many historians state.[122] Moreover, there was no issue at all about most aspects of secular life. The debate concerned largely the right of the emperor to intervene in certain aspects of religious life, and only under specific circumstances. Most of what the emperor did elsewhere, including most of the political sphere, was understood as secular and thus not problematic. (There was a debate also about the extent to which clergy could participate in certain state activities, especially war and capital punishment, and this drew boundaries from the other side.)[123]

The polity of the Romans was always inflected religiously, whether in a pagan or Christian way, but it was not defined by religion, much less by any particular religion. During its long history, Roman identity survived through many religious developments, shifts, and conversions. The Christian Church and its religious modes started out as non-Roman but eventually became essential to the republic. Still, they never constituted its totality. The republic was constituted as a political and not a religious community. It was secular not in the sense that it *excluded* religion through some kind of modern "separation" (a red herring), but in that it was not *defined* by it. Being Orthodox was only one aspect of being a Roman in the Byzantine republic, a necessary one perhaps in the minds of most but not a sufficient one. In fact, to the degree that the Church was a "department of state" and mostly subject to the authority of imperial institutions—to a degree that we still do not understand—the polity subsumed its religion as an attribute and property of itself.[124] We saw in Chapter 1 how Syrianos (in the ninth century) included priests among the many constituent elements of the *politeia*, alongside lawyers, merchants, soldiers, and others, each of whom promoted the common good in his own way.[125]

Some Byzantines thought piety was a more important virtue for their rulers to have, others less. Some chose to devote more of their lives to religion, others less. There were other things to do than be Christian. Consider Petronas, the uncle of the emperor Michael III and a leading general of his age. When he was about to die, a friend begged the holy man Antonios to pay him a visit. But Antonios refused, saying, "These secular types don't keep faith" (οἱ κοσμικοὶ πιστὰ οὐ φυλάσσουσι). Eventually he went, whereupon Petronas told him, "Holy father, I am dying." Antonios: "It is not a Christian man who is dying." Petronas: "I confess that I am a Christian, though I am all too aware that I have never done what Christians should do."[126] The same could be said by many or even by most Byzantines, though their views have not survived, unlike the views of saints and bishops.[127]

Therefore, in looking at Byzantium as a political culture, I agree with what Ray Van Dam has recently written (about Constantine no less), namely, that we can and must "discard the obsession with Christianity . . . the single-minded focus on Christianity."[128] I would like to close with a survey of some Byzantine secular thinking regarding the strength of the empire, which refutes Paul Alexander's negative thesis. I suspect that imperial planners thought in secular terms as a rule, but we can rarely glimpse their deliberations. Most of our sources reflect the religious bias of later authors whom religious institutions chose to preserve. For example, modern historians are unanimous that one of the factors that enabled the Byzantine state to survive was its efficient tax system. A vast apparatus was deployed to operate it, but we have only the barest records from it. Here again we run into the gap between what we know was the case and what surviving sources say. Yet if Alexander was right and the Byzantines could not think in secular terms, how did they operate this fiscal system? Fortunately we do not have to guess: the emperors themselves and many other writers are on record. I quoted Justinian on the importance of arms and laws above. Not only could the Byzantines think in secular terms about both the strength and failures of their state, they regularly linked their thoughts on these topics to the conception of the Byzantine republic to which this book has been devoted. I will focus first on their fiscal system, then move to other secular aspects of Byzantine strength.

It was well understood that the state needed money to carry out its basic functions. Justinian explained that tax evasion threatened the cohesion of "our *politeia*."[129] In 566 his successor Justin II noted that the bankrupt imperial finances he had inherited were jeopardizing the ability of the army to perform.[130] Basileios I complained to the senate upon his accession that there was not enough money to pay public obligations.[131] Alexios I found himself facing the Norman invasion with no money and so no army.[132] In 569 Justin II had explained at length how taxes worked, affirming, in the process, the impersonality of the republic (note the highlighted words):

> These provisions relate not only to governors; they also apply to the assessors and officials of every magistrate, no matter who he may be . . . our only aim is that the provinces may be governed by good laws and that persons may reside there in safety and enjoy the blessings of justice as dispensed by the governors, and that the public taxes may be collected without controversy; for when this is not done, it will be impossible for the government to be preserved. It is because of the pay re-

ceived by them that soldiers are enabled to resist the enemy and defend citizens from the invasions and cruelty of the barbarians, and protect fields and towns from the attacks of robbers and others living a disorderly life. It is also by means of taxation that the other cohorts receive what is allotted to them, that walls are repaired, cities fortified, public baths warmed, and, finally, the theatres intended for the diversion of our subjects supported. Thus the taxes paid by our subjects are used and expended, partly for themselves, and partly indirectly on their account, *for we do not derive any benefit from them, and are only charged with their administration;* still, we are fully rewarded for our trouble by the infinite blessings which our Lord and Savior Jesus Christ has bestowed upon us through the greatness of his clemency.[133]

This does not reveal a weaker understanding of the basis of empire than the famous and often-quoted statement by Cerialis in Tacitus, namely, that you cannot have peace without soldiers; or soldiers without pay; or pay without taxation.[134] This seems to have been a diachronic maxim of Roman governance.[135]

Leon VI (late ninth century) advised his generals to "be concerned about the farmers. I think that these two pursuits are truly essential for the constitution and permanence of a nation *(ethnos):* farming nourishes and strengthens the soldiers, whereas the military avenges and protects the farmers. The other life-pursuits impress me as second to these" (but in different rhetorical context later in the same text, he puts religion and the priests "above everything else").[136] In his legislation regarding the military lands, Leon's son Konstantinos VII began by stating that "as the head is to the body, so is the army to the *politeia* . . . He who does not subject these matters to great care *(pronoia)* errs with respect to his own safety, especially if he regards the common interest *(to koinon)* as his own realm of security."[137] Even demographic arguments are attested. In his great *Novel* of 934 barring the "powerful" from acquiring lands in village communes, Romanos I recognized the link between population and demography on the one hand and taxes and the military on the other:

For population settlements demonstrate the great benefit of their function—the contribution of taxes and the fulfillment of military obligations—which will be completely lost should the common people disappear. Those concerned with the stability of the state must eliminate the cause of disturbance, expel what is harmful, and support the common good *(to koinon)*.[138]

Other writers also explained how imperial systems of governance worked. In his survey of the different classes contributing to the republic, Syrianos (ninth century) explains the function of the state fiscal system:

> The fiscal system (τὸ χρηματικὸν) was set up to take care of matters of public importance that arise on occasion, such as the building of ships and walls. But it is principally concerned with paying the soldiers. Each year most of the public revenues are spent for this purpose.[139]

He then specifies the skills that fiscal officials must have:

> They must have some knowledge of surveying, of agricultural methods, and of accounting. For the amounts assessed for tax purposes are based upon the area of land, and upon its quality as well, and its productivity in crops or resources in metal. They must be able to estimate the effects of climate, topography [and so on].[140]

John Haldon has written that "the Byzantine army was perceived as a distinct branch of the state apparatus, composed of subjects of the emperor, equipped and supported by the state through its taxes, recruited and paid to carry out a specific and limited set of tasks."[141]

To be sure, it was always possible to argue that what "really" counted was prayer and not money, armies, or alliances, and we saw that even Justinian was prepared to say that.[142] It is more correct to say, rather, that there were rhetorical moments in which some people occasionally deployed such arguments. It is not clear that anyone ever "believed" them or put them into practice; besides, they would have been difficult to evaluate as no one was seriously prepared to test a "prayer only" strategy. When Konstantinos IX decided to dispense with guards and trust only in God, Psellos tried to talk sense into him by saying that ship captains, architects, and generals also trust in God but implement practical measures relating to their art.[143]

Psellos had a secular view of the workings of the empire and offers us a secular explanation for its decline during the eleventh century. Konstantinos IX failed to realize that two things support Roman power, its system of offices and money, plus one more: their intelligent oversight and rational distribution.[144] Too many emperors thought that they were safe so long as they won over the civil officials, but in fact they needed to gain and keep the favor of the populace of the City, the senate, and the armies.[145] (As we have seen, Psellos was entirely correct about this.) When Isaakios Komnenos decided to rebel in Asia Minor, he wisely cut communications to the capital and appropriated the tax revenues in order to pay his army and reward his supporters, but he also made sure that tax registers were kept up to date so that no one would have grievances later.[146] Finally, at the end of the original version of his *Chronographia*, Psellos pauses to look back over the past thirty years (1025–1057) and explain what went wrong with "the body of the republic" (τὸ τῆς πολιτείας σῶμα). He offers an astute argument about the mismanagement of the system of government, focusing on fiscal waste, the multiplication of salaried titles, and the neglect of the armies.[147] It is an entirely secular analysis; not only does Psellos not bring theodicy into it, he consistently criticizes emperors for spending money on monasteries and the like.[148]

The same period of decline was analyzed by Psellos's contemporary and acquaintance Attaleiates. His *History* likewise stressed the theme of irrational mismanagement and blamed the Romans' woes not on God's anger but on their own rotten political culture.[149] He was explicit that heresy and such theological crimes had nothing to do with it: it was all the fault of bad Roman leadership.[150] For example, Konstantinos X paid too little attention to the armies, with the result that provincials were exposed to enemy invasions just as they were seeing their taxes rise.[151] Nikephoros Bryennios's critique of the failures of Nikephoros III Botaneiates likewise revolved around Botaneiates's bad fiscal policies.[152]

Though they are but a sample, the passages and authors presented above demonstrate that the Byzantines could explain the strengths and failures of their empire in more or less the same ways as modern historians. As has been noted in connection with western Medieval Studies, "the ideology presented by [modern] historians of medieval political ideas has sometimes seemed divorced not only from the realities described by historians of medieval politics but from the ideas of most of those involved in medieval government."[153]

Many Byzantine historians and other authors too treated the emperor not as God's anointed but as a manager and steward of public resources.[154] This was not because their elite education made them more sophisticated. This book has demonstrated that vigorous debate and dynamic exchanges characterized the political sphere of Byzantium on all levels and at all times. The common people of Constantinople and other major cities could just as easily switch from praising the emperor as God's anointed to protesting against his financial or religious policies, and to insulting him sexually. In his letter of advice to Boris, the king of Bulgaria, Photios says of those who govern that "even a small mistake of theirs is inflated, talked about everywhere by everyone, and so it becomes notorious."[155] Psellos expanded on this idea, explaining that this was because of the acerbic nature of public debate in Byzantium: even if you tried to do good, people would be found to twist it around. Emperors, it seems, could not catch any breaks.[156] We are back to what Cheynet exposed as "the versatility of public opinion and the fragility of imperial power."[157] No emperor could wrap himself in enough God-talk to feel safe from the perils of the republic, and even a decent man could be regarded as inadequate to the managerial tasks of the office.[158] It was understood that emperors were only mortal men with vices and flaws. Probably the most pessimistic thing said by one emperor to another was that "many emperors have lived in this palace, but few have lived in the kingdom of heaven."[159]

In the end, the imperial idea was but one modality in the complex system of roles, rights, and responsibilities that held the republic together and ensured its vitality. We should stop using it as our Archimedean point, for the Byzantines themselves did not. Even when they said they did.

Conclusion

Byzantine Studies is a field that operates on two levels. Its scholars produce excellent work on any specific topic to which they turn their attention, but when they have to say something about how the culture worked as a whole, the basic premises on which it rested, and the ideologies that most of its people accepted, they continue to rely on stereotypes from the 1930s that were produced in questionable ways and that survive today because they are uncritically recycled. They acquire momentum and the status of known facts. The whole of our apparatus of general terms belongs in this category, and I list here the main ones that I intend to interrogate in the sequel: "emperor" and "empire" (do they translate *basileus* and *basileia?*), "multiethnic empire" (but what were the Romans of Byzantium?), and "ecumenical" or "universal" (whose usage by scholars seems to be a modern invention). These concepts have placed a mask on the face of Byzantium; it is time to start peeling it off, layer by layer.

Having invented these categories, we have then ostracized many of the terms by which the Byzantines understood themselves and their place in the world: "Roman" (which did not mean the same as Christian), "secular" (which is a fundamental category of Christian thought), and the one on which this book has focused, the *politeia* or "republic" that constituted the Byzantines' political sphere. An imaginary modern construct labeled "Byzantium," identified with theocracy and absolutism, has come to stand between us and the vibrant political culture of the east Romans. We identify their culture with its religion, first, because various western powers appropriated its Roman legacy during the course of the Middle Ages and denied it to the eastern empire; second, because having such a Christian theocracy of the imagination was good for Enlightenment philosophers to think with, for their own purposes, not because they wanted to understand that specific historical society any better. But unfortunately we still lack a history of Byzantine Studies that would explain how past stereotypes and prejudices have come to constitute the foundations of the field. Byzantium has played the role of "the absolutist Orthodox Christian empire" in the western imagination for so long that it is hard to think of it as anything else. No small dose of Orientalism has been poured into this recipe.

The best way out of this predicament is to reclaim the Roman identity of Byzantium. The norms of the ancient *res publica* were firmly embedded in the ideology of its political sphere. Popular sovereignty lacked institutions of governance but found expression in the continual referendum to which emperors were subject. Politics was the threat of civil war. Legitimacy was popularity. What we call Byzantium was a turbulent, politically dynamic, but ultimately stable monarchical republic in the Roman tradition masquerading, to itself as much as to others, as an imperial theocracy.

Notes

Preface

1. Ostrogorsky, *History,* 27.
2. They include Cyril Mango, Michael Angold, Averil Cameron, and Paul Magdalino.
3. Cameron, *The Byzantines,* 14.
4. This was pioneered by Dölger, "Rom in der Gedankenwelt."
5. A nice phrase by Horden, "The Confraternities," 32.
6. Cameron, *The Byzantines,* 12.
7. Anastos, "Byzantine Political Theory," 13.
8. For example, it informs Runciman's *The Byzantine Theocracy,* though few Byzantinists would go as far as he in stressing the Byzantines' Roman identity.
9. Some of his main ideas were accepted by I. Karagiannopoulos, P. Pieler, E. Chrysos, and I. Medvedev, but their publications on the topic (which are few, mostly not in English, and not always in accessible volumes) have impacted the field even less than his.
10. Chiefly in Beck's *Res Publica Romana* (an essay) and in the first part of *Das byzantinische Jahrtausend.* See the engaging introduction to the man himself by one of his students, Falkenhausen, "Hans-Georg Beck." Few scholars have engaged with his alternate view of the culture, e.g., Fögen, "Das politische Denken der Byzantiner," 78–82, but this discussion is too limited in scope to reach the fundamental problems of interpretation; it does, however, identify problems in the way Beck cast his thesis. A summary of the dispute, which sides mostly against Beck, is in Angelov, *Imperial Ideology,* 11–13; also 253–255, 347.
11. The expression is by Hammer, *Roman Political Thought,* 7.
12. For the early Roman context, see Richardson, *The Language of Empire.*
13. Van Dam, *Remembering Constantine,* 222.
14. Kaegi, *Byzantine Military Unrest,* 6.

15. I would advocate an expanded "early Byzantium" beginning in the second century AD.

1. Introducing the Byzantine Republic

1. Haldon is a rare exception, e.g., in "Toward a Social History," 10–11.
2. In quoting the works of scholars who use the term "ideology" in this sense, I will assume that readers will be able to adjust between their usage and mine.
3. Compare Revell, *Roman Imperialism*, 13: "not in the narrow sense of political ideologies, but in the broader concept of beliefs about how the world should be organized. Ideologies underpinned the shared culture of the empire: ideas [about] the correct ways of living, hierarchies of social position and political power" (also 15; and note the studies cited there).
4. J. Bell Burnell quoted in Richardson, *The Language of Empire*, 6–7. We are interested specifically in the political sphere, not in the many other sites of the culture where other ideologies may have been operative (e.g., in gender relations).
5. Eagleman, *Incognito*, 88.
6. I have benefited from an exchange on this with my colleague Will Batstone, who produced this formulation (pers. comm.).
7. Beck, *Das byzantinische Jahrtausend*, 42.
8. For studies of such texts, see Bell, *Three Political Voices*; Fögen, "Das politische Denken," 72–78; Angelov, *Imperial Ideology*; Triantari, *Πολιτική ρητορική*; Guran, "Une théorie politique." For how I would read these works against the background of the Roman polity, see Kaldellis, "Aristotle's *Politics* in Byzantium." Hans-Georg Beck fell into the trap of these treatises, turning to them in the hope of extracting the norms of the polity.
9. For approaches based on these different bodies of evidence, see Hunger, *Prooimion*, for the legal sources; Treitinger, *Die oströmische Kaiser- und Reichsidee*, and MacCormack, *Art and Ceremony*, for ceremony; while Païdas, *Τα Βυζαντινά «Κάτοπτρα ηγεμόνος»*, 9, believes that the Mirrors hold the key. Ahrweiler, *L'idéologie politique*, and Pertusi, *Il pensiero politico bizantino*, are surveys, conventional in their basic assumptions.
10. This is either explicit in the title, e.g., Kolb, *Herrscherideologie*, or emerges in the course of the discussion, e.g., in Koutrakou, *La propagande impériale*, 49 ("the image of the emperor"); and Angelov, *Imperial Ideology*, throughout.
11. Kazhdan and Epstein, *Change in Byzantine Culture*, 110.
12. I cite two of many possible studies: MacCormack, *Art and Ceremony*, 185, does not pick up on the phrase "according to the wishes of the *res publica*" and focuses, throughout her study, on the theological aspect; Boeck, "Engaging the Byzantine Past," 230, who cites Theophylaktos saying that the

emperor's "basis is the good will of the masses and the concurrence of the people," in support of her view that "the emperor was divinely chosen . . . and derived his power from God."

13. Mango, *Byzantium*, 219.
14. On this point, see now Lilie, "Der Kaiser in der Statistik."
15. James, "Byzantium," 7.
16. Brubaker, "The *Christian Topography*," 3.
17. Reynolds likewise argued that the widespread view that "skepticism was impossible in the Middle Ages" is a function of modent mentalities, not medieval ones: "Social Mentalities."
18. See Troianos, Οι Νεαρές Λέοντος, 17–26. I will cite the *Novels* by number and then by the pages of this edition and translation.
19. See chiefly Michaélidès-Nouaros, "Les idées philosophiques" (who thought highly of Leon); Fögen, "Gesetz und Gesetzgebung" (argues for a symbolic interpretation); eadem, "Legislation und Kodifikation" (on their relation to the *Basilika*); Dagron, "Lawful Society"; Magdalino, "The Non-Juridical Legislation"; and the studies appended to Troianos, Οι Νεαρές Λέοντος, 415–577, who cites additional general studies at 17–18 n. 1.
20. Ἐπεὶ δὲ καὶ ἐν ταῖς κρατούσαις συνηθείαις ἐφάνησάν τινες οὐ παράλογοι οὐδὲ τοιαῦται οἵας ἂν νοῦς συνετὸς ἀτιμάσειε, καὶ ταύτας νόμου προνομίῳ τετιμηκότες, ἀντὶ δὲ συνηθείας ἀλόγου εἰς νόμου πρόσταξιν καὶ τιμὴν ἀνηγάγομεν.
21. In ancient Greek, πολιτεῦσθαι means "no more and no less than conducting oneself as if in a *polis*": Ando, "The Roman City." For the way in which Roman usage began to change the meaning of these Greek terms, see Ando, "Imperial Identities," 38, and later in Chapter 1.
22. For Leon and Justinian, see Prinzing, "Das Bild Justinians I.," 56–57; Magdalino, "The Non-Juridical Legislation"; Tougher, "The Imperial Thought-World"; Troianos, Οι Νεαρές Λέοντος, 445–467.
23. ἄρτι δὲ ὑπὸ συνηθειῶν ἀθεσπίστων καὶ μόνην προβαλλομένων ἰσχὺν τὴν τῶν ὄχλων ἀρέσκειαν, πολλῆς ἐπιγενομένης καινοτομίας.
24. For the same reasoning, see *Novel* 57 (pp. 194–195).
25. *Novel* 18 (pp. 86–89). See also, e.g., *Novels* 48, 57, 66, 95, 100, and the list in Michaélidès-Nouaros, "Les idées philosophiques," 45–50 (= 120–126).
26. *Novel* 19 (pp. 88–93).
27. Dagron, "Lawful Society," 44.
28. *Novel* 38 (pp. 148–149).
29. E.g., *Novels* 25, 99, 107, 108.
30. Εἰ γὰρ ὅπερ πατὴρ τέκνοις, τοῦτο δεῖ τοῖς πολίταις εἶναι τοὺς νόμους, πρὸς ἓν μόνον τὸ συμφέρον καὶ σωτήριον τῶν πολιτευομένων ὁρῶντας . . .
31. See also Beck, *Das byzantinische Jahrtausend*, 45.
32. Lokin, "The Significance of Law," 86; but at 81–82 he toys with theology.
33. *Novels* 58 (pp. 196–197), 91 (pp. 258–259).
34. *Novel* 60 (pp. 200–201).

35. *Novel* 59 (pp. 198–199).
36. *Novel* 19 (pp. 88–89).
37. *Novels* 36 (pp. 142–143) and 67 (pp. 216–217).
38. E.g., *Novels* 30, 46.
39. As noted by Simon, "Legislation," 19–21.
40. Dagron, "Lawful Society," 46–47.
41. Haldon, *Byzantium in the Seventh Century,* 259.
42. Harries, *Law and Empire,* 2–3; for custom and Roman law specifically, see 31–34, citing the relevant passages of the *Corpus,* especially *Digest* 1.3.32–41 and *CJ* 8.52.1–3; in the sixth to eighth centuries, see Haldon, *Byzantium in the Seventh Century,* 266–267; in later commentators, Simon, "Balsamon und Gewohnheitsrecht." For the notion of custom as an unwritten law, see the ancient and Byzantine sources cited by Steinwenter, "Zur Lehre vom Gewohnheitsrechte," 430–431; for the origin of this legal approach to "custom" in the aftermath of the *Constitutio Antoniniana,* see Ando, *Law, Language, and Empire,* 30–34 (previously non-Roman law became, by legal definition, Roman custom after 212).
43. *Basilika* 2.1.41, based on *Digest* 1.3.32: Περὶ ὧν ἔγγραφος οὐ κεῖται νόμος, παραφυλάττειν δεῖ τὸ ἔθος καὶ τὴν συνήθειαν . . . Ἡ παλαιὰ συνήθεια ἀντὶ νόμου φυλάττεται. Ὥσπερ ἡ θέσις τοῦ νόμου ἢ ἔγγραφός ἐστιν ἢ ἄγραφος, οὕτω καὶ ἡ ἀναίρεσις αὐτοῦ ἢ δι' ἐγγράφου γίνεται νόμου ἢ δι' ἀγράφου, τουτέστι τῆς ἀχρησίας.
44. Konstantinos VII, *Novel* 5 (= *Macedonian Legislation,* p. 118; trans. p. 71). For imperial concessions to legal reality in the Macedonian period, see Oikonomides, "The 'Peira' of Eustathios Romaios," 186.
45. Zonaras, *Chronicle* 17.8: καὶ τό τε στρατιωτικὸν τό τε πολιτικὸν οὐ πρὸς τὸ κρατῆσαν ἔθος, ὃ καὶ νόμον δοκεῖν τοῖς νομοθέταις τεθέσπισται, διεξάγειν ἤθελεν, ἀλλὰ πρὸς τὴν οἰκείαν κρίσιν καὶ τὸ θέλημα ἑαυτοῦ. Magdalino has shown how Zonaras altered the wording in his source (Psellos) to emphasize his legal critique: "Aspects of Twelfth-Century Byzantine *Kaiserkritik,*" 346. So while this is not a reliable assessment of Basileios II, it does reflect the legal opinion of Zonaras.
46. I thank Scott Kennedy for this astute observation.
47. Haldon, *Byzantium in the Seventh Century,* 258–259.
48. A school of (German) "constitutionalist" thought is largely based on the mistranslation of Byzantine *politeia* as "state": Pieler, "Verfassung und Rechtsgrundlagen," 215. But the problem is not limited there. To cite only one of countless instances, see Canepa, *The Two Eyes of the World,* 102, who translates both *politeia* and *to pragma dêmosion* as "state." More examples will be cited throughout this book.
49. See below for the distinction between state and civil society. See also Habermas, *The Structural Transformation,* 4, 12, 19, 29–31.
50. For the date, see Baldwin, "On the Date"; Lee and Shepard, "A Double Life"; Cosentino, "The Syrianos's 'Strategikon'"; and Rance, "The Date"; for the attribution to Syrianos, Zuckermann, "The Compendium."

51. Syrianos, *On Strategy* 4 (pp. 18–19): τῶν πολιτευομένων τὸ πλῆθος κατὰ τὸ ἄοπλον μέρος.

52. Leon VI, *Novel* 27 (pp. 114–115): Καὶ καλῶς πρέπον ὑπάρχει τὴν ὠφέλειαν ἐν κοινῷ κατατίθεσθαι τοὺς ὄφελός τι ἐξευρεῖν τῷ βίῳ σπουδαῖς οἰκείαις προθυμηθέντας ἢ τὸ βούλεσθαι μέχρις ἐνίων προσώπων περιορίζειν, τοὺς δ' ἄλλους ἀμετόχους ταύτης ἐᾶν· πολὺ δὲ πλέον προσῆκε τὴν ἐκ τῶν νόμων εὐεργεσίαν εἶναι κοινήν. Ὥσπερ γὰρ ἐπὶ ἄρχοντος ἀρετῆς, οὕτω καὶ ἐπὶ νόμων ὀφείλομεν κοινῇ τοῦ ἐκεῖθεν ἀπολαύειν καλοῦ ἅπαν τὸ ἀρχόμενόν τε καὶ ὑποκείμενον.

53. We naturally tend to think the same, but modern philosophy has worked hard to sever the link between *is* and *ought*. See MacIntyre, *After Virtue*.

54. Corippus, *In Praise of Justin II* 2.175–274 (*res publica*: 2.245) (trans. pp. 97–99).

55. *Geoponica*, preface 6: εἰδὼς εἰς τρία ταῦτα τὴν πολιτείαν διῃρημένην, στρατείαν τέ φημι καὶ ἱερωσύνην καὶ γεωργίαν. The preface is contemporary, unlike most of the contents of this collection. See, in general, Lemerle, *Byzantine Humanism,* 332–336. According to Lydos (sixth century), the "custom among the Romans used to be to order their *politeia* in three parts," the soldiers, the farmers, and the hunters: *On the Months* 4.158.

56. Attaleiates, *History* 281, at least in the eyes of the emperor Nikephoros III Botaneiates; see Vryonis, "Byzantine ΔΗΜΟΚΡΑΤΙΑ," 309–312.

57. Leon VI, *Taktika* pr. 3: τῶν περὶ τὴν πολιτείαν πραγμάτων and τὰ Ῥωμαίων πράγματα.

58. *Naumachika for the patrikios and parakoimomenos Basileios,* pr. 1 (p. 61): τῷ βίῳ λυσιτελεῖν οἶδε καὶ συνιστᾶν πολιτείαν; for the date, Mazzucchi, "Dagli anni di Basilio," 304–306.

59. Theophanes Continuatus, *Konstantinos VII* 14 (p. 446): πολλῶν δὲ ἐν τῇ πολιτείᾳ ἡμῶν καλῶν καὶ ἀξιεπαινέτων γνώσεις καὶ λογικαὶ τέχναι καὶ ἐπιστῆμαι, τούτων οὐκ οἶδ' ὅπως ἀμεληθέντων καὶ παροραθέντων τί σοφίζεται ὁ φιλοσοφώτατος ἐκεῖνος νοῦς; . . . καὶ τὴν πολιτείαν Ῥωμαίων τῇ σοφίᾳ κατεκόσμησεν καὶ κατεπλούτισεν.

60. *Eisagoge* 3.8 (p. 242) (formerly known as *Epanagoge*): Τῆς πολιτείας ἐκ μερῶν καὶ μορίων ἀναλόγως τῷ ἀνθρώπῳ συνισταμένης, τὰ μέγιστα καὶ ἀναγκαιότατα μέρη βασιλεύς ἐστι καὶ πατριάρχης. In general, see Troianos, *Οι πηγές του βυζαντινού δικαίου,* 171–176; for the authorship, see Schminck, *Studien,* 14.

61. Psellos, *Encomium for Konstantinos Leichoudes,* p. 399 (trans. p. 93): ἐπειδὴ πολυμερὲς αὐτῷ τὸ τῆς βασιλείας ἔδοξε πρᾶγμα, καὶ τὸ μὲν πρὸς μάχας εὔθετον καὶ πολέμους ὑπερορίους, τὸ δὲ πρὸς εἰρήνην ῥέπον καὶ οἰκονομίαν πραγμάτων, καὶ ἄλλο πρὸς ἄλλό τι ὁρῶν, τῷ μὲν ἐφίστησι στρατηγούς, τῷ δὲ δικαστάς, τῷ δὲ ῥήτορας, τῷ δὲ συμβούλους δεξιούς· καὶ ἵνα μὴ διασπᾶτο τὸ κράτος τοῖς μέρεσι, μηδὲ ἡ μία τῶν ὅλων ἀρχὴ ἀναγκαίως συνδιαιροῖτο τοῖς πολλοῖς μερισμοῖς, ἐγνώκει καὶ συνάψαι τὰ πολλὰ ταῦτα εἰς ἕνα δεσμόν.

62. Psellos, *Chronographia* 7.51–59.

63. Psellos used the ailing body of his emperors as a parallel metaphor for this development: Jouanno, "Le corps du prince," 217: a symbolic image, the emperor becomes *un corps politique*.

64. Psellos, *Chronographia* 7.55, with an acknowledgment that he is switching metaphors.

65. E.g., Attaleiates, *History* 44, 121, 135.

66. For this sense of *politeia*, see Aristotle, *Politics* 3.6, 4.1; Plutarch, *On Monarchy and Democracy and Oligarchy* (= *Moralia* 826a–827c), with a brief introduction defining other senses of the term; see Ruppel, "Politeuma"; Romilly, *The Rise and Fall of States*, 30–40; Hankins, "Exclusivist Republicanism," 456.

67. Adams, *Bilingualism*, 471; also Ando, "Was Rome a Polis?" 15, and the studies cited there. In general, see Mason, *Greek Terms*, 202.

68. The preceding terms were also used in the Greek translation of Eutropius's *Breviarium* made in the late fourth century: Tribolis, *Eutropius Historicus;* Fisher, "Greek Translations," 189–193; and Roberto, "Il *Breviarium* di Eutropio." Important here are the Greek versions of Justinian's *Novels* and other legal texts, which translate *res publica* as *politeia*. For ancient inscriptions, see Sherk, *Roman Documents*.

69. Lind, "The Idea of the Republic," 46–51, is not as useful as one would hope and has a "Republican" bias (see below). See also Drexler, "Res publica"; Suerbaum, *Vom antiken zum frühmittelalterlichen Staatsbegriff*.

70. Flower, *Roman Republics*, 12.

71. Cicero, *Republic* 1.39 (I have here preferred the Keyes trans. p. 65): *res publica res populi, populus autem non omnis hominum coetus quoquo modo congregatus, sed coetus multitudinis iuris consensu et utilitatis communione sociatus*. See also 3.43; Augustine, *City of God against the Pagans* 2.21, 19.21, 19.24; Isidorus of Seville, *Etymologiae* 9.4.2.

72. See, e.g., Sharples, "Cicero's Republic"; Frede, "Constitution and Citizenship." There are some classical authors in which *koinon* or *politeia* veers near to what a Roman would call a *res publica* (e.g., Lysias and Demosthenes), but usually only because they are using the term vaguely without specifying that they mean *democratic* values and institutions, i.e., the *politeia* of their city.

73. Cicero, *Republic* 1.42 (I here use the Rudd trans. p. 20); See also Augustine, *City of God against the Pagans* 2.21, 19.21, 19.24.

74. Schofield, "Cicero's Definition," 191–193.

75. Cicero, *Republic* 1.54, 2.43.

76. Cicero, *Pro Sestio* 137: "They established the Senate as the guardian, and president, and protector of the republic; they chose the magistrates to depend on the authority of this order, and to be, as it were, the ministers of this most dignified council; and they contrived that the Senate itself should be strengthened by the high respectability of those ranks which came nearest to it, and so be able to defend and promote the liberties and interests of the common people" (Yonge trans.).

77. Skinner, "The State"; see also "A Model of Sovereignty" in Chapter 4 for Rousseau.
78. Hankins, "Exclusivist Republicanism."
79. Schofield, "Cicero's Definition." For the incommensurability of Greek and Roman theoretical vocabulary on this point, see Ando, "Was Rome a Polis?" 7–8, 13–16.
80. *Dialogue on Political Science* 5.41.
81. Gowing, "The Imperial Republic."
82. Ando, *Law, Language, and Empire,* 114.
83. Bardill, *Constantine,* 18 (for "monarchical republic").
84. Flower, *Roman Republics,* 19; see 10 for modern usage. See also 15: "Roman history has not well been served by a simplistic and sharply drawn dichotomy between 'republic' and 'empire' as chronological terms."
85. *Digest* 1.11.
86. For a typological survey, see Suerbaum, *Vom antiken zum frühmittelalterlichen Staatsbegriff.*
87. For the debate over what Augustus might have meant by *res publica,* see Gowing, *Empire and Memory,* 4–5, citing previous scholarship.
88. Tacitus, *Annals* 1.3.7: *quotus quisque reliquus qui rem publicam vidisset?* Syme, *The Roman Revolution,* 513: "his purpose was expressly to deny the Republic of Augustus." See also Caesar in Suetonius, *Julius* 77.
89. Their story is told by MacMullen, *Enemies,* 18–45.
90. Tacitus, *Annals* 1.7: *Tiberius cuncta per consules incipiebat, tamquam* vetere *re publica et ambiguus imperandi.*
91. Tacitus, *Annals* 1.9.5.
92. On retrospective views of Republican "freedom," see the sources and studies discussed in Sion-Jenkis, *Von der Republik zum Prinzipat,* 131–158; and Gowing, *Empire and Memory,* 24–25, 78–79; Hankins, "Exclusivist Republicanism," 457 (*res publica* and *libertas* not the same in Livius); Gallia, *Remembering the Roman Republic,* 17–18, 35.
93. E.g., Sarris, *Empires of Faith,* 8. Note how Gallia, *Remembering the Roman Republic,* 23–24 gets tangled up between *res publica* and *libertas,* but that is only because he thinks the former means "a form of government." Finally, he seeks refuge: "technically speaking, the *res publica* continued to exist after Actium." (His book is otherwise an excellent study.)
94. Tacitus, *Annals* 1.2.
95. Gowing, *Empire and Memory,* 43; in general on the continuity of the *res publica,* 34–48.
96. Eutropius, *Breviarium* 7.9–10; for his Greek translations, see n. 68 above.
97. Cline and Graham, *Ancient Empires,* 220. See also Flower, *Roman Republics,* 98: "a system of one-man rule that provided a much more stable and equitable administration of the provinces."
98. Cicero, *Republic* 5.2. This was noted by Augustine, *City of God against the Pagans* 2.21. Roman political debate, under both the Republic and the empire,

was always about the current state of the *res publica;* e.g., Batstone and Damon, *Caesar's Civil War,* 41, 49, 54, 58–60.

99. Lind, "The Idea of the Republic," 49 n. 17.

100. See, e.g., Eder, "Augustus and the Power of Tradition," 83–84; Winterling, *Politics and Society.*

101. Flower, *Roman Republics,* 155.

102. Toner, *Homer's Turk,* 107–108, 123. I am aware of no proof that Orthodox Christians are easier to cow than ancient pagan Romans.

103. Heather, *The Fall of the Roman Empire,* 23. As far as I can tell, a total ignorance of the Byzantine sources lies behind this, and a reliance on F. Dvornik (for whose work see Chapter 6).

104. Pazdernik, "Justinianic Ideology," 188–189. The textual basis for the period-name comes from Aurelius Victor, *De Caesaribus* 39, who noted that Diocletian, like Caligula and Domitian, liked to be addressed as *dominus* and inaugurated a more pretentious courtly style (Victor otherwise admired him). This was vaguely "periodized" by Lydos, *On the Magistracies of the Roman State* 1.4, but to polemicize against Justinian: Kaldellis, "Republican Theory." Alföldi, *Die monarchische Repräsentation,* argued that this change had been long in the making, and effectively folded the Principate into the Dominate; for a lucid exposition of his argument, see Agamben, *The Kingdom and the Glory,* 175–177. Kolb, *Herrscherideologie,* has shown that there was no radical break even at the level of court ceremony and ideology, and de Ste. Croix, *The Class Struggle,* 373, argued against rupture on economic grounds.

105. Despotism: Magdalino, "Court and Capital," 132; theocracy: idem, "Knowledge in Authority," 194.

106. Canepa, *The Two Eyes of the World,* 3. Canepa discusses various attempts to periodize at 228–229 n. 5. For the transition from Republic to Principate, see Ando, "From Republic to Empire," 39–40.

107. Also Seneca, *Letter 71: quidni ille mutationem rei publicae forti et aequo pateretur animo?* Suetonius, *Augustus* 28: a *novus status* of the *res publica* under Augustus; *Claudius* 1.4: Germanicus *pristinum se rei publicae statum, quandoque posset, restituturum.* The Greek equivalents are found in Kassios Dion, *Roman History* 52.7.1: μεταβολῇ πολιτείας; 53.11.1: τῇ μεταστάσει τῆς πολιτείας. See, in general, Sion-Jenkis, *Von der Republik zum Prinzipat,* 20–30 for the Latin authors.

108. Plutarch, *Caesar* 28.6: πολλοὶ δ᾽ ἦσαν οἱ καὶ λέγειν ἐν μέσῳ τολμῶντες ἤδη, πλὴν ὑπὸ μοναρχίας ἀνήκεστον εἶναι τὴν πολιτείαν.

109. Appianos, *Roman History,* pr. 22–23: Γάιός τε Καῖσαρ, ὑπὲρ τοὺς τότε δυναστεύσας καὶ τὴν ἡγεμονίαν κρατυνάμενός τε καὶ διαθέμενος ἐς φυλακὴν ἀσφαλῆ, τὸ μὲν σχῆμα τῆς πολιτείας καὶ τὸ ὄνομα ἐφύλαξεν, μόναρχον δ᾽ ἑαυτὸν ἐπέστησε πᾶσι. καὶ ἔστιν ἥδε ἡ ἀρχὴ μέχρι νῦν ὑφ᾽ ἑνὶ ἄρχοντι.

110. Appianos, *Civil War* 1.4: πόθῳ τῆς πατρίου πολιτείας.

111. Appianos, *Civil War* 1.6: Ὧδε μὲν ἐκ στάσεων ποικίλων ἡ πολιτεία Ῥωμαίοις ἐς ὁμόνοιαν καὶ μοναρχίαν περιέστη. In general, see Bucher, "The Origins, Program, and Composition," especially 431 and n. 51: "I cannot agree that Appian favored the Republic: what he admired in the Romans is independent of the form of their constitution." See also Sion-Jenkis, *Von der Republik zum Prinzipat*, 38–43.

112. Kassios Dion, *Roman History* 53.19.1: ἡ μὲν οὖν πολιτεία οὕτω τότε πρός τε τὸ βέλτιον καὶ πρὸς τὸ σωτηριωδέστερον μετεκοσμήθη· καὶ γάρ που καὶ παντάπασιν ἀδύνατον ἦν δημοκρατουμένους αὐτοὺς σωθῆναι. For his classification and sequence of Roman regimes, see Manuwald, *Cassius Dio und Augustus*, 77–100; Fechner, *Untersuchungen zu Cassius Dios*, 8–11; Rich, *Cassius Dio*; Sion-Jenkis, *Von der Republik zum Prinzipat*, 43–50; in general, Gowing, *The Triumviral Narratives*.

113. Kassios Dion, *Roman History* 56.43.4.

114. Dionysios of Halikarnassos, *Roman Antiquities* 1.8.2: πολιτειῶν τε ἰδέας διέξειμι πάσας ὅσαις ἐχρήσατο βασιλευομένη τε καὶ μετὰ τὴν κατάλυσιν τῶν μονάρχων, καὶ τίς ἦν αὐτῶν ἑκάστης ὁ κόσμος; see also Romulus at 2.3.7–8 and Brutus at 4.72–75. See Pelling, "The Greek Historians of Rome," 254.

115. For a detailed reading, see Kaldellis, "Republican Theory."

116. Georgios Synkellos, *Chronographia* p. 365: καὶ ἐλθὼν εἰς Ῥώμην τὴν τῶν ὑπάτων ἀρχὴν καταλύει σύνεγγυς ἔτι κατασχοῦσαν μετὰ Ταρκύινον Σούπερβον, πρῶτος μοναρχήσας Ῥωμαίων, ἔτι φιλανθρωπότατος γενόμενος τῶν πώποτε βεβασιλευκότων.

117. Georgios Synkellos, *Chronographia* p. 368: Ἀπὸ Γαΐου Ἰουλίου Καίσαρος οἱ μετέπειτα Ῥωμαίων βασιλεῖς Καίσαρες ὠνομάσθησαν, ἀπὸ δὲ Αὐγούστου Αὔγουστοι. ἐπὶ τούτου τὰ Ῥωμαϊκὰ ἤκμασεν.

118. Georgios Monachos, *Chronicle*, v. 1, p. 293: Τὰ δὲ Ῥωμαίων πράγματα διοικεῖτο πρῶην ὑπὸ ὑπάτων ἐπὶ ἔτη τξδʹ ἕως Ἰουλίου Καίσαρος.

119. Georgios Monachos, *Chronicle*, v. 2, pp. 557–558: Οὐαλεντινιανὸς ὁ μέγας τῇ πίστει τῆς εὐσεβείας τέλειος καὶ ἀκέραιος τῇ παλαιᾷ τῆς τῶν Ῥωμαίων βασιλείας αὐθεντίᾳ τὴν πολιτείαν ἐκυβέρνα καλῶς.

120. Psellos, *Historia Syntomos* 8: Ἡ βασιλικὴ Ῥωμαίων πολιτεία διαμείνασα μετὰ τὸν οἰκισμὸν τῆς Ῥώμης ἐτῶν τεσσάρων καὶ τεσσαράκοντα καὶ διακοσίων ἀριθμόν, ἐπὶ δὲ τοῦ τελευταίου βασιλέως Ταρκυνίου τυραννὶς γενομένη, ὑπὸ γενναιοτάτων κατελύθη ἀνδρῶν καὶ παυσαμένης αὐτῇ τῆς μοναρχίας ἤτοι βασιλείας εἰς ἀριστοκρατίαν τὸ κράτος μετέπεσε. See also Dzelabdzic, "Η δημοκρατική Ρώμη."

121. Psellos, *Historia Syntomos* 16: Οὗτος πρῶτος ὁ Καῖσαρ ὕπατος μετὰ Βιβούλου γενόμενος τῶν Ῥωμαίων τὴν ἀριστοκρατίαν εἰς μοναρχίαν μετέστησε καὶ τὴν ὑπατείαν εἰς βασιλείαν μετήλλαξε.

122. Xiphilinos, *Epitome of Kassios Dion*, v. 3, p. 526: τὸ μὲν οὖν σύμπαν οὕτω τὴν ἀρχὴν διῴκησε, λέξω δὲ καὶ καθ᾽ ἕκαστον ὅσα ἀναγκαῖόν ἐστι καὶ νῦν μάλιστα, διὰ τὸ πάμπολυ ἀπηρτῆσθαι τῶν καιρῶν ἐκείνων τὸν καθ᾽ ἡμᾶς βίον καὶ τὸ πολίτευμα, μνημονεύεσθαι· λέγω γὰρ τοῦτο οὐκέτι ὡς ὁ Δίων ὁ

Προυσαεὺς ὁ ἐπὶ τοῦ Σευήρου καὶ Ἀλεξάνδρου τῶν αὐτοκρατόρων γενόμενος, ἀλλ᾽ ὡς Ἰωάννης ὁ Ξιφιλῖνος ἀδελφόπαις ὢν Ἰωάννου τοῦ πατριάρχου, ἐπὶ δὲ Μιχαὴλ αὐτοκράτορος τοῦ Δούκα τὴν ἐπιτομὴν ταύτην τῶν πολλῶν βιβλίων τοῦ Δίωνος συντατόμενος.

123. Zonaras, *Chronicle*, pr. 4: ὡς εἰς τυραννίδα τὴν βασιλείαν ὁ Σούπερβος Ταρκύνιος μεταγαγὼν καθηρέθη . . . ὡς εἰς ἀριστοκρατίαν, εἶτα καὶ δημοκρατίαν μετηνέχθη Ῥωμαίοις τὰ πράγματα, ὑπάτων καὶ δικτατώρων, εἶτα καὶ δημάρχων τὴν τῶν κοινῶν ποιουμένων διοίκησιν . . . καὶ ὅπως ὕστερον ἐκ τούτων εἰς μοναρχίαν ἡ ἀρχὴ τοῖς Ῥωμαίοις μετέπεσε.

124. Zonaras, *Chronicle*, 3.3: Εἰ μὲν οὖν πρὸς τὴν προτέραν κατάστασιν τῆς Ῥωμαίων ἡγεμονίας ἀναγαγεῖν τις βουληθείη τὸ ὅραμα, ὅτε ἡ γερουσία καὶ οἱ δικτάτωρες καὶ οἱ ὕπατοι καὶ οἱ δήμαρχοι καὶ ὁ δῆμος τῆς τῶν πολιτικῶν πραγμάτων ἀντείχοντο διοικήσεως . . . εἰ δὲ πρὸς τὴν ὑστέραν, ὅτε πρὸς μοναρχίαν ἐξ ἀριστοκρατίας μετήνεκτο Ῥωμαίοις τὰ πράγματα, καὶ πρὸς τὴν εἰσέπειτα τῆς βασιλείας κατάστασιν, καὶ τότε πλείστην ἂν καταλάβοι τῇ πολιτείᾳ προξενήσασαν βλάβην τὴν πρὸς ἀλλήλους τῶν Ῥωμαίων διχόνοιαν (a history that, he indicates, extends to his own time, by using a νῦν). This passage is based on Theodoretos's *Interpretation of Daniel* in PG 81.1420, but is expanded.

125. A good one in Bessarion, *Encomium for Trebizond*, p. 51.

2. The Emperor in the Republic

1. Cheynet, "Les limites du pouvoir," 28.
2. Lendon, *Empire of Honour*, 18; see also 236.
3. This is the point on which I would differ from the otherwise excellent analysis in Neville, *Authority*. But it is a typical double-standard. Haldon, "Social Élites," 184, writes, "Differentiating between 'the state' and the social élite of the empire is to create an artificial separation between the two, since they overlapped in so many ways." This is true, but nearly universally so, even today. What is missing from all these observations is the Byzantine concept of the *politeia*.
4. Haldon and Brubaker, *Byzantium in the Iconoclast Era*, 724.
5. Ibid., 796.
6. Bjornlie, *Politics and Tradition*, 58; also 43.
7. Millar, *The Roman Republic*, 55.
8. Skinner, "The State," 90; see also Mansfield, *Taming the Prince*, 158: "In Machiavelli's writings the word *stato* always refers to somebody's state—a prince's or an oligarchy's or a people's. After Machiavelli, and already in Bodin, 'state' begins to signify an impersonal entity belonging to no one, just as we use it today."
9. Reynolds, *Fiefs and Vassals*, 27. For an argument supporting the existence of an ancient Athenian state, see Anderson, "The Personality of the Greek State."

10. Haldon, "The Byzantine State," 5; also idem, *Warfare,* 10; and in many other publications. Some historians are more enthusiastic: Antoniadis-Bibicou, "Introduction," 15: "Avec le cas byzantine, nous avons la genèse d'un État au plein sens du term, par mutation; la mutation de la *Pars Orientis* de l'Empire romain en État indépendant dont les institutions, tout en étant d'origine romaine, se transforment lentement . . . une civilisation politique qui, contrairement à des clichés déformant à satiété les réalités telles que nous pouvons les percevoir à travers les sources, nous autorise à évoquer 'le premier État moderne' après les grandes invasions."

11. Skinner, "The State," 112.

12. Ibid., 108–109, 112–116, 122; for republican theorists, see also Skinner, "A Genealogy," 332–340.

13. Anderson, "The Personality of the Greek State," 6.

14. Geuss, *History and Illusion,* 43.

15. E.g., Haldon, "Comparative State Formation," 1122–1123.

16. The only text to do so that I have found is Ovid, *Tristia* 4.4.15: *res est publica Caesar,* which is grammatically ambiguous and is deliberately making an extreme point; see also Gowing, *Empire and Memory,* 151–152. See later in Chapter 2 for Zonaras and Choniates.

17. Leon VI, *Taktika* 4.1 and 13.4, respectively.

18. Haldon, *State, Army and Society,* II, 161; Beck, *Res Publica Romana,* 22–24, had no problem using the correct term.

19. Campbell, *The Emperor and the Roman Army,* 19–25, concedes that soldiers swore an oath to the emperor and the *res publica* but tries hard to minimize the significance of the latter (e.g., 7, 13, 156) because of his Republican bias and what he thinks is a clear-headed, cynical approach to imperial politics. He misleadingly calls the imperial army a private mercenary force (198, 302), which is refuted by part 2 of his book, which demonstrates that Roman soldiers were governed by a law of persons that fully integrated them into the *res publica* (e.g., 260, 280, 297). See also the sources that he presents at 151, 289, 384, and 422–423 and those in Millar, "Imperial Ideology," 16. For military oaths in late antiquity, see Lee, *War in Late Antiquity,* 52–53, 177, 184. The *res publica* is in the military oath cited by Vegetius, *Epitome of Military Science* 2.5 (late fourth century); Servius, *Commentary on Virgil's Aeneid* 8.1; and the military and civilian oaths in pseudo-Zacharias, *Ecclesiastical History* 7.8 (referring to 511); on the latter, see Chrysos, "Ἔνας ὅρκος πίστεως," especially 9 n. 6, 17 n. 1, and 21–22, arguing for continuity between Rome and Byzantium on this point. M. Kruse has suggested (pers. comm.) that when Constantius addresses the soldiers as *optimi rei publicae defensores* in Ammianus, *Res Gestae* 15.8.2–6 (355 AD), he is alluding to their military oath. This had ancient roots: Caesar, *Gallic War* 4.25, refers to a standard-bearer who leapt into battle with the cry that he would do his duty "for the republic and the general" *(rei publicae atque imperatori);* also Appianos, *Civil War* 5.17. Late

antique consuls entering office on 1 January took vows *pro salute rei publicae* and two days later *pro salute imperatorum:* Salzman, *On Roman Time,* 81–82. The oath taken at the accession of Leon I in 457 was "not to plot against him or the *politeia*": Konstantinos VII, *Book of Ceremonies* 1.91 (v. 1, 416), a wording that was still relevant in the tenth century when the book was compiled. Ioannes Lydos, *On the Months* 4.10, says that "consuls used to perform sacrifices on behalf of the *politeia* and the Roman *populus*" (ἱερούργουν δὲ καὶ οἱ ὕπατοι ὑπὲρ τῆς πολιτείας καὶ τοῦ δήμου τοῦ Ῥωμαϊκοῦ). Justinian required officials to swear an oath to *basileia* and *politeia* (*imperio atque respublica* in the Latin version): *Novel* 8, appendix; and *Institutes* 1.25 refers to slain soldiers as *pro re publica ceciderunt.* Prayers said upon the birth of a male heir mentioned both "the *basileia* and *politeia* of the Romans": Konstantinos VII, *Book of Ceremonies* 2.21 (v. 1, 616). Oaths taken by subjects in the middle period are understudied: Svoronos, "Le serment de fidélité," especially 135; for the later period, Angelov, *Imperial Ideology,* ch. 10, especially 326–344. See now the papers in Auzépy and Saint-Guillain, *Oralité et lien social.* Judging from the evidence of Leon VI (above), military oaths of the middle period mentioned the *politeia.* According to Konstantinos VII, *Book of Ceremonies* 1.91, all magistrates swore an oath not to plot against either the emperor or the *politeia,* and the emperor kept copies of these oaths (δεῖ δὲ εἰδέναι, ὅτι ὅρκον οἱ ἄρχοντες τοῦ παλατίου παρέχουσιν, ὡς οὐκ ἐπιβουλεύουσιν αὐτῷ ἢ τῇ πολιτείᾳ, καὶ τὸ περὶ τούτου ὁρκοσκοπικὸν φυλάττεται παρὰ τῷ βασιλεῖ). This is said in the section that follows the account of the accession of Leon I, which has been "generalized" for future use: see Kaldellis, *Procopius of Caesarea,* 259 n. 53. For oaths taken by emperors to serve the *politeia,* see "Popular Acclamations and Imperial Accession" in Chapter 4.

20. Jordanes, *Romana* 357: *non rei publica sed regi infestus.*
21. Leon VI, *Taktika* 4.3: τῇ Ῥωμαϊκῇ ἡμῶν πολιτείᾳ.
22. *Campaign Organization* 28 (pp. 320–321). The parallel contemporary text *On Skirmishing* 19 (pp. 216–217) leaves only the holy emperors in its version; for the patriotism of this text, see Ševčenko, "Constantinople Viewed from the Eastern Provinces," 731.
23. Theophylaktos, *History* 3.1.11–12 (trans. p. 73). For the context, see Kaegi, *Byzantine Military Unrest,* 68–72.
24. Euagrios, *Ecclesiastical History* 6.11 (trans. pp. 302–303): δεδείχατε γὰρ ὡς εἰ καὶ πρὸς τοὺς στρατηγήσαντας ὑμῶν τὴν λύπην ἐκληρώσασθε, οὐδὲν ὑμῖν τοῦ πολιτεύματος προὐργιαίτερον.
25. τὴν ἐς τὴν πολιτείαν ὑμῶν εὔνοιαν, mentioned again later in the same text.
26. καὶ ἑαυτοῖς καὶ τῷ πολιτεύματι τὸ συνοῖσον σκοπήσωμεν; see Leppin, "Roman Identity," 251–253, for this speech. For appeals to heroes of the Republic in military harangues of the later empire, see also Ammianus, *Res Gestae* 23.5.19–20; see also 25.9.8–11.

27. Psellos, *Chronographia* 5.2: ἢ περὶ τῆς βασιλείας ἢ περὶ τῆς τοῦ κοινοῦ καταστάσεως.

28. Psellos, *Chrysoboullon of Michael VII Doukas to Robert Guiscard* 136–137 (p. 181).

29. Skylitzes, *Synopsis: Michael III* 14 (p. 101).

30. Respectively, Attaleiates, *History* 11, 52, 66, 180, 182, and 297. For these terms in Attaleiates, see Kaldellis, "The Date of Psellos' Death," 656–657; in Prokopios, idem, "The Date and Structure," 590–591; for the middle period in general, Christou, *Αὐτοκρατορική εξουσία,* where dozens of similar expressions are quoted.

31. Cicero, *Tusculan Disputations* 5.72.

32. Theophanes Continuatus, *Konstantinos VII* 8 (p. 442): ὃς λύμη καὶ νόσος τῇ πολιτείᾳ Ῥωμαίων γέγονεν.

33. Theophanes Continuatus, *Romanos II* 1 (p. 470): καλῶς τῇ πολιτείᾳ ἐνήργουν; Attaleiates, *History* 53: κἄν τε σπουδαῖον τῇ πολιτείᾳ εἰσήνεγκαν, κἄν τε δεινὸν ἢ καὶ ἄπρακτον.

34. Mauropous, *Letter* 6 (p. 57): ὁ τῆς πολιτείας λαμπρὸς καὶ διαυγὴς ὀφθαλμός.

35. Psellos, *Chronographia* 6.154: εἰμὶ γὰρ εἴπερ τις ἄλλος φιλορώμαιος καὶ φιλόπατρις; 6.190: ἐπεί με ᾔδει φιλόπολίν τε ὄντα καὶ φιλορώμαιον.

36. Psellos, *Chronographia* 7.19: καὶ οὗτος φιλορώμαιός τις, said of a colleague in precisely such critical circumstances.

37. Psellos, *When he refused from the position of* protoasekretis 139–141 (p. 34) = *Oratoria minora* 8: πολλά γέ τοι τούτῳ καὶ τῶν κοινῶν συνέπραξα καὶ περὶ πολιτείας ὑπεθέμην ἀρίστης καὶ πᾶσιν οἷς ἐμφαίνεται μοναρχία, ὥς γέ μοι δοκεῖ, συνήρμοσα. The passage can be translated in other ways, but this seems to be the idea behind it.

38. The man with whom Psellos most associated this ideal was Konstantinos Leichoudes, but it was also meant autobiographically. See Criscuolo, "Tardoantico e umanesimo bizantino," 20–22; "πολιτικὸς ἀνήρ"; "Pselliana," 207–214; *Michele Psello,* 15–16, 60–72; Kaldellis, *The Argument,* 154–166; Ljubarski, *Η προσωπικότητα και το έργο,* 92–95.

39. Zonaras, *Chronicle* pr. 1 (p. 3): τῶν πραγμάτων ἀφέμενον καὶ τυρβάζεσθαι ἀποσχόμενον καὶ τοῦ μέσου μεταναστεύσαντα καὶ καθ᾽ ἑαυτὸν ἑλόμενον ζῆν.

40. For emperors, see, e.g., *Life of Basileios I* 72 (p. 246); χρὴ δὲ αὖθις τὸν λόγον ἀναδραμεῖν ἐπὶ τὰς πράξεις ἐκείνας, ὧν αὐτουργὸς ὁ βασιλεὺς ἐχρημάτιζεν, καὶ . . . ὅπως ἀεὶ τοῖς κοινοῖς ἐνασχολούμενος πράγμασι καὶ πρὸς τὴν κοσμικὴν ἐπιμέλειαν τεταμένην ἔχων διηνεκῶς τὴν διάνοιαν; and Romanos I in Skylitzes, *Synopsis: Konstantinos VII* (again) 1 (pp. 233–234): τὴν πᾶσαν τῶν πραγμάτων διεκόσμει διοίκησιν.

41. E.g., Nikolaos Mystikos, *Letter* 16 (p. 108); Theophanes Continuatus, *Michael III* 19 (p. 169); Psellos, *Letter S* 112 (p. 358); *Chronographia* 1.3, 1.19; Zonaras, *Chronicle* 14.16, 18.3.

42. This is a point that I will develop in a separate study; for now, see Kaldellis, *Hellenism,* 65–66.

43. κηδεμῶν τῆς πολιτείας: Simon, "Zur Ehegesetzgebung der Isaurier," 21–22 (or else it was Leon V); for the debate over the date of this edict, Kresten, "Datierungsprobleme," 37–106.

44. Psellos, *Chronographia* 4.14; the same image, slightly varied, at 7.57 for Isaakios I.

45. Doukas, *History* 39.1: Τὸ δὲ τὴν πόλιν σοι δοῦναι, οὐτ' ἐμόν ἐστιν οὐτ' ἄλλου τῶν κατοικούντων ἐν ταύτῃ· κοινῇ γὰρ γνώμῃ πάντες αὐτοπροαιρέτως ἀποθανοῦμεν καὶ οὐ φεισόμεθα τῆς ζωῆς ἡμῶν.

46. *Basilika* 46.3.1 = *Digest* 1.8.1: Τὰ δὲ ἀνθρώπεια ἢ δημόσιά εἰσιν ἢ ἰδιωτικά. Τὰ δημόσια οὐδενός εἰσιν, ἀλλὰ τῆς κοινότητος· τὰ δὲ ἰδιωτικὰ τῶν καθ' ἕκαστόν εἰσι. For lists of the things held in common by the citizens, see *Digest* 1.8.6.1; Cicero, *De officiis* 1.53; *De Inventione* 2.168 (though the latter are not offered as technical legal definitions); Appianos, *Civil Wars* 1.10–11. In general, see Ando, "The Roman City in the Roman Period," 114–115. For relating Roman terms to modern ones, especially beyond property, see Sessa, *The Formation of Papal Authority,* 23–24, citing previous scholarship. In the late fourteenth century, Nikolaos Kabasilas wrote extensively on the distinction between private and public property: see Siniossoglou, *Radical Platonism,* 364–367.

47. Ulpianus in *Digest* 1.1.1.2.

48. The antiquarian Pompeius Festus (second century AD) in Cameron, *The Last Pagans,* 47; for examples of public rituals from the fourth century, identified as such in the sources, see ibid., 66; Salzman, *On Roman Time,* 153–154.

49. Kassios Dion, *Roman History* 38.43.4: οὔτε γὰρ ἐγὼ αὐτὸν μετεπεμψάμην, ἀλλ' ὁ Ῥωμαῖος, ὁ ἀνθύπατος, αἱ ῥάβδοι, τὸ ἀξίωμα, τὰ στρατόπεδα, οὔτε ἐγὼ μετεπέμφθην ὑπ' αὐτοῦ, ἀλλὰ ταῦτα πάντα. ἰδίᾳ μὲν γὰρ ἐμοὶ πρὸς αὐτὸν οὐδέν ἐστι συμβόλαιον· κοινῇ δὲ δὴ πάντες καὶ εἴπομέν τι καὶ ἐποιήσαμεν καὶ ἀντηκούσαμεν καὶ ἐπάθομεν (Caesar). For this distinction in Byzantium, see Holmes, "Political Elites"; Haldon and Brubaker, *Byzantium in the Iconoclast Era,* 608.

50. Sand, *Invention,* 41: "historical kingdoms belonged to the monarchs . . . not to the societies that bore these persons on their productive backs. Modern democratic political entities, by contrast, are perceived by the masses to be their collective property." This view of the premodern state is pervasive among theorists, including Skinner, as mentioned earlier in Chapter 2.

51. See, e.g., Leon VI, *Novel* 51.

52. One western theorist tried to make that argument, based on the Roman laws of inheritance: Folz, *The Concept of Empire,* 93.

53. Justin II, *Novel* 149.2.

54. Tiberios II, *Novel* in Zepos, eds., *Jus Graecoromanum,* v. 1, 20: ἐπεὶ μηδὲ τὰ τῶν θείων οἴκων πράγματα μόνοις ἡμῖν, κοινὰ δὲ τοῦ καθ' ἡμᾶς πολιτεύματος ἐννοεῖσθαι προσήκει.

55. Romanos I, *Novel* (of 934) 7.1 (= *Macedonian Legislation*, p. 91; trans. p. 59).
56. Maniatis, "On the Validity," 580, discussing the *Novel* of 996 AD; see also Beck, *Res Publica Romana*, 40. See also Aristotle, *Politics* 1314b5–10 on rulers behaving as custodians of public property.
57. Angelov, *Imperial Ideology*, 254 n. 5, also 292–294.
58. Euagrios, *Ecclesiastical History* 4.30: εἴπερ ἐξ οἰκείων δρῷεν. For the same concern, see the roughly contemporary *Dialogue on Political Science* 5.38: "others shall not add to their private property out of public funds" (trans. p. 153).
59. Skylitzes, *Synopsis: Michael IV 7* (pp. 397–398): κἀκ τῶν δημοσίων καὶ κοινῶν . . . ἀλλοτρίοις χρήμασιν ὠνούμενον τὴν μετάνοιαν. The distinction between private and public funds is made often in the *Life of Basileios I*, e.g., at 20, 21, 29.
60. Psellos, *Chronographia* 6.57, 6.62–63, 6.153–154; see Laiou, "Imperial Marriages," 176.
61. For this genre in general, see Prinzing, "Beobachtungen zu 'integrierten' Fürstenspiegeln"; Čičurov, "Gesetz und Gerechtigkeit"; and the surveys by Païdas, *Η θεματική των βυζαντινών «Κατόπτρων ηγεμόνος»*, and *Τα Βυζαντινά «Κάτοπτρα ηγεμόνος»*. The coherence of the genre is questioned by Odorico, "Les mirrors des princes."
62. Basileios I, *Hortatory Chapters* 24* (pp. 156–157).
63. Basileios I, *Hortatory Chapters* 41* (pp. 186–187): σήμερον γάρ εἴσι τὰ βασίλεια σὰ καὶ αὔριον ἔσονται οὐ σά, μετὰ δὲ τὴν αὔριον ἑτέρου, καὶ τὴν μετ' ἐκείνην τοῦ μετ' ἐκεῖνον, ὥστε οὐκ εἰσὶν οὐδέποτε οὐδενός. εἰ γὰρ καὶ πολλοὺς ἀμείβουσι τοὺς δεσπότας, οὐδένα ἄρα τὸν γνήσιον ἔχουσι δεσπότην.
64. The literature on the family-based Komnenoi regime is vast. The most important study is Magdalino, *The Empire of Manuel I*, ch. 3.
65. So Angelov, *Imperial Ideology*, 253–255. See also below.
66. Gautier, "Diatribes de Jean l'Oxite," 41–43. See, in general, Magdalino, *The Empire of Manuel I*, 269–272.
67. See "'Republic' and 'State' in Byzantium" in Chapter 2.
68. Zonaras, *Chronicle* 18.29: βασιλεῖ δὲ πρὸς τούτοις καὶ ἡ τῆς δικαιοσύνης φροντὶς καὶ ἡ τῶν ὑπηκόων προμήθεια καὶ ἡ τῶν παλαιῶν ἠθῶν τοῦ πολιτεύματος τήρησις. τῷ δὲ μέλημα μᾶλλον ἡ τῶν ἀρχαίων ἐθῶν γέγονε τῆς πολιτείας ἀλλοίωσις . . . καὶ τοῖς πράγμασιν οὐχ ὡς κοινοῖς οὐδ' ὡς δημοσίοις ἐκέχρητο καὶ ἑαυτὸν οὐκ οἰκονόμον ἥγητο τούτων, ἀλλὰ δεσπότην, καὶ οἶκον οἰκεῖον ἐνόμιζε καὶ ὠνόμαζε τὰ βασίλεια . . . ταύτης γὰρ ἴδιον τὸ τοῦ κατ' ἀξίαν ἑκάστῳ διανεμητικόν· ὁ δὲ τοῖς μὲν συγγενέσι καὶ τῶν θεραπόντων τισὶν ἁμάξαις ὅλαις παρεῖχε τὰ δημόσια χρήματα.
69. Magdalino, "Aspects of Twelfth-Century Byzantine *Kaiserkritik*," 330, 346, where he shows how Zonaras altered the wording in his sources to highlight this aspect of his criticisms. Also Beck, *Res Publica Romana*, 16.
70. For this concept, see Chapter 3.

71. Zonaras, *Chronicle* 13.3: οἵπερ ἤδη καὶ παρερρυήκεσαν πρὸ πολλοῦ. ἢ γοῦν ἐψευσμένην ὑποληπτέον τὴν τοῦ Οὐάλεντος πρόρρησιν καὶ διημαρτημένην τὴν τέχνην ἢ ἐκεῖνα νομιστέον ἐκεῖνον εἰπεῖν τὰ ἔτη, ἐν οἷς τὰ τῆς πολιτείας ἔθη ἐτηρεῖτο καὶ ἡ κατάστασις καὶ ἡ γερουσία τετίμητο καὶ οἱ ταύτης ἤνθουν πολῖται καὶ ἔννομος ἦν ἐπιστασία, τὸ κράτος δὴ τὸ βασίλειον, ἀλλ' οὐκ ἄντικρυς τυραννίς, ἴδια τὰ κοινὰ τῶν κρατούντων λογιζομένων καὶ εἰς οἰκείας ἀπολαύσεις χρωμένων αὐτοῖς. For Valens, see Magdalino, *L'Orthodoxie des astrologues*, 87–88.
72. Choniates, *History* 143: ὡς πατρῷον κλῆρον καθηδυπαθεῖν μονώτατοι τὰ δημόσια καὶ ὡς ἀνδραπόδοις χρᾶσθαι τοῖς ἐλευθέροις.
73. Magdalino, "Aspects of Twelfth-Century Byzantine *Kaiserkritik*," 337–338.
74. Angelov, *Imperial Ideology*, 269–280, 300–303; at 253–255 he refers to "the flickering survival of Roman ideological and legalistic notions of public power" but then claims that "old Roman notions of public power remained embedded in political vocabulary and the language of government." He nowhere discusses what the Byzantines meant when they said they were Romans nor refers to them as such. For the Palaiologan writers, see also Païdas, *Τὰ Βυζαντινὰ «Κάτοπτρα ἡγεμόνος»*, 100, 120, 135–136, 164–165.
75. Kassios Dion, *Roman History* 57.2.3 and 72.33.2.
76. So Talbert, *The Senate*, 377.
77. Regarding the popular acclamations of the emperor, compare Kaegi, *Heraclius*, 83. And it would last for centuries more!
78. Ammianus, *Res Gestae* 26.4 and 26.5.13.
79. Prokopios, *Secret History* 2.21: ὅτι δὴ τῆς πολιτείας τὰ καιριώτατα αὐτὸς περὶ ἐλάσσονος πραγμάτων τῶν κατὰ τὴν οἰκίαν πεποίηται, regarding military operations on the one hand and the affairs of his wife Antonina on the other.
80. Attaleiates, *History* 100: συνέδοξε τὴν ὑπὲρ τῶν ὅλων κρατῆσαι πρόνοιαν, καὶ τῆς εἰδικῆς καὶ ἐπιθανατίου παραγγελίας τὸ κοινῇ συμφέρον ἐπιεικῶς προτιμήσασθαι, ὅτι τὰ εἰδικὰ σύμφωνα τὰ πρὸς δημοσίαν συντέλειαν ἀφορῶντα περιτρέπειν δεδύνηνται· τὸ γὰρ μὴ γίνεσθαι βασιλέα διὰ τὸν τῆς μίξεως ζῆλον κοινὴ συμφορὰ καὶ καθαίρεσις τῆς Ῥωμαίων ἀρχῆς ἐγινώσκετο. δόξαν οὖν οὕτω κεκράτηκεν ἡ τοιαύτη γνώμη; compare Zonaras, *Chronicle* 18.10; see Oikonomides, "Le serment."
81. Eustathios of Thessalonike, *Capture of Thessalonike* 60 and 68 (pp. 74–75 and 88–89).
82. Attaleiates, *History* 195. For the context of this passage, see Kaldellis, "A Byzantine Argument."
83. Attaleiates, *History* 220.
84. Nikolaos Mystikos, *Letter* 164 (pp. 490–491).
85. Psellos, *Chronographia* 7.61: ἀπολογία γὰρ αὐτάρκης τοῖς διαβάλλειν ἐθέλουσι τὴν πρᾶξιν ὁ δημόσιος καθειστήκει. See, in general, Stănescu, "Les réformes d'Isaac Comnène."
86. Alexios I, *Chrysoboullon* of 1102, line 57 (p. 286).

87. Anna Komnene, *Alexiad* 4.2.2: ὁπόσα τῶν θελημάτων αὐτῶν μὴ ἐπισφαλῆ τῇ τῶν Ῥωμαίων ἀρχῇ εἶεν.

88. Wiseman, *Remembering the Roman People,* 226.

89. Konstantinos VII, *De administrando imperio* pr. 13–15: περὶ τὰς βελτίστας βουλὰς καὶ τὸ κοινῇ συμφέρον μὴ διαμαρτάνειν· πρῶτα μὲν ποῖον ἔθνος κατὰ τί μὲν ὠφελῆσαι δύναται Ῥωμαίους, κατὰ τί δὲ βλάψαι.

90. References in Kaldellis, "A Byzantine Argument," 11 n. 16.

91. Psellos, *Chronographia* 7B.42.1–8: τὸ δ' ἐντεῦθεν ὀκνεῖ περαιτέρω χωρεῖν καὶ διηγήσασθαι πρᾶξιν, ἣν οὐκ ἔδει μὲν γενέσθαι, ἵνα δὴ παρὰ βραχὺ ταυτολογήσας ἐρῶ, ἔδει δὴ γενέσθαι παντάπασι, τὸ μὲν διὰ τὴν εὐσέβειαν καὶ τὴν πρὸς τὸ δεινὸν εὐλάβειαν, τὸ δὲ διὰ τὴν τῶν πραγμάτων περίστασιν καὶ τὴν τοῦ καιροῦ περιπέτειαν; discussion in Kaldellis, *The Argument,* 46–47. Psellos makes a similar argument in his *Funeral Oration for Ioannes Xiphilinos* p. 450: "the patriarch's requests were just, but the emperor too was right not to grant them. The former put in front of the emperor God himself as an example, but the emperor hastened to do what was safe for his kingdom. The words and the desires of each were appropriate to their station in life." For another case, see Chomatenos writing to Theodoros Laskaris in "The Emperor and the Law" in Chapter 3.

92. Mansfield, *Taming the Prince,* 158.

93. Dagron, *Emperor and Priest,* 21–22.

94. See the discussion in Chapter 6.

95. Magdalino, "Honour among Romaioi," 186.

96. Veyne, *Bread and Circuses,* 292–295.

97. See "A Model of Sovereignty" in Chapter 4.

98. Aischylos, *Persians* 213.

99. Revell, *Roman Imperialism,* 52; for the oaths taken by magistrates, see n. 19 above.

100. Ma, *Antiochos III,* 3–4, 150–174, and throughout (see also 173: "the constitution of a supra-*polis* state without having to dissolve the local communities in a fully constituted territorial state"); Errington, *A History,* 72–73. For good surveys of Hellenistic kingship, see Walbank, "Monarchies"; Gruen, "Hellenistic Kingship"; Virgilio, *Lancia, diadema e porpora.*

101. Walbank, "Monarchies," 64–65: "There was certainly a closer relationship between the king of Macedon and his people than existed elsewhere; to that extent it was a national monarchy." There are five known inscriptions in which the king calls himself "king of the Macedonians."

102. Savalli-Lestrade, *Les philoi;* Errington, *A History,* 66–67.

103. Ma, *Antiochos III,* ch. 4.

104. For these aspects, see Gehrke, "Der siegreiche König"; Chaniotis, "The Divinity of Hellenistic Rulers."

105. Spawforth, *Augustus,* 235.

106. Galerius in Lactantius, *On the Deaths of the Persecutors* 34.1; Eusebios, *Ecclesiastical History* 8.17.6 (likewise Maximinus in 9.10.7–8).

107. Eusebios, *Life of Constantine* 1.11: πρὸς τὴν τῶν κοινῶν διόρθωσιν πρός τε τὸ συμφέρον ἑκάστου διωρισμένα νόμων τε διατάξεις, ἃς ἐπὶ λυσιτελείᾳ τῆς τῶν ἀρχομένων πολιτείας συνετάττετο. For links between Constantine and Augustus on this point, see Potter, *Constantine,* 168.

108. Eunapios, *History* fr. 28.1 (pp. 42–43): οὐχ ὅτι ἦρα βασιλείας ... οὐχ ὅτι ἐβούλετο δημαγωγεῖν, ἀλλ᾿ ὅτι τοῦτο ἠπίστατο τοῖς κοινοῖς συμφέρειν (Blockley translates *koina* as "the state").

109. Anastasios I in Konstantinos VII, *Book of Ceremonies* 1.92 (v. 1, 424): ὁπόσον μοι βάρος ὑπὲρ τῆς κοινῆς πάντων σωτηρίας ἐπετέθη, οὐκ ἀγνοῶ, and ἀλλὰ τὸν Θεὸν τὸν παντοκράτορα δυσωπῶ, ὅπως, οἷόν με ἐν ταύτῃ τῇ κοινῇ ἐκλογῇ γενέσθαι ἠλπίσατε, τοιοῦτον τῇ τῶν πραγμάτων ἐργασίᾳ κατανοήσητε. For imperial "elections" and the role of the *demos,* see Chapter 4.

110. Ševčenko, "The Title and Preface," 82: τί γὰρ τοιοῦτον ἐξασκεῖν αὐτοκράτορα δεῖ, ὃ τῇ πολιτείᾳ ἐπιφέρει τὴν ὄνησιν μετὰ λόγου γινομένον; at 85, Ševčenko translates *politeia* as "society" or "state."

111. A curiously understudied genre is the emperor's accession speech; see, e.g., Anastasios in Konstantinos VII, *Book of Ceremonies* 1.92 (v. 1, 424); Justin II in Corippus, *In Praise of Justin II* 2.174–273 and 2.333–357; Konstantinos X Doukas in Attaleiates, *History* 70–71; and the proclamation that Psellos wrote for Konstantinos X = Psellos, *Oratoria Minora* 5 (pp. 16–18). From an earlier period, there are a number in Ammianus's *Res Gestae.*

112. These expressions are conveniently collected in Hunger, *Prooimion,* 84–154.

113. For a list of sources and such expressions, see also Koutrakou, *La propagande impériale,* 120–122.

114. Troianos, *Οι πηγές του βυζαντινού δικαίου,* 30; Köpstein, "Μερικές παρατηρήσεις," 409; in general, Karagiannopoulos, *Η πολιτική θεωρία,* 25–29.

115. Leon III, *Ekloge* pr. 30–31 (p. 162).

116. Simon, "Zur Ehegesetzgebung der Isaurier," 21–22; for the debate over the date, Kresten, "Datierungsprobleme."

117. Psellos, *Orationes Panegyricae* 2.673–674 (p. 44).

118. Leon VI, *Taktika* pr. 2.

119. In legislation, including Justinian's *Novels* (especially 8 and 114), see Hunger, *Prooimion,* 94–100; see also Prokopios, *Secret History* 12.20, 12.27, 13.28–30; and Croke, "Justinian the 'Sleepless Emperor.'"

120. Respectively: Leon III, *Ekloge* pr. 32–33 (p. 162): πρὸς τὴν εὕρεσιν τῶν ἀρεσκόντων θεῷ καὶ τῷ κοινῷ συμφερόντων ἀκοίμητον τὸν νοῦν; *Life of Basileios I* 30 (p. 116) and 72 (p. 250); Attaleiates, *History* 312.

121. Psellos, *Letter S* 170 (p. 433).

122. For an example from the Mirrors of Princes, see Theophylaktos of Ohrid, *Oration to Konstantinos Doukas* p. 207.

123. Ioannes Lydos, *On the Magistracies of the Roman State* 3.15; Psellos, *Oratoria minora* 11 (pp. 44–46); Attaleiates, *History* 316. For their experience, see Kelly, *Ruling the Later Roman Empire;* Guillou, "Functionaries."

124. Nikephoros, *Short History* 15.
125. For the translation, and references to editions and scholarship, see Stephenson, *The Legend of Basil,* 49.
126. Psellos, *Letters S* 69 (p. 302) and 170 (p. 433).
127. Psellos, *Encomium for Konstantinos Leichoudes* pp. 398–399.
128. Psellos, Selention *on behalf of the Emperor Diogenes* 4, 38, 51–54 = *Oratoria minora* 4–6. A *silention* was an imperial address, either to the senate or the populace at large: Christophilopoulou, "Σιλέντιον."
129. Psellos, *Orationes panegyricae* 19 (p. 181).
130. Attaleiates, *History* 176.
131. See "The Byzantine Concept of the *Politeia*" in Chapter 1.
132. *On Skirmishing* 19 (pp. 216–217): παρὰ φορολόγων ἀνθρωπαρίων, καὶ μηδεμίαν τῷ κοινῷ προξενούντων ὠφέλειαν. See also Justin II on his official Ioannes in Menandros, *History,* fr. 9.2 (pp. 102–105).
133. See, e.g., Angelov, *Imperial Ideology,* 81–82, 136–140; Kiousopoulou, *Βασιλεύς ή οικονόμος,* 198–200, 219 n. 139, though her theme can be traced throughout the Byzantine centuries and was not distinctive of the early fifteenth century; e.g., the notion of the common good was not a result of the influence of Aquinas (199).
134. Skoutariotes (?), *Historical Synopsis* p. 463. For the debate over the authorship of this text, see Macrides, *George Akropolites,* 65–71, who doubts it was Skoutariotes.
135. Synesios, *On Kingship* 18.
136. Synesios, *On Kingship* 15: πάτρια δὲ ἡγοῦ Ῥωμαίων, οὐ τὰ χθὲς καὶ πρώην εἰς ἐκδεδιῃτημένην ἤδη παρελθόντα τὴν πολιτείαν, ἀλλ᾽ ἐν οἷς ὄντες ἐκτήσαντο τὴν ἀρχήν.
137. Heather, "The Anti-Scythian Tirade"; Cameron and Long, *Barbarians and Politics,* ch. 4; Karamboula, *Staatsbegriffe,* 30–52; Païdas, *Η θεματική των βυζαντινών «Κατόπτρων ηγεμόνος».*
138. Prokopios, *Secret History* 30.25.
139. Psellos, *Chronographia* 6.47.
140. E.g., Psellos, *Chronographia* 4.9–10.
141. Angelov, *Imperial Ideology,* 192–193, 197, 292–294; Kiousopoulou, *Βασιλεύς ή οικονόμος,* 187–191.
142. Dagron, *Emperor and Priest,* 57.

3. Extralegal Authority in a Lawful Polity

1. The fuller version is preserved in Konstantinos VII's *Excerpta,* in the collection *On Plots,* pp. 165–166; a slightly more condensed version in Theophanes, *Chronographia* p. 129; the ultimate source is Malalas, *Chronicle* 15.13, but its surviving abridgment merely notes the existence of the letter. The Konstantinian version is Αἰλία Βηρίνα ἡ ἀεὶ Αὐγούστα Ἀντιοχεῦσι πολίταις ἡμετέροις. ἴστε ὅτι τὸ βασίλειον μετὰ τὴν ἀποβίωσιν Λέοντος τοῦ

τῆς θείας λήξεως ἡμέτερόν ἐστιν. προεχειρισάμεθα δὲ βασιλέα
Στρακωδίσσεον τὸν μετὰ ταῦτα κληθέντα Ζήνωνα, ὥστε τὸ ὑπήκοον
βελτιωθῆναι καὶ πάντα τὰ στρατιωτικὰ τάγματα. ὁρῶσι νῦν τὴν πολιτείαν
ἅμα τῷ ὑπηκόῳ κατόπιν φερομένην ἐκ τῆς αὐτοῦ ἀπληστίας ἀναγκαῖον
ἡγησάμεθα βασιλέα ὑμῖν στέψαι εὐσεβῆ δικαιοσύνῃ κεκοσμημένον, ἵνα τὰ
τῆς Ῥωμαϊκῆς πολιτείας περισώσῃ πράγματα καὶ τὸ πολέμιον ἥσυχον ἄξει,
τοὺς δὲ ὑπηκόους ἅπαντας μετὰ τῶν νόμων διαφυλάξῃ· ἐστέψαμεν Λεόντιον
τὸν εὐσεβέστατον, ὃς πάντας ὑμᾶς προνοίας ἀξιώσει.᾽ καὶ εὐθέως ἔκραξεν ὁ
δῆμος τῶν Ἀντιοχέων ἅπας ὑφ᾽ ἓν ἀναστάς· μέγας ὁ θεός, καί· κύριε ἐλέησον,
τὸ καλὸν καὶ τὸ συμφέρον παράσχου.

2. For the date, and a general evaluation, see Treadgold, *The Early Byzantine Historians*, 100.

3. Priskos, *History* fr. 11.2 (pp. 266–273). In general, see Maas, "Fugitives and Ethnography"; Kelly, *Attila the Hun*, 147–155, 229–230; Kaldellis, *Ethnography*, 7–8, 12–17.

4. Priskos, *History* fr. 11.2.488–490.

5. Priskos, *History* fr. 11.2.504–510: καὶ ὃς δακρύσας ἔφη ὡς οἱ μὲν νόμοι καλοὶ καὶ ἡ πολιτεία Ῥωμαίων ἀγαθή, οἱ δὲ ἄρχοντες οὐχ ὅμοια τοῖς πάλαι φρονοῦντες αὐτὴν διαλυμαίνονται.

6. For early modern theorists who thought along similar lines, see Skinner, "A Genealogy," 334.

7. Prokopios, *Wars* 1.3.3–5 (trans. H. B. Dewing, modified): οὐ γὰρ νομάδες εἰσὶν ὥσπερ τὰ ἄλλα Οὐννικὰ ἔθνη, ἀλλ᾽ ἐπὶ χώρας ἀγαθῆς τινος ἐκ παλαιοῦ ἵδρυνται . . . μόνοι δὲ Οὔννων οὗτοι λευκοί τε τὰ σώματα καὶ οὐκ ἄμορφοι τὰς ὄψεις εἰσίν. οὐ μὴν οὔτε τὴν δίαιταν ὁμοιότροπον αὐτοῖς ἔχουσιν οὔτε θηρίου βίον τινὰ ᾗπερ ἐκεῖνοι ζῶσιν, ἀλλὰ καὶ πρὸς βασιλέως ἑνὸς ἄρχονται καὶ πολιτείαν ἔννομον ἔχοντες ἀλλήλοις τε καὶ τοῖς πέλας ἀεὶ ὀρθῶς καὶ δικαίως ξυμβάλλουσι, Ῥωμαίων τε καὶ Περσῶν οὐδέν τι ἧσσον.

8. The latest discussion, citing previous bibliography, is Canepa, *The Two Eyes of the Earth*.

9. Agathias, *Histories* 2.25.3: ἄλλην γὰρ οὕτω πολιτείαν οὐκ οἶδα ἐς πλείστας μορφάς τε καὶ σχήματα μεταβαλοῦσαν καὶ ἐν ταὐτῷ μένειν ἐπὶ πλεῖστον οὐ διαρκέσασαν.

10. For the Persians, see Theophylaktos, *History* 3.15, 4.3, 4.7, 4.10.

11. Agathias, *Histories* 1.2.3–5: εἰσὶ γὰρ οἱ Φράγγοι οὐ νομάδες, ὥσπερ ἀμέλει ἔνιοι τῶν βαρβάρων, ἀλλὰ καὶ πολιτείᾳ ὡς τὰ πολλὰ χρῶνται Ῥωμαϊκῇ καὶ νόμοις τοῖς αὐτοῖς καὶ τὰ ἄλλα ὁμοίως ἀμφί τε τὰ συμβόλαια καὶ γάμους καὶ τὴν τοῦ θείου θεραπείαν νομίζουσιν. Χριστιανοὶ γὰρ ἅπαντες τυγχάνουσιν ὄντες καὶ τῇ ὀρθοτάτῃ χρώμενοι δόξῃ· ἔχουσι δὲ καὶ ἄρχοντας ἐν ταῖς πόλεσι καὶ ἱερεῖς καὶ τὰς ἑορτὰς ὁμοίως ἡμῖν ἐπιτελοῦσι καὶ ὡς ἐν βαρβάρῳ γένει ἔμοιγε δοκοῦσι σφόδρα εἶναι κόσμιοί τε καὶ ἀστειότατοι καὶ οὐδέν τι ἔχειν τὸ διαλλάττον ἢ μόνον τὸ βαρβαρικὸν τῆς στολῆς καὶ τὸ τῆς φωνῆς ἰδιάζον. ἄγαμαι γὰρ αὐτοὺς ἐς τὰ μάλιστα ἔγωγε τῶν τε ἄλλων ὧν ἔχουσιν ἀγαθῶν καὶ τῆς ἐς ἀλλήλους δικαιοσύνης τε καὶ ὁμονοίας. For Agathias on

the Franks, see Cameron, "Agathias on the Early Merovingians" (a useful fact-checking analysis); see Kaldellis, "The Historical and Religious Views," for a different view of the religious component of the argument.

12. For closer readings of this aspect of the texts, see Kaldellis, *Procopius of Caesarea*, 69–75; and *Ethnography*, 17–25.

13. Orosius, *Seven Books of History against the Pagans* 7.43.4–6: *sine quibus respublica non est respublica.*

14. For an analysis of his *On the Magistracies*, see Kaldellis, "Republican Theory."

15. Prokopios, *Secret History* 15.16: ἐς δουλοπρέπειαν γὰρ ἡ πολιτεία ἦλθε, δουλοδιδάσκαλον αὐτὴν ἔχουσα; for the text's representation of tyranny, see Kaldellis, *Procopius of Caesarea*, ch. 4. For the link between law and *politeia*, see, e.g., *Secret History* 7.31, 7.39, 9.32, 19.8.

16. For Justinian's side of the story, see Pazdernik, "Justinianic Ideology" and, for freedom, "Procopius and Thucydides."

17. Cicero, *Republic* 5.2.

18. Corippus, *In Praise of Justin II* 2.175–274 (*res publica:* 2.245) (trans. pp. 97–99), and throughout.

19. See, e.g., Severus in Rowan, *Under Divine Auspices*, 88; Constantine in Van Dam, *Remembering Constantine;* Justinian in many of his *Novels* and other pronouncements; Herakleios to Phokas in Nikephoros, *Short History* 1 (οὕτως, ἄθλιε, τὴν πολιτείαν διῴκησας;). The motif can be traced throughout the Byzantine period, especially in panegyrics.

20. Schminck, "Ein rechtshistorischer 'Traktat,'" 82.

21. E.g., Photios, *Letter* 46 (v. 1, p. 93): μετὰ τῶν νόμων.

22. Beaucamp, "Byzantine Egypt," 273. For a detailed look at the day-to-day workings of these reciprocal expectations, see Connolly, *Lives behind the Laws.*

23. Cicero, *Republic* 1.43.

24. Cicero, *Republic* 1.50.

25. Synesios, *On Kingship* 6: βασιλέως μέν ἐστι τρόπος ὁ νόμος, τυράννου δὲ ὁ τρόπος νόμος.

26. Ioannes Lydos, *On the Magistracies of the Roman State* 1.3; Konstantinos IX, *Novel on the Nomophylax* 2; see, in general, Païdas, *Η θεματική των βυζαντινών «Κατόπτρων ηγεμόνος»*, 93–95, 113–116.

27. Photios in *Eisagoge*, title 2.1 (p. 240): βασιλεύς ἐστιν ἔννομος ἐπιστασία, κοινὸν ἀγαθὸν πᾶσι τοῖς ὑπηκόοις, a rare attempt to *define* the imperial office; in *Novels* by Nikephoros II, Konstantinos IX, Alexios I, and the Palaiologan emperors cited in Hunger, *Prooimion*, 119–122; and Manuel I in Macrides, "Justice under Manuel I," 122, citing the precedent of Basileios of Kaisareia, *Homily on Psalm 32* 9, in *PG* 29.345a; *Homily 12 on Proverbs* 2, in *PG* 31.389b; quoted by Maximos the Confessor in *PG* 91.776b. In general, see Simon, "Princeps legibus solutus," 479–485; Fögen, "Das politische Denken," 69–72.

28. *CJ* 1.14.4: *Digna vox maiestate regnantis legibus alligatum se principem profiteri: Adeo de auctoritate iuris nostra pendet auctoritas. Et re vera maius imperio est submittere legibus principatum. Et oraculo praesentis edicti quod nobis licere non patimur indicamus* (trans. Scott); see *Basilika* 2.6.9: καὶ κατὰ βασιλέως οἱ γενικοὶ κρατείτωσαν νόμοι· καὶ πᾶσα παράνομος ἐκβαλλέσθω ἀντιγραφή.

29. Harries, *Law and Empire*, 37 n. 4.

30. Lanata, *Legislazione e natura*, 165.

31. See Aristotle, *Nikomachean Ethics* 1137b26–32.

32. In the *Novels:* Hunger, *Prooimion*, 117–122. In general, Steinwenter, "ΝΟΜΟΣ ΕΜΨΥΧΟΣ"; Aalders, "ΝΟΜΟΣ ΕΜΨΥΧΟΣ"; Dvornik, *Early Christian and Byzantine Political Philosophy*, 245–248; Anastos, "Byzantine Political Theory," 20–26. For the ancient sources, see Dagron, "Lawful Society," 34 n. 30.

33. Themistios, *Orr.* 1.15b, 16.212d, 19.227d–228a; see also Aalders, "ΝΟΜΟΣ ΕΜΨΥΧΟΣ," 314. For Themistios as a panegyrist, see Heather and Moncour, *Politics, Philosophy, and Empire*.

34. *Digest* 1.3.31: *Princeps legibus solutus est* = *Basilika* 2.6.1. See also Kassios Dion, *Roman History* 53.18.1: λέλυνται τῶν νόμων.

35. Peachin, *Iudex vice Caesaris*, 10–13; Kelly, *Ruling the Later Roman Empire*.

36. In general, see Dagron, "La règle et l'exception"; for the ecclesiastical context, see Konidaris, "The Ubiquity of Canon Law," 131–135; Kazhdan, "Some Observations," 203 n. 6, and discussion at 204–206. Provincial judges: Neville, *Authority in Byzantine Provincial Society*, 101–102.

37. Leon VI, *Novel* 109 (pp. 300–303).

38. Theodoros Balsamon in Rallis and Potlis, Σύνταγμα τῶν ἱερῶν καὶ θείων κανόνων, v. 3, 349 (commentary on Carthage canon 16); see Simon, "Princeps legibus solutus," 475–477; Dagron, "Lawful Society," 34. For Balsamon as a theorist of imperial power, especially within the Church, see Dagron, *Emperor and Priest*, ch. 8.

39. *Digest* 1.4.1: *quod principi placuit legis habet vigorem.*

40. *Basilika* 2.6.2: Ὅπερ ἀρέσει τῷ βασιλεῖ νόμος ἐστίν.

41. Ammianus, *Res Gestae* 14.1.5. See also Constantius in Athanasios, *History of the Arians* 33.7: whatever I want, let that be deemed a canon; see Flower, *Emperors and Bishops*, 21 n. 70.

42. Simon, "Legislation."

43. Haldon, *Byzantium in the Seventh Century*, 254–264, notes the changes and offers an explanation.

44. Burgman, "A Law for Emperors."

45. Simon, "Princeps legibus solutus," focuses on an attempt by Demetrios Chomatenos (thirteenth century); for western efforts, see Pennington, *The Prince and the Law.*

46. *Institutes* 2.17.8: *licet legibus soluti sumus, at tamen legibus vivimus*, ascribed to Severus and Alexander; Greek trans. in Theophilos, *Institouta* 2.17.8 (Lokin pp. 374–375; Zepos p. 110). See also *CJ* 6.23.3 (232 AD): *licet enim lex*

imperii sollemnibus iuris imperatorem solverit, nihil tamen tam proprium imperii est, ut legibus vivere; Digest 32.23: *decet enim tantae maiestati eas servare leges, quibus ipse solutus esse videtur* ("It is proper that so great a majesty should observe the laws from which he is deemed to be himself exempt"); also in the *Epitome of the Laws* 1.29 in Zepos, *Jus Graecoromanum*, v. 4, 276-585, here 290; see also Manuel I, *Novel* (of 1158), in Zepos, *Jus Graecoromanum*, v. 1, 385-386. The first attestation that I have found is by Nero in Seneca's *De clementia:* Fears, *Princeps a Diis Electus,* 138. By the time of Ambrose, the idea was a commonplace: *Letter* 21.9 (*PL* 16.1047a); in general, see Anastos, "Byzantine Political Theory," 27-28.

47. Trajan: Pliny, *Panegyricus* 63-65 *(ipse te legibus subiecisti);* Julian: Ammianus, *Res Gestae* 22.7.2 (he fined himself for an infraction; but compare 22.10.6), and the emperor's *Letter to Themistios,* especially 261a, 262a-b, on which see Kaldellis, "Aristotle's *Politics* in Byzantium"; for Julian, see Dvornik, "The Emperor Julian"; idem, *Early Christian and Byzantine Political Philosophy,* 659-672; in general, Wallace-Hadrill, "Civilis Princeps." Also Justin II in Corippus, *In Praise of Justin II* 2.380-381: *et se pietate subegit legibus ultro suis.*

48. Pazdernik, "Justinianic Ideology," 189-190.

49. Nikolaos Mystikos, *Letter* 32.91-95 (pp. 220-221): "If the emperor is the enemy and opponent of the laws, who shall fear those laws? Does it not follow that, if the ruler puts himself in enmity and opposition to them, then the subject will be of a like disposition toward them, even without compulsion of any kind?" See also idem, *Tract on the Tetragamy* 25 (pp. 52-53): "If he is the first himself to make nonsense of what his own law prescribes by scorning its command, is it not evident that he encourages the public to transgress the law rather than to observe it?"

50. *CJ* 1.22.6. The first such that we have is Constantine in *Codex Theodosianus* 1.2.2: judges should follow the laws, not imperial rescripts that may go contrary to them.

51. Manuel I in Zepos, *Jus Graecoromanum*, v. 1, 385-386; also in Macrides, "Justice under Manuel I," 118-121 and 168-172 for discussion; and Simon, "Princeps legibus solutus," 462-467.

52. See the case in Ammianus, *Res Gestae* 28.1.24, on which Harries, *Law and Empire,* 40; see also Prokopios, *Wars* 1.11.

53. Eustathios Romaios, *Peira* 63.1; ed. in Zepos, *Jus Graecoromanum*, v. 4, 235 (the emperor is Romanos III); see the discussion by Troianos in Grammatikopoulou, ed., 98; also Simon, "Princeps legibus solutus," 474-475. Normally in the *Peira* the word of the emperor is final: Oikonomides, "The 'Peira' of Eustathios Romaios," 187. See also the court of the "General Judges of the Romans" instituted by Andronikos II in 1296, whose verdicts could not be appealed: Angelov, *Imperial Ideology,* 354-355; "Introduction," 3-4.

54. Harries, *Law and Empire,* 26 on "the full strength of the Roman legal tradition."

55. Dagron, *Emperor and Priest,* 19.
56. Maniatis, "On the Validity of the Theory," 610–611, 627, but he goes on to list the grounds on which confiscations could be legal and justified; see also 617–618 for their rarity.
57. Laiou, "Economic Thought and Ideology," 1126.
58. E.g., Beck, *Res Publica Romana,* 43–45; Karamboula, *Η νομοθετική δραστηριότητα,* 400.
59. Cicero, *On the Laws* 3.8. Flower, *Roman Republics,* 147 hyperbolically says that this claim "portended the end of constitutional government." In fact, Rome never had a constitutional government. The statement was still relevant later: see Ammianus, *Res Gestae* 23.1.7: *lex una sit et perpetua, salutem omni ratione defendere, nihil remittente vi mortis.*
60. McGuckin, *The Ascent of Christian Law,* 93.
61. Cicero, *Republic* 1.39; see "The *Politeia* between Republic and Empire" in Chapter 1.
62. Trans. in Johnson, *Ancient Roman Statutes,* 149–150, modified. See Brunt, "Lex de imperio Vespasiani," 107–109.
63. *CJ* 3.1.8 (314 AD).
64. Noted by Simon, "Legislation," 9–10. For Prokopios's engagement with Justinian's laws, see, in more detail, Kaldellis, *Procopius of Caesarea,* 150–159, 223–228.
65. Syros, "An Early Modern," 825, with full references. His claim about Islamic cities is doubtful, but the philosopher is likely constructing heuristic ideals.
66. Harries, *Law and Empire,* 41 and especially 58.
67. Kekaumenos, *Strategikon* 77. In general, see Medvedev, "Le pouvoir," 75–81; Chrysos, "Το δικαίωμα της αντίστασης."
68. Nikolaos Mystikos, *Letter* 32.89–91 (pp. 220–221): 'Βασιλεύς', φασίν, 'ἄγραφος νόμος', οὐχ ἵνα παρανομῇ καὶ πράττῃ ἁπλῶς τὰ δοκοῦντα, ἀλλ' ὥστε τοιοῦτον εἶναι διὰ τῶν ἔργων αὐτοῦ τῶν ἀγράφων οἷος ὁ νόμος ὁ ἔγγραφος.
69. Nikolaos Mystikos, *Letter* 32.309–324, 345–347 (pp. 232–235).
70. A theory of resistance to power on religious grounds was also articulated in the fourteenth century by Demetrios Kydones, *Apologia,* p. 400; and as early as Tertullianus, *Apologeticus* 4, on whom see McGuckin, *The Ascent of Christian Law,* 104–105. For religious resistance to imperial power through the rhetoric of martyrdom in the fourth century, see Flower, *Emperors and Bishops,* 26, citing previous scholarship.
71. Ammianus, *Res Gestae* 16.5.12.
72. Kazhdan, "Some Observations," 204–206.
73. Laiou, "Imperial Marriages."
74. Skylitzes, *Synopsis: Konstantinos IX* 7 (p. 434).
75. Psellos, *Chronographia* 1.31, 1.34.
76. *Life of Basileios I* 26–27 (pp. 100–109).

77. *Life of Basileios I* 20 (pp. 80–83).

78. Theophanes Continuatus, *Michael III* 24 (p. 78): ὁ δὲ τοὐναντίον ἢ ὡς οἱ πολιτικοὶ θεσμοὶ βούλονται . . . ἔπραττέ τε καὶ ἐπεπολίτευτο.

79. Chomatenos, *Ponema* 110; see Prinzing, "The Authority of the Church," 150.

80. Attaleiates, *History* 206–207; see also 98, the trial and accession of Romanos Diogenes; and the condemnation and pardon of Michael Anemas in Anna Komnene, *Alexiad* 12.5–6, discussed by Mavromattis, "Τὰ ὅρια ανοχῆς," 29–32.

81. Angelov, *Imperial Ideology,* 140–145, with examples at 236, 242, 244.

82. Ibid., 192–194, 197.

83. Simon, "Princeps legibus solutus," 484; Pliny, *Panegyric for Trajan* 65.1–2.

84. Magdalino, "In Search of the Byzantine Courtier," 146.

85. Prokopios of Gaza, *Panegyric for Anastasios* 1; trans. in MacCormack, *Art and Ceremony,* 69.

86. Psellos, *Orationes Panegyricae* 12.6–7 and 21.28 (pp. 124 and 186).

87. E.g., Theophilos, *Institouta* 2.17.8 (Lokin pp. 374–375; Zepos p. 110); *Epitome of the Laws* 1.29, in Zepos v. 4, 290; Theodoros of Nikaia, *Letter* 42.98–99 (p. 313).

88. Theophanes, *Chronographia* p. 488 (trans. p. 671).

89. Justinian, *Novel* 22.7; Leon VI, *Novel* 33.

90. Balsamon, *Answers to the Questions of Markos, Bishop of Alexandria* 4 (p. 451). Similar expressions in Agapetos, *Advice to the Emperor* 28: κἂν γάρ τις πολιτεύηται μὲν ἐνθέσμως; Photios, *Letter* 1.893: τῶν μηδὲν ἀδικούντων, ἀλλὰ κατὰ τοὺς νόμους πολιτευομένων.

91. The *Book of the Eparch* refers in its title to how the guilds of the City ought to πολιτεύεσθαι. But some cases are problematic, e.g., one from the fifth century to which Cameron gives the sense "hold political office": *Circus Factions,* 288–289.

92. Attaleiates, *History* 52: τὸν νόμον ποιούμενος βούλημα, πᾶσαν εὐταξίαν καὶ εὐνομίαν πεποίηκε πολιτεύεσθαι.

93. *Hortatory Chapters* 32 (pp. 170–171); see Čičurov, "Gesetz und Gerechtigkeit," 40–43.

94. Dagron, "Lawful Society," 32.

95. Attaleiates, *Ponema nomikon* 2.43, in Zepos, *Jus Graecoromanum,* v. 7, 497: τουτέστιν, ἐὰν ἁμάρτῃ, οὐ κολάζεται.

96. E.g., Campbell, *The Emperor and the Roman Army,* 393–394, 400, 427; Kelly, *Ruling the Later Roman Empire,* throughout; McCormick, *Eternal Victory,* 185; Haldon, *State, Army and Society,* I, 163–164; Cheynet, "Les limites du pouvoir."

97. Revell, *Roman Imperialism,* 80.

98. Agamben, *State of Exception,* 1.

99. Ibid., 4.

100. Ibid., 22–23.

101. Ibid., 69; for the emperors, see also 38, 46, 81–82.
102. Ibid., 2.
103. These two are regularly confused, e.g., in Christophilopoulou, "Αἱ βάσεις τοῦ βυζαντινοῦ πολιτεύματος" and *Τὸ πολίτευμα καὶ οἱ θεσμοί*, 36; Charanis, "The Role of the People," 69.
104. Agapetos, *Advice to the Emperor* 27; see also 49 (trans. p. 109). In general, see Čičurov, "Gesetz und Gerechtigkeit," 34–35.
105. Agapetos, *Advice to the Emperor* 35 (trans. p. 111); see Bell, *Three Political Voices*, 47: "We should see Agapetus as providing not simply sensible advice and a moral guide, but an (elegant) survival manual for an embattled emperor."
106. Scott, *Hidden Transcripts*, 96.

4. The Sovereignty of the People in Theory

1. Wiseman, *Remembering the Roman People*, 237; see also the discussion at 119–122.
2. The main sources are Psellos, *Chronographia* 5.16–50; Attaleiates, *History* 12–18; Skylitzes, *Epitome: Michael V* (pp. 416–420). They are *almost* in complete agreement about the course of events; see Karpozilos, *Βυζαντινοὶ ἱστορικοὶ*, v. 3, 292–299. Lounghis, "Χρονικόν περί της αναιρέσεως," and more generally in "The Byzantine Historians," believes that the sources have covered up what really happened, which was covert class warfare.
3. Vryonis, "Byzantine ΔΗΜΟΚΡΑΤΙΑ," especially 302. Vryonis generally blurs the distinction between the guilds and the populace in 1042, but in fact the latter turned against the former in the forum of Constantine, and the sources are unanimous and clear that the entire populace was involved. Charanis, "The Role of the People," 69–70, believes that "the people" did not mean everyone but some subsection (the merchants and some others), but he is not clear as to which section he means and why he thinks so. None of the sources authorize such qualifications. Hendy, *Studies*, 572–580, does not take into consideration the increase in the number of sources for this period and makes too much of the low birth of certain imperial associates (which had always been a feature of imperial politics); see also Angold, "The Byzantine State," 24–26; and Cheynet, "La colère du peuple," which offers a survey but does not regard these disturbances as primarily political. Garland, "Political Power and the Populace," offers another survey, and questions the "guilds" interpretation (46), but accepts the idea of eleventh- and twelfth-century exceptionalism. Krallis, "'Democratic' Action," refers to "the rise of the urban strata" as a new phenomenon. Shepard, "Aspects of Moral Leadership," 11, refers to the events as the exception rather than the norm but concedes the lack of detailed sources for earlier periods (13). For earlier periods the populist case had been made by Diehl, "Le sénat et le peuple," but those events are

again treated as exceptions by Angold, "The Byzantine Political Process," 7 ("Popular participation in the political process was thereafter marginal"). See also Syros, "Between Chimera and Charybdis," 454: "the people's role in Byzantine politics was often nothing more than cosmetic." Cameron, *The Byzantines,* 69–70: "popular movements of opposition are not to be expected in such a society"; this refers to the lack of movements to abolish the monarchy but still reflects a failure to consider the sheer number of movements opposing specific emperors.

4. Psellos, *Chronographia* 4.23.
5. Skylitzes, *Epitome: Michael V* 1 (p. 416).
6. Psellos, *Chronographia* 5.5. For acclamations, see later in Chapter 4.
7. Psellos, *Chronographia* 4.22 (words spoken by Ioannes *orphanotrophos* to Michael IV).
8. Psellos, *Chronographia* 5.15–16.
9. Skylitzes, *Epitome: Michael V* 1 (p. 417): ἀποπειραθῆναι τῶν πολιτῶν πρότερον, οἵαν ἔχουσι περὶ αὐτοῦ γνώμην . . . κρίνας τῆς γνώμης τῶν πολιτῶν.
10. Psellos, *Chronographia* 5.23: τοῦ δημοτικοῦ πλήθους ἀποπειρᾶται . . . διέλυσέ τε καὶ τοῦτον τὸν σύλλογον.
11. Psellos, *Chronographia* 5.25. See also Psellos, *Funeral Oration for Michael Keroularios,* pp. 322–323: "the entire City . . . not only the anonymous types but also those in office and the well-known."
12. Skylitzes, *Epitome: Michael V* 1 (p. 418): ἅπας ὁ λαός; Attaleiates, *History* 14–15: βουλόμενος καταστεῖλαι τὸ φλεγμαῖνον πάθος τῶν Βυζαντίων. For "Dig up his bones," see also Theophanes, *Chronographia* p. 369, relating to the events of 695 and p. 375, relating to the events of 705. For the events of those years, see Chapter 5. For the increased importance of the forum of Constantine for communication between emperors and subjects, see Christophilopoulou, *Τὸ πολίτευμα καὶ οἱ θεσμοὶ,* 213–214.
13. Attaleiates, *History* 15.
14. Psellos, *Chronographia* 5.32.
15. Krallis, "'Democratic' Action." See, in general, Garland, "Political Power and the Populace," 47.
16. Psellos, *Chronographia* 5.28; Attaleiates, *History* 15.
17. It did not reflect a belief by the historians in divine causation: Kaldellis, *The Argument,* 101–109.
18. Psellos, *Chronographia* 5.5 and 5.24 (τὸ μέγα καὶ δημοσιώτατον μυστήριον).
19. Beck, *Senat und Volk,* 41–47.
20. Psellos, *Chronographia* 5.26.
21. Psellos, *Chronographia* 5.37; Attaleiates, *History* 16. A chronicle reports that "commoners of the people" burst into Hagia Sophia and forced the patriarch to crown Theodora: Schreiner, *Die byzantinischen Kleinchroniken,* v. 1, 166.
22. Skylitzes, *Epitome: Michael V* 2 (p. 420).

23. For Greece, see Davies, "On the Non-Usablity of the Concept of 'Sovereignty,'" 60–62; for Rome, Ando, *Law, Language, and Empire,* 69–70.

24. Ostwald, *From Popular Sovereignty,* likewise never defines sovereignty but treats the term as shorthand for whatever elements of the state he intuits had more political power at any time.

25. Schmitt, *Political Theology.*

26. Rousseau, *Discourse on Sciences and Arts* 1.20.

27. Rousseau, *The Social Contract* 1.5.

28. Rousseau, *The Social Contract* 2.12.

29. Rousseau, *The Social Contract* 2.6.

30. Rousseau, *The Social Contract* 3.1; see also 3.18.

31. Rousseau, *The Social Contract* 3.14.

32. See the discussion of Skinner in "'Republic' and 'State' in Byzantium" in Chapter 2. Compare Wallerstein, *World-Systems Analysis,* 42: "Sovereignty was a concept that was invented in the modern world-system. Its prima facie meaning is totally autonomous state power." However, it was not so much invented then as theorized.

33. Hobbes, *Leviathan* 2.18.3. In general, see Skinner, "The Genealogy," 329, 342–348.

34. Hobbes, *Leviathan* 2.18.6; see also 2.30.20: no law of the monarch can be unjust; and 2.26.6 and 2.29.9: the monarch is absolutely not bound by the laws.

35. Hobbes, *Leviathan* 2.30.9. For the right in the republican tradition to replace abusers of power, see Skinner, "The State," 112–113, 115.

36. Hobbes, *Leviathan* 2.19.10–12.

37. Hobbes, *Leviathan* 2.29–30. At 2.19.9 he discusses the dictators, which is as close as he comes to the emperors. For an exposition on the Roman model, in which kings are subjects and not sovereigns, see *The Elements of Law II: De Corpore Politico* 21.9–10.

38. Hobbes, *Leviathan* 2.21.9.

39. Brunt, "Lex de imperio Vespasiani," 107; Ando, *Law, Language, and Empire,* 100–107. Early third century: Kassios Dion, *Roman History* 53.18.4. For the survival of the assemblies, see Millar, "Imperial Ideology." Gallia, *Remembering the Roman Republic,* 31 n. 72: "a formality, but not a mere formality." For the sacrifices of the Arval brethren associated with these elections, see Ando, "The Origins and Import," 104.

40. One can view our elections as ceremonies to ratify choices made in advance by the real holders of power; we are presented with two candidates who, despite personal differences, will pursue almost identical policies, not all of which are in the people's interest. A debate is also raging about the degree to which the Roman Republic was a popular regime. It is commonly presented as a de facto oligarchy, but recent work by Millar and others has stressed the democratic aspects of its politics: Millar, *The Crowd in Rome;* Wiseman, *Remembering the Roman People.* More studies on both sides of this issue are cited by Hammer, *Roman Political Thought,* 246 n. 29.

41. Wiseman, *Remembering the Roman People,* 198. For Cicero's similar argument in the *De lege Manilia,* see Ando, "The Origins and Import," 108.

42. Brunt, "Lex de imperio Vespasiani," 114.

43. Campbell, *The Emperor and the Roman Army,* 410–411; also Millar, *The Roman Republic,* 53–55.

44. Millar, "Imperial Ideology," 13, 15.

45. Veyne, *L'empire gréco-romain,* 15–18, 28–30.

46. *Digest* 1.4.1 (Ulpian): "A decision given by the emperor has the force of a law. This is because the populace entrusts to him its own entire *imperium* and *potestas,* doing this by the *lex regia* which is passed concerning his *imperium.*" Also *Institutes* 1.2.6; *Deo Auctore (Digest)* 7; *CJ* 1.17.1.7; Justinian, *Novel* 62, pref.: "the legal authority *(ius)* of the people and the Senate was transferred to the imperial majesty for the sake of the happiness of the *res publica*"; Gaius, *Institutes* 1.1.5: "the emperor receives his *imperium* by a *lex*"; and Ammianus, *Res Gestae* 14.6.5. See also Anastos, "Byzantine Political Theory," 30–31.

47. Theophilos, *Institouta* 1.2.6 (Lokin pp. 12–13; Zepos p. 9); see also Eustathios Romaios, *Peira,* in Zepos, *Jus Graecoromanum,* v. 4, p. 143: καὶ τὰ δημόσια δὲ ἐκεῖνα ἔλεγεν εἶναι δημόσια ἅπερ τὸ πάλαι πρὸ τοῦ γενέσθαι βασιλέα εἶχεν ὁ δημόσιος καὶ ἐκαρποῦτο, τῆς δὲ βασιλείας κατασταθείσης προσεγένοντο αὐτῇ. For the *lex regia* in the west, see Folz, *The Concept of Empire,* 91–97, 123–131.

48. See how this was imagined in the third century by Kassios Dion, *Roman History* 53.17–18.

49. Cicero, *Republic* 2.37–38.

50. Manasses, *Short Chronicle* 1688–1690: τότε δὴ πάντες εἰς ταὐτὸ Ῥωμαῖοι συνελθόντες / κατάλυσιν ψηφίζονται τοῦ βασιλείου κράτους, / κυροῦσι δὲ προβάλλεσθαι κατ' ἔτος κονσιλίους.

51. Theophylaktos of Ohrid, *Oration to Konstantinos Doukas,* p. 195. This pseudo-etymology came from the Byzantine dictionaries and passed, from Theophylaktos, into the Mirrors.

52. Theophylaktos of Ohrid, *Oration to Konstantinos Doukas,* p. 195: ὁ τύραννος ἐπὶ τὴν ἀρχὴν ἐκβιάζεται· οὐ γὰρ ὑπὸ τῶν πολιτῶν τὰ χαλινὰ τῆς ἀρχῆς ἐκδέχεται, ἀλλ' αὐτὸς ἁρπάζει ταῦτα σφαγαῖς τε καὶ αἵμασι.

53. Theophylaktos of Ohrid, *Oration to Konstantinos Doukas,* p. 199: εὐνοίᾳ πλήθους καὶ λαοῦ συνδρομῇ.

54. Theophylaktos of Ohrid, *Oration to Konstantinos Doukas,* p. 201: πᾶν τὸ πλῆθος ἡγεμόνα τοῦτον πεποίηται.

55. Medvedev, "Y avait-il une constitution à Byzance?" 388: "une curieuse thèse sur le charactère légal et pacifique de l'accession au trône, dont la condition est 'la bienvellance d'un grand nombre, la participation raisonnable du peuple.'"

56. Dagron, *Emperor and Priest,* 66 n. 56. The basic study is Christophilopoulou, *Ἐκλογή, ἀναγόρευσις καὶ στέψις,* followed by "Περὶ τὸ πρόβλημα τῆς

ἀναδείξεως," based on the assumptions of a previous phase of scholarship, for example, in the search for formal constitutional criteria; also, in
general, Beck, *Das byzantinische Jahrtausend,* 60–70 (who highlights the republican aspect); Dagron, *Emperor and Priest,* 54–83 (who sidelines the republican aspect). A good summary is Chrysos, "Τὸ δικαίωμα τῆς
ἀντίστασης," 36–39; for the Roman origins of acclamation, see Aldrete,
Gestures and Acclamation; for late antiquity, Roueché, "Acclamations in the
Later Roman Empire"; Wiemer, "Voces populi"; for the ceremonial aspects, MacCormack, *Art and Ceremony,* 240–266 (who misses the republican dimension, focusing on panegyrical rather than historical sources);
Bauer, "Urban Space and Ritual"; and Trampedach, "Kaiserwechsel und
Krönungsritual." Additional bibliography is cited by Williams, "Hymns
as Acclamations," 110 n. 7.

57. Instinsky, "Consensus universorum"; MacCormack, *Art and Ceremony,*
272–275; Roueché, "Acclamations in the Later Roman Empire," 187–188;
Harries, *Law and Empire,* 25, 66–69; in other sites of the culture, Oehler,
"Der consensus universorum." The concept has not yet been studied in its
middle Byzantine phase, though it exists in the sources (in the form *koinê
gnômê* or the like).

58. Corippus, *In Praise of Justin II* 1.345–347 (trans. p. 94).

59. For rebels and the *populus,* see Chapter 5.

60. The three elements are schematized as early as the accession of Tiberius
in Tacitus, *Annals* 1.7, to whom they swore allegiance; see also Galba's presentation of Piso to the same elements in Tacitus, *Histories* 1.17. They re-
cur in later sources, e.g., Sidonius, *Carm.* 5.386–388 for Majorianus, on
which see MacCormack, *Art and Ceremony,* 224. The Byzantine *locus classi-
cus* is Psellos, *Chronographia* 7.1 (though referring less to "constitutional"
legitimacy than the practical matter of ensuring support so as not to be
toppled); the standard discussion is by Beck, *Das byzantinische Jahrtausend,*
52–59.

61. For the early period, see MacCormack, *Art and Ceremony,* 254–255;
Canepa, *The Two Eyes of the World,* 11.

62. Well put by Dagron, *Emperor and Priest,* 81; Trampedach, "Kaiserwechsel
und Krönungsritual," 277.

63. As do Christophilopoulou, Ἐκλογή, ἀναγόρευσις καὶ στέψις; and Beck,
Senat und Volk.

64. As does Beck, *Das byzantinische Jahrtausend,* 67.

65. For previous efforts, see Bury, "The Constitution"; Ensslin, "The Emperor," though in spirit both are largely correct. After Beck, it has remained a largely German fixation, e.g., Pieler, "Verfassung und Rechtsgrundlagen," based on the mistranslation of *politeia* as "state" (especially
215); see now the reflections in Medvedev, "Y avait-il une constitution à
Byzance?," writing in the same tradition. The only Byzantine text that
comes close to resembling a constitution is the ninth-century *Eisagoge,*

probably written by Photios, which was an eccentric composition that seems to have had no impact: Medvedev, "Le pouvoir," 76–77; Troianos, Οἱ πηγές του βυζαντινού δικαίου, 173–174; and Stolte and Meijering, "The Prooimion of the Eisagoge."

66. Theophylaktos, *History* 3.11.

67. Euagrios, *Ecclesiastical History* 5.13, mentions the palace guard in addition to the patriarch and the magistrates, and Yuhannan of Amida (John of Ephesos), *Ecclesiastical History* 3.5, ascribes the initiative not to Justin but to the senate and empress, and he speaks of multitudes being present. In general, see Cameron, "An Emperor's Abdication."

68. Manasses, *Short Chronicle* 3413–3414.

69. Christophilopoulou, Ἐκλογή, ἀναγόρευσις καὶ στέψις, 53.

70. Flower, *Emperors and Bishops*, 41, 43.

71. Ando, *Imperial Ideology*, 205.

72. Konstantinos VII, *Book of Ceremonies* 1.92 (v. 1, pp. 417–425). The account is even more detailed than necessary for our purposes. See Lilie, "Die Krönung des Kaisers Anastasios I."; Haarer, *Anastasius I*, 1–6; Meier, *Anastasios I*, 65–75. Debate has focused on the question of whether Anastasios signed a profession of Orthodoxy, which is immaterial to our theme but would actually strengthen my reading if it were true: the emperor was expected to abide by the norms of the polity in all ways, including religion.

73. Konstantinos VII, *Book of Ceremonies* 1.92 (covering so far pp. 417–421). For Ioulianos, see Martindale, *The Prosopography of the Later Roman Empire*, v. 2, 639 (Iulianus 14).

74. The reason why this was necessary is explained by a number of episodes; see, e.g., Ammianus, *Res Gestae* 25.5.8; Eunapios, *History*, fr. 5.1; Prokopios, *Wars* 5.4.7; Cassiodorus, *Variae* 10.5.

75. Konstantinos VII, *Book of Ceremonies* 1.92 (covering pp. 421–425): ὁπόσον μοι βάρος ὑπὲρ τῆς κοινῆς πάντων σωτηρίας ἐπετέθη, οὐκ ἀγνοῶ, and ἀλλὰ τὸν Θεὸν τὸν παντοκράτορα δυσωπῶ, ὅπως, οἷόν με ἐν ταύτῃ τῇ κοινῇ ἐκλογῇ γενέσθαι ἠλπίσατε, τοιοῦτον τῇ τῶν πραγμάτων ἐργασίᾳ κατανοήσητε.

76. Konstantinos VII, *Book of Ceremonies* 1.93 (p. 426).

77. Did other Byzantine emperors swear an oath of office? This is an unstudied question, though it is noted by Medvedev, "Le pouvoir," 79–80. We can be certain about Anastasios, and his is the accession we know the most about. If others also did, it may simply not be recorded in the vague terms in which their accessions are typically recorded. The *Panegyric of Maximian* 6.3 (= *Panegyrici Latini* 10) claims that Maximian made his vows on behalf of the *res publica* when he entered upon the consulship: *Vidimus te, Caesar, eodem die pro re publica et uota suscipere et conuicta debere.* This is relevant but is not an oath associated with his elevation to the throne; see also the same in Pliny, *Panegyric for Trajan* 65.2: *iurat in leges attendentibus dis*, etc. In Corippus, *In Praise of Justin II,* there is no explicit mention of the

new emperor swearing an oath, but at 2.7 he goes to the church to pray and *effusis precibus Christo sua vota dicaret*. What ensues is not an oath of office, but this poem, which is highly stylized, would not be above subsuming a republican convention within a lofty religious rhetoric. Michael V, we saw at the beginning of Chapter 4, swore an oath to Zoe before his elevation, and it may have had more provisions than our sources record. It is likely that there was no fixed rule: some emperors-elect were required to swear oaths or give guarantees to various effect (dynastic, religious, immunity to opponents, etc.) depending on circumstances. Religious issues naturally attracted more attention in the sources than banal oaths to serve the *politeia,* which may simply have been too routine to mention. For the profession of faith that some were required to submit (not necessarily accompanied by oaths), see Sickel, "Das byzantinische Krönungsrecht," 547 n. 78; for oaths that emperors gave for various reasons after their accession, Troianos, "Συμβολὴ εἰς τὴν ἔρευναν," but see 155–156 for guarantees given before their accession; Laiou, "The Emperor's Word" (who seems not to know Troianos's fundamental, albeit inaccessible study); Rochette, "Empereurs et serment," 160–166.

78. Konstantinos VII, *Book of Ceremonies* 1.93 (pp. 426–429, here 426): ὁ δεσπότης ἡμῶν, ὡς ἄνθρωπος, ἐτελεύτησεν· δεῖ οὖν ἡμᾶς πάντας κοινῇ βουλεύσασθαι, καὶ τὸν τῷ Θεῷ ἀρέσκοντα καὶ τῇ πολιτείᾳ συμφέροντα ἐπιλέξασθαι; see now Croke, "Justinian under Justin," 16–22.

79. See, e.g., Campbell, *The Emperor and the Roman Army,* 375–382; Veyne, *L'empire gréco-romain,* 22–25, who believes that universal consensus was a fiction and Byzantium was basically a theocracy.

80. See, e.g., Adcock, *Roman Political Ideas,* 95, 103; Fears, *Princeps a Diis Electus,* 141, 143, 168–169, 218; Wallace-Hadrill, "Civilis Princeps"; but see also Ando, *Imperial Ideology,* 33.

81. Grig and Kelly, "Introduction," 19.

82. Ammianus, *Res Gestae* 15.8.8, 20.5.3, 20.5.6, 26.2.2, 27.6.8.

83. Magdalino, "Court and Capital," 132.

84. Liebeschuetz, *The Decline and Fall,* 211, for the period after the mid-fifth century.

85. Corippus, *In Praise of Justin II* 1.130–132 (trans. p. 89).

86. Leon the Deacon, *History* 2.12 (trans. pp. 85–86): δεῖ Ῥωμαίους ὄντας ἡμᾶς, καὶ θείοις ῥυθμιζομένους προστάγμασι, τὰ νεογνὰ τοῦ αὐτοκράτορος Ῥωμανοῦ τέκνα, ἐπεὶ πρὸς ἡμῶν καὶ τοῦ δήμου παντὸς ἀνερρέθησαν αὐτοκράτορες, εἰς τὴν προγονικὴν τιμὴν συντηρεῖν καὶ σέβας ἀπονέμειν.

87. Psellos, *Funeral Oration for Michael Keroularios* p. 366.

88. Attaleiates, *History* 58; for more on this event, see "Public Opinion and Contests for Power" in Chapter 5.

89. Psellos, *Funeral Oration for Michael Keroularios* p. 366.

90. Attaleiates, *History* 169: ἐπληροφορήθη, καὶ ὡς τοῖς πολίταις καὶ τοῖς ἀνακτόροις ἐπικεκήρυκται.

91. Choniates, *History* 455: Ἤδη γὰρ καὶ τὸ τῆς πολιτείας αὐτὸν ἀνευφήμησε πλήρωμα καὶ πρὸς τῆς γυναικὸς Εὐφροσύνης ἡ τούτου προητοίμαστο εἴσοδος τό τε τῆς συγκλήτου μέρος, εἰ καὶ μὴ ἅπαν, ἱλαρῶς ὅσα οἱ ξυνενήνεκται ἤνεγκε καὶ τῶν ἐκ τοῦ δήμου πρὸς τὴν ἀκοὴν τῶν ἠγγελμένων οὐδέν τις ἀτάσθαλον ἐνεόχμωσεν, ἀλλ᾽ ἠρέμησαν πρῶτα μὲν πάντες καὶ συνεπηυδόκησαν τοῖς ἀκουσθεῖσι, μήτε βατταρίσαντες, μήτ᾽ ἀναφλεγέντες πρὸς δικαίαν ὀργήν, οἷς εἰωθὸς αὐτοῖς βασιλέα χειροτονεῖν, ὑπὸ τῶν στρατοπέδων καὶ τοῦτο ἀφῄρηνται.
92. See Choniates, *History* 233–234.
93. Genesios, *On the Reigns of the Emperors* 4.1; Skylitzes, *Synopsis: Michael III* 1 (p. 81); for Manuel, see Grégoire, "Manuel et Théophobe," but now Signes Codoñer, "Dead or Alive?"; for the events of 842, see Christophilopoulou, *Ἐκλογή, ἀναγόρευσις καὶ στέψις,*' 88–89.
94. Wood, *"We Have No King but Christ,"* 135.
95. Ibid., 137.
96. Ibid., 155–157; at the same time, "the text emphasizes that both Rome and Edessa were ruled by Christ, rather than by the emperor." Emperors are therefore to be acclaimed, or not, within that framework.
97. Pacatus, *Panegyric of Theodosius* 3.5–6 (= *Panegyrici Latini* 2) (trans. p. 451, slightly modified).
98. E.g., Prokopios of Gaza, *Panegyric for Anastasios* 5, discussed by MacCormack, *Art and Ceremony,* 248. In one account, Leon III was elected while in Anatolia by a committee in the capital: Nikephoros, *Short History* 52 (εἰς ψῆφον ἐληλυθότων τοῦ βασιλεύσαντος). See also Skylitzes, *Synopsis: Michael III* 1 (p. 81): the regents τὸν δῆμον ἐκκλησιάσαντες in the hippodrome. We need a study of the uses and variations of this language. There are at least two sources that complain that a vote by the senate to recognize a successor was not free of coercion and thereby invalid: Prokopios, *Secret History* 9.52: δειμάτων περιουσίᾳ ἐπὶ ταύτην ἠγμένοι τὴν ψῆφον; and, after our period, Nikephoros Gregoras, discussed in Angelov, *Imperial Ideology,* 281. But the people assembled in numbers could not easily be coerced, only manipulated. "Voting" was also a basic procedural aspect of ecclesiastical meetings throughout Byzantium (derived from the procedures of the Roman senate, which ecclesiastical committees in the Roman world followed): MacMullen, *Voting about God;* Preiser-Kapeller, "He ton pleionon psephos." For universal consent in the election of patriarchs: Psellos, *Funeral Oration for Ioannes Xiphilinos* p. 448 (κοινὸν ὁμολόγημα παρὰ πάντων).
99. See, for example, the language in which Psellos presents the appointment of Michael Keroularios as the leader of a conspiracy against Michael IV: *Funeral Oration for Keroularios* pp. 313–315, including (but not limited to) the phrase κοινῇ πάντες ψηφίζονται; on the conspiracy, see Cheynet, *Pouvoir et contestations,* 51–52.
100. Jones, *The Later Roman Empire,* 322; Beck, *Das byzantinische Jahrtausend,* 57–59. Obviously, those who did receive power from a popular ancestor

presented themselves as heirs, *kleronomoi*, e.g., Michael VII in Psellos, *Letter S* 143, pp. 385–386. For a cousin of Konstantinos IX who tried to make good on his claim and failed, see "Public Opinion and Contests for Power" in Chapter 5. It was with the Komnenoi that notions of a hereditary right to the throne begin to appear in conjunction with the establishment of a family: see, e.g., Bryennios, *Materials for a History*, pr. 9–10, though this text probably has an ambivalent view of the matter: Neville, *Heroes and Romans;* for reactions to the Palaiologoi, see Angelov, *Imperial Ideology*, 280–285. In Skylitzes, *Synopsis: Konstantinos VII* (first) 10 (pp. 205–206) such beliefs are presented as a form of delusion (as Phokas did not have imperial ancestors).

101. E.g., Choniates, *Orations*, p. 130 (on Laskaris); Bessarion, *Encomium of Trebizond*, pp. 57–61 (on the Komnenoi).
102. For a comparative assessment, see West, "Dynastic Historical Writing," 514.
103. Dagron, *Emperor and Priest*, 23 (the best discussion of the topic).
104. Ibn Khordadbeh and Marvazi in Kaegi, *Byzantine Military Unrest*, 277; McCormick, *Eternal Victory*, 131; Cheikh, *Byzantium*, 88–89.
105. Dagron, *Emperor and Priest*, 13, with full references; also Kazhdan and Constable, *People and Power*, 146.
106. Ibn Shahram's report was embedded in al-Rudhrawari, *Continuation*, 23–34, here p. 31; for the date of the embassy, see Forsyth, *The Byzantine-Arab Chronicle*, 410–411, and 407, 455 n. 88 for the possible textual problems; the basic study is Beihammer, "Der harte Sturz."
107. Rousseau, *The Social Contract* 3.18.
108. Discussed by Angelov, *Imperial Ideology*, 280–285.
109. Kaegi, *Heraclius*, 83.
110. Ando, "From Republic to Empire," 61.
111. Angold, "The Byzantine Political Process," 13, said of the events of 713 but generally true.

5. The Sovereignty of the People in Practice

1. For the factions, see Cameron, *Circus Factions;* Whitby subsequently argued that their activities either could be political or provided the opportunity for political acts: "The Violence of the Circus Factions"; for one suggestion regarding the terminology for the factions and people, see Dagron, "The Urban Economy," 414–417.
2. One more emperor struck back at a popular uprising, Alexios III Angelos in 1201, but it seems to have involved a relatively small number of people and dissipated after one day: Choniates, *History* 525–526.
3. Theodoros Anagnostes, *Ecclesiastical History* p. 138: ἀνάξιος (= Theophanes, *Chronographia* p. 154). See the analysis of this episode by Chrysos, "Ἕνας ὅρκος πίστεως," 6; and Dijkstra and Greatrex, "Patriarchs and Poli-

tics," 235–239; for the context, Haarer, *Anastasius I,* 147–151. For Theodoros Anagnostes, see Karpozilos, Βυζαντινοὶ ἱστορικοὶ, v. 1, 221–224. For the popular dimension of the religious controversies in the early period, see Gregory, *Vox Populi.*

4. Pseudo-Zacharias, *Ecclesiastical History* 7.7–8 (trans. 251–264). For the violence of the factions against Anastasios, see Meijer, *Chariot Racing,* 138–140.

5. Malalas, *Chronicle* 16.19; see Haarer, *Anastasius I,* 156–157; Meier, "Σταυρωθεὶς δι' ἡμᾶς."

6. Well put by Guran, "Genesis and Function," 293, but I am not convinced by eschatological interpretations of Roman political history.

7. Christophilopoulou, Ἐκλογή, ἀναγόρευσις καὶ στέψις, 49–51.

8. Prokopios, *Wars* 1.24. His account must be supplemented by other sources, especially Malalas, *Chronicle* 18.71; *Chronicon Paschale* pp. 620–629; see, in general, Greatrex, "The Nika Riot." Meier, "Die Inszenierung," has argued that this was not a popular revolt but a ploy to draw out Justinian's enemies. This view will probably not gain many adherents: Evans, *The Power Game,* 229 n. 27.

9. Yuhannan of Amida (John of Ephesos), *Ecclesiastical History,* part III, 3.30–33; Euagrios, *Ecclesiastical History* 5.18 (whose account is less detailed but provides the information that the emperor had also been denounced); see Rochow, "Die Heidenprozesse."

10. Theophylaktos, *History* 8.1.10; for the context and other sources, see Kaegi, *Byzantine Military Unrest,* 108–115. Whitby, *The Emperor Maurice,* 122–124, doubts the truth of the betrayal but does not say whether the entire story including the commission was fabricated. Even then, the story would have been written with an eye to what readers would believe the urban populace could do.

11. Nikephoros, *Short History* 8. This is not mentioned in other sources. For the context and a discussion, see Kaegi, *Heraclius,* 88–89.

12. Nikephoros, *Short History* 28. For events later in that year when the people forced the hands of the patriarch and then the emperor in the making of co-emperors, see *Short History* 31.

13. Hatlie, *The Monks and Monasteries,* 222–223.

14. Skylitzes, *Epitome: Konstantinos IX* 7 (p. 434).

15. Choniates, *History* 478 (trans. pp. 262–263). This type of assembly, summoned by the emperor, seems to have been unprecedented: Kyritses, "The Imperial Council," 63.

16. Choniates, *History* 560–562 (trans. pp. 306–307, modified).

17. Gregory, *Vox Populi,* 216.

18. Ibid., 219–221.

19. McGuckin, *The Ascent of Christian Law,* 238 n. 2.

20. Quoted by Karlin-Hayter, "L'enjeu," 85, from the transcript of an unpublished course.

21. Cheynet, *Pouvoir et contestations,* 202–205 (the people) and 161–162 (propaganda = oracles). Other studies of plots and rebellions include K. A. Bourdara, *Καθοσίωσις καί τυραννίς* (parts 1 and 2); 'Το ἔγκλημα καθοσιώσεως'; Ferluga, "Aufstände im byzantinischen Reich"; and Savvides, *Βυζαντινὰ στασιαστικὰ καὶ αὐτονομιστικὰ κινήματα.* For earlier centuries, see now Szidat, *Usurpator tanti nominis;* and Kaegi, *Byzantine Military Unrest.*

22. Cheynet, *Pouvoir et contestations,* 13.

23. Veyne, *Bread and Circuses,* 295–296.

24. For the ancient Romans, see now Toner, *Popular Culture,* on which see later in Chapter 5; for Koutrakou on the Byzantines, see later in Chapter 5.

25. E.g., Habermas, *The Structural Transformation,* 25–26, 29–31; among more popular books, Saul, *Voltaire's Bastards,* 320.

26. Sand, *Invention of the Jewish People,* 124: "a sovereign's dependence on his subjects' goodwill is also a modern phenomenon . . . Kings did not need to rally the masses around a national politics." See also 315: "Before the rise of modernity, there was no class of individuals whose task it was to express or represent the opinion of the 'people.'"

27. Skylitzes, *Synopsis: Michael VI* 1 (pp. 481–482).

28. Zonaras, *Chronicle* 18.1; for such political ditties, see below.

29. Nikephoros, *Short History* 40; Theophanes, *Chronographia* p. 369. For the common source on which these reports are based, see Treadgold, "Trajan the Patrician"; for the events themselves, Cameron, *Circus Factions,* 267–269; Angold, "The Byzantine Political Process," 11.

30. Choniates, *History* 230–238.

31. Garland, "Political Power and the Populace," 35.

32. Choniates, *History* 341–344: πρωΐας δὲ γενομένης οὐκ ἦν ὅστις οὐ παρῆν οἰκήτωρ τῆς πόλεως, οὐδ' ἐθεοκλύτει αὐτοκρατορήσειν μὲν Ἰσαάκιον, Ἀνδρόνικον δὲ καθαιρεθῆναι τῆς βασιλείας καὶ συλληφθέντα παθεῖν ὁπόσα δέδρακε τῇ τῶν ὅλων σχεδὸν ἐπιβουλεύων ζωῇ.

33. Choniates, *History* 344–351.

34. Bryennios, *Materials for a History* pr. 4. For the confusion surrounding this man's identity, see Polemis, *The Doukai,* 51 n. 17.

35. Choniates, *History* 428.

36. "John of Nikiu," *Chronicle* 120.61–62 (trans. pp. 198–199).

37. *The Armenian History Attributed to Sebeos* 44 (trans. p. 106, with the commentary at pp. 255–256). For this source, see now Howard-Johnston, *Witnesses to a World Crisis,* ch. 3.

38. Liudprand, *Antapodosis* 5.21.

39. For a recent and rather extreme version of this tendency, see Stouraitis, "Bürgerkrieg." The way Stouraitis presents these events, Byzantine civil wars could have been avoided if only there were a reliable oracle to indicate God's will.

40. Theophanes Continuatus, *Michael II* 11, 13 (pp. 52–53, 58–59): ἅμα δὲ τῷ εἰς ὄψιν ἐποφθῆναι τῶν πολιτῶν τὰς πύλας αὐτῷ ἀναπετάσαι οἰόμενος, μίσει

δὴ τῷ πρὸς Μιχαήλ. ἐπεὶ δὲ ταύτης τῆς ἐλπίδος διέπεσεν, μᾶλλον μὲν οὖν καὶ ὕβρεσι τούτων καὶ λοιδορίαις ἐπλύνετο, τότε μὲν δὴ τὴν στρατηγικὴν σκηνὴν, etc.; the same in Genesios, *On the Reigns of the Emperors* 2.5; Skylitzes, *Synopsis: Michael II* 8 (p. 34); Zonaras, *Chronicle* 15.23. The basic study is still Lemerle, "Thomas le Slave."

41. Leon the Deacon, *History* 3.7 (trans. pp. 95–97); Skylitzes, *Synopsis: Basileios II and Konstantinos VIII* 7 (pp. 257–259).

42. Konstantinos VII, *Book of Ceremonies* 1.96 (v. 1, pp. 435–439).

43. Psellos, *Chronographia* 6.106.

44. Zonaras, *Chronicle* 17.23.

45. Psellos, *Chronographia* 6.109; see also Attaleiates, *History* 24; Skylitzes, *Synopsis: Konstantinos IX* 8 (p. 440): the message was meant for both citizens and soldiers.

46. Lefort, "Rhétorique et politique."

47. Psellos, *Chronographia* 6.114. Citizen defense is stressed also by Skylitzes, *Synopsis: Konstantinos IX* 8 (p. 440).

48. Psellos, *Chronographia* 6.117.

49. Skylitzes, *Synopsis: Michael VI* 11 (p. 495).

50. Psellos, *Chronographia* 7.33.

51. Skylitzes, *Synopsis: Michael VI* 11 (p. 497); Attaleiates, *History* 58.

52. Skylitzes, *Synopsis: Michael VI* 12 (pp. 497–498).

53. Psellos, *Funeral Oration for Michael Keroularios* pp. 365–366.

54. Attaleiates, *History* 58.

55. Skylitzes, *Synopsis: Michael VI* 12 (p. 500).

56. Attaleiates, *History* 250–252; a more positive version in Bryennios, *Materials for a History,* 3.11–12.

57. Attaleiates, *History* 293.

58. Attaleiates, *History* 258.

59. Attaleiates, *History* 256; see Krallis, "'Democratic' Action." The term *dêmokratia* appears in many Byzantine texts, in a wide variety of contexts. Each one, however, has to be understood in its particular context. In my opinion there is no coherent meaning behind the term, so I will not fill this note with references. They would not illuminate this usage here (nor it them). Some scholars have tried to extract a single sense, representing *the* Byzantine view of *dêmokratia,* but they invariably give privilege to one sense (or text) over the others.

60. Attaleiates, *History* 256–257.

61. Attaleiates, *History* 267–273. A different version, more favorable to Bryennios, with less popular enthusiasm for Botaneiates, is in Bryennios, *Materials for a History* 3.18–24.

62. See n. 3 of Chapter 4.

63. For the latter, in addition to the instances mentioned above, see also the events of 1201 in Choniates, *History* 525–526.

64. E.g., icons: Alexander, *Nicephorus,* 125 n. 1–2.

65. In general, see Koutrakou, *La propagande impériale,* 303. "Unworthy!" was also chanted in ecclesiastical controversies: Niketas David, *Life of Ignatios* 33 (p. 51).
66. Martindale, *The Prosopography of the Later Roman Empire,* v. 2, 1172–1173.
67. Especially Angold, "The Byzantine Political Process," 7.
68. Nikephoros, *Short History* 42.
69. Zonaras, *Chronicle* 14.24: ἀπεπειρᾶτο τῶν πολιτῶν, αὐτοῖς ἐκ τοῦ τείχους προκύπτουσιν ὁμιλῶν. οἱ δὲ οὐ μόνον αὐτὸν οὐ προσίεντο, ἀλλὰ καὶ ὕβρεις αὐτοῦ κατέχεον πλημμελεῖς.
70. Treadgold, "Trajan the Patrician."
71. Theophanes, *Chronographia* p. 374.
72. Theophanes, *Chronographia* p. 400.
73. Nikephoros, *Short History* 57.
74. Zonaras, *Chronicle* 15.2: οἰόμενος παρὰ τοῦ λαοῦ προσδεχθήσεσθαι. τῶν δὲ τῆς πόλεως μὴ ἐπιστρεφομένων αὐτοῦ, οἱ Βούλγαροι τοῦτον πολλῶν χρημάτων τῷ Λέοντι προύδωκαν. In general, see Kaegi, *Byzantine Military Unrest,* 211–212.
75. Garland, "Political Power and the Populace," 46–51. Garland does not engage with political ideology or with our understanding of what type of regime the Byzantine empire was; most of her article is a summary of events.
76. Scott, *Hidden Transcripts,* 52.
77. Kaldellis, "The Byzantine Role."
78. Garland, "Political Power and the Populace," 20.
79. Lactantius, *On the Deaths of the Persecutors* 18.
80. Agathias, *Histories* 5.20.5: ἐπὶ τῇ τοῦ ὁμίλου εὐνοίᾳ (among other terms).
81. Psellos, *Funeral Oration for Michael Keroularios* p. 316: τῆς τῶν πολλῶν περὶ τὸν ἄνδρα κρίσεως (among other terms).
82. Choniates, *History* 143–146.
83. Koutrakou, *La propagande impériale,* at 56–67; see also 317–319. Chrysos, "Τὸ δικαίωμα της αντίστασης στο Βυζάντιο," is excellent. Garland, "Political Power and the Populace," comes close to formulating a concept of public opinion but prefers to summarize the sources.
84. Koutrakou, *La propagande impériale,* 60.
85. Ibid., 317–320, here 319.
86. Choniates, *History* 6.
87. E.g., Bryennios, *Materials for a History* 4.1, on Nikephoros III Botaneiates. See also the episodes discussed in the preceding section of this chapter, "Public Opinion and Contests for Power."
88. Agapetos, *Advice to the Emperor* 35 (trans. p. 111); see also the translator's introduction at 47: "We should see Agapetus as providing not simply sensible advice and a moral guide, but an (elegant) survival manual for an embattled emperor."
89. *Hortatory Chapters* 21 (pp. 146–147): δεινὸν γὰρ πως τὸ ὑπήκοον τὰς τῶν ἀρχόντων πράξεις λογοθετεῖν.

90. Theophylaktos, *History* 1.1.15–20. On the ironies in this work, see Efthymiades, "A Historian and His Tragic Hero."

91. Theodoros Stoudites, *Letter* 7: οὕτω φυλάττεταί σου ἀρραγὲς τὸ βασίλειον, οὕτω εἴκει καὶ πείθεταί σοι ἀσμένως τὸ ὑπήκοον.

92. For example, see Tougher, *The Reign of Leo VI,* on how Leon VI tried to "sell" his marriages. Drake, "Lessons from Diocletian's Persecution," 55, argues that the persecutions failed because they failed to create a popular consensus through the use of force.

93. Zonaras, *Chronicle* 18.9.

94. Anastos, "Byzantine Political Theory," 17.

95. Theophanes Continuatus, *Leon V* 19 (p. 31).

96. Theophanes Continuatus, *Theophilos* 1 (p. 85); see also Skylitzes, *Synopsis: Theophilos* 1 (p. 49).

97. Theophanes, *Chronographia* p. 351; see also Ekonomou, *Byzantine Rome and the Greek Popes,* 179–180.

98. E.g., Herrin, *Margins and Metropolis,* 182: "Due to Justinian's unpopularity, Philippikos was welcomed into the city"; also 193 for the fall of Philippikos himself. Louth, *Greek East and Latin West,* 64: "Constantine's unpopularity increased to such an extent that, on 15 August 797, at the orders of his mother, Constantine was blinded."

99. Theophanes Continuatus, *Leon V* 3 (p. 8).

100. Leon the Deacon, *History* 4.6; Skylitzes, *Synopsis: Nikephoros II* 18 (pp. 273–274); see Morris, "The Two Faces"; and "Succession and Usurpation."

101. Psellos, *Chronographia* 7.60; Zonaras, *Chronicle* 18.4.

102. Attaleiates, *History* 75: μερική τις δυσβουλία καὶ συνέλευσις συνετάραξε τὸ ὑπήκοον, οὐχὶ συνθήκη κοινὴ καὶ συγκίνησις ἐξεπολέμωσε τοῦτον, καὶ θάρσους ἐνεπλήσθησαν.

103. Attaleiates, *History* 258.

104. Eustathios, *Capture of Thessalonike* 24, 27, 33. For Andronikos and the people, see Garland, "Political Power and the Populace," 35–38.

105. Eustathios, *Capture of Thessalonike* 20.

106. *Life of Basileios I* 18 (pp. 70–75). For Michael III, who has gradually been rehabilitated in modern scholarship, see now Varona Codeso, *Miguel III.*

107. *Life of Basileios I* 19 (pp. 78–79).

108. *Life of Basileios I* 24 (pp. 90–93).

109. Criscuolo, "Tardoantico e umanesimo bizantino," 20–22; "πολιτικὸς ἀνήρ"; "Pselliana," 207–214; *Michele Psello,* 15–16, 60–72; Kaldellis, *The Argument,* 154–166; Ljubarski, *Η προσωπικότητα και το έργο,* 92–95.

110. Psellos, *Chronographia* 7.66.

111. Psellos, *Historia Syntomos* 3.

112. Eustathios, *Capture of Thessalonike* 50 (pp. 58–61; for this Alexios, see pp. 234–235, appendix 2).

113. Garland, "Political Power and the Populace," 46.

114. Reynolds, *Kingdoms and Communities,* 4.

115. See now Baun, *Tales from Another Byzantium*, though limited in scope, despite its length. For an older encyclopedic compilation, useful but uncritical and incoherent, see Koukoules, Βυζαντινῶν βίος.
116. Yavetz, *Plebs and Princeps*, 13.
117. Toner, *Popular Culture*, 7 (also 35) and 10.
118. Ibid., 179. For a longer and more theoretical exposition of this argument, see Ando, *Imperial Ideology*.
119. Toner, *Popular Culture*, 27, referring to the cases cited by MacMullen, *Roman Social Relations*, 171 n. 30; also 118 on riots and crowds; 163 and 183 on passive resistance to elite authority.
120. Toner, *Popular Culture*, 97–101. For negative acclamations, see also Aldrete, *Gestures and Acclamations*, 118–127, 159–164.
121. Toner, *Popular Culture*, 181–183, 188.
122. O'Neill, "Going Round in Circles."
123. See Beck, *Geschichte der byzantinischen Volksliteratur*, 25–28 for a list; for individual cases or general studies, see Morgan, "A Byzantine Satirical Song?" (Tzimiskes and Theophano); Jeffreys, "The Nature and Origins"; Koutrakou, *La propagande impériale*, 169–175 (including polemical poems written by elite opposition); Horrocks, *Greek: A History*, 256–261 (close reading of those about Maurikios and Theophano); and Garland, "Political Power and the Populace," 30–33 for the reign of Alexios (many incidents) and 49–50 in general. Chorikios claimed that mimes and the stage in general ridiculed political leaders: Webb, *Demons and Dancers*, 118–119. A classic case from late antiquity is the mockery that Julian encountered at Antioch and countered with his *Misopogon*. For epigrams hostile to Anastasios, see *Greek Anthology* 11.270–271, neither inscribed nor chanted according to Iliev, "Literary Memory."
124. Choniates, *History* 520 (or, "mind justice").
125. Scott, *Hidden Transcripts*, 51. I have refrained from using his work more extensively because I do not think that the popular culture of Constantinople was as hidden as the cases he studies; it was simply not reported that often in elite literature, which is a different matter. Scott addresses the latter issue at 87.
126. Garland, "Political Power and the Populace," 20; also "'And His Bald Head.'"
127. Fuhrmann, *Policing the Roman Empire*, 139.
128. Suetonius, *Tiberius* 25.1.
129. Williams, "Hymns as Acclamations," 119–120.
130. See the studies cited by Fagan, *The Lure of the Arena*, 18, 140, 146; also Millar, *The Emperor*, 368–375; Toner, *Popular Culture*, 120, 153, 157–158; and Meijer, *Chariot Racing*, 97–98 with 131 for intensification in late antiquity; for the later periods, see Cameron, *Circus Factions*, especially ch. 7; Roueché, "Acclamations in the Later Roman Empire," 183 and 198; Heucke, *Circus*

und Hippodrom, a systematic collection of the evidence, especially 265–310 for subjects' demands; and Vespignani, *Il circo di Costantinopoli,* focusing on late antiquity; for its political use, see Dagron, *L'hippodrome de Constantinople,* ch. 6–7. Special mention must be made of Cameron's book, whose relevance to the present discussion can be misunderstood. His concern is to show that we must not see the *factions* as expressing any kind of popular sovereignty (3), to which I have no objection, though his view of Byzantium as an "oriental despotism" (181–182) is a different matter.

131. From assemblies to games: Fagan, *The Lure of the Arena,* 259–260; from assemblies to theaters: Wallace-Hadrill, *Rome's Cultural Revolution,* 167: "both orders are Roman."

132. Van Nuffelen, "Playing the Ritual Game," 184–185.

133. Cameron, *Circus Factions,* 231.

134. *Patria of Constantinople* 3.201 (pp. 220–221).

135. For those events, see the preceding section of this chapter, "Public Opinion and Contests for Power."

136. Proverbs 14.2.

137. Choniates, *History* 233–234. For a study of such attitudes, see Magdalino, "Byzantine Snobbery."

138. For a partial response to Choniates, see Garland, "Political Power and the Populace," 47.

139. See "Patterns of Popular Intervention" earlier in Chapter 5.

140. Angold, "The Byzantine Political Process," 5–6.

141. Magdalino, "Byzantium = Constantinople," and much prior scholarship, e.g., Nystazopoulou-Pelekidou, "Constantinople centre du pouvoir."

142. Beck, *Das byzantinische Jahrtausend,* 56.

143. Such a situation had existed before in Roman history, for example, after the Social War (91–87 BC) and the extension of the franchise to most of Italy: voting rights in that phase of the Roman Republic could mostly be exercised at Rome itself.

144. Treadgold, "Byzantium, the Reluctant Warrior," 225.

145. Ibid., 226–227; for different ways of parsing the same statistics, see Lilie, "Der Kaiser in der Statistik."

146. Penna and Morrisson, "Usurpers and Rebels."

147. A point well made by McCormick, *Eternal Victory,* 233, 253–258; for the acclamation of the rebel, see also Christophilopoulou, Ἐκλογή, ἀναγόρευσις καὶ στέψις, 149. Some of those became permanent separate capitals after ca. 1200. My analysis is limited to the period of imperial coherence before that.

148. Athens: Theophanes Continuatus, *Konstantinos VII* 9 (p. 388). Naupaktos: Skylitzes, *Synopsis: Konstantinos VIII* 1 (p. 372). Nikopolis: Skylitzes, *Synopsis: Michael IV* 25 (pp. 411–412). In what follows, I exclude incidents in Italy

and anywhere after 1199, when the empire was coming apart: see Savvides, Βυζαντινὰ στασιαστικὰ καὶ αὐτονομιστικὰ κινήματα.

149. Skylitzes, *Synopsis: Michael IV* 25 (pp. 411–412).
150. Kekaumenos, *Strategikon* 74; for the fiscal context, see Harvey, *Economic Expansion*, 114–115, 221–222; Neville, *Authority in Byzantine Provincial Society*, 116–117; for the ethnic dimension, Curta, *Southeastern Europe*, 280–281.
151. Kekaumenos, *Strategikon* 20.
152. Attaleiates, *History* 23.
153. Attaleiates, *History* 28.
154. Attaleiates, *History* 244–245; see also Krallis, "'Democratic' Action," 44–45.
155. Attaleiates, *History* 201–204.
156. Bryennios, *Materials for a History* 3.9–10.
157. Attaleiates, *History* 300.
158. Anna Komnene, *Alexiad* 2.6.10.
159. Bryennios, *Materials for a History* 2.22–23; Anna Komnene, *Alexiad* 1.2; see the extensive discussion of prior scholarship in Leveniotis, *Τὸ στασιαστικό κίνημα*, 176–184. It has been noted that the people of Amaseia were sup-porting a Latin in this case: Magdalino, "The Byzantine Army," 29; Hal-don, *Warfare, State, and Society*, 269.
160. Neville, *Authority in Byzantine Provincial Society*, 95–97; Lefort, "The Rural Economy," 279–283; Harvey, "The Village." Discussions of local institu-tions focus on the Palaiologan period, simply because that is where the evidence is, yet older scholarship is not reliable: Tsirpanlis, "Byzantine Parliaments"; Charanis, "The Role of the People," 76 for Amaseia; Shaw-cross, "'Do Thou Nothing without Counsel,'" 117–118. Baun, *Tales from Another Byzantium*, 6, 319, 385, counters the model of a society held to-gether only by top-down hierarchies by showcasing strong local communities.
161. Koutrakou, *La propagande impériale*, 322.
162. Theophanes, *Chronographia* pp. 386–388, with Kaegi, *Byzantine Military Unrest*, 193–194, 210.
163. Theophanes Continuatus, *Michael II* 20 (p. 71); Genesios, *On the Reigns of the Emperors* 2.8–9.
164. Skylitzes, *Synopsis: Michael II* 20 (p. 47).
165. E.g., Anna Komnene, *Alexiad* 4.1.3 (Dyrrachion), 10.3.4 (Adrianople); while both were foreign invasions, they can be used here because the in-vaders had with them Byzantine pretenders who tried to persuade these cities to join them.
166. Choniates, *History* 285–288.
167. Haldon, *Warfare, State and Society*, 259.
168. Haldon, *State, Army and Society*, II 140–141, also 172, 185, 187; *Byzantium in the Seventh Century*, 266, 268–269, 373–374.

169. Haldon and Brubaker, *Byzantium in the Iconoclast Era,* 628; see also 26–28.

170. Christophilopoulou, "Αἱ βάσεις τοῦ βυζαντινοῦ πολιτεύματος," 218; Koutrakou, *La propagande impériale,* 330.

171. Neville, *Authority in Byzantine Provincial Society,* 44–45.

172. Diehl, "Le sénat et le peuple," 213.

173. Manojlović, "Le peuple de Constantinople," especially 687–704. Regarding the factions, he was set straight by Cameron.

174. Hammer, *The* Iliad *as Politics,* 26–27.

175. Harries, *Law and Empire,* 97, obviously using sovereignty in a slightly different sense.

176. E.g., in 963: Skylitzes, *Synopsis: Basileios II and Konstantinos VIII* 7 (p. 258). I am not including the violence of the factions in the early period, as they were not the *dêmos.*

177. Leon the Deacon, *History* 6.1 (trans. p. 144). We need a study of such transitional moments.

178. Choniates, *History* 525–527.

179. Skylitzes, *Synopsis: Michael VI* 12 (p. 499), here called Theodoros.

180. Choniates, *History* 235 (trans. p. 133, modified).

181. E.g., Greatrex, "Roman Identity"; and Page, *Being Byzantine,* with my review in *Medieval Review* 09.04.10 (September 4, 2010), focusing on this question.

182. Agamben, *State of Exception,* 1, quoting F. Saint-Bonnet.

183. Agamben, *State of Exception,* 2; see also 10–11.

184. Applied to Byzantium by Bury, "The Constitution"; Ensslin, "The Emperor"; and Beck, *Senat und Volk,* 1.

6. The Secular Republic and the Theocratic "Imperial Idea"

1. See, for example, the discussion in Bell, *Social Conflict,* 304.

2. Alexander, "The Strength of Empire," 348.

3. Spanos and Zarras, "Representations of Emperors as Saints," 63–64 (a useful examination of a neglected question).

4. Heather, *The Fall of the Roman Empire,* 23.

5. Menze, *Justinian,* 6.

6. Haldon and Brubaker, *Byzantium in the Iconoclast Era,* 11 n. 2. The last item is Baynes, "Eusebius and the Christian Empire," reprinted in his *Byzantine Studies,* 168–172. It is still cited as if it were an adequate study of Eusebios (it is not). Another foundational study was Dölger, "Die Kaiserurkunde," originally published in 1938.

7. Cameron, *The Byzantines,* 97, also 68. Similar quotations can be offered from the work of many scholars.

8. This is from Magdalino, "The Medieval Empire," 206.

9. Grabar, *L'empereur dans l'art byzantin.* Art history being a more theoretical and self-reflexive discipline than other subfields of Byzantine Studies,

Grabar's ideology has received critical scrutiny, e.g., in Mathews, *The Clash of Gods,* 16–20; Walker, *The Emperor and the World,* 12–17.

10. Johnston, forthcoming.

11. Alföldi's studies from 1934 and 1935 were later published in his *Die monarchische Repräsentation.* Treitinger's studies from 1938 and 1940 were later published in his *Die oströmische Kaiser- und Reichsidee.*

12. Freeman, *The Horses of St. Mark's,* 64 (see also 63: "Byzantium was a theocratic empire"); not a Byzantinist, but expressing well what he has learned from them.

13. For accessible introductions to recent research, see Kurzban, *Why Everyone (Else) Is a Hypocrite;* Eagleman, *Incognito.*

14. Walden, *God Won't Save America,* 182: "Doesn't God usually get what he wants?"

15. Choniates, *History* 444.

16. Choniates, *History* 419, 446–447.

17. Konstantinos: Psellos, *Chronographia* 6.132–133; Romanos: Kaldellis, *The Argument,* 28–30.

18. For sources, see Païdas, *Η θεματική των βυζαντινών «Κατόπτρων ηγεμόνος»,* 45, 63, 70, 106, 155–157, 177, 241, 302–303; and *Τα Βυζαντινά «Κάτοπτρα ηγεμόνος»,* 115, 124.

19. Cameron, *Last Pagans,* 95; see also Beck, *Das byzantinische Jahrtausend,* 105–107 on political sedition regarded as a religious sin.

20. Harris, *Constantinople,* compare 61–62 with 138–139.

21. Cameron, *The Byzantines,* 68–69.

22. Cameron, "The Construction of Court Ritual," 124; see also Canepa, *The Two Eyes of the World,* 1: "the dissonance between historical fact and ideological fiction often illuminates what lies behind the rhetoric." Yes, but *what* lies behind the rhetoric? How do we access it?

23. Beck, *Das byzantinische Jahrtausend,* 60–61; ch. 8 is a key discussion; also Karagiannopoulos, *Η πολιτική θεωρία,* 35–36.

24. This was even the case when an emperor viewed in retrospect as orthodox was replaced by a "heretic": it was the former who was the "tyrant," i.e., the illegitimate usurper. The orthodox emperor had lost; therefore he had not been favored by God, even if on religious grounds he should have been. See Koutrakou, *La propagande impériale,* 297, for the case of Artabasdos; also 281. A case has been made that the imperial idea did have an impact on the polity, but a negative one, namely, that it encouraged civil wars (because gaining the throne against a sitting emperor meant that you were God's favorite), and also that it made the Byzantines attack their emperors especially when the empire was being defeated by barbarians, i.e., at the worst possible time, because those emperors were perceived as having lost God's favor: Treadgold, "Byzantium, the Reluctant Warrior," 228.

25. Prokopios, *Buildings* 1.1.21.

26. *Chronicon Paschale* p. 622.

27. Cameron, *Last Pagans*, 53–55.
28. A draft form of this idea has been (independently) proposed by Angelov, "Byzantinism," 16–17, albeit in a bare outline. Angelov does not think that Byzantium was either Roman or republican.
29. Shumate, *Nation, Empire, Decline*, 30.
30. Fears, *Princeps a diis electus*, e.g., 44 (the Hellenistic context), 56, 60 (Alexander and Darius), 92 (Sulla), 171–174 (the Roman dynasts and emperors, "lacked a dynastic claim," the idea "clusters around the founder of a dynasty," etc.), 262 (Septimius Severus, who had been the first in a long time to use violence to seize power), 281 (after Valerian's capture). See also Bardill, *Constantine*, 58–68, for the same underlying argument; and Cline and Graham, *Ancient Empires*, 90 for ancient Babylon.
31. Fears, *Princeps a diis electus*, 217.
32. Ibid., 11–12, 141, 190, 216.
33. Stephenson, *Constantine*, 75.
34. Ibid., 71–86, 90–91, 129–140, 172–174; for the evolution of ideas of divine election and support in late antiquity, see also Fears, *Princeps a diis electus*, 277–317; Digeser, *The Making of a Christian Empire*, 3, 15, 20–30, 121–122; Kolb, *Herrscherideologie*, who stresses continuity with the Principate; for the Severan dynasty as transitional, see Rowan, *Under Divine Auspices*, 6, 249; for Gallienus, see Canepa, *The Two Eyes of the World*, 81, who also discusses (throughout) rivalry with the divinely appointed shahs of Iran. The Republican background is discussed by Clark, *Divine Qualities*.
35. Van Dam, *Roman Revolution*, 21, 97, 126–129, 248, 292–304 (Maxentius tried to do the same: ch. 9); *Remembering Constantine*, 132–154.
36. Drake, "Lessons," 53–54 for a discussion of the third-century context.
37. Fears, *Princeps a diis electus*, 252, also 279, 281, 283, 294, 305, 317–318; see also Sarris, *Empires of Faith*, 16; Drake, "Lessons," 53–54, citing previous discussions; Digeser, *The Making of a Christian Empire*, 20–30, 142.
38. Anonymous Post Dionem, *History* fr. 10.6 (p. 197). For the general argument, see Digeser, *The Making of a Christian Empire*, 3 (Aurelian), 28 and 38–39 (Diocletian).
39. Both pagan and Christian: Sarris, *Empires of Faith*, 22. Fears surveys precrisis expressions of the idea in Roman literature. Christian ones can be found too, e.g., Romans 13.1–2, on which see Harrill, *Paul the Apostle*, 91–94; Theophilos of Antioch (ca. 170), *To Autolykos* 1.11.
40. Canepa, *The Two Eyes of the World*, 100; see also 81: "fluctuations in divinities notwithstanding." Also Heather, *The Fall of the Roman Empire*, 123: "The presiding divinity was recast as the Christian God," and 232; Haldon and Brubaker, *Byzantium in the Iconoclast Era*, 782.
41. Lenski, "Constantine and Slavery," 246, discussing the concept of *libertas*.
42. Agamben, *The Kingdom and the Glory*, 11.
43. Johnson, *Ethnicity and Argument*, ch. 6.

44. Van Dam, *Roman Revolution,* 232; *Remembering Constantine,* 79–80, 88–89; *Rome and Constantinople,* 26.

45. Van Dam, *Roman Revolution,* 286; in general, 283–293, 310–316; *Remembering Constantine,* 76–79. For the blurring of Constantine and Christ, see also Martin, *Inventing Superstition,* 220.

46. Van Dam, *Roman Revolution,* 330–344; *Remembering Constantine,* 55.

47. In 1 Samuel 8, God instructs Samuel to listen to his people's persistent demand for a king. The institution of the kingship is thereby presented as both populist and divine.

48. Konstantinos VII, *Book of Ceremonies* 1.92 (v. 1, 424); with Anastos, "Vox Populi," 196 n. 38, I read προηγουμένης for προηγουμένως.

49. Konstantinos VII, *Book of Ceremonies* 1.93 (v. 1, 429). See also Niketas David, *Life of Patriarch Ignatios* 2 (p. 5): Michael I was proclaimed by God and the senators.

50. *Lex regia:* see "A Model of Sovereignty" in Chapter 4; God and the *politeia:* see, e.g., *Novels* 86 pr.; 81 pr. Karagiannopoulos, *Η πολιτική θεωρία,* 28, says that it was only after the Nika riots that he began to shift the grounds of his power from the people to God. This seems too neat.

51. *Dialogue on Political Science* 5.17, 5.46–47, 5.52.

52. Attaleiates, *History* 293.

53. Anastos, "Vox Populi," 182.

54. E.g., Runciman, *The Byzantine Theocracy;* Karagiannopoulos, *Η πολιτική θεωρία,* 19–20.

55. E.g., Ensslin, "The Emperor," 268–273, overall an excellent discussion.

56. Christophilopoulou, *Ἐκλογή, ἀναγόρευσις καὶ στέψις,* 25 (in her treatment of the early period).

57. Christophilopoulou, *Τὸ πολίτευμα καὶ οἱ θεσμοὶ,* 31–32.

58. E.g., in Anastos, "Vox Populi"; Heim, "Vox exercitus"; Medvedev, "Ἡ συνοδικὴ ἀπόφαση," 231. Canepa, *The Two Eyes of the World,* 8, refers to "a harmonious semantic whole."

59. MacCormack, *Art and Ceremony,* 243. I am also much less convinced than MacCormack that imperial subjects "believed" the rhetoric.

60. Ibid., 253.

61. Ibid., 162.

62. *Pangyrici Latini* 6.3.1 *(Panegyric of Constantine).*

63. Themistios, *Oration* 6.73c *(Philadelphoi).*

64. Justin II to Tiberios II in Theophylaktos Simokattes, *History* 3.1.8.

65. Psellos, *Letter S* 207 (p. 508).

66. Michael VIII Palaiologos, *Regarding His Own Life* 453, 456.

67. Shumate, *Nation, Empire, Decline,* 30.

68. E.g., Heather, "Liar in Winter," 199–200 (Themistios); Kaldellis, *Ethnography,* 120–125 (Mauropous).

69. Tacitus, *Histories* 1.4.2.

70. Mansfield, *Taming the Prince,* 3.

71. Scott, *Hidden Transcripts,* 56.
72. Kaldellis, *Ethnography,* 78–79.
73. Photios, *Letter* 187 (lines 186–193): ὁ σωτὴρ ἡμῶν καὶ θεὸς τῶν μὲν πολιτικῶν τύπων καὶ τῆς περὶ αὐτὰ τάξεως οὐκ ἔσχε προηγούμενον τὸν σκοπόν; ᾔδει γάρ, ᾔδει τοὺς ἀνθρώπους ἱκανὴν τῇ πείρᾳ παρασκευὴν πρὸς ταῦτα λαβεῖν, τῆς χρείας καὶ τῆς ἀνάγκης τὴν μάθησιν αὐτοῖς ὁσημέραι ῥᾳδίαν παρεχομένης, καὶ τῶν προλαβόντων τὰ πταίσματα ἀποχρῶσαν τοῖς ἐσομένοις ἐπὶ τῶν ὁμοίων ἀντεισάγειν τὴν διόρθωσιν ... προηγουμένη δὲ τῷ σωτῆρι φροντὶς ἡ τῶν ψυχῶν ὑπῆρχε σωτηρία. For a parallel argument, see Ioannes Philoponos, *On the Creation of the World* 6.16 (p. 263): kingship is not a natural fact, but created by the will of men, which is often rotten.
74. Julian's work is lost, but fragments have been salvaged from the refutation by Cyril of Alexandria: see especially *Against the Galilaians* 178a–194d, 221e, 229e.
75. Photios, *Letter* 187.180–182.
76. Magdalino, "The History of the Future," 57. He is referring to Ioannes Oxeites, *Oration to Alexios Komnenos* 21–23.
77. Cutler, "On Byzantine Boxes," 45–46.
78. Maguire and Maguire, *Other Icons,* 3.
79. Walker, *The Emperor and the World,* 17–18.
80. Beck, *Byzantinisches Erotikon;* see also idem, *Das byzantinische Jahrtausend,* 7: the Byzantines were more worldly than we imagine.
81. Beck, *Das byzantinische Jahrtausend,* 85–86.
82. Alexander, "The Strength of Empire," 340 n. 4: "Constantine Porphyrogenitus seems to be the only mid-Byzantine author with a favorable view of the Hellenic name"; 341: "the term *Romania* is first found in the more popular language of Malalas to designate the Byzantine empire."
83. Alexander, "The Strength of Empire," 339; see also 356: "the failure of Byzantine intellectuals to analyze the sources of Byzantine greatness in secular terms." Cyril Mango is another often-cited scholar who has argued that Byzantium was "not classical" and restricted to supernatural modes of thought.
84. Haldon, *Warfare, State, and Society,* 23.
85. Whittow, *The Making of Byzantium,* 134–135.
86. E.g., Shepard, "Past and Future," 174.
87. Crowley, *Constantinople,* 19; see also 20: "The Byzantines were superstitiously obsessed with prophecy."
88. Reynolds, "Social Mentalities."
89. Justinian, *Deo Auctore* pr. (*Digest*).
90. Justinian, *Summa* pr. (*CJ*); and *Novel* 24 pr. For the historical analysis that Justinian gives here, see Kruse, "A Justinianic Debate," who answers the astute questions posed by Simon, "Legislation," 2. For "arms and laws," see also *Deo Auctore* pr. (*Digest*); *Tanta* pr. (*Digest*). It was a cliché in late antique sources: Honoré, *Tribonian,* 35 n. 373.

91. Haldon, *Byzantium in the Seventh Century*, 25.

92. Haldon and Brubaker, *Byzantium in the Iconoclast Era*, 11–15, 18–22.

93. Ibid., 73; compare 78: "But the political insecurity and ideological frailty of the usurper's position was not easily pushed into the background."

94. One occasionally encounters pleas for secular culture despite the religious slant of the sources: Merrills and Miles, *The Vandals*, 192, 227.

95. See my review in the *Ancient History Bulletin* 19 (2005): 97–101.

96. Dagron, *Emperor and Priest*, 21.

97. Ibid., 113.

98. MacCormack, *Art and Ceremony*, 242. See also Macrides, "Nomos and Kanon," 61: "If, as in theological thought and political theory, it is true that the Byzantine state and church were neither separate nor separable institutions but manifestations of one and the same Christianity . . ." But how could the state have been "a manifestation of Christianity"? The "if" suggests that Macrides is casting this as a conventional view, not necessarily her own.

99. Zonaras, *Chronicle* 13.11.

100. Jordanes, *Romana* 304; additional sources in Kaldellis, *Hellenism*, 145; Kekaumenos, *Strategikon* 88, cites him as a positive example; see also Augustine, *City of God* 5.21.

101. Zonaras, *Chronicle* 14.3.

102. Patriarch Nikephoros in Genesios, *On the Reigns of the Emperors* 1.16; Theophanes Continuatus, *Leon V* 30–31 (pp. 19–20); Zonaras, *Chronicle* 15.20.

103. This is true of almost all texts about Theophilos, even later ones such as the *Timarion;* Zonaras, *Chronicle* 15.25–26; Manasses, *Short Chronicle* 4711–4715; see Vlysidou, "L'empereur Théophile," especially 449; and Markopoulos, "The Rehabilitation."

104. Pseudo-Symeon, *Chronicle: Michael III and Theodora* 3 (p. 651); for another version of that event, see the *Life of David, Symeon, and Georgios of Lesbos* 27 (trans. pp. 214–215).

105. Niketas David, *Life of Patriarch Ignatios* 17 (p. 25).

106. Popović, "Zum Bild des römischen Kaisers Trajan," with many citations but almost no analysis of the significance of this phenomenon.

107. Tatianos and others: Digeser, *The Making of a Christian Empire*, 51; Eusebios: Johnson, *Ethnicity and Argument*, 179–181, 184, and the rest of that chapter; Gregorios of Nazianzos, *Letter* 78.6, on which Harries, *Law and Empire*, 150.

108. Revell, *Roman Imperialism and Local Identities*, 111.

109. Van Dam, *Roman Revolution*, 146–147, citing previous scholarship.

110. Galerius: Digeser, *The Making of a Christian Empire*, 56; Lactantius is discussed throughout, and see 141–142 for a summary; McGuckin, *The Ascent of Christian Law*, 115–116.

111. An obstacle is posed by the modern term "Caesaropapism," deemed a bad thing in the modern Catholic-Protestant West. In their rush to "rehabilitate" Byzantium on western terms, historians have rejected its applicabil-

ity and have thereby made themselves unable to explain the emperor's position vis-à-vis the Church. The impasse results from the following logic: if western scholars think it's bad, then it can't have been true of Byzantium, which we now want to show was not bad. But why should we care what Catholic-Protestant thinkers believe is right for Church-State relations? The Byzantines, being Romans, had their own ideas about this.

112. For a brief survey, see Vryonis, "The Patriarchate."
113. Eusebios, *Life of Constantine* 3.12.2.
114. Photios, *Bibliotheke* cod. 67 (Sergios).
115. E.g., Niketas David, *Life of Patriarch Ignatios* 21 (p. 36) (κοσμικοί ἄρχοντες . . . Ἐκκλησία), citing the relevant canon law at 31 (p. 48).
116. E.g., Leon VI, *Novels* 14, 16, 75, 96. See also Justinian, *Novel* 6 pr. with a distinction between human and divine things in jurisdictional terms.
117. Especially in his patriarchal orations, e.g., Psellos, *Funeral Oration for Michael Keroularios* p. 312.
118. Theophylaktos of Ohrid, *Defense of Eunuchs* pp. 312–315. The "rulers of the world" is from 1 Corinthians 2.6. For this text, see Messis, "Public hautement affiché."
119. The major moments in this permanent debate are surveyed by Runciman, *The Byzantine Theocracy*. See also the important comments by Haldon, *Byzantium in the Seventh Century*, 282–285.
120. Ioannes of Damascus, *On Divine Images* 2.12.
121. Pseudo-Symeon, *Chronicle: Leon V* 6 (p. 608).
122. For a formulation by a mainstream Byzantinist, see Pitsakis, "Ἀντίσταση κατά της εξουσίας," 50: "the issue [of Church-State relations] is not only not posed, it did not exist; it could not even enter the minds of the Byzantines." It depends, of course, on what we take "the issue" to have been. It is usually not defined (nor is it here).
123. E.g., Theodoros Stoudites, *Letter* 455, on which see Panagiotopoulos, *Περί Ἀθίγγανων*, 109–110; and the question of fighting priests: Kolbaba, *The Byzantine Lists*, 50–51; for Keroularios's political ambitions, see Dagron, *Emperor and Priest*, ch. 7.
124. Haldon, *Byzantium in the Seventh Century*, 284: "the Church within the East Roman empire became the East Roman imperial Church—the two were initially by no means the same." Department of state: Charanis, "On the Question"; and Macrides, "Nomos and Kanon," 61.
125. Syrianos, *On Strategy* 1–3 (pp. 10–15).
126. *Life of Antonios the Younger* (addit.) 10: Χριστιανὸς μὲν εἶναι ὁμολογῶ· οὐδέποτε δὲ τὰ χριστιανῶν οἶδα ἐμαυτὸν ἐργασάμενον.
127. Kaldellis, "The Hagiography of Doubt."
128. Van Dam, *Remembering Constantine*, 222.
129. Justinian, *Edict* 13 pr.
130. Justin II, *Novel* 148 pr. For the expression about wealth as the sinews of war, see the sources cited by Kaegi, *Byzantine Military Unrest*, 133.

131. Skylitzes, *Epitome: Michael III and Theodora* 10 (p. 97).
132. Anna Komnene, *Alexiad* 3.11.5.
133. Justin II, *Novel* 149.2.
134. Tacitus, *Histories* 4.74. I prefer the late third-century Kallinikos, *Patria of Rome* (= FGrH 281 F 1): "The collection of taxes is not an occasion for avarice on your part nor for harming those who pay them, but they are spent on the fighting men and, through them, returns to those who pay them, so that which is given is more like a loan than a taking-away of taxes."
135. Heather, *The Fall of the Roman Empire,* 120–121 (citing also Ammianus, *Res Gestae* 20.11.5, 22.3.7–8), and 297 citing a mid-fifth-century law admitting failure on this front. See also Karamboula, *Η νομοθετική δραστηριότητα,* 400 (Diocletian).
136. Leon VI, *Taktika* 11.9 (also 20.209); compare Epilogue 8 of the same work.
137. Konstantinos VII, *Novel* 5 (= *Macedonian Legislation,* p. 118; trans. p. 71). For the army as "the sinews of the Romans," see *Life of Basileios I* 51 (p. 288); Theodosios the Deacon, *The Capture of Crete* 1.73–74, 2.140; Psellos, *Chronographia* 4.19.
138. Romanos I, *Novel* 3.A2 (= *Macedonian Legislation,* p. 85; trans. p. 55, modified); for the context, see Kaplan, *Les hommes,* 185, 421–426. The background of social transformation is much debated. For other arguments from demography, see Theophylaktos of Ohrid, *Defense of Eunuchs* pp. 312–315.
139. Syrianos, *On Strategy* 2 (pp. 12–13).
140. Syrianos, *On Strategy* 3 (pp. 14–15).
141. Haldon, *Warfare, State, and Society,* 257.
142. In addition to Justinian, *Deo Auctore* pr. *(Digest),* see *Codex Theodosianus* 16.2.16; Photios, *Homily* 4.6 (with a pun on *rhomê* perhaps); Ioannes Oxeites, *Oration to Alexios Komnenos* p. 41; see McCormick, *Eternal Victory,* 237–252. But with them compare Plutarch, *Sulla* 19.5 (ὡς οὐχ ἧττον εὐτυχίᾳ κατορθώσας ἢ δεινότητι καὶ δυνάμει τὸν πόλεμον); Plotinos, *Ennead* 3.2.8.36–39; Ioannes Lydos, *On the Magistracies* 1.38 ("for those who have recourse to prayers in a time of war clearly expect defeat").
143. Psellos, *Chronographia* 6.132–133. Leon VI argued the same: *Taktika* 20.77.
144. Psellos, *Chronographia* 6.29.
145. Psellos, *Chronographia* 7.1.
146. Psellos, *Chronographia* 7.7.
147. Psellos, *Chronographia* 7.52–59. He was followed here by Zonaras, *Chronicle* 18.3.
148. See Kaldellis, *The Argument,* for how Psellos promotes his secular and antimonastic priorities.
149. Krallis, *Michael Attaleiates;* Kaldellis, "A Byzantine Argument."
150. Attaleiates, *History* 97.
151. Attaleiates, *History* 77.
152. Bryennios, *Materials for a History* 4.1.

153. Nelson, "The Lord's Annointed," 105.

154. For the early Palaiologan period, see Angelov, *Imperial Ideology,* e.g., 292–294 (on tax policy). Kiousopoulou, *Βασιλεύς ή οικονόμος,* highlights that aspect of the office in late Byzantium, but seems to regard it as a distinctive development of that period.

155. Photios, *Letter* 1.541–543 (καὶ τὸ μικρὸν τῶν πταισμάτων εἰς μέγεθος αἴρεται καὶ πανταχοῦ φέρεται καὶ πᾶσι γίνεται περιβόητον).

156. Psellos, *Chronographia* 6.27; see also Zonaras, *Chronicle* 18.29.

157. Cheynet, *Pouvoir et contestations,* 13.

158. E.g., Zonaras, *Chronicle* 14.28, on Theodosios III's unsuitability for the διοίκησις πραγμάτων.

159. *Hortatory Chapters* 41* (pp. 186–187). Saint Antony called the emperor Constantine "a mere man": Athanasios, *Life of Antony* 81.

Bibliography

Abbreviations

BF   *Byzantinische Forschungen*
BMGS *Byzantine and Modern Greek Studies*
BZ   *Byzantinische Zeitschrift*
DOP   *Dumbarton Oaks Papers*
FM   *Fontes Minores*
GRBS *Greek, Roman, and Byzantine Studies*
JRS   *Journal of Roman Studies*
PG   J.-P. Migne, ed., *Patrologiae cursus completus, Series graeca* (Paris)
REB   *Revue des études byzantines*

Primary Sources

The following bibliography does not include standard texts from classical antiquity. I cite English translations where available, for the convenience of the interested reader even when I have not quoted from them directly. I use "v." to designate specific volumes within a multivolume publication, and "vols." to designate the total number of volumes. "Ed." means only that the publication contains the original text, not necessarily the most recent critical edition (though often that is the case). Byzantine authors are listed by their family or second names, unless they are conventionally known by their first names or are emperors.

Agapetos the Deacon. *Advice to the Emperor.* Ed. R. Riedinger, *Agapetos Diakonos: Der Fürstenspiegel für Kaiser Iustinianos,* Athens, 1995; trans. P. N. Bell, *Three Political Voices from the Age of Justinian,* 99–122.

Agathias. *Histories.* Ed. R. Keydell, *Agathiae Myrinaei Historiarum Libri Quinque,* Berlin, 1967; trans. J. D. Frendo, *Agathias: The Histories,* Berlin, 1976.

Alexios I. *Chrysoboullon* of 1102. Ed. P. Lemerle et al., *Actes de Lavra,* v. 1: *Des origines à 1204,* Paris, 1970, 282–287.

Anna Komnene. *Alexiad*. Ed. D. R. Reinsch and A. Kambylis, *Annae Comnenae Alexias*, Berlin, 2001; trans. E. R. A. Sewter, rev. P. Frankopan, *Anna Komnene: Alexiad*, London, 2009.

Anonymous Post Dionem. *History*. Fr. ed. C. Müller, *Fragmenta Historicorum Graecorum*, v. 4. Paris, 1868, 192–199.

The Armenian History Attributed to Sebeos. Trans. R. W. Thomson, with notes by J. Howard-Johnston. Liverpool, 1999.

Athanasios. *History of the Arians*. Ed. H. G. Opitz, *Athanasius Werke*, v. 2.1. Berlin, 1940, 183–230.

Attaleiates, Michael. *History*. Ed. and trans. I. Pérez Martín, *Miguel Ataliates: Historia*, Madrid, 2002; ed. and trans. A. Kaldellis and D. Krallis, *Michael Attaleiates: History*, Washington, DC, 2012.

Aurelius Victor. *De Caesaribus*. Trans. H. W. Bird. Liverpool, 1994.

Balsamon, Theodoros. *Answers to the Questions of Markos, Bishop of Alexandria*. Ed. G. A. Rallis and M. Potlis, *Σύνταγμα τῶν ἱερῶν καὶ θείων κανόνων*, v. 4. Athens, 1852–1859, 447–496.

Basileios I. *Hortatory Chapters*. Ed. and trans. K. Païdas, [*Βασίλειος Α΄ Μακεδών*]: *Δύο παραινετικά κείμενα προς τον αὐτοκράτορα Λέοντα ϛ΄ τον Σοφό*. Athens, 2009.

Basilika. Ed. H. J. Scheltema et al., *Basilicorum Libri LX*, 8 vols. Groningen, 1953–.

Bessarion. *Encomium for Trebizond*. Ed. O. Lampsides, "Ὁ «εἰς Τραπεζοῦντα» λόγος τοῦ Βησσαρίωνος," *Ἀρχεῖον Πόντου* 39 (1984): 3–75.

Book of the Eparch. Ed. J. Koder, *Das Eparchenbuch Leons des Weisen*. Vienna, 1991.

Bryennios, Nikephoros. *Materials for a History*. Ed. and trans. P. Gautier, *Nicephori Bryennii Historiarum libri quattuor (Nicéphore Bryennios: Histoire)*. Brussels, 1975.

Campaign Organization. Ed. and trans. G. T. Dennis, *Three Byzantine Military Treatises*. Washington, DC, 1985, 246–335.

Chomatenos, Demetrios. *Ponemata*. Ed. G. Prinzing, *Demetrii Chomateni Ponemata Diaphora*. Berlin, 2002.

Choniates, Niketas. *History*. Ed. J.-L. van Dieten, *Nicetae Choniatae Historia*, Berlin, 1975; trans. H. J. Magoulias, *O City of Byzantium, Annals of Niketas Choniates*, Detroit, 1984.

——. *Orations*. Ed. J.-L. van Dieten, *Nicetae Choniatae orationes et epistulae*. Berlin, 1972.

Chronicon Paschale. Trans. M. and M. Whitby. Liverpool, 1989.

Cicero. *Republic*. Ed. and trans. C. W. Keyes, *Cicero: De re publica, De legibus*, Cambridge, MA, 1928; trans. N. Rudd, *Cicero: The Republic and the Laws*, Oxford, 1998.

CJ = Codex Iustinianus. Ed. P. Krueger, *Corpus Iuris Civilis*, v. 2, Berlin, 1895; trans. S. P. Scott, *The Civil Law*, v. 12–15, Cincinnati, 1932.

Codex Theodosianus. Ed. T. Mommsen, *Theodosiani libri XVI*, Berlin, 1905; trans. C. Pharr, *The Theodosian Code and Novels and the Sirmondian Constitutions*, Princeton, NJ, 1952.

Corippus, Flavius Cresconius. *In Praise of Justin II*. Ed. and trans. A. Cameron, *In laudem Iustini Augusti minoris libri IV*. London, 1976.

Dialogue on Political Science. Ed. and trans. C. M. Mazzucchi, *Menae patricii cum Thoma referendario de scientia politica dialogus,* Milan, 1982; trans. P. N. Bell, *Three Political Voices from the Age of Justinian,* Liverpool, 2009, 123–188.

Digest. Ed. T. Mommsen, *Corpus Iuris Civilis,* v. 1, pt. 2, Berlin, 1899; trans. A. Watson, ed., *The Digest of Justinian,* Philadelphia, 1985.

Doukas. *History.* Ed. and trans. V. Grecu, *Istoria Turco-Bizantina,* Bucharest, 1958; trans. H. Magoulias, *Decline and Fall of Byzantium to the Ottoman Turks, by Doukas,* Detroit, MI, 1975.

Eisagoge. Ed. I. and P. Zepos, *Jus Graecoromanum,* v. 2. Athens, 1931, 236–368.

Euagrios. *Ecclesiastical History.* Ed. J. Bidez and L. Parmentier, *The Ecclesiastical History of Evagrius,* London, 1898; trans. M. Whitby, *The Ecclesiastical History of Evagrius Scholasticus,* Liverpool, 2000.

Eunapios. *History.* Ed. and trans. R. C. Blockley, *The Fragmentary Classicising Historians of the Later Roman Empire: Eunapius, Olympiodorus, Priscus and Malchus,* 2 vols. Liverpool, 1981–1983, v. 2, 2–150.

Eusebios. *Ecclesiastical History.* Ed. and trans. K. Lake and J. E. L. Oulton, 2 vols. Cambridge, MA, 1926–1932.

——. *Life of Constantine.* Trans. A. Cameron and S. G. Hall, *Eusebius: Life of Constantine.* Oxford, 1999.

Eustathios of Thessalonike. *Capture of Thessalonike.* Ed. and trans. J. Melville-Jones, *Eustathios of Thessaloniki: The Capture of Thessaloniki.* Canberra, 1988.

Eutropius. *Breviarium.* Trans. H. W. Bird. Liverpool, 1993.

Genesios, Ioseph. *On the Reigns of the Emperors.* Ed. A. Lesmüller-Werner and I. Thurn, *Josephi Genesii regum libri quattuor,* Berlin, 1978; trans. A. Kaldellis, *Genesios: On the Reigns of the Emperors,* Canberra, 1998.

Geoponica. Ed. H. Beckh, Leipzig, 1895; trans. A. Dalby, *Geoponica: "Farm Work" or "Agricultural Pursuits,"* Devon, UK, 2010.

Georgios Monachos. *Chronicle.* Ed. C. de Boor, rev. P. Wirth, *Georgii Monachi Chronicon,* 2 vols. Stuttgart, 1978.

Georgios Synkellos. Ed. A. Mosshammer, *Ecloga chronographica,* Leipzig, 1984; trans. W. Adler and P. Tuffin, *The Chronography of George Synkellos: A Byzantine Chronicle of Universal History from the Creation,* Oxford, 2002.

Institutes. Ed. P. Krueger, trans. P. Birks and G. McLeod, *Justinian's Institutes.* Ithaca, NY, 1987.

Ioannes of Damaskos. *On Divine Images.* Ed. B. Kotter, *Die Schriften des Johannes von Damaskos,* v. 3, Berlin, 1975; trans. D. Anderson, *St. John of Damascus: On the Divine Images,* Crestwood, NY, 1980.

Ioannes Oxeites. Ed. P. Gautier, "Diatribes de Jean l'Oxite contre Alexis Ier Comnène," *Revue des études byzantines* 28 (170): 5–55.

"John of Nikiu." *Chronicle.* Trans. R. H. Charles, *The Chronicle of John, Coptic Bishop of Nikiu.* Amsterdam, 1916.

Jordanes. *Romana* and *Getica.* Ed. T. Mommsen, *Iordanis Romana et Getica.* Berlin, 1882 = *Monumenta Germaniae Historica, Auctores Antiquissimi* v. 5.

Julian. *Against the Galilaians*. Ed. and trans. W. C. Wright, *The Works of the Emperor Julian*. Cambridge, MA, 1913, v. 3, 318–433.

——. *Letter to Themistios* and *Misopogon*. Ed. and trans. idem, v. 2, 202–237 and 420–511.

Justin II. *Novels*. See Justinian, *Novels*.

Justinian. *Novels and Edicts*. Ed. R. Schoell and G. Kroll, *Corpus Iuris Civilis*, v. 3, Berlin, 1899; trans. S. P. Scott, *The Civil Law*, v. 16–17, Cincinnati, 1932.

Kallinikos. *Patria of Rome (FGrH* 281 F 1). Ed. and trans. A. Kaldellis in I. Worthington, ed., *Brill's New Jacoby*, published online by Brill, www.brill.com.

Kekaumenos. *Strategikon*. Ed. and trans. M. D. Spadaro, *Cecaumeno: Raccomandazioni e consigli di un galantuomo*. Alessandria, 1998.

Konstantinos VII Porphyrogennetos. *Book of Ceremonies*. Ed. J. J. Reiske, *Constantini Porphyrogeniti imperatoris de cerimoniis aulae byzantinae*, 2 vols., Bonn, 1829–1830; text and trans. A. Moffatt and M. Tall, *Constantine Porphyrogennetos: The Book of Ceremonies*, 2 vols., Canberra, 2012.

——. *De administrando imperio*. Ed. G. Moravcsik and trans. R. J. H. Jenkins, *Constantine Porphyrogenitus: De administrando imperio*, Washington, DC, 1967; annotated trans. K. Belke and P. Soustal, *Die Byzantiner und ihre Nachbarn: Die De administrando imperio genannte Lehrschrift des Kaisers Konstantinos Porphyrogennetos für seinen Sohn Romanos*, Vienna, 1995.

——. *On Embassies*. Ed. C. de Boor, *Excerpta historica iussu imp. Constantini Porphyrogeniti confecta*, v. 1: *Excerpta de legationibus*. Berlin, 1903.

——. *On Plots*. Ed. C. de Boor, *Excerpta historica iussu imp. Constantini Porphyrogeniti confecta*, v. 3: *Excerpta de insidiis*. Berlin, 1905.

Konstantinos IX Monomachos. *Novel on the Nomophylax*. Ed. A. Salač, *Novella constitutio saec. XI medii*. Prague, 1954.

Kydones, Demetrios. *Apologia for His Faith*. Ed. G. Mercati, *Notizie di Procoro e Demetrio Cidone, Manuele Caleca e Teodoro Meliteniota*, Vatican City, 1931, 359–437; trans. (based on a German trans.) in J. Likoudis, *Ending the Byzantine Greek Schism*, New Rochelle, NY, 1992, 22–70.

Lactantius. *On the Deaths of the Persecutors*. Ed. and trans. J. L. Creed, *Lactantius: De Mortibus Persecutorum*. Oxford, 1984.

Leon III. *Ekloge*. Ed. L. Burgmann, *Ecloga: Das Gesetzbuch Leons III. und Konstantinos' V.* Frankfurt, 1983.

Leon VI. *Novels*. Ed. P. Noailles and A. Dain, *Les Novelles de Léon VI le Sage*, Paris, 1944; ed. and trans. S. N. Troianos, *Οι Νεαρές Λέοντος ς΄ του Σοφού*, Athens, 2007; trans. S. P. Scott, *The Civil Law*, v. 17, Cincinnati, 1932.

——. *Taktika*. Ed. and trans. G. T. Dennis, *The Taktika of Leo VI*. Washington, DC, 2010.

Leon the Deacon. *History*. Ed. C. B. Hase, *Leonis diaconi Historae libri X*, Bonn, 1828; trans. A.-M. Talbot and D. F. Sullivan, *The History of Leo the Deacon: Byzantine Military Expansion in the Tenth Century*, Washington, DC, 2005.

Life of Antonios the Younger (addit.). Ed. F. Halkin, "Saint Antoine le Jeune et Petronas le vainqueur des Arabes en 863," *Analecta Bollandiana* 62 (1944): 210–223.

Life of Basileios I. Ed. and trans. I. Ševčenko, *Chronographiae quae Theophanis Continuati nomine fertur liber quo Vita Basilii imperatoris amplectitur.* Berlin, 2011.

Life of David, Symeon, and Georgios of Lesbos. Ed. J. van den Gheyn, "Acta graeca ss. Davidis, Symonis et Georgii Mitylenae in insula Lesbo," *Analecta Bollandiana* 18 (1899): 209–259; trans. D. Domingo-Forasté in A.-M. Talbot, ed., *Byzantine Defenders of Images: Eight Saints' Lives in English Translation,* Washington, DC, 1998, 143–241.

Liudprand of Cremona. Trans. P. Squatriti, *The Complete Works of Liudprand of Cremona.* Washington, DC, 2007.

Lydos, Ioannes. *On the Magistracies of the Roman State.* Ed. and trans. A. Bandy, *Ioannes Lydus: On Powers or The Magistracies of the Roman State.* Philadelphia, 1983.
———. *On the Months.* Ed. R. Wuensch, *Ioannis Laurentii Lydi Liber de mensibus.* Leipzig, 1898.

Macedonian Legislation. Ed. N. Svoronos, *Les Novelles des empereurs macédoniens concernant la terre et les stratiotes,* Athens, 1994; trans. E. McGeer, *The Land Legislation of the Macedonian Emperors,* Toronto, 2000.

Malalas, Ioannes. *Chronicle.* Ed. I. Thurn, *Ioannis Malalae Chronographia,* Berlin and New York, 2000; trans. E. Jeffreys et al., *The Chronicle of John Malalas,* Melbourne, 1986.

Manasses, Konstantinos. *Short Chronicle.* Ed. O. Lampsides, *Constantini Manassis Breviarium Chronicum,* 2 vols. Athens, 1996.

Mauropous, Ioannes. *Letters.* Ed. and trans. A. Karpozilos, *The Letters of Ioannes Mauropous, Metropolitan of Euchaita.* Thessalonike, 1990.

Menandros. *History.* Ed. and trans. R. C. Blockley, *The History of Menander the Guardsman.* Liverpool, 1985.

Michael VIII Palaiologos. *Regarding His Own Life.* Ed. and trans. H. Grégoire, "Imperatoris Michaelis Palaeologi De vita sua," *Byzantion* 29–30 (1959–1960): 447–476.

Naumachika for the patrikios and parakoimomenos Basileios. Ed. A. Dain, *Naumachica.* Paris, 1943.

Nikephoros, patriarch of Constantinople. *Short History.* Ed. and trans. C. Mango. Washington, DC, 1990.

Niketas David. *Life of Patriarch Ignatios.* Ed. and trans. A. Smithies, with notes by J. M. Duffy. Washington, DC, 2013.

Nikolaos Mystikos. *Letters.* Ed. and trans. R. J. H. Jenkins and L. G. Westerink, *Nicholas I Patriarch of Constantinople: Letters.* Washington, DC, 1973.
———. *Tract on the Tetragamy.* Ed. and trans. L. G. Westerink, *Nicholas I, Patriarch of Constantinople: Miscellaneous Writings.* Washington, DC, 1981, 36–55.

On Skirmishing. Ed. and trans. in G. Dennis, *Three Byzantine Military Treatises.* Washington, DC, 1985, 143–239.

Orosius. *Seven Books of History against the Pagans.* Trans. A. T. Fear. Liverpool, 2010.

Panegyrici Latini. Ed. and trans. C. E. V. Nixon and B. S. Rodgers, *In Praise of Later Roman Emperors: The Panegyrici Latini.* Berkeley, CA, 1994.

Patria of Constantinople. Ed. and trans. A. Berger, *Accounts of Medieval Constantinople: The Patria.* Washington, DC, 2013.

Philoponos, Ioannes. *On the Creation of the World.* Ed. G. Reichardt, *Ioannes Philoponus: De opificio mundi.* Leipzig, 1897.

Photios. *Bibliotheke.* Ed. and trans. R. Henry, *Photius: Bibliothèque,* 8 vols. Paris, 1959–1977; partial trans. N. G. Wilson, *Photius: The Bibliotheca,* London, 1993.

——. *Homilies.* Ed. S. Aristarchos, Τοῦ ἐν ἁγίοις πατρὸς ἡμῶν Φωτίου πατριάρχου Κωνσταντινουπόλεως λόγοι καὶ ὁμιλίαι, 2 vols., Constantinople, 1900; trans. C. Mango, *The Homilies of Photius Patriarch of Constantinople,* Cambridge, MA, 1958.

——. *Letters.* Ed. B. Laourdas and L. G. Westerink, *Photii Patriarchae Constantinopolitani Epistulae et Amphilochia,* 3 vols. Leipzig, 1983–1987.

Priskos. *History.* Ed. and trans. R. C. Blockley, *The Fragmentary Classicising Historians of the Later Roman Empire: Eunapius, Olympiodorus, Priscus and Malchus,* 2 vols. Liverpool, 1981–1983, v. 2, 222–400.

Prokopios. *Wars* and *Secret History.* Ed. J. Haury, rev. G. Wirth, *Procopii Caesariensis opera omnia,* 4 vols., Leipzig, 1962–1964; trans. H. B. Dewing, *Procopius,* 6 vols., Cambridge, MA, 1914–1935; trans. A. Kaldellis, *Prokopios: The Secret History with Related Texts,* Indianapolis, 2010.

Prokopios of Gaza. *Panegyric for Anastasios.* Ed. and trans. A. Chauvot, *Procope de Gaza, Priscien de Césarée: Panégyriques de l'empereur Anastase Ier.* Bonn, 1986.

Psellos, Michael. *Chronographia.* Ed. S. Impellizeri and trans. S. Ronchey, *Michele Psello: Imperatori di Bisanzio (Cronografia),* 2 vols., Milan, 1984; trans. E. R. A. Sewter, *Michael Psellus: Fourteen Byzantine Rulers,* London, 1966.

——. *Chrysoboullon of Michael VII Doukas to Robert Guiscard.* Ed. G. T. Dennis, *Michaelis Pselli orationes forenses et acta.* Stuttgart, 1994, 176–181.

——. *Encomium for Konstantinos Leichoudes.* Ed. K. Sathas, Μεσαιωνικὴ Βιβλιοθήκη, v. 4, Paris, 1874, 388–421; trans. U. Criscuolo, *Michele Psello: Orazione in Memoria di Costantino Lichudi,* Messina, 1983.

——. *Funeral Oration for Ioannes Xiphilinos.* Ed. K. Sathas, Μεσαιωνικὴ Βιβλιοθήκη, v. 4. Athens, 1874, 421–462.

——. *Funeral Oration for Michael Keroularios.* Ed. K. Sathas, Μεσαιωνικὴ Βιβλιοθήκη, v. 4. Athens, 1874, 303–387.

——. *Historia Syntomos.* Ed. and trans. W. J. Aerts, *Michaelis Pselli Historia syntomos.* Berlin, 1990.

——. *Letters S.* Ed K. N. Sathas, Μεσαιωνικὴ Βιβλιοθήκη, v. 5. Venice, 1876.

——. *Orationes Panegyricae.* Ed. G. T. Dennis, *Michaelis Pselli orationes panegyricae.* Stuttgart, 1994.

——. *Oratoria Minora.* Ed. A. R. Littlewood, *Michaelis Psellis oratoria minora.* Leipzig, 1985.

Pseudo-Symeon. *Chronicle.* Ed. in I. Bekker, *Theophanes Continuatus, Ioannes Cameniata, Symeon Magister, Georgius Monachus.* Bonn, 1838.

Pseudo-Zacharias. *Ecclesiastical History*. Ed. G. Greatrex, trans. R. R. Phenix and C. B. Horn, *The Chronicle of Pseudo-Zachariah Rhetor: Church and War in Late Antiquity*. Liverpool, 2011.

al-Rudhrawari. *Continuation of Miskawayh's Experiences of the Nations*. Trans. D. S. Margoliouth, in idem and H. F. Amedroz, *The Eclipse of the 'Abbasid Caliphate: Original Chronicle of the Fourth Islamic Century*, v. 6. Oxford, 1921.

Skoutariotes, Theodoros. *Historical Synopsis*. Ed. K. Sathas, *Μεσαιωνικὴ Βιβλιοθήκη*, v. 7. Venice, 1894.

Skylitzes, Ioannes. *Synopsis of Histories*. Ed. J. Thurn, *Ioannis Scylitzae Synopsis Historiarum*, Berlin, 1973; trans. J. Wortley, *John Skylitzes: A Synopsis of Byzantine History, 811–1057*, Cambridge, 2010.

Synesios. *On Kingship*. Ed. N. Terzaghi, *Synesii Cyrenensis opuscula*. Rome, 1944, 5–62.

Syrianos. *On Strategy*. Ed. and trans. in G. Dennis, *Three Byzantine Military Treatises*. Washington, DC, 1985, 9–135.

Themistios. *Orations*. Ed. G. Downey and A. F. Norman, *Themistii Orationes*, 2 vols. Leipzig, 1951–1970.

Theodoros Anagnostes. *Ecclesiastical History*. Ed. C. Hansen, *Theodoros Anagnostes: Kirchengeschichte*. Berlin, 1971.

Theodoros of Nikaia. *Letters*. Ed. J. Darrouzès, *Épistoliers byzantines du Xe siècle*. Paris, 1960, 261–316.

Theodoros Stoudites. *Letters*. Ed. G. Fatouros, *Theodori Studitae Epistulae*, 2 vols. Berlin, 1992.

Theodosios the Deacon. *The Capture of Crete*. Ed. U. Criscuolo, *Theodosius Diaconus: De Creta Capta*. Leipzig, 1979.

Theophanes. *Chronographia*. Ed. C. de Boor, *Theophanis Chronographia*, 2 vols., Leipzig, 1883–1885; trans. C. Mango and R. Scott, *The Chronicle of Theophanes Confessor: Byzantine and Near Eastern History AD 284–813*, Oxford, 1997.

Theophanes Continuatus. Ed. I. Bekker. Bonn, 1838.

Theophilos. *Institouta*. Ed. J. H. A. Lokin et al., *Theophili Antecessoris Paraphrasis Institutionum*, Groningen, 2010; also ed. in I. and P. Zepos, *Jus Graecoromanum*, v. 3, Athens, 1931, 3–271.

Theophylaktos of Ohrid. *Defense of Eunuchs*. Ed. and trans. P. Gautier, *Théophylacte d'Achrida: Discours, traités, poésies*. Thessalonike, 1980, 287–331.

——. *Letters*. Ed. and trans. P. Gautier, *Théophylacte d'Achrida: Lettres*. Thessalonike, 1986.

——. *Oration to Konstantinos Doukas*. Ed. and trans. P. Gautier, *Théophylacte d'Achrida: Discours, traités, poésies*. Thessalonike, 1980, 177–211.

Theophylaktos Simokattes. *History*. Ed. C. de Boor, rev. P. Wirth, *Theophylacti Simocattae Historiae*, Stuttgart, 1972; trans. M. and M. Whitby, *The History of Theophylact Simocatta*, Oxford, 1986.

Vegetius. *Epitome of Military Science*. Trans. N. P. Milner. Liverpool, 1993.

Xiphilinos, Ioannes. *Epitome of Kassios Dion*. Ed. U. P. Boissevain, *Cassii Dionis Cocceiani historiarum romanarum quae supersunt*, v. 1. Berlin, 1901.

Yuhannan of Amida (John of Ephesos). *Ecclesiastical History: Part Three.* Trans. R. P. Smith, *The Third Part of the Ecclesiastical History of John, Bishop of Ephesus.* Oxford, 1860.

Zonaras, Ioannes. *Chronicle.* Ed. *PG* 134–135. Ed. M. Pinder and T. Büttner-Wobst, *Ioannis Zonarae Epitomae historiarum,* 3 vols. Berlin, 1841–1897.

Modern Scholarship

Aalders, G. J. D. "ΝΟΜΟΣ ΕΜΨΥΧΟΣ." In P. Steinmetz, ed., *Politeia und Res Publica: Beiträge zum Verständnis von Politik, Recht und Staat in der Antike.* Wiesbaden, 1969, 315–329.

Adams, J. N. *Bilingualism and the Latin Language.* Cambridge, 2004.

Adcock, F. E. *Roman Political Ideas and Practice.* Ann Arbor, MI, 1964.

Agamben, G. *State of Exception.* Trans. K. Attell. Chicago, 2005.

——. *The Kingdom and the Glory: For a Theological Genealogy of Economy and Government.* Trans. L. Chiesa. Stanford, CA, 2011.

Ahrweiler, H. *L'idéologie politique de l'Empire byzantin.* Paris, 1975.

Aldrete, G. S. *Gestures and Acclamations in Ancient Rome.* Baltimore, MD, 1999.

Alexander, P. *The Patriarch Nicephorus of Constantinople: Ecclesiastical Policy and Image Worship in the Byzantine Empire.* Oxford, 1958.

——. "The Strength of Empire and Capital as Seen through Byzantine Eyes." *Speculum* 37 (1962): 339–357; reprinted in idem, *Religious and Political History and Thought in the Byzantine Empire,* London, 1978, III; and in J. Shepard, ed., *The Expansion of Orthodox Europe: Byzantium, the Balkans and Russia,* Ashgate, 2007, 9–28.

Alföldi, A. *Die monarchische Repräsentation im römischen Kaiserreiche.* Darmstadt, 1970.

Anastos, M. "Vox populi voluntas Dei and the Election of the Byzantine Emperor." In J. Neusner, ed., *Christianity, Judaism and Other Greco-Roman Cults: Studies for Morton Smith at Sixty,* v. 2. Leiden, 1975, 181–207.

——. "Byzantine Political Theory: Its Classical Precedents and Legal Embodiment." In S. Vryonis, ed., *The "Past" in Medieval and Modern Greek Culture.* Malibu, CA, 1978, 13–53.

Anderson, G. "The Personality of the Greek State." *Journal of Hellenic Studies* 129 (2009): 1–22.

Ando, C. "Was Rome a Polis?" *Classical Antiquity* 18 (1999): 5–34.

——. *Imperial Ideology and Provincial Loyalty in the Roman Empire.* Berkeley, CA, 2000.

——. "Imperial Identities." In T. Whitmarsh, ed., *Local Knowledge and Microidentities in the Imperial Greek World.* Cambridge, 2010, 17–45.

——. "The Roman City in the Roman Period." In S. Benoist, ed., *Rome, a City and Its Empire in Perspective: The Impact of the Roman World through Fergus Millar's Research.* Leiden, 2012, 109–124.

——. *Law, Language, and Empire in the Roman Tradition.* Philadelphia, 2011.

——. "From Republic to Empire." In M. Peachin, ed., *The Oxford Handbook of Social Relations in the Roman World.* Oxford, 2011, 37–66.

——. "The Origins and Import of Republican Constitutionalism." *Cardozo Law Review* 34 (2012–2013): 101–119.

Angelov, D. "Byzantinism: The Imaginary and Real Heritage of Byzantium in Southeastern Europe." In D. Keridis et al., eds., *New Approaches to Balkan Studies.* Dulles, VA, 2003, 3–23.

——. *Imperial Ideology and Political Thought in Byzantium, 1204–1330.* Cambridge, 2007.

——. "Introduction." In idem, ed., *Church and Society in Late Byzantium.* Kalamazoo, MI, 2009, 1–7.

Angold, M. "The Byzantine State on the Eve of the Battle of Manzikert." *BF* 26 (1991): 9–34.

——. "The Byzantine Political Process at Crisis Point." In P. Stephenson, ed., *The Byzantine World.* London, 2010, 5–21.

Antoniadis-Bibicou, H. "Introduction: Byzance entité historique médiane dans le temps et dans l'espace." In eadem, ed., *Byzance et l'Europe: Colloque à la Maison de l'Europe.* Paris, 2001, 13–26.

Auzépy, M.-F., and G. Saint-Guillain, eds. *Oralité et lien social au Moyen Âge (Occident, Byzance, Islam): Parole donné, foi jurée, serment.* Paris, 2008.

Baldwin, B. "On the Date of the Anonymous περὶ στρατηγικῆς." *BZ* 81 (1988): 290–293.

Bardill, J. *Constantine: Divine Emperor of the Christian Golden Age.* Cambridge, 2012.

Batstone, W. W., and C. Damon. *Caesar's Civil War.* Oxford, 2006.

Bauer, F. A., "Urban Space and Ritual: Constantinople in Late Antiquity." In J. R. Brandt and O. Steen, eds., *Imperial Art as Christian Art—Christian Art as Imperial Art: Expression and Meaning in Art and Architecture from Constantine to Justinian.* Rome, 2001, 27–61.

Baun, J. *Tales from Another Byzantium: Celestial Journey and Local Community in the Medieval Greek Apocrypha.* Cambridge, 2007.

Baynes, N. H. *Byzantine Studies and Other Essays.* London, 1955.

Beaucamp, J. "Byzantine Egypt and Imperial Law." In R. S. Bagnall, ed., *Egypt in the Byzantine World, 300–700.* Cambridge, 2007, 271–287.

Beck, H.-G. *Senat und Volk von Konstantinopel: Probleme der byzantinischen Verfassungsgeschichte.* Munich, 1966.

——. *Res Publica Romana: Vom Staatsdenken der Byzantiner.* Munich, 1970.

——. *Geschichte der byzantinischen Volksliteratur.* Munich, 1971.

——. *Das byzantinische Jahrtausend.* Munich, 1978.

——. *Byzantinisches Erotikon: Orthodoxie, Literatur, Gesellschaft.* Munich, 1984.

Beihammer, A. "Der harte Sturz des Bardas Skleros: Eine Fallstudie zu zwischenstaatliche Kommunikation und Konfliktführung in der byzantinisch-arabischen Diplomatie des 10. Jahrhunderts." *Römische historische Mitteilungen* 45 (2003): 21–57.

Bell, P. N. *Three Political Voices from the Age of Justinian.* Liverpool, 2009.

——. *Social Conflict in the Age of Justinian: Its Nature, Management, and Mediation.* Oxford, 2013.

Billig, M., et al. *Ideological Dilemmas: A Social Psychology of Everyday Thinking.* London, 1988.

Bjornlie, M. S. *Politics and Tradition between Rome, Ravenna and Constantinople: A Study of Cassiodorus and the* Variae, *527–554.* Cambridge, 2013.

Boeck, E. "Engaging the Byzantine Past: Strategies of Visualizing History in Sicily and Bulgaria." In R. Macrides, ed., *History as Literature in Byzantium.* Burlington, VT, 2010, 215–235.

Bourdara, K. A. *Καθοσίωσις καί τυραννίς κατά τούς μέσους βυζαντινούς χρόνους: Μακεδονική δυναστεία (867–1056).* Athens, 1981.

——. *Καθοσίωσις καί τυραννίς κατά τούς μέσους βυζαντινούς χρόνους: 1056–1081.* Athens, 1984.

——. "Το έγκλημα καθοσιώσεως κατά την περίοδο της βασιλείας των Αγγέλων (1185–1204)." In *Τιμαί Ιωάννου Τριανταφυλλόπουλου.* Athens, 2000, 437–464.

Brubaker, L. "The *Christian Topography* (Vat. gr. 699) Revisited: Image, Text, and Conflict in Ninth-Century Byzantium." In E. Jeffreys, ed., *Byzantine Style, Religion and Civilization: In Honour of Sir Steven Runciman.* Cambridge, 2006, 3–24.

Brunt, P. A. "Lex de imperio Vespasiani." *JRS* 67 (1977): 95–116.

Bucher, G. S. "The Origins, Program, and Composition of Appian's Roman History." *Transactions of the American Philological Association* 130 (2000): 411–458.

Burgman, L. "A Law for Emperors: Observations on a Chrysobull of Nikephoros III Botaneiates." In P. Magdalino, ed., *New Constantines: The Rhythm of Imperial Renewal in Byzantium, 4th–13th Centuries.* Brookfield, VT, 1994, 247–257.

Bury, J. B. "The Constitution of the Later Roman Empire." In H. Temperley, ed., *Selected Essays of J. B. Bury.* Cambridge, 1930, 99–125.

Cameron, Alan. *Circus Factions: Blues and Greens at Rome and Byzantium.* Oxford, 1976.

——. *The Last Pagans of Rome.* Oxford, 2011.

Cameron, Alan, and J. Long. *Barbarians and Politics at the Court of Arcadius.* Berkeley, CA, 1993.

Cameron, Averil. "Agathias on the Early Merovingians." *Annali della Scuola Normale Superiore di Pisa. Classe di lettere e filosofia* ser. 2, 37 (1968): 95–140.

——. "An Emperor's Abdication." *Byzantinoslavica* 37 (1976): 161–167.

——. "The Construction of Court Ritual: The Byzantine *Book of Ceremonies.*" In D. Cannadine and S. Price, eds., *Rituals of Royalty: Power and Ceremonial in Traditional Societies.* Cambridge, 1987, 106–136.

——. *The Use and Abuse of Byzantium: An Essay in Reception.* London, 1992.

——. *The Byzantines.* Malden, MA, 2006.

Campbell, J. B. *The Emperor and the Roman Army, 31 BC–AD 235.* Oxford, 1984.

Canepa, M. P. *The Two Eyes of the World: Art and Ritual of Kingship between Rome and Sasanian Iran.* Berkeley, CA, 2009.

Chaniotis, A. "The Divinity of Hellenistic Rulers." In A. Erskine, ed., *A Companion to the Hellenistic World.* Oxford, 2003, 431–445.

Charanis, P. "The Role of the People in the Political Life of the Byzantine Empire: The Period of the Comneni and the Palaeologi." *Byzantine Studies* 5 (1978): 69-79.

———. "On the Question of the Evolution of the Byzantine Church into a National Greek Church." *Βυζαντιακά* 2 (1982): 95-109.

El Cheikh, N. M. *Byzantium Viewed by the Arabs.* Cambridge, MA, 2004.

Cheynet, J.-C. *Pouvoir et contestations à Byzance (963–1210).* Paris, 1990.

———. "La colère du peuple a Byzance (Xe–XIIe siècle)." *Société française d'histoire urbaine* 3 (2001): 25-38.

———. "Les limites du pouvoir à Byzance: une forme de tolérance?" In A. Nikolaou, ed., *Ανοχή και καταστολή στους μέσους χρόνους: Μνήμη Λένου Μαυρομάτη.* Athens, 2002, 15-28.

Christophilopoulou, A. "Σιλέντιον." *BZ* 44 (1951): 79-85.

———. *Ἐκλογή, ἀναγόρευσις καὶ στέψις τοῦ βυζαντινοῦ αὐτοκράτορος.* Athens, 1956.

———. "Περὶ τὸ πρόβλημα τῆς ἀναδείξεως τοῦ βυζαντινοῦ αὐτοκράτορος." *Ἐπιστημονικὴ Ἐπετηρὶς τῆς Φιλοσοφικῆς Σχολῆς τοῦ Πανεπιστημίου Ἀθηνῶν* 12 (1961-1962): 471-492.

———. "Αἱ βάσεις τοῦ βυζαντινοῦ πολιτεύματος." *Ἐπιστημονικὴ Ἐπετηρὶς τῆς Φιλοσοφικῆς Σχολῆς τοῦ Πανεπιστημίου Ἀθηνῶν* 22 (1971-1972): 201-223.

———. *Τὸ πολίτευμα καὶ οἱ θεσμοὶ τῆς βυζαντινῆς αὐτοκρατορίας, 324–1204.* Athens, 2004.

Christou, E. *Αυτοκρατορική εξουσία και πολιτική πρακτική: Ο ρόλος του παραδυναστεύοντος στη βυζαντινή διοίκηση (τέλη 8ου–αρχές 11ου αιώνα).* Athens, 2008.

Chrysos, E. "Ἕνας ὅρκος πίστεως στὸν αὐτοκράτορα Ἀναστάσιο." In V. Kremmydas et al., eds., *Ἀφιέρωμα στον Νίκο Σβορώνο.* Rethymno, 1986, v. 1, 5-22.

———. "Το δικαίωμα της αντίστασης στο Βυζάντιο." In E. Grammatikopoulou, ed., *Αμφισβήτηση της εξουσίας.* Athens, 2003, 35-48.

Čičurov, I. "Gesetz und Gerechtigkeit in den byzantinischen Fürstenspiegeln des 6.-9. Jahrhunderts." In L. Burgmann et al., eds., *Cupido Legum.* Frankfurt, 1985, 33-45.

Clark, A. J. *Divine Qualities: Cult and Community in Republican Rome.* Oxford, 2007.

Cline, E. H., and M. W. Graham. *Ancient Empires from Mesopotamia to the Rise of Islam.* Cambridge, 2011.

Connolly, S. *Lives behind the Laws: The World of the* Codex Hermogenianus. Bloomington, IN, 2010.

Cosentino, S. "The Syrianos's 'Strategikon': A 9th Century Source?" *Byzantinistica: Rivista di studi bizantini e slavi* 2 (2000): 243-280.

Criscuolo, U. "Tardoantico e umanesimo bizantino: Michele Psello." *Koinonia* 5 (1981): 7-23.

———. "πολιτικὸς ἀνήρ: Contributo al pensiero politica di Michele Psello." *Rendiconti dell'Accademia di Archeologia, Lettere e Belle Arti di Napoli* 57 (1982): 129-163.

———. "Pselliana." *Studi italiani di filologia classica* 4 (1982): 194-215.

——. *Michele Psello: Orazione in Memoria di Costantino Lichudi*. Messina, 1983.

Croix, G. E. M. de Ste. *The Class Struggle in the Ancient Greek World: From the Archaic Age to the Arab Conquests*. Ithaca, NY, 1989.

Croke, B. "Justinian under Justin: Reconfiguring a Reign." *BZ* 100 (2007): 13–56.

——. "Justinian, the 'Sleepless Emperor.'" In G. Nathan and L. Garland, eds., *Basileia: Essays on Imperium and Culture in Honour of E. M. and M. J. Jeffreys*. Brisbane, 2011, 103–108.

Crowley, R. *Constantinople: The Last Great Siege, 1453*. New York, 2005.

Curta, F. *Southeastern Europe in the Middle Ages, 500–1250*. Cambridge, 2006.

Cutler, A. "On Byzantine Boxes." *Journal of the Walters Art Gallery* 42–43 (1984–1985): 32–47.

Dagron, G. "La règle et l'exception: Analyse de la notion d'économie." In D. Simon, ed., *Religiöse Devianz: Untersuchungen zu sozialen, rechtlichen und theologischen Reaktionen auf religiöse Abweichung im westlichen und östlichen Mittelalter*. Frankfurt, 1990, 1–18.

——. "Lawful Society and Legitimate Power: Ἔννομος πολιτεία, ἔννομος ἀρχή." In A. E. Laiou and D. Simon, eds., *Law and Society in Byzantium: Ninth–Twelfth Centuries*. Washington, DC, 1994: 27–51.

——. "The Urban Economy, Seventh–Twelfth Centuries." In A. E. Laiou, ed., *The Economic History of Byzantium from the Seventh through the Fifteenth Century*. Washington, DC, 2002, v. 2, 393–461.

——. *Emperor and Priest: The Imperial Office in Byzantium* Trans. J. Birrell. Cambridge, 2003.

——. *L'hippodrome de Constantinople: Jeux, peuple et politique*. Paris, 2011.

Davies, J. K. "On the Non-Usablity of the Concept of 'Sovereignty' in an Ancient Greek Context." In L. A. Foresti, ed., *Federazioni e federalismo nell'Europa antica*. Milan, 1994, 51–65.

Diehl, C. "Le sénat et le peuple byzantin aux VIIe et VIIIe siècles." *Byzantion* 1 (1924): 201–213.

Digeser, E. D. *The Making of a Christian Empire: Lactantius and Rome*. Ithaca, NY, 2000.

Dijkstra, J., and G. Greatrex. "Patriarchs and Politics in Constantinople in the Reign of Anastasius (with a Reedition of *O.Mon.Epiph.* 59)." *Millennium* 6 (2009): 223–264.

Dölger, F. "Die Kaiserurkunde der Byzantiner als Ausdruck ihrer politischen Anschauungen." In idem, *Byzanz und die europäische Staatenwelt*. Ettal, 1953, 9–33.

——. "Rom in der Gedankenwelt der Byzantiner." Ibid., 70–115.

Drake, H. A. "Lessons from Diocletian's Persecution." In D. V. Twomey and M. Humphries, eds., *The Great Persecution*. Dublin, 2009, 49–60.

Drexler, H. "Res publica." *Maia* 9 (1957): 247–281 and 10 (1958): 3–37.

Dvornik, F. "The Emperor Julian's 'Reactionary' Ideas on Kingship." In K. Weitzmann, ed., *Late Classical and Mediaeval Studies in Honor of Albert Matthias Friend*. Princeton, NJ, 1955, 71–81.

———. *Early Christian and Byzantine Political Philosophy: Origins and Background.* Washington, DC, 1966.

Dzelabdzic, D. "Η δημοκρατική Ρώμη στην πολιτική σκέψη του Μιχαήλ Ψελλού." *Zbornik radova Visantološkog instituta* 42 (2005): 23–34.

Eagleman, D. *Incognito: The Secret Lives of the Brain.* New York, 2011.

Eder, W. "Augustus and the Power of Tradition: The Augustan Principate as Binding Link between the Republic and Empire." In K. Raaflaub and M. Toher, eds., *Between Republic and Empire: Interpretations of Augustus and His Principate.* Berkeley, CA, 1990, 71–122.

Efthymiades, S. "A Historian and His Tragic Hero: A Literary Reading of Theophylact Simocatta's Ecumenical History." In R. Macrides, ed., *History as Literature in Byzantium.* Burlington, VT, 2010, 169–185.

Ekonomou, A. J. *Byzantine Rome and the Greek Popes: Eastern Influences on Rome and the Papacy from Gregory the Great to Zacharias,* A.D. *590–752.* Lanham, MD, 2007.

Ensslin, W. "The Emperor and the Imperial Administration." In N. H. Baynes and H. St. L. B. Moss, eds., *Byzantium: An Introduction to East Roman Civilization.* Oxford, 1949, 268–307.

Errington, R. M. *A History of the Hellenistic World, 323–30* BC. Oxford, 2008.

Evans, J. A. *The Power Game in Byzantium: Antonina and the Empress Theodora.* London, 2011.

Fagan, G. G. *The Lure of the Arena: Social Psychology and the Crowd at the Roman Games.* Cambridge, 2011.

von Falkenhausen, V. "Hans-Georg Beck." In P. Armstrong, ed., *Authority in Byzantium.* Farnham, Surrey, 2013, 337–344.

Fears, J. R. *Princeps a diis electus: The Divine Election of the Emperor as a Political Concept at Rome.* Rome, 1977.

Fechner, D. *Untersuchungen zu Cassius Dios Sicht der römischen Republik.* Hildesheim, 1986.

Ferluga, J. "Aufstände im byzantinischen Reich zwischen den Jahren 1025 und 1081: Versuch einer Typologie." *Rivista di studi bizantini e slavi* 5 (1985): 137–165.

Fisher, E. "Greek Translations of Latin Literature in the Fourth Century A.D." *Yale Classical Studies* 27 (1982): 173–215.

Flower, H. I. *Roman Republics.* Princeton, NJ, 2010.

Flower, R. *Emperors and Bishops in Late Roman Invective.* Cambridge, 2013.

Fögen, M. T. "Gesetz und Gesetzgebung in Byzanz: Versuch einer Funktionsanalyse." *Jus Commune* 14 (1987): 137–158.

———. "Legislation und Kodifikation des Kaisers Leon VI." *Subseciva Groningana* 3 (1989): 23–35.

———. "Das politische Denken der Byzantiner." In I. Fetscher and H. Münkler, eds., *Pipers Handbuch der politischen Ideen.* Munich, 1993, v. 2, 41–85.

Folz, R. *The Concept of Empire in Western Europe from the Fifth to the Fourteenth Century.* Trans. S. A. Ogilvie. London, 1969.

Forsyth, J. H. *The Byzantine-Arab Chronicle (938–1034) of Yahya b. Saʿid al-Antaki,* 2 vols. PhD thesis: University of Michigan 1977.

Frede, D. "Constitution and Citizenship: Peripatetic Influence on Cicero's Political Conceptions in the *De re publica*." In W. W. Fortenbaugh and P. Steinmetz, eds., *Cicero's Knowledge of the Peripatos.* New Brunswick, NJ, 1989, 77–100.

Freeman, C. *The Horses of St. Mark's: A Story of Triumph in Byzantium, Paris, and Venice.* New York, 2004.

Fuhrmann, C. J. *Policing the Roman Empire: Soldiers, Administration, and Public Order.* Oxford, 2012.

Gallia, A. B. *Remembering the Roman Republic: Culture, Politics, and History under the Principate.* Cambridge, 2012.

Garland, L. "'And His Bald Head Shone Like a Full Moon . . .': An Appreciation of the Byzantine Sense of Humour as Recorded in Historical Sources of the Eleventh and Twelfth Centuries." *Parergon* 8 (1990): 1–31.

———. "Political Power and the Populace in Byzantium Prior to the Fourth Crusade." *Byzantinoslavica* 53 (1992): 17–52.

Gautier, P. "Diatribes de Jean l'Oxite contre Alexis Ier Comnène." *REB* 28 (1970): 5–55.

Gehrke, H.-J. "Der siegreiche König: Überlegungen zur hellenistischen Monarchie." *Archiv fürKulturgeschichte* 64 (1982): 247–277.

Geuss, R. *History and Illusion in Politics.* Cambridge, 2001.

Gowing, A. M. *The Triumviral Narratives of Appian and Dio Cassius.* Ann Arbor, MI, 1992.

———. *Empire and Memory: The Representation of the Roman Republic in Imperial Culture.* Cambridge, 2005.

———. "The Imperial Republic of Velleius Paterculus." In J. Marincola, ed., *A Companion to Greek and Roman Historiography.* Malden, MA, 2011, 411–418.

Grabar, A. *L'empereur dans l'art byzantin: Recherches sur l'art officiel de l'empire d'Orient.* Paris, 1936.

Greatrex, G. "The Nika Riot: A Reappraisal." *Journal of Hellenic Studies* 117 (1997): 60–86.

———. "Roman Identity in the Sixth Century." In S. Mitchell and G. Greatrex, eds., *Ethnicity and Culture in Late Antiquity.* London, 2000, 267–292.

Grégoire, H. "Manuel et Théophobe ou le concurrence de deux monastères." *Byzantion* 9 (1934): 183–204.

Gregory, T. E. *Vox Populi: Popular Opinion and Violence in the Religious Controversies of the Fifth Century* A.D. Columbus, OH, 1979.

Grig, L., and G. Kelly. "Introduction." In *Two Romes: Rome and Constantinople in Late Antiquity.* Oxford, 2012, 3–30.

Gruen, E. S. "Hellenistic Kingship: Puzzles, Problems, and Possibilities." In P. Bilde et al., eds., *Aspects of Hellenistic Kingship.* Aarhus, 1996, 116–125.

Guillou, A. "Functionaries." In G. Cavallo, ed., *The Byzantines.* Chicago, 1997, 197–229.

Guran, P. "Genesis and Function of the 'Last Emperor' Myth in Byzantine Eschatology." *Bizantinistica: Rivista di studi Bizantini e Slavi*, ser. 2, 8 (2006): 273–303.

———. "Une théorie politique du serment au XIVe siècle: Manuel Moschopoulos." In M.-F. Auzépy and G. Saint-Guillain, eds., *Oralité et lien social au Moyen Âge (Occident, Byzance, Islam): Parole donné, foi jurée, serment*. Paris, 2008, 169–185.

Haarer, F. K. *Anastasius I: Politics and Empire in the Late Roman World*. Liverpool, 2006.

Habermas, J. *The Structural Transformation of the Public Sphere: An Inquiry into a Category of Bourgeois Society*. Trans. T. Burger. Cambridge, MA, 1991.

Haldon, J. *Byzantium in the Seventh Century: The Transformation of a Culture*. Cambridge, 1990.

———. *State, Army and Society in Byzantium: Approaches to Military, Social and Administrative History, 6th–12th Centuries*. Brookfield, VT, 1995.

———. "The Byzantine State in the Ninth Century: An Introduction." In L. Brubaker, ed., *Byzantium in the Ninth Century: Dead or Alive?* Brookfield, VT, 1998, 3–10.

———. *Warfare, State, and Society in the Byzantine World, 565–1204*. London, 1999.

———. "Toward a Social History of Byzantium." In idem, ed., *A Social History of Byzantium*. Chichester, UK, 2009, 1–30.

———. "Social Élites, Wealth, and Power." In idem, ed., *A Social History of Byzantium*. Chichester, UK, 2009, 168–211.

———. "Comparative State Formation: The Later Roman Empire in the Wider World." In S. F. Johnson, ed., *The Oxford Handbook of Late Antiquity*. Oxford, 2012, 1111–1147.

Haldon, J., and L. Brubaker. *Byzantium in the Iconoclast Era, c. 680–850: A History*. Cambridge, 2011.

Hammer, D. *The* Iliad *as Politics: The Performance of Political Thought*. Norman, OK, 2002.

———. *Roman Political Thought and the Modern Theoretical Imagination*. Norman, OK, 2008.

Hankins, J. "Exclusivist Republicanism and Non-Monarchical Republic." *Political Theory* 38 (2010): 452–482.

Harries, J. *Law and Empire in Late Antiquity*. Cambridge, 1999.

Harrill, J. A. *Paul the Apostle: His Life and Legacy in Their Roman Context*. Cambridge, 2012.

Harris, J. *Constantinople: Capital of Byzantium*. London, 2007.

Harvey, A. *Economic Expansion in the Byzantine Empire, 900–1200*. Cambridge, 1989.

———. "The Village." In E. Jeffreys, ed., *The Oxford Handbook of Byzantine Studies*. Oxford, 2008, 328–333.

Hatlie, P. *The Monks and Monasteries of Constantinople, ca. 350–850*. Cambridge, 2007.

Heather, P. "The Anti-Scythian Tirade of Synesius' *De Regno*." *Phoenix* 42 (1988): 152–172.

——. *The Fall of the Roman Empire: A New History.* London, 2005.

——. "Liar in Winter: Themistius and Theodosius." In S. McGill et al., eds., *From the Tetrarchs to the Theodosians: Later Roman History and Culture, 284–450 CE.* Cambridge, 2010 = *Yale Classical Studies* v. 34, 185–213.

Heather, P., and D. Moncour. *Politics, Philosophy, and Empire in the Fourth Century: Select Orations of Themistius.* Liverpool, 2001.

Heim, F. "Vox exercitus, Vox Dei: La désignation de l'empereur charismatique au IVe siècle." *Revue des études latines* 68 (1990): 160–172.

Hendy, M. *Studies in the Byzantine Monetary Economy, c. 300–1450.* Cambridge, 1985.

Herrin, J. *Margins and Metropolis: Authority across the Byzantine Empire.* Princeton, NJ, 2013.

Heucke, C. *Circus und Hippodrom als politischer Raum: Untersuchungen zum grossen Hippodrom von Konstantinopel und zu entsprechenden Anlagen in spätantiken Kaiserresidenzen.* Hildesheim, 1994.

Hobbes, T. *The Elements of Law II: De Corpore Politico.* Ed. J. C. A. Gaskin, *Human Nature and De Corpore Politico.* Oxford, 1994.

——. *Leviathan.* Ed. J. C. A. Gaskin. Oxford, 1996.

Holmes, C. "Political Elites in the Reign of Basil II." In P. Magdalino, ed., *Byzantium in the Year 1000.* Leiden, 2003, 35–70.

Honoré, T. *Tribonian.* Ithaca, NY, 1978.

Horden, P. "The Confraternities of Byzantium." *Studies in Church History* 23 (1986): 25–45.

Horrocks, G. *Greek: A History of the Language and Its Speakers.* London, 1997.

Howard-Johnston, J. *Witnesses to a World Crisis: Historians and Histories of the Middle East in the Seventh Century.* Oxford, 2010.

Hunger, H. *Prooimion: Elemente der byzantinischen Kaiseridee in den Arengen der Urkunden.* Vienna, 1964.

Iliev, D. "Literary Memory: A Case of Its Application in a Late Antique Epigram." In A. Milanova et al., eds., *Memory and Oblivion in Byzantium.* Sofia, 2011, 7–13.

Instinsky, H. U. "Consensus universorum." *Hermes* 75 (1940): 265–278.

James, L. "Byzantium: A Very, Very Short Introduction." In eadem, ed., *A Companion to Byzantium.* Chichester, UK, 2010, 1–8.

Jeffreys, M. "The Nature and Origins of the Political Verse." *DOP* 28 (1974): 141–195.

Johnson, A. C. *Ancient Roman Statutes: A Translation.* Austin, TX, 1961.

Johnson, A. P. *Ethnicity and Argument in Eusebios' Praeparatio Evangelica.* Oxford, 2006.

Johnston, S. I. "Ritual's Handmaid." In eadem, *Narrating Myth*, forthcoming.

Jones, A. H. M. *The Later Roman Empire, 284–602: A Social, Economic, and Administrative Survey.* Norman, OK, 1964.

Jouanno, C. "Le corps du prince dans la *Chronographie* de Michel Psellos." *Kentron: Revue du monde antique et de psychologie historique* 19 (2003): 205–221.

Kaegi, W. E. *Byzantine Military Unrest, 471–843: An Interpretation*. Amsterdam, 1981.

——. *Heraclius: Emperor of Byzantium*. Cambridge, 2003.

Kaldellis, A. *The Argument of Psellos' Chronographia*. Leiden, 1999.

——. "The Historical and Religious Views of Agathias: A Reinterpretation." *Byzantion* 69 (1999): 206–252.

——. *Procopius of Caesarea: Tyranny, History, and Philosophy at the End of Antiquity*. Philadelphia, 2004.

——. "Republican Theory and Political Dissidence in Ioannes Lydos." *Byzantine and Modern Greek Studies* 29 (2005): 1–16.

——. "A Byzantine Argument for the Equivalence of All Religions: Michael Attaleiates on Ancient and Modern Romans." *International Journal of the Classical Tradition* 14 (2007): 1–22.

——. *Hellenism in Byzantium: The Transformations of Greek Identity and the Reception of the Classical Tradition*. Cambridge, 2007.

——. "The Date and Structure of Prokopios' *Secret History* and His Projected Work on Church History." *GRBS* 49 (2009): 585–616.

——. "Aristotle's *Politics* in Byzantium." In V. Syros, ed., *Well Begun Is Only Half Done: Tracing Aristotle's Political Ideas in Medieval Arabic, Syriac, Byzantine, Jewish, and Indo-Persian Sources*. Tempe, AZ, 2011, 121–143.

——. "The Date of Psellos' Death, Once Again: Psellos Was Not the Michael of Nikomedeia Mentioned by Attaleiates." *BZ* 104 (2011): 649–661.

——. "The Byzantine Role in the Making of the Corpus of Classical Greek Historiography: A Preliminary Investigation." *Journal of Hellenic Studies* 132 (2012): 71–85.

——. *Ethnography after Antiquity: Foreign Peoples and Places in Byzantine Literature*. Philadelphia, 2013.

——. "The Hagiography of Doubt and Skepticism." In S. Efthymiades, ed., *The Ashgate Research Companion to Byzantine Hagiography*, v. 2. Aldershot, 2014, 453–477.

Kaplan, M. *Les hommes et la terre à Byzance du VIe au XIe siècle*. Paris, 1992.

Karagiannopoulos, I. E. *Η πολιτική θεωρία των Βυζαντινών*. Thessalonike, 1992.

Karamboula, D. *Staatsbegriffe in der frühbyzantinischen Zeit*. Vienna, 1993.

——. *Η νομοθετική δραστηριότητα επι Διοκλητιανού και η κρατική παρέμβαση στον τομέα του δικαίου: Ο Γρηγοριανός και ο Ερμογενειανός κώδικας*. Athens, 2008.

Karlin-Hayter, P. "L'enjeu d'une rumeur: Opinion et imaginaire à Byzance au IXe s." *Jahrbuch der österreichischen Byzantinistik* 41 (1991): 85–111.

Karpozilos, A. *Βυζαντινοὶ ἱστορικοὶ καὶ χρονογράφοι*, 3 vols. Athens, 1997–2009.

Kazhdan, A. P. "Some Observations on the Byzantine Concept of Law: Three Authors of the Ninth through the Twelfth Centuries." In A. E. Laiou and D. Simon, eds., *Law and Society in Byzantium: Ninth–Twelfth Centuries*. Washington, DC, 1994, 199–216.

Kazhdan, A. P., and G. Constable. *People and Power in Byzantium: An Introduction to Modern Byzantine Studies*. Washington, DC, 1982.

Kazhdan, A. P., and A. W. Epstein. *Change in Byzantine Culture in the Eleventh and Twelfth Centuries.* Berkeley, CA, 1985.

Kelly, C. *Ruling the Later Roman Empire.* Cambridge, MA, 2004.

———. *Attila the Hun: Barbarian Terror and the Fall of the Roman Empire.* London, 2009.

Kiousopoulou, A. *Βασιλεύς ή οικονόμος: Πολιτική εξουσία και ιδεολογία πριν από την άλωση.* Athens, 2007.

Kolb, F. *Herrscherideologie in der Spätantike.* Berlin, 2001.

Kolbaba, T. M. *The Byzantine Lists: Errors of the Latins.* Urbana, IL, 2000.

Konidaris, I. M. "The Ubiquity of Canon Law." In A. E. Laiou and D. Simon, eds., *Law and Society in Byzantium: Ninth–Twelfth Centuries.* Washington, DC, 1994, 131–150.

Köpstein, H. "Μερικές παρατηρήσεις για τη νομική κατάσταση των δούλων κατά την πείρα." In C. Angelidi, ed., *Ἡ καθημερινὴ ζωὴ στὸ Βυζάντιο.* Athens, 1989, 409–419.

Koukoules, Ph. *Βυζαντινῶν βίος καὶ πολιτισμός.* 6 vols. Athens, 1949–1955.

Koutrakou, N.-C. *La propagande impériale byzantine: Persuasion et réaction (VIIIe–Xe siècles).* Athens, 1994.

Krallis, D. "'Democratic' Action in Eleventh-Century Byzantium: Michael Attaleiates's 'Republicanism' in Context." *Viator* 40 (2009): 35–53.

———. *Michael Attaleiates and the Politics of Imperial Decline in Eleventh-Century Byzantium.* Tempe, AZ, 2012.

Kresten, O. "Datierungsprobleme 'isaurischer' Eherechtsnovellen I. Coll. 1 26." *FM* 4 (1981): 37–106.

Kruse, M. "A Justinianic Debate across Genres on the State of the Roman Republic." In Greatrex, H. Elton, and L. McMahon, eds., *Shifting Frontiers in Late Antiquity X: Shifting Genres in Late Antiquity,* forthcoming.

Kurzban, R. *Why Everyone (Else) Is a Hypocrite: Evolution and the Modular Mind.* Princeton, NJ, 2012.

Kyritzes, D. "The Imperial Council in Byzantium." In D. Angelov and M. Saxby, eds., *Power and Subversion in Byzantium.* Farnham, Surrey, 2013, 57–70.

Laiou, A. E. "Imperial Marriages and Their Critics in the Eleventh Century." *DOP* 46 (1992): 165–176.

———. "Economic Thought and Ideology." In eadem, ed., *The Economic History of Byzantium from the Seventh through the Fifteenth Century.* Washington, DC, 2002, v. 3, 1123–1144.

———. "The Emperor's Word: Chrysobulls, Oaths and Synallagmatic Relations in Byzantium (11th–12th C.)." *Travaux et Mémoires* 14 (2002): 347–362.

Lanata, G. *Legislazione e natura nelle Novelle Giustinianee.* Naples, 1984.

Lee, A. D. *War in Late Antiquity: A Social History.* Malden, MA, 2007.

Lee, D., and J. Shepard. "A Double Life: Placing the Peri Presbeon." *Byzantinoslavica* 52 (1991): 14–39.

Lefort, J. "Rhétorique et politique: Trois discours de Jean Mauropous en 1047." *Travaux et mémoires* 6 (1976): 265–303.

———. "The Rural Economy, Seventh-Twelfth Centuries." In A. Laiou, ed., *The Economic History of Byzantium from the Seventh through the Fifteenth Century*. Washington, DC, 2002, v. 1, 231-310.

Lemerle, P. "Thomas le Slave." *Travaux et mémoires* 1 (1965): 255-297.

———. *Byzantine Humanism: The First Phase (Notes and Remarks on Education and Culture in Byzantium from Its Origins to the 10th Century)*. Trans. H. Lindsay and A. Moffatt. Canberra, 1986.

Lendon, J. E. *Empire of Honour: The Art of Government in the Roman World*. Oxford, 1997.

Lenski, N. "Constantine and Slavery: *Libertas* and the Fusion of Roman and Christian Values." *Atti dell'Accademia Romanistica Costantiniana* 18 (2011): 235-260.

Leppin, H. "Roman Identity in a Border Region: Evagrius and the Defense of the Roman Empire." In W. Pohl et al., eds., *Visions of Community in the Post-Roman World: The West, Byzantium and the Islamic World, 300–1100*. Burlington, VT, 2012, 241-258.

Leveniotis, G. A. *Το στασιαστικό κίνημα του Νορμανδού Ουρσελίου (Ursel de Bailleul) στην Μικρά Ασία (1073–1076)*. Thessaloniki, 2004.

Liebeschuetz, J. H. W. G. *The Decline and Fall of the Roman City*. Oxford, 2001.

Lilie, R.-J. "Die Krönung des Kaisers Anastasios I. (491)." *Byzantinoslavica* 56 (1995): 3-12.

———. "Der Kaiser in der Statistik: Subversive Gedanken zur angeblichen Allmacht der byzantinischen Kaiser." In C. Stavrakos et al., eds., *Hypermachos: Studien zu Byzantinistik, Armenologie und Georgistik. Festschrift für Werner Seibt zum 65. Geburtstag*. Wiesbaden, 2008, 211-233.

Lind, L. R. "The Idea of the Republic and the Foundations of Roman Political Liberty." *Studies in Latin Literature and Roman History* 4 (1986): 44-108.

Ljubarski, J. N. *Η προσωπικότητα και το έργο του Μιχαήλ Ψελλού: Συνεισφορά στην ιστορία του βυζαντινού πολιτισμού*. Trans. A. Tzelesi. Athens, 2004.

Lokin, J. H. A. "The Significance of Law and Legislation in the Law Books of the Ninth to Eleventh Centuries." In A. E. Laiou and D. Simon, eds., *Law and Society in Byzantium: Ninth–Twelfth Centuries*. Washington, DC, 1994, 71-91.

Lounghis, T. "Χρονικόν περί της αναιρέσεως του Αποβασιλέως Κύρου Μιχαήλ του Καλαφάτου." *Byzantiaka* 18 (1998): 75-104.

———. "The Byzantine Historians on Politics and People from 1042 to 1081." *Byzantion* 72 (2002): 381-403.

Louth, A. *Greek East and Latin West: The Church AD 681–1071*. Brookline, MA, 2007.

Ma, J. *Antiochos III and the Cities of Western Asia Minor*. Oxford, 1999.

Maas, M. "Fugitives and Ethnography in Priscus of Panium." *BMGS* 19 (1995): 146-160.

MacCormack, S. *Art and Ceremony in Late Antiquity*. Berkeley, CA, 1981.

MacIntyre, A. *After Virtue: A Study in Moral Theory*, 2nd ed. Notre Dame, IN, 1984.

MacMullen, R. *Enemies of the Roman Order: Treason, Unrest, and Alienation in the Empire*. London, 1966.

———. *Roman Social Relations, 50 B.C. to A.D. 284.* New Haven, CT, 1974.

———. *Voting about God in Early Church Councils.* New Haven, CT, 2006.

Macrides, R. "Justice under Manuel I Komnenos: Four Novels on Court Business and Murder." *FM* 6 (1984): 99–204.

———. "Nomos and Kanon on Paper and in Court." In R. Morris, ed., *Church and People in Byzantium.* Birmingham, UK, 1990, 61–86.

———. *George Akropolites: The History.* Oxford, 2007.

Magdalino, P. "Aspects of Twelfth-Century Byzantine *Kaiserkritik.*" *Speculum* 58 (1983): 326–346.

———. "Byzantine Snobbery." In M. Angold, ed., *The Byzantine Aristocracy: IX to XIII Centuries.* Oxford, 1984, 58–78.

———. "Honour among Romaioi: The Framework of Social Values in the World of Digenes Akrites and Kekaumenos." *BMGS* 13 (1989): 183–218.

———. *The Empire of Manuel I Komnenos, 1143–1180.* Cambridge, 1993.

———. "The Non-Juridical Legislation of Leo VI." In S. Troianos, ed., *Analecta Atheniensia ad ius byzantinum spectantia.* Athens, 1997, 169–182.

———. "In Search of the Byzantine Courtier: Leo Choirosphaktes and Constantine Manasses." In H. Maguire, ed., *Byzantine Court Culture from 829 to 1204.* Washington, DC, 1997, 141–165.

———. "The Byzantine Army and the Land: From *stratiotikon ktema* to Military *pronoia.*" In K. Tsiknakis, ed., *Το εμπόλεμο Βυζάντιο (9ος–12ος αι.).* Athens, 1997, 15–36.

———. "The Medieval Empire (780–1204)." In C. Mango, ed., *The Oxford History of Byzantium.* Oxford, 2002, 169–213.

———. *L'Orthodoxie des astrologues: La science entre le dogme et la divination à Byzance (VIIe–XIVe siècle).* Paris, 2006.

———. "The History of the Future and Its Uses: Prophecy, Policy and Propaganda (with Postscipt)." In J. Shepard, ed., *The Expansion of Orthodox Europe: Byzantium, the Balkans and Russia.* Aldershot, 2007, 29–63.

———. "Byzantium = Constantinople." In L. James, ed., *A Companion to Byzantium.* Malden, MA, 2010, 43–54.

———. "Court and Capital in Byzantium." In J. Duindam et al., eds., *Royal Courts in Dynastic States and Empires: A Global Perspective.* Leiden, 2011, 132–144.

———. "Knowledge in Authority and Authorized History: The Imperial Intellectual Programme of Leo VI and Constantine VII." In P. Armstrong, ed., *Authority in Byzantium.* Farnham, Surrey, 2013, 187–209.

Maguire, H., and E. D. *Other Icons: Art and Power in Byzantine Secular Culture.* Princeton, NJ, 2007.

Mango, C. *Byzantium: The Empire of New Rome.* New York, 1980.

Maniatis, G. C. "On the Validity of the Theory of Supreme State Ownership of All Land in Byzantium." *Byzantion* 77 (2007): 566–634.

Manojlović, G. "Le peuple de Constantinople." *Byzantion* 11 (1936): 617–716.

Mansfield, H. C. *Taming the Prince: The Ambivalence of Modern Executive Power.* Baltimore, MD, 1989.

Manuwald, B. *Cassius Dio und Augustus: Philologische Untersuchungen zu den Büchern 45–46 des dionischen Geschichtswerkes.* Wiesbaden, 1979.

Markopoulos, A. "The Rehabilitation of the Emperor Theophilus." In L. Brubaker, ed., *Byzantium in the Ninth Century: Dead or Alive?* Aldershot, 1998, 37–49.

Martin, D. B. *Inventing Superstition: From the Hippocratics to the Christians.* Cambridge, MA, 2004.

Martindale, J. R., ed. *The Prosopography of the Later Roman Empire*, v. 2: A.D. 395–527. Cambridge, 1980.

Mason, H. J. *Greek Terms for Roman Institutions: A Lexicon and Analysis.* Toronto, 1974.

Mathews, T. F. *The Clash of Gods: A Reinterpretation of Early Christian Art.* Princeton, NJ, 1993.

Mavromattis, L. "Τα όρια ανοχής της εκτροπής στο ύστερο Βυζάντιο." In A. Nikolaou, ed., *Ανοχή και καταστολή στους μέσους χρόνους: Μνήμη Λένου Μαυρομάτη.* Athens, 2002, 29–36.

Mazzucchi, G. M. "Dagli anni di Basilio Parakimomenos (cod. *Ambr.* B 119 sup.)." *Aevum* 52 (1978): 267–316.

McCormick, M. *Eternal Victory: Triumphal Rulership in Late Antiquity, Byzantium and the Early Medieval West.* Cambridge, 1986.

McGuckin, J. A. *The Ascent of Christian Law: Patristic and Byzantine Formulations of a New Civilization.* Yonkers, NY, 2012.

Medvedev, I. "Ἡ συνοδικὴ ἀπόφαση τῆς 24 Μαρτίου 1171 ὡς νόμος γιὰ τὴ διαδοχὴ στὸ θρόνο τοῦ Βυζαντίου." In N. Oikonomides, *Τὸ Βυζάντιο κατὰ τὸν 12ο αἰώνα: Κανονικὸ δίκαιο, κράτος και κοινωνία.* Athens, 1991, 229–238.

———. "Le pouvoir, la loi et le *jus resistendi* à Byzance." *Byzantinoslavica* 56 (1995): 75–81.

———. "Y avait-il une constitution à Byzance? Quelques considérations." In A. Avramea et al., eds., *Βυζάντιο: Κράτος και Κοινωνία. Μνήμη Νίκου Οικονομίδη.* Athens, 2003, 383–391.

Meier, M. "Die Inszenierung einer Katastrophe: Justinian und der Nika-Aufstand." *Zeitschrift für Papyrologie und Epigraphik* 142 (2003): 273–300.

———. "Σταυρωθεὶς δι' ἡμᾶς—Der Aufstand gegen Anastasius im Jahr 512." *Millennium* 4 (2007): 157–237.

———. *Anastasios I: Die Entstehung des Byzantinischen Reiches.* Stuttgart, 2009.

Meijer, F. *Chariot Racing in the Roman Empire.* Trans. L. Waters. Baltimore, MD, 2010.

Menze, V. L. *Justinian and the Making of the Syrian Orthodox Church.* Oxford, 2008.

Merrills, A., and R. Miles. *The Vandals.* Oxford, 2010.

Messis, C. "Public hautement affiché et public réellement visé: Le cas de l'*Apologie de l'eunuchisme* de Théophylacte d'Achrida." In P. Odorico, ed., *La face cachée de la littérature byzantine: Le texte en tant que message immédiat.* Paris, 2012, 41–86.

Michaélidès-Nouaros, G. "Les idées philosophiques de Léon le Sage et son attitude à l'égard de la coutume." Ἐπιστημονικὴ Ἐπετηρὶς Σχολῆς Νομικῶν καὶ Οἰκονομικῶν Ἐπιστημῶν Ἀριστοτελείου Πανεπιστημίου Θεσσαλονίκης 8 (1960-1963) 25-54 = "Αἱ φιλοσοφικαὶ καὶ κοινωνιολογικαὶ ἰδέαι Λέοντος ϛ' τοῦ Σοφοῦ ἐπὶ τῶν ὁρίων τῆς νομοθετικῆς ἐξουσίας," in idem, Δίκαιον καὶ κοινωνικὴ συνείδησις, Athens, 1972, 99-129.

Millar, F. The Emperor in the Roman World (31 BC–AD 337). Ithaca, NY, 1977.

———. "Imperial Ideology in the Tabula Siarensis." In J. González and J. Arce, eds., Estudios sobre la Tabula Siarensis. Madrid, 1988, 11-19.

———. The Roman Republic in Political Thought. Hanover, NH, 2002.

———. The Crowd in Rome in the Late Republic. Ann Arbor, MI, 2002.

Morgan, G. "A Byzantine Satirical Song?" BZ 47 (1954): 292-297.

Morris, R. "The Two Faces of Nikephoros Phokas." BMGS 12 (1988): 83-115.

———. "Succession and Usurpation: Politics and Rhetoric in the Late Tenth Century." In P. Magdalino, ed., New Constantines: The Rhythm of Imperial Renewal in Byzantium, 4th–13th Centuries. Aldershot, UK, 1994, 199-214.

Nelson, J. L. "The Lord's Annointed and the People's Choice: Carolingian Royal Ritual." In idem, The Frankish World. London, 1996, 99-132.

Neville, L. Authority in Byzantine Provincial Society, 950–1100. Cambridge, 2004.

———. Heroes and Romans in Twelfth-Century Byzantium: The "Material for History" of Nikephoros Bryennios. Cambridge, 2012.

Nystazopoulou-Pelekidou, M. "Constantinople centre du pouvoir et d'autorité." Byzantiaka 5 (1985): 13-32.

Odorico, P. "Les mirrors des princes à Byzance: Une lecture horizontale." In idem, ed., "L'éducation au gouvernement et à la vie": La tradition des "Régles de vie" de l'antiquité au Moyen-Âge. Paris, 2009, 223-246.

Oehler, K. "Der consensus universorum als Kriterium der Wahrheit in der antiken Philosophie und der Patristik." Antike und Abendland 10 (1961): 103-129.

Oikonomides, N. "Le serment de l'impératrice Eudocie (1067)." REB 21 (1963): 101-128.

———. "The 'Peira' of Eustathios Romaios: An Abortive Attempt to Innovate in Byzantine Law." FM 7 (1986): 169-192.

O'Neill, P. "Going Round in Circles: Popular Speech in Ancient Rome." Classical Antiquity 22 (2003): 135-166.

Ostrogorsky, G. History of the Byzantine State. Trans. J. Hussey. New Brunswick, NJ, 1969.

Ostwald, M. From Popular Sovereignty to the Sovereignty of Law: Law, Society, and Politics in Fifth-Century Athens. Berkeley, CA, 1986.

Page, G. Being Byzantine: Greek Identity before the Ottomans. Cambridge, 2008.

Païdas, K. D. S. Η θεματική των βυζαντινών «Κατόπτρων ηγεμόνος» της πρώιμης και μέσης περιόδου (398–1085): Συμβολή στην πολιτική θεωρία των Βυζαντινών. Athens, 2005.

——. *Τα Βυζαντινά «Κάτοπτρα ηγεμόνος» της ύστερης περιόδου (1254–1403): Εκφράσεις του βυζαντινού βασιλικού ιδεώδους.* Athens, 2006.

Panagiotopoulos, I. A. *Περί Αθίγγανων: πολιτική και θρησκεία στη Βυζαντινή Αυτοκρατορία.* Thessalonike, 2008.

Pazdernik, C. "Procopius and Thucydides on the Labors of War: Belisarius and Brasidas in the Field." *Transactions of the American Philological Association* 130 (2000): 149–187.

——. "Justinianic Ideology and the Power of the Past." In M. Maas, ed., *Cambridge Companion to the Age of Justinian.* Cambridge, 2005, 185–212.

Peachin, M. *Iudex vice Caesaris: Deputy Emperors and the Administration of Justice during the Principate.* Stuttgart, 1996.

Pelling, C. "The Greek Historians of Rome." In J. Marincola, ed., *A Companion to Greek and Roman Historiography.* Malden, MA, 2011, 244–258.

Penna, V., and C. Morrisson. "Usurpers and Rebels in Byzantium: Image and Message through Coins." In D. Angelov and M. Saxby, eds., *Power and Subversion in Byzantium.* Farnham, Surrey, 2013, 21–42.

Pennington, K. *The Prince and the Law, 1200–1600: Sovereignty and Rights in the Western Legal Tradition.* Berkeley, 1993.

Pertusi, A. *Il pensiero politico bizantino.* Bologna, 1990.

Pieler, P. "Verfassung und Rechtsgrundlagen des byzantinischen Staates." *Jahrbuch der österreichischen Byzantinistik* 31 (1981): 213–231.

Pitsakis, K. G. "Αντίσταση κατά της εξουσίας και επανάσταση στο Βυζάντιο: Η θέση του δικαίου της Εκκλησίας." In E. Grammatikopoulou, ed., *Αμφισβήτηση της εξουσίας.* Athens, 2003, 48–65.

Polemis, D. I. *The Doukai: A Contribution to Byzantine Prosopography.* London, 1968.

Popović, M. "Zum Bild des römischen Kaisers Trajan in der byzantinischen Literatur." In W. Hörandner et al., *Wiener Byzantinistik und Neogräzistik.* Vienna, 2004 = *Byzantina et neogreca vindobonensia* v. 24, 337–347.

Potter, D. *Constantine the Emperor.* Oxford, 2013.

Preiser-Kapeller, J. "He ton pleionon psephos: Der Mehrheitsbeschluss in der Synode von Konstantinopel in spätbyzantinischer Zeit—Normen, Strukturen, Prozesse." In E. Flaig, ed., *Genesis und Dynamiken der Mehrheitsentscheidung.* Munich, 2013, 203–227.

Prinzing, G. "Das Bild Justinians I. in der Überlieferung der Byzantiner vom 7. bis 15. Jahrhundert." *FM* 7 (1986): 1–99.

——. "Beobachtungen zu 'integrierten' Fürstenspiegeln der Byzantiner." *Jahrbuch der österreichischen Byzantinistik* 38 (1988): 1–31.

——. "The Authority of the Church in Uneasy Times: The Example of Demetrios Chomatenos, Archbishop of Ohrid, in the State of Epiros 1216–1236." In P. Armstrong, ed., *Authority in Byzantium.* Farnham, Surrey, 2013, 137–150.

Rallis, G. A., and M. Potlis, eds. *Σύνταγμα τῶν ἱερῶν καὶ θείων κανόνων,* 7 vols. Athens, 1852–1859.

Rance, P. "The Date of the Military Compendium of Syrianus Magister (formerly the Sixth-Century Anonymus Byzantinus)." *BZ* 100 (2007): 701–737.

Revell, L. *Roman Imperialism and Local Identities.* Cambridge, 2009.

Reynolds, S. "Social Mentalities and the Case of Medieval Scepticism." *Transactions of the Royal Historical Society* 6th ser., 1 (1991): 21–41.

———. *Fiefs and Vassals: The Medieval Evidence Reinterpreted.* Oxford, 1994.

———. *Kingdoms and Communities in Western Europe, 900–1300,* 2nd ed. Oxford, 1997.

Rich, J. W. *Cassius Dio: The Augustan Settlement* (Roman History *53–55.9*). Warminster, 1990.

Richardson, J. *The Language of Empire: Rome and the Idea of Empire from the Third Century* BC *to the Second Century* AD. Cambridge, 2008.

Roberto, U. "Il *Breviarium* di Eutropio nella cultura greca tardoantica e bizantina: la versione attribuita a Capitone Licio." *Medioevo Greco* 3 (2003): 241–271.

Rochette, R. "Empereurs et serment sous les Paléologues." In M.-F. Auzépy and G. Saint-Guillain, eds., *Oralité et lien social au Moyen Âge (Occident, Byzance, Islam): Parole donné, foi jurée, serment.* Paris, 2008, 157–167.

Rochow, I. "Die Heidenprozesse unter Kaisern Tiberios II. Konstantinos und Maurikios." In H. Köpstein and F. Winkelmann, eds., *Studien zum 7. Jahrhundert in Byzanz: Probleme der Herausbildung des Feudalismus.* Berlin, 1976, 120–130.

de Romilly, J. *The Rise and Fall of States according to Greek Authors.* Ann Arbor, MI, 1977.

Roueché, C. "Acclamations in the Later Roman Empire: New Evidence from Aphrodisias." *JRS* 74 (1984): 181–199.

Rousseau, J.-J. *Discourse on the Sciences and Arts.* Trans. V. Gourevitch, *Rousseau: The Discourses and Other Early Political Writings.* Cambridge, 1997.

———. *The Social Contract.* Trans. V. Gourevitch, *Rousseau:* The Social Contract *and Other Later Political Writings.* Cambridge, 1997.

Rowan, C. *Under Divine Auspices: Divine Ideology and the Visualisation of Imperial Power in the Severan Period.* Cambridge, 2012.

Runciman, S. *The Byzantine Theocracy.* Cambridge, 1977.

Ruppel, W. "Politeuma: Bedeutungsgeschichte eines staatsrechtlichen Terminus." *Philologus* 82 (1927): 268–312, 434–454.

Salzman, M. R. *On Roman Time: The Codex-Calendar of 354 and the Rhythms of Urban Life in Late Antiquity.* Berkeley, CA, 1990.

Sand, S. *The Invention of the Jewish People.* London: 2009.

Sarris, P. *Empires of Faith: The Fall of Rome to the Rise of Islam, 500–700.* Oxford, 2011.

Saul, J. R. *Voltaire's Bastards: The Dictatorship of Reason in the West.* London: 1992.

Savalli-Lestrade, I. *Les philoi royaux dans l'Asie hellénistique.* Geneva, 1998.

Savvides, A. G. K. Βυζαντινὰ στασιαστικὰ καὶ αὐτονομιστικὰ κινήματα στὰ Δωδεκάνησα καὶ στὴ Μικρὰ Ἀσία, 1189–c.1240 μ.X. Athens, 1987.

Schminck, A. Studien zu mittelbyzantinischen Rechtsbüchern. Frankfurt, 1986.

———. "Ein rechtshistorischer 'Traktat' im Cod. Mosq. gr. 445." FM 9 (1993): 81-96.

Schmitt, C. Political Theology: Four Chapters on the Concept of Sovereignty. Trans. G. Schwab. Cambridge, MA, 1985.

Schofield, M. "Cicero's Definition of res publica." In idem, Saving the City: Philosopher-Kings and Other Classical Paradigms. London, 1999, 178-194.

Schreiner, P. Die byzantinischen Kleinchroniken, 3 vols. Vienna, 1975.

Scott, J. C. Hidden Transcripts: Domination and the Arts of Resistance. New Haven, CT, 1990.

Sessa, T. The Formation of Papal Authority in Late Antique Italy. Cambridge, 2012.

Ševčenko, I. "Constantinople Viewed from the Eastern Provinces in the Middle Byzantine Period." Harvard Ukrainian Studies 3-4 (1978-1980): 712-747.

———. "The Title and Preface to Theophanes Continuatus." In S. Lucá and L. Perria, eds., Opora: Studi in onore di mgr Paul Canart per il LXX compleanno. Rome, 1998, v. 2, 77-93.

Sharples, R. W. "Cicero's Republic and Greek Political Theory." Polis 5.2 (1986): 30-50.

Shawcross, T. "'Do Thou Nothing without Counsel': Political Assemblies and the Ideal of Good Government in the Thought of Theodore Palaeologus and Theodore Metochites." Al-Masaq 20 (2008): 89-118.

Shepard, J. "Past and Future in Middle Byzantine Diplomacy: Some Preliminary Observations." In M. Balard et al., eds., Byzance et le monde extérieur: Contacts, relations, échanges. Paris, 2005, 171-191.

———. "Aspects of Moral Leadership: The Imperial City and Lucre from Legality." In P. Armstrong, ed., Authority in Byzantium. Farnha, Surrey, 2013, 9-30.

Sherk, R. K. Roman Documents from the Greek East: Senatus Consulta and Epistulae to the Age of Augustus. Baltimore, MD, 1969.

Shumate, N. Nation, Empire, Decline: Studies in Rhetorical Continuity from the Romans to the Modern Era. London, 2006.

Sickel, W. "Das byzantinische Krönungsrecht bis zum 10. Jahrhundert." BZ 7 (1898): 511-557.

Signes Codoñer, J. "Dead or Alive? Manuel the Armenian's (After)life after 838." In C. Gastgeber et al., eds., Pour l'amour de Byzance: Hommage à Paolo Odorico. Frankfurt am Main, 2013, 231-242.

Simon, D. "Zur Ehegesetzgebung der Isaurier." FM 1 (1976): 16-43.

———. "Princeps legibus solutus: Die Stellung des byzantinischen Kaisers zum Gesetz." In D. Nörr and D. Simon, eds., Gedächtnisschrift für Wolfgang Kunkel. Frankfurt, 1984, 449-492.

——. "Balsamon und Gewohnheitsrecht." In W. J. Aerts et al., eds., *Scholia: Studia ad criticam interpretationemque textuum Graecorum et ad historiam iuris Graeco-Romani pertinentia viro doctissimo D. Holwerda oblata.* Groningen, 1985, 119–133.

——. "Legislation as Both a World Order and a Legal Order." In A. E. Laiou and D. Simon, eds., *Law and Society in Byzantium: Ninth–Twelfth Centuries.* Washington, DC, 1994, 1–25.

Siniossoglou, N. *Radical Platonism in Byzantium: Illumination and Utopia in Gemistos Plethon.* Cambridge, 2011.

Sion-Jenkis, K. *Von der Republik zum Prinzipat: Ursachen für den Verfassungswechsel in Rom im historischen Denken der Antike.* Stuttgart, 2000.

Skinner, Q. "The State." In T. Ball et al., eds., *Political Innovation and Conceptual Change.* Cambridge, 1989, 90–131.

——. "A Genealogy of the Modern State." *Proceedings of the British Academy* 162 (2009): 325–370.

Spanos, A., and N. Zarras. "Representations of Emperors as Saints in Byzantine Textual and Visual Sources." In M. Borgolte and B. Schneidmüller, eds., *Hybride Kulturen im mittelalterlichen Europa.* Berlin, 2010, 63–78.

Spawforth, A. *Augustus and the Greek Cultural Revolution.* Cambridge, 2012.

Stănescu, E. "Les réformes d'Isaac Comnène." *Revue des études sud-est européennes* 4 (1966): 35–69.

Steinwenter, A. "Zur Lehre vom Gewohnheitsrechte." In *Studi in onore di Pietro Bonfante.* Milan, 1930, v. 2, 419–440.

——. "ΝΟΜΟΣ ΕΜΨΥΧΟΣ: Zur Geschichte einer politischen Theorie." *Anzeiger der österreichischen Akademie der Wissenschaften, philosophisch-historische Klasse* 83 (1946): 250–268.

Stephenson, P. *The Legend of Basil the Bulgar Slayer.* Cambridge, 2003.

——. *Constantine: Unconquered Emperor, Christian Victor.* London, 2009.

Stolte, B. H., and R. Meijering, eds. "The Prooimion of the Eisagoge: Translation and Commentary." *Subseciva Groningana* 7 (2001): 91–155.

Stouraitis, I. "Bürgerkrieg in ideologischer Wahrnehmung durch die Byzantiner (7.–12. Jahrhundert): Die Frage der Legitimierung und Rechtfertigung." *Jahrbuch der österreichischen Byzantinistik* 60 (2010): 149–172.

Suerbaum, W. *Vom antiken zum frühmittelalterlichen Staatsbegriff: Über Verwendung und Bedeutung von res publica, regnum, imperium und status von Cicero bis Jordanis,* 3rd ed. Münster, 1977.

Svoronos, N. G. "Le serment de fidélité à l'empereur byzantine et sa signification constitutionnelle." *REB* 9 (1952): 106–142.

Syme, R. *The Roman Revolution.* Oxford, 1939.

Syros, V. "Between Chimera and Charybdis: Byzantine and Post-Byzantine Views on the Political Organization of the Italian City-States." *Journal of Early Modern History* 14 (2010): 451–504.

——. "An Early Modern South Asian Thinker on the Rise and Decline of Empires: Shāh Walī Allāh of Delhi, the Mughals, and the Byzantines." *Journal of World History* 23 (2012): 793–840.

Szidat, J. *Usurpator tanti nominis: Kaiser und Usurpator in der Spätantike (337–476 n. Chr.)*. Stuttgart, 2010.

Talbert, R. J. A. *The Senate of Imperial Rome*. Princeton, NJ, 1984.

Toner, J. *Popular Culture in Ancient Rome*. Malden, MA, 2009.

———. *Homer's Turk: How Classics Shaped Ideas of the East*. Cambridge, MA, 2013.

Tougher, S. *The Reign of Leo VI (886–912): Politics and People*. Leiden, 1997.

———. "The Imperial Thought-World of Leo VI: The Non-Campaigning Emperor of the Ninth Century." In L. Brubaker, ed., *Byzantium in the Ninth Century: Dead or Alive?* Brookfield, VT, 1998, 51–60.

Trampedach, K. "Kaiserwechsel und Krönungsritual im Konstantinopel des 5. bis 6. Jahrhunderts." In M. Steinicke and S. Weinfurter, eds., *Investitur- und Krönungsrituale: Herrschaftseinsetzungen im kulturellen Vergleich*. Böhlau, 2005, 275–290.

Treadgold, W. "Byzantium, the Reluctant Warrior." In N. Christie and M. Yazigi, eds., *Noble Ideals and Bloody Realities: Warfare in the Middle Ages*. Leiden, 2006, 209–233.

———. *The Early Byzantine Historians*. New York, 2007.

———. "Trajan the Patrician, Nicephorus, and Theophanes." In D. Bumazhnov et al., eds., *Bibel, Byzanz und christlicher Orient: Festschrift für Stephen Gero zum 65. Geburtstag*. Louvain, 2011, 589–623.

Treitinger, O. *Die oströmische Kaiser- und Reichsidee nach ihrer Gestaltung im höfischen Zeremoniell*. Darmstadt, 1969.

Triantari, S. A. *Πολιτική ρητορική και επικοινωνία τον 14ο αιώνα*, 2nd ed. Thessalonike, 2010.

Tribolis, D. N. *Eutropius Historicus καὶ οἱ Ἕλληνες μεταφρασταὶ τοῦ Breviarium ab Urbe Condita*. Athens, 1941.

Troianos, S. N. "Συμβολὴ εἰς τὴν ἔρευναν τῶν ὑπὸ τῶν βυζαντινῶν αὐτοκρατόρων παρεχομένων ἐνόρκων ἐγγυήσεων." *Ἐπετηρὶς τοῦ Κέντρου Ἐρεύνης τῆς Ἱστορίας τοῦ Ἑλληνικοῦ Δικαίου τῆς Ἀκαδημίας Ἀθηνῶν* 12 (1965): 130–168.

———. *Οι πηγές του βυζαντινού δικαίου*, 2nd ed. Athens, 1999.

———. Untitled contribution in E. Grammatikopoulou, ed., *Αμφισβήτηση της εξουσίας*. Athens, 2003, 98.

———. *Οι Νεαρές Λέοντος ϛ΄ του Σοφού*. Athens, 2007.

Tsirpanlis, C. N. "Byzantine Parliaments and Representative Assemblies from 1081 to 1351." *Byzantion* 43 (1973): 432–481.

Tylor, T. R. *Why People Obey the Law*. New Haven, CT, 1990.

Van Dam, R. *The Roman Revolution of Constantine*. Cambridge, 2007.

———. *Rome and Constantinople: Rewriting Roman History during Late Antiquity*. Waco, TX, 2010.

———. *Remembering Constantine at the Milvian Bridge*. Cambridge, 2011.

Van Nuffelen, P. "Playing the Ritual Game in Constantinople (379–457)." In L. Grig and G. Kelly, eds., *Two Romes: Rome and Constantinople in Late Antiquity*. Oxford, 2012, 183–200.

Varona Codeso, P. *Miguel III (842–867): Construcción histórica y literaria de un reinado*. Madrid, 2009.

Versnel, H. S. *Coping with the Gods: Wayward Readings in Greek Theology*. Leiden, 2011.

Vespignani, G. *Il circo di Costantinopoli nuova Roma*. Spoleto, 2001.

Veyne, P. *Bread and Circuses: Historical Sociology and Political Pluralism*. Trans. B. Pearce. London, 1990.

———. *L'empire gréco-romain*. Paris, 2005.

Virgilio, B. *Lancia, diadema e porpora: Il re e la régalità ellenistica*. Pisa, 1999.

Vlysidou, V. N. "L'empereur Théophile 'chérissant les nations' et ses relations avec la classe supérieure de la société byzantine." In E. Kountoura-Galake, ed., *Οι σκοτεινοί αιώνες του Βυζαντίου (7ος–9ος αι.)*. Athens, 2001, 443–453.

Vryonis, S. "Byzantine ΔΗΜΟΚΡΑΤΙΑ and the Guilds in the Eleventh Century." *DOP* 17 (1963): 287–314.

———. "The Patriarchate of Constantinople and the State." In V. Hotchkiss and P. Henry, eds., *Orthodoxy and Western Culture: A Collection of Essays Honoring Jaroslav Pelikan on the Eightieth Birthday*. Crestwood, NY, 2005, 109–123.

Walbank, F. W. "Monarchies and Monarchic Ideas." *Cambridge Ancient History* 7.1 (1984): 62–100.

Walden, G. *God Won't Save America: Psychosis of a Nation*. London, 2006.

Walker, A. *The Emperor and the World: Exotic Elements and the Imaging of Middle Byzantine Imperial Power, Ninth to Thirteenth Centuries C.E.* Cambridge, 2012.

Wallace-Hadrill, A. "Civilis Princeps: Between Citizen and King." *JRS* 72 (1982): 32–48.

———. *Rome's Cultural Revolution*. Cambridge, 2008.

Wallerstein, I. *World-Systems Analysis: An Introduction*. Durham, NC, 2004.

Webb, R. *Demons and Dancers: Perforance in Late Antiquity*. Cambridge, MA, 2008.

West, C. "Dynastic Historical Writing." In S. Foot and C. F. Robinson, eds., *The Oxford History of Historical Writing*, v. 2. Oxford, 2012, 496–516.

Whitby, M. *The Emperor Maurice and His Historian: Theophylact Simocatta on Persian and Balkan Warfare*. Oxford, 1988.

———. "The Violence of the Circus Factions." In K. Hopwood, ed., *Organized Crime in Antiquity*. London, 1998, 229–253.

Whittow, M. *The Making of Byzantium, 600–1025*. Berkeley, CA, 1996.

Wiemer, H.-U. "Voces populi: Akklamationen als Surrogat politischer Partizipation." In E. Flaig, ed., *Genesis und Dynamiken der Mehrheitsentscheidung*. Munich, 2013, 173–202.

Williams, M. S. "Hymns as Acclamations: The Case of Ambrose of Milan." *Journal of Late Antiquity* 6 (2013): 108–134.

Winterling, A. *Politics and Society in Imperial Rome*. Malden, MA, 2009.

Wiseman, T. P. *Remembering the Roman People: Essays on Late-Republican Politics and Literature*. Oxford, 2009.

Wood, P. *"We Have No King but Christ": Christian Political Thought in Greater Syria on the Eve of the Arab Conquest (c. 400–585)*. Oxford, 2010.

Yavetz, Z. *Plebs and Princeps*. Oxford, 1969.

Zepos, I. and P., eds. *Jus Graecoromanum,* 8 vols. Athens, 1931.

Zuckermann, C. "The Compendium of Syrianus Magister." *Jahrbuch der österreichischen Byzantinistik* 40 (1990): 209–224.

Acknowledgments

The ideas presented in this book have taken shape over the course of two decades and have been honed in presentations, discussions, and debates with dozens of colleagues, friends, and interested parties. It would serve no purpose to list them all here. Rather than implicate the guiltiest parties here, I will give them a copy of the book. I am especially grateful to those who took the trouble to challenge me with arguments and specific source-citations. The study of Byzantium now more than ever needs precisely the spirit of vigorous debate that you embody. I thank the three anonymous readers for Harvard University Press who made valuable suggestions for improving the book, especially its conceptual clarity. It was also a pleasure and great honor to work with Sharmila Sen, who has made a mark by fostering scholarship that rethinks basic paradigms in each field and restores agency to groups that are often left out or represented as silent or passive. This book is dedicated to another of her authors, who has patiently endured my obsession with "the Romans."

Index